A GRAMMAR OF NESE

A GRAMMAR OF NESE

LANA GRELYN TAKAU

ANU PRESS

ASIA-PACIFIC LINGUISTICS

ANU PRESS

Published by ANU Press
The Australian National University
Canberra ACT 2600, Australia
Email: anupress@anu.edu.au

Available to download for free at press.anu.edu.au

ISBN (print): 9781760465551
ISBN (online): 9781760465568

WorldCat (print): 1354992474
WorldCat (online): 1354992454

DOI: 10.22459/GN.2023

This title is published under a Creative Commons Attribution-NonCommercial-NoDerivatives 4.0 International (CC BY-NC-ND 4.0) licence.

The full licence terms are available at
creativecommons.org/licenses/by-nc-nd/4.0/legalcode

Cover design and layout by ANU Press. Cover photograph: simanlaci/Bigstock.com.

This book is published under the aegis of the Asia-Pacific Linguistics editorial board of ANU Press.

This edition © 2023 ANU Press

Contents

List of illustrations	vii
Author biography	ix
Acknowledgements	xi
Abbreviations	xiii
1. Introduction	**1**
1.1 Vanuatu language setting	1
1.2 Malekula and its language setting	11
1.3 The present work	26
2. Phonology	**31**
2.1 Introduction	31
2.2 Phonemic inventory	32
2.3 Phonotactics	49
2.4 Stress	57
2.5 Morphophonemic processes	58
2.6 Orthography	87
3. Word classes	**89**
3.1 Introduction	89
3.2 Nouns	90
3.3 Verbs	99
3.4 Pronouns	103
3.5 Prepositions	106
3.6 Adverbs	108
3.7 Quantifiers and numerals	110
3.8 Conjunctions and subordinators	114
3.9 Relational classifiers	120
3.10 Directionals	120
3.11 Demonstratives	122
3.12 Negative particles	128
3.13 Verbal affixes	128
3.14 Greetings and leavetakings	129
3.15 Lexical interjections	129
3.16 Flexibility of word class membership	130

4. The noun phrase — **135**
- 4.1 Introduction — 135
- 4.2 Order of noun phrase constituents — 135
- 4.3 Functions of noun phrases — 140
- 4.4 Words and bound pro-indexes functioning as heads of noun phrases — 143
- 4.5 Modification of the head — 147
- 4.6 Discourse role of pronouns — 179
- 4.7 Nominalisation — 183

5. The verb complex — **187**
- 5.1 Introduction — 187
- 5.2 Order of elements in the Nese verb complex — 188
- 5.3 Heads of verb complex — 188
- 5.4 Argument indexing — 190
- 5.5 Modification of the head verb — 199
- 5.6 Serial verb constructions — 226
- 5.7 Valency — 233

6. Simple sentences — **237**
- 6.1 Introduction — 237
- 6.2 Verbal clauses — 237
- 6.3 Non-verbal clauses — 239
- 6.4 Existential clauses — 244
- 6.5 Topicalisation and left dislocation — 245
- 6.6 Adjuncts — 248
- 6.7 Interrogative clauses — 271
- 6.8 Imperative clauses — 278
- 6.9 Comparative clauses — 280
- 6.10 Passive clauses — 280

7. Complex sentences — **283**
- 7.1 Introduction — 283
- 7.2 Coordinate clauses — 283
- 7.3 Conjunctive coordination — 284
- 7.4 Disjunctive *deve* 'or' — 290
- 7.5 Subordinate clauses — 291

References — 329

List of illustrations

Figures

Figure 1.1: First language learned	4
Figure 1.2: Oceanic subgroup within the Austronesian language family	8
Figure 1.3: Lynch's (2006) tentative subgrouping of Malekula languages	15
Figure 1.4: Malekula languages subgrouping	16
Figure 1.5: The Matanvat people living in Port Vila, singing a Christian song in Nese	17
Figure 1.6: Three Nese speakers (left to right): Aklyn Silas, Louis Ross and late Chief Gregoire Salyor	22
Figure 1.7: The late Annie Hymak, one of the last fluent Nese speakers, in her home at Senbokhas	22
Figure 4.1: NP heads and modifiers	136
Figure 4.2: Constituents of a noun phrase	137
Figure 4.3: Nominalisation	183
Figure 5.1: Verb complex constituents	188

Maps

Map 1.1: Vanuatu within Oceania	2
Map 1.2: The Austronesian language family	7
Map 1.3: Vanuatu and Malekula	12
Map 1.4: Linguistic subdivisions of Malekula	13
Map 1.5: The Matanvat area	19

Author biography

Lana Takau is a freelance linguistics researcher working for the Max Planck Institute for Evolutionary Anthropology. A native Ni-Vanuatu originating from Paama and Pentecost parentage, she has a PhD in linguistics from the University of Newcastle in Australia and this manuscript has been developed out of her PhD thesis on the highly endangered Nese language, which is spoken on the island of Malekula in Vanuatu. She lives in Vanuatu with her daughter and loves being outdoors in nature.

Acknowledgements

This work developed from my PhD thesis, and I am grateful to my supervisors Dr Catriona Malau, Dr Bill Palmer and Dr Åshild Næss, the University of Newcastle, the University of London's Endangered Languages Documentation Programme, the Nese speaking community in Malekula in Vanuatu and my friends in Vanuatu and abroad during the thesis-writing stage.

A great number of people have contributed in one way or another in the preparation of this manuscript and, although they are nonetheless important, space does not allow me to acknowledge each and every one of them. First of all, I would like to thank Professor Russell Gray, Dr Mary Walworth and the Max Planck Institute of Evolutionary Anthropology for the assistance provided during the editing of this manuscript. I am also grateful to the late Professor John Lynch, who initially linked me with Asia-Pacific Linguistics, and to the two anonymous reviewers who provided insightful comments on the draft of this manuscript.

It would not have been possible for me to complete this book without the support of my close relatives and friends here in Vanuatu. I would like to thank my cousin, Vanessa Tanghwa, for printing some draft copies for revision, and my aunt, Laelyn Mahit, for encouraging me in this endeavour. I am also grateful to my daughter, Lasandra, and my two nephews, Bill and Noel, for easing the writing of this book by filling the experience with their laughter, warmth and smiles. Finally, to some of my close friends: Susan Kaltovei, Linam Lui, Leah Mary and Qwelen Daniel – thank you so much for being a wonderful support system. Thanks be to God who makes all things work together for good.

Abbreviations

1	first person
2	second person
3	third person
ADV	adverb
ADVS	adversative
ART	article
ASP	aspect
CLED	classifier edible items
CLGEN	classifier general items
CLLIQ	classifier liquids
CONJ	conjunction
DEHORT	dehortative
DEM	demonstrative
DEM:LOC	local adverbial demonstrative
DIR	directional
EXCL	exclusive
EXCLAM	exclamation
GENMOD	general modifier
HESIT	hesitation marker
INCL	inclusive
INT	interrogative
IRR	irrealis
LOC	locational
NEG1	first element of negative discontinuous marker

NEG2	second element of negative discontinuous marker
NOM	nominalisation
NP	noun phrase
OBJ	object
PERS.PRON	personal pronoun
PL	plural
POSS	possessive
POT	potential
PREP1	first prepositional form
PREP2	second prepositional form
PROHIB	prohibitative
PURP1	first purposive form
PURP2	second purposive form
REAL	realis
REDUP	reduplication
SG	singular
SIM	similitive
SUB	subordinator
TAM	tense aspect mood
V1	verb 1 or the first verb in the sequence
V2	verb 2 or the second verb in the sequence
VC	verb complex
VP	verb phrase

1

Introduction

1.1 Vanuatu language setting

Nese is spoken on the island of Malekula in central Vanuatu. The Vanuatu archipelago (formerly known as the New Hebrides) is located in the South Pacific Ocean, northeast of New Caledonia and southeast of Solomon Islands, as shown in Map 1.1. The islands lie in a Y shape and stretch over an area of approximately 700,000 square kilometres. Geographically, Vanuatu has Solomon Islands, Fiji, New Caledonia and Papua New Guinea as its nearest neighbours. These countries make up the Melanesian sociocultural and linguistic grouping, which is differentiated from the Micronesian and Polynesian cultural groups.

Vanuatu gained its independence on 30 July 1980 from France and England, who had established a joint rule over the islands in 1906, an arrangement known as the Anglo-Franco condominium. Although self-determination has been achieved, a legacy of the colonial rule can be seen in the current dual education system where French is the language of instruction in schools that are located in areas that were originally colonised by the French, and English is the language of instruction in areas where the English language is dominant. In 2012, the Vanuatu government contemplated the use of vernacular education from kindergarten to grade 3 classes, whereby the vernacular languages were to become the languages of instruction in schools in the rural areas and Bislama would be adopted as the language of instruction in schools in the urban areas (Ministry of Education and Training, 2012, p. 2). The endeavour was implemented and banned by the Vanuatu Prime Minister in early 2023.

Map 1.1: Vanuatu within Oceania

Source: Copyright Bruce Jones Design Inc. 2011. Used with permission from www.freeusandworldmaps.com/html/WorldRegions/WorldRegionsPrint.html

Vanuatu comprises approximately 80 islands and its capital, Port Vila, is located on Efate, an island situated in central Vanuatu. According to the 2020 Vanuatu population preliminary findings, the country's population is 301,695, of which roughly 23 per cent live in urban areas while the remaining 77 per cent live in rural areas (Vanuatu Population, 2021). Vanuatu has a tropical climate, characterised by two seasons, which are dry (cool) and wet/cyclone (hotter). The former begins around May and lasts till October, while the latter extends from November to April. However, being located near the equator, a relatively uniform temperature is experienced throughout the year.

It is believed that the islands forming the Vanuatu archipelago have been inhabited since 1200BC (Spriggs, 2006, p. 123). The first recorded European explorer to set foot on Vanuatu was De Quiros, who landed on the island of Santo in 1568, followed by Louis Antoine De Bougainville in 1768 (Crowley, 1990, p. 51). During the 18th and 19th centuries, the islands were visited by whalers and traders in search of sandalwood, bêche-de-mer and labourers who were hired to work on the sandalwood and bêche-de-mer stations erected on certain islands within Vanuatu and abroad (Crowley, 1990, p. 58). These social conditions engendered the development of a contact language from which the current lingua franca creole, Bislama, is descended.

1.1.1 Linguistic situation in Vanuatu

There are approximately 138 languages spoken in Vanuatu (François et al., 2015, p. 3) and, consequently, with a total population of 301,695, this means that each language has approximately 2,190 speakers. This figure places Vanuatu as having the highest density of languages per capita in the world. While this may arouse a Ni-Vanuatu's linguistic pride, the reality is that this somewhat common knowledge amongst linguists is unknown in the Ni-Vanuatu lay milieu and, furthermore, the Vanuatu linguistic arena portrays a rather unbalanced scene with respect to local languages.

Bislama is by far the most widely used language in Ni-Vanuatu urban society. While it has been claimed that Bislama is the primary language, used by 74 per cent of the total population of those aged 5+ years in Vanuatu, recent findings indicate that this variety of Melanesian Pidgin is perhaps not gaining the foothold in the linguistic scene in urban areas as is widely believed (Vanuatu National Statistics Office, 2012, p. 95).

Figure 1.1 suggests that an overwhelming proportion of urban dwellers (86 per cent) learnt an indigenous language as their first language, although the proportion of rural dwellers learning an indigenous language is slightly higher (94 per cent). The figure for rural dwellers does not come as a surprise given that it is expected that the use of indigenous languages is more widespread in rural areas. However, the urban statistics imply that Bislama is not a serious threat to the acquiring of indigenous languages in the urban areas, an observation that contradicts the commonly held perception that the overwhelming use of Bislama is a primary factor in the falling use of indigenous languages in urban areas (Vandeputte-Tavo, 2014 as cited in François et al., 2015, p. 12). More surprisingly, Figure 1.1 shows that only 13 per cent of urban dwellers learnt Bislama as a first language, while the figure for rural dwellers is 6 per cent. The somewhat intriguing scenario depicted in the statistics for the urban dwellers could be attributed to the fact that the majority of survey respondents have just recently immigrated to the urban area from rural areas.

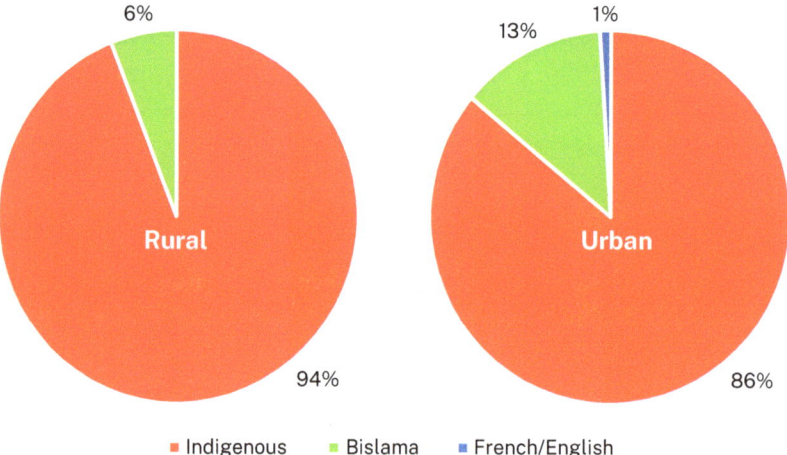

Figure 1.1: First language learned
Source: Vanuatu National Statistics Office (2012, p. 97)

Competency in a language in the Vanuatu context implies possessing a good command of a language and in relation to Bislama and the local languages, it means being proficient in speaking rather than in writing the language. While it is conceivable that most ordinary educated adult Ni-Vanuatus may be able to write in Bislama in one way or another, it is difficult to assess whether their written composition of the language is correct, given that there is no standardised Bislama orthography currently being used by the public at large. For example, the lexeme *sapos* 'if' may be orthographically represented as *spos*, *sipos*, *spose* or even by the phonologically reduced variant *sos*. In this context, correctness is perhaps evaluated on the basis of whether a written composition in Bislama is understood by the addressee.

Similarly, while orthographies of certain local languages may have been developed, the employment of these orthographies by speakers of the language is perhaps restricted to those involved in teaching these local languages and they are not adopted by the general speaker population to be used on a daily basis. For example, the Nese spelling system is currently being used primarily by only one of the Nese speakers who is a language activist in the community; her work involves composing stories, songs and poems in Nese for her kindergarten students. Other fluent speakers are not using the orthography for various reasons, one of which is that writing is not a primary means of communication within that cultural milieu.

According to Article 3 of Chapter 1 of the Constitution of the Republic of Vanuatu: 'the national language of the Republic of Vanuatu is Bislama. The official languages are Bislama, English and French. The principal languages of education are English and French'. Although the label 'national language' gives Bislama a somewhat more prestigious position compared to English and French, this is arguably not the reality from certain perspectives. To begin with, the language is not yet standardised. It may be argued, however, that standardisation efforts have been made with the publication of Crowley's (2003) Bislama dictionary and, more recently, in connection to the implementation of Bislama as a language of instruction. Nevertheless, the institutions and the general public in Vanuatu do not adhere to one specific single spelling system and there are differences in pronunciation and grammar from island to island. In a similar vein, varying degrees of comprehension in the language exists, which is partly due to the degree of exposure to Bislama and perhaps town life. Furthermore, the common perception amongst Ni-Vanuatus regarding the notion of 'bilingual' in Vanuatu seems to imply that Bislama may not be considered a language in its own right. One only has to look at job adverts in the newspaper to see that the term 'bilingual' refers to someone with the knowledge of both English and French rather than English and Bislama or French and Bislama or even Bislama and a local language. This restricted application of the term 'bilingual' in the Vanuatu context highlights the fact that Bislama and the local languages have not yet acquired equal status, in relation to the recognition of the value of bilingualism in official contexts.

Perhaps the most important article in the Constitution of the Republic of Vanuatu in relation to the local vernaculars is Article 2, which clearly states that the 'local languages shall be protected and preserved'. While this article suggests the local languages ought to be 'protected and preserved', it perhaps conveys a zeal in black and white that is not reflected in reality. To begin with, whilst loss of language seems to be a concern for the public at large, and even more so for speakers whose language is facing immediate extinction, it is perhaps seen as a somewhat trivial issue compared to other practical issues, such as efforts to stabilise the economy and corruption in politics, to name but a few. Even in the local music industry, the renowned string band groups rarely if ever sing songs relating to language loss, while love songs, corruption in politics and results of poor education are the frequent themes that surface in the composers' lyrics.

1.1.2 Subgrouping

All of the 138 indigenous languages of Vanuatu (François et al., 2015, p. 3) belong to the Oceanic subgroup of the Austronesian language family, which has approximately 1,200 member languages (Lynch, Ross & Crowley, 2002, p. 1). The languages of the Austronesian family have approximately 270 million speakers, its members covering an enormous area, from Malagasy to Easter Island, Taiwan and Hawai'i to New Zealand. Its geographical range is shown in Map 1.2. The Austronesian language family has nine first order subgroups (Lynch et al., 2002, p. 4). These are:

1. Formosan languages
2. Proto Malayo Polynesian
3. Western Malayo Polynesian languages
4. Proto Central/Eastern Malayo Polynesian
5. Central Malayo Polynesian languages
6. Proto Eastern Malayo Polynesian
7. Proto South Halamhera/Irian Jaya
8. Proto Oceanic

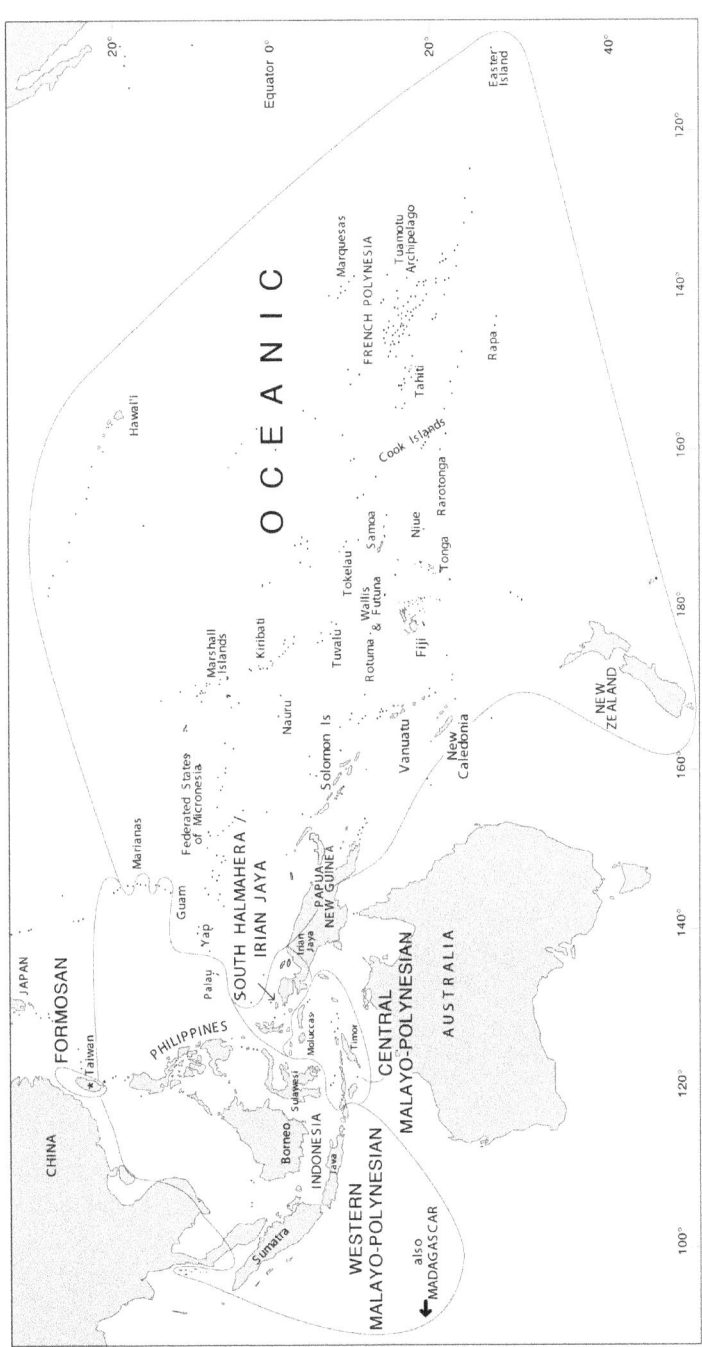

Map 1.2: The Austronesian language family
Source: Lynch, Ross and Crowley (2011, p. 3), used with permission

The existence of Oceanic as a subgroup of the Austronesian language family has gained consensual status amongst linguists. However, it is not a direct subgroup of the Austronesian language family but a subgroup of the Malayo Polynesian branch. Vanuatu languages belong to the Southern Oceanic linkage, which is one of the five groupings within the Central Eastern Oceanic subgrouping (Lynch et al., 2002, p. 112).

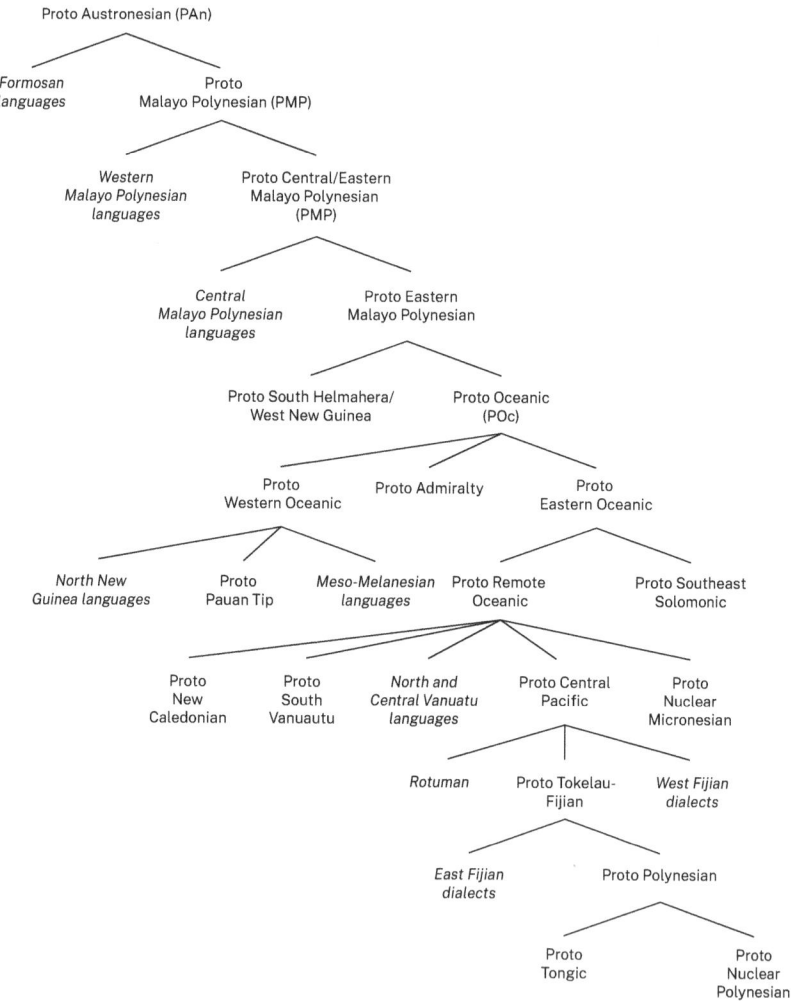

Figure 1.2: Oceanic subgroup within the Austronesian language family
Source: Ross, Pawley and Osmond (2011, p. 7)

Ross, Pawley and Osmond (2011, p. 7) provide a contrasting schema of the diversification of Austronesian languages as shown in Figure 1.2, where the immediate descendant of Proto Oceanic is Proto Eastern Malayo Polynesian. Proto Oceanic has three daughter nodes, one of which is Proto Eastern Oceanic, the immediate ancestor of Proto Remote Oceanic. Vanuatu languages belong to two subgroups emanating from Proto Remote Oceanic. These two subgroups are Proto South Vanuatu and North and Central Vanuatu languages. Figure 1.2 has the latter subgroup in italics, an indication that the subgroup has no exclusively shared common ancestor. Other subgroups within the same order as the two Vanautu subgroups mentioned are Proto New Caledonian, Proto Central Pacific and Proto Nuclear Micronesian. Diverging from the canonical hierarchy concept, François et al. (2015) propose that Vanuatu languages form a single linkage instead of a set of clearly delimited and hierarchically arranged subgroups.

1.1.3 Vanuatu internal subgrouping

The internal classification of Vanuatu languages is an issue that has been subject to a great deal of debate (Capell, 1962; Tryon, 1976, 1996; Guy, 1982; Clark, 1985; Lynch & Tryon, 1985; Lynch & Crowley, 2001) ever since Ray's (1926) discussion of the three divisions: the North, Central and Southern subgroups. The putative subgroups of the Vanuatu languages arising from these discussions comprise a North and Central Vanuatu and the Southern Vanuatu family. Tryon (1996, p. 170) suggests that the Vanuatu languages come under one single higher-level Vanuatu group that further divides into two subgroups called North-Central Vanuatu and Southern Vanuatu. The former is then further divided into two groups called Northern Vanuatu and Central Vanuatu, respectively. The Northern subgroup includes all languages of the Torres and Banks islands, Maewo, Ambae, northern Pentecost and Santo, while the Central group comprises of Malekula languages, central southern Pentecost, Ambrym, Paama, Epi, the Shepherd Islands and Efate (Tryon, 1996, p. 170). Emae and Mele-Ifira are Polynesian outliers. The Southern subgroup consists of all the languages south of Efate except Futuna-Aniwa which are part of the Polynesian outliers (Tryon, 1996, p. 172).

The subgroup directly relevant to this research is the North and Central Vanuatu subgroup. Clark (2009, p. 2) asserts that the existence of the North and Central subgroup and the separate division between North and Central is now widely accepted among linguists. He classes Malekula as an individual division within the Central Vanuatu subgroup, along with other subgroups comprising central and south Pentecost, Ambrym, Paama, Epi, the Shepherd group and Efate. Lynch (2006) disagrees that this set of languages form a separate subgroup within the Central Vanuatu grouping.

1.1.4 Previous linguistic work on Vanuatu languages

It was the arrival and establishment of missionary activity in the late 1800s and 1900s in Vanuatu that sparked the first linguistic work. Missionaries developed orthographies that were used to write songs, amongst other things, in the local vernaculars. However, the main pioneers of linguistic description in Vanuatu were Codrington (1885), Macdonald (1891) and Ray (1926). Codrington (1885) wrote sketch grammars of the languages of the Torres islands, Maewo, Ambae, Santo, Ambrym, Efate and Aneityum in southern Vanuatu. Macdonald (1891) discussed grammatical aspects of the Efate, Erromangan and Santo languages. Ray's (1926) comparative study of Melanesian languages was a comprehensive linguistic description of languages in Melanesia, covering several languages spoken in northern, central and southern Vanuatu.

These studies were then followed by Ivens' (1937–39) description of the Lamalanga (Raga/Hano) language of North Pentecost; Lobaha (Ivens, 1940–42), which is spoken in Ambae, and Lotora of North Maewo (Ivens, 1940–42). While others have carried out studies on individual Vanuatu languages, it was Tryon's (1976) investigation of more than 100 languages of Vanuatu that laid the foundation for comparative linguistic work on languages of the area. Since then, linguistic description of Vanuatu languages has increased with a considerable amount of input from John Lynch and Terry Crowley: grammars or dictionaries now exist for Lenakel (Lynch, 1977, 1978), Paamese (Crowley, 1992), Kwamera (Lindstrom, 1986), Bislama (Crowley, 1995), Sye (Crowley, 1998) and Ura (Crowley, 1999). Other major contributions that came about in the 21st century include Lynch and Crowley's survey of Vanuatu languages (2001), the detailed grammar of North-East Ambae (Hyslop, 2001) and a grammar of Mwotlap (François, 2001). Furthermore, François also produced a short grammar and dictionary of Araki (2002), along with the pioneering study done by Thieberger on the South Efate language containing example constructions linked to audio and video files attached with the publication (2006) and Crowley's posthumous publications on four Malekula languages, namely Avava (2006a), Naman (2006b), Nese (2006c) and Tape (2006d), which were edited by John Lynch. A few other grammars on Vanuatu languages, which have been the subject of PhD dissertations, are the descriptions of Namakir (Sperlich, 1994), Lewo (Early, 1994), Tamambo (Jauncey, 1997) and Raga (Bogiri, 2013).

In terms of language description, like most Malekula languages, the Nese language has received very minimal linguistic attention beyond Crowley's (2006c) sketch grammar of 81 pages. In fact, Crowley's descriptive work on the language is the only descriptive work ever written on the languages of the Northern subgroup of Malekula languages. The other languages in this subgroup – namely Vovo, Botovoro and Vao – have not yet been subject to descriptive linguistic work, although research has been carried out on Malua Bay by Kanauhea Wessels (2013). Subsequent reviews of Crowley's (2006c) work were made by François (2007) and Guerin (2010). Jean Louis Riallou, a French anthropologist, has also done some work on the Nese culture, in particular the Namangi system, and his work contains a few texts in the Nese language and information on the history of the Matanvat area, where Nese is spoken. These texts are written in a French-based orthography and are translated and glossed in the French language. Another contribution is Lynch's (2005) discussion of the apicolabial shift in Nese. Outside of academia, World Vision (n.d.) developed a booklet entitled 'Kasem smol save long lanwis, Smol buk blong kakae and buk blong raet: Matanvat', which contains Nese vocabulary. In addition to this, Seventh-day Adventist missionaries to Matanvat have developed an orthography for Nese that has been used to write religious songs in Nese to be used in the church; however, these booklets are no longer available.

1.2 Malekula and its language setting

Malekula island (Map 1.3) is located at 16.30°S, 167.50°E and lies south of the island of Santo and west of the island of Ambrym. The islands of Vanuatu have been divided into six provinces since 1994 and Malekula hosts the capital of the Malampa province, which comprises Malekula, Paama and Ambrym islands and encompasses an area of 2,779 km². According to the Vanuatu National Statistics Office statistics, the total population in Malekula stood at approximately 30,981 (2016, pp. 29–30), the majority (23 per cent) of whom resided in Northeast Malekula. Malekula alone has approximately 77 per cent of the province's population (40,928).

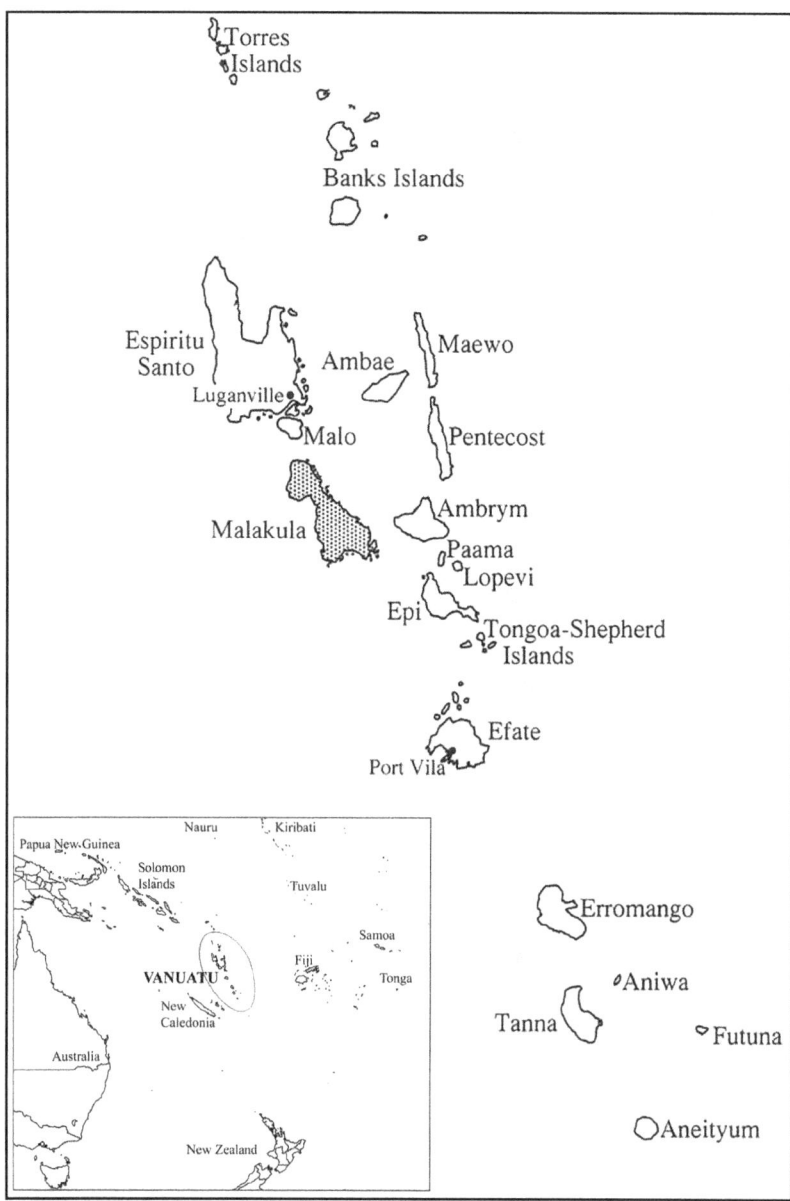

Map 1.3: Vanuatu and Malekula
Source: Dimock (2009, p. 2)

1. INTRODUCTION

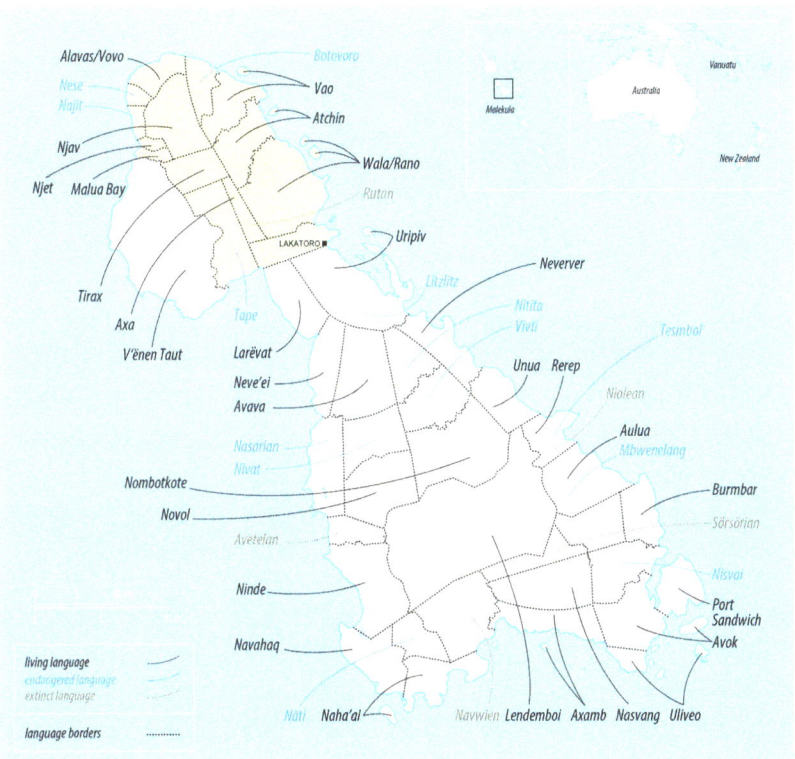

Map 1.4: Linguistic subdivisions of Malekula
Source: Walworth et al. (2021)

The capital of the island, and its main administrative centre, is known as Lakatoro and is situated on the eastern coast of the island, boasting several retail shops, an open-air market, a supermarket, a bank, a primary school and two internet cafes, at the time of writing. Lakatoro has a population of approximately 705 people. A secondary school and the main hospital of the island, and indeed of the province as a whole, are located at Norsup village on the mainland of Malekula. Norsup has the largest coconut plantation in Vanuatu. The interior of the island is covered with rainforest and is mountainous.

Walworth et al. (2021, p. 8) propose that there are 30 living languages, 13 endangered languages and five extinct languages on Malekula, as shown in Map 1.4. Bislama is the main language used at the administrative centre of Lakatoro and surrounding villages such as Tautu. English and French are also used. Lakatoro has a mixed population consisting of people from different parts of Malekula and from other islands around

13

Vanuatu. However, people living there who come from the same language communities also speak their local language amongst themselves. There are schools in Malekula that have French as the medium of instruction and those that have English as the medium of instruction.

Nese is classified as moribund and has been labelled as a communalect alongside other neighbouring communalects, namely Njav, Njet, Najit and Naha (Crowley, 2006c, p. 1). It is mainly spoken in the area called Matanvat, although a few speakers are scattered around the area extending from Lerrongrrong to Tontarr Asakh. However, given that the majority of speakers are located in the Matanvat area, it is widely known as the language of Matanvat. The northwestern area of Malekula is divided into two sociocultural groups, namely the Big Nambas and the Small Nambas. Nese is located in the area occupied by the Small Nambas people. In the Norsup/Lakatoro area where all other government services are located, such as the Norsup hospital, post office and bank, Bislama, English and French are used as there is a mixed population in these two areas, although some people use their vernacular languages in their homes and with visiting speakers of their language.

1.2.1 Internal classification of Malekula languages

The internal classification of Malekula languages remains an unresolved issue mainly due to the absence of detailed descriptions of the majority of the languages spoken on the island. Out of the 39 identified languages (Lynch & Crowley, 2001, pp. 67–69), less than 50 per cent have received linguistic attention; these include Aulua (Ray, 1893), V'ënen Taut (Fox, 1979), V'ënen Taut (Dodd, 2015), Port Sandwich (Charpentier, 1979), Avava (Crowley, 2006a), Naman (Crowley, 2006b), Nese (Crowley, 2006c; Takau, 2016), Tape (Crowley, 2006d), Neve'ei (Musgrave, 2007), Neverver (Barbour, 2012), Unua (Pearce, 2015), Tirax (Brotchie, 2009), Maskelynes (Healey, 2013), Espigles Bay (Holmes, 2014) and Malua Bay (Wessels, 2013). Charpentier (1982) is another contribution in the descriptive work on Malekula languages, specifically focusing on southern Malekula languages.

Despite this gap in the body of knowledge on Malekula languages, there have been attempts at classifying languages of this island. Tryon (1976, p. 309) proposes a North Malekula subgroup and a South Malekula subgroup, the latter he describes as lexically and morphologically aberrant compared to languages in the North Malekula subgroup. Lynch

(2006, p. 19) further refines this classification, proposing a three-way subdivision: northern, eastern and western. The eastern and western groups are each further divided into two groups: the northeastern and southeastern, and the core and peripheral western groups respectively. Lynch's classification is based on phonological and lexical innovations, although he also discusses morphological innovations. However, it reveals a few discrepancies, in that some languages such as Vao, Larëvat, Avava and Neverver have links to two subgroups and the Aulua language cannot be assigned to a lower-level group. These discrepancies, along with the fact that other undescribed languages cannot be classified, clearly reflect the need for more in-depth data on Malekula languages. Figure 1.3 schematises this classification and the languages involved; the brackets signify languages that are also present in another subgroup. Their names also appear in the other subgroup but without the brackets.

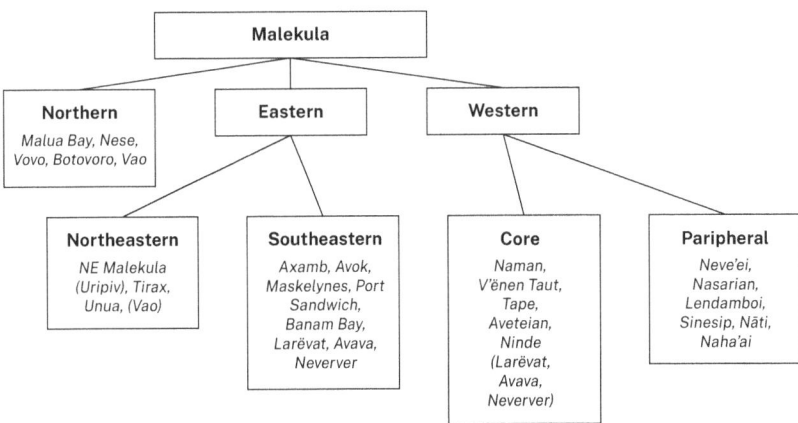

Figure 1.3: Lynch's (2006) tentative subgrouping of Malekula languages

More recently, Lynch (2016) offers another hypothesis on the subgrouping of Malekula languages that is schematised in Figure 1.3, based only on phonological innovations, with the only lexical innovations used in connection to establishing membership within the Eastern languages. Innovations in the North Coast subgroup include conditioned vowel loss occurring in the North Coast subgroup with Malua Bay securing a position within the Northern Malekula subgroup owing to the presence of *i being backed and rounded before a consonant followed by *o and to the presence of *d, *dr and *r (*R) (Lynch, 2016). As shown in Figure 1.3 the Northern Malekula subgroup is depicted in a single line contrasting from the Eastern and Western Malekula linkages, which are represented by double lines (Lynch, 2016).

A GRAMMAR OF NESE

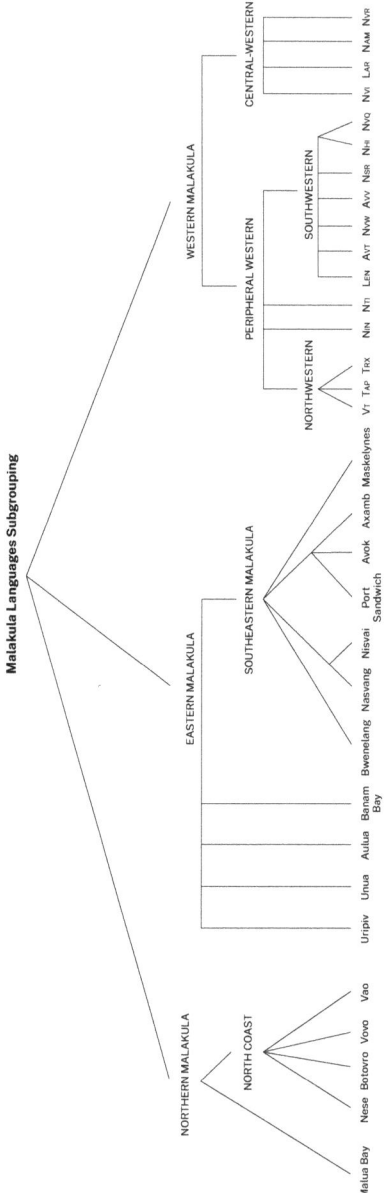

Figure 1.4: Malekula languages subgrouping

Source: Lynch (2016)

Full names of abbreviated forms in Figure 1.4 are VT: V'ënen Taut, TAP: Tape, TRX: Tirax, NIN: Ninde, NTI: Nāti, LEN: Lendamboi, AVT: Aveteian, NVW: Navwien, AVV: Avava, NSR: Nasarian, NHI: Naha'ai, NVQ: Nahavaq, NVI: Neve'ei, LAR: Larëvat, NAM: Naman and NVR: Neverver (Lynch, 2016).

1.2.2 Sociolinguistic overview of Matanvat

The moribund language of Nese is spoken by a very small number of speakers who live in the area known as Matanvat, which is located at the North Western tip of Malekula island. Approximately 300 people currently live in the Matanvat area, although only 34 per cent are native to Matanvat, a slight increase from the 10 per cent native population that lived in Matanvat with the commencement of migration from 'man kam' (see below). There is a Matanvat community in Port Vila whose total population is roughly 30 people, some of whom are represented in Figure 1.5, in which they are rehearsing a Christian song in the Nese language for a church program in 2012. These Matanvat natives have migrated to Port Vila for work and educational purposes. The elderly people in the Port Vila Matanvat community speak Nese to varying degrees, although the majority are not competent in the language. There are also a couple of speakers living in Santo. Due to inter-island marriages Matanvat men and women are also dispersed throughout the islands of Vanuatu.

Figure 1.5: The Matanvat people living in Port Vila, singing a Christian song in Nese
Source: The author

The migration of men and women from other villages into Matanvat is known to have culminated in the 1930s and 1940s with the establishment of a cooperative and the arrival of foreigners bringing Christianity to the area (G. Salyor, personal communication, 2013). These foreigners, or 'man kam', arrived from areas of Malekula such as South West Bay, Tisvel, Vinmavis, Lambumbu, Tenmaru, Amok, Makawe, Vakas, Tilamet and Nirenbas. The chief ruling at that time, Kaku Salyor, established a political movement called Malamko, which not only sought to gain independence, but also established Matanvat as a booming economic centre. A cooperative was set up in the Tontarr area which bought copra and cotton from the two locals and these two products were exported. The harbour provided an avenue for the shipment of cotton and copra to Australia. This was another factor that attracted 'man kam' to the Matanvat area.

Furthermore, the fact that the area was relatively peaceful while tribal wars raged in the neighbouring villages attracted foreigners to the area. The earliest mission to arrive was the Seventh-day Adventists (SDA), who arrived in the mid-1910s, followed by the Catholics. The missionaries encouraged the composition of Christian songs in the Matanvat language, to be used in church services, although it was also common for churchgoers to sing songs written in the language of the area in which the mission was formerly based. Therefore, those attending the Catholic Church would sing songs written in the Vao language, given that the mission was at Vao prior to its establishment at Matanvat, and the Seventh-day Adventists would sing songs written in the Atchin language, since the SDA church was formerly based in Atchin.

1.2.3 Matanvat today

The Matanvat area covers a 40 km stretch of land from Lerrongrong to Tontarr Asakh. The inhabited areas include Lerrongrong, Senbokhas, Matanvat Presbyterian and Matanvat SDA or Tontarr Asakh (see Map 1.5). It is served by one dirt road, a link to the provincial capital, Lakatoro, and to the Big Nambas area, with numerous bush tracks leading to the garden areas established by the villagers. The area is mostly covered with coconut plantations and dense forest, although it has a surprisingly flat topography. Villagers prefer to live in the coastal areas rather than inland, perhaps due to the opportunities afforded by coastal living such as easy access to road transport services and schools.

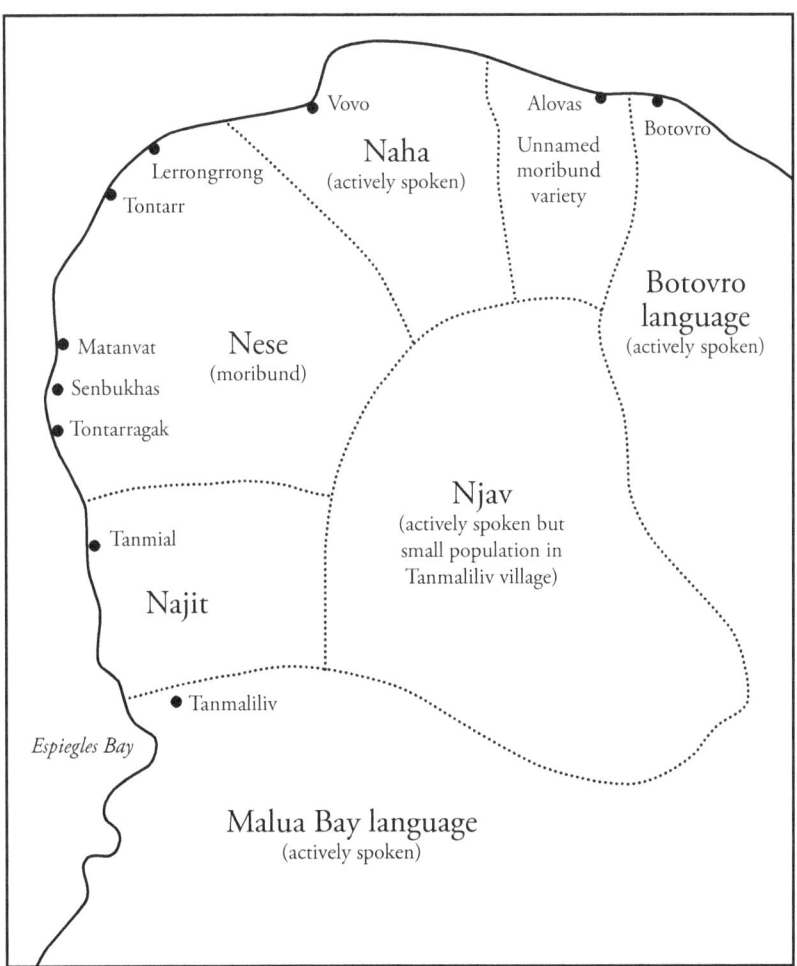

Map 1.5: The Matanvat area
Source: Crowley (2006c, p. 3)

Most people in Matanvat village today thrive on subsistence farming, copra and cocoa beans. While subsistence farming contributes to the daily food consumption, the farming of copra and cocoa generates the monetary means through which school fees, transport costs and household purchases are met. Up until early 2019, copra prices used to range from 15,000–60,000 vatu per tonne, currently dropping to a fixed price of 25,000 vatu per tonne. The most common food is plantain bananas, along with root crops such as taro, yams, sweet potato and fruits such as pawpaw, mandarins, mango and Canarium nuts, to name but a few. Yam is a most highly prized food item, usually eaten on special occasions, when it is prepared in the traditional dish commonly called *sosor* 'yam pudding with coconut cream'. Fish, caught using fishing nets, fish lines and knives, is also eaten along with other sea creatures such as sea urchins. Imported foods such as white rice, canned fish, noodles and salt are also widely eaten. Kava[1] is now consumed by young teenagers and the elderly alike. Leafy greens such as 'island cabbage' are also a common source of protein, although they can be scarce during the dry season.

Water from the rain and wells is used for all purposes. During the dry season when there is a shortage of rainfall, people drink water from the wells. Aid agencies have established water pumps that pump water from underground in certain areas in Matanvat, but for other areas that do not have water pumps, wells are dug to retain water. Apart from underground wells and water pumps, water tanks are also used, and drums and containers are used to collect and store water. While most houses are made from local materials such as thatch, bamboo and coral, there seems to be a recent general trend towards cement floors.

Life in the Matanvat area revolves around community work. Most individual responsibilities are fulfilled through communal support; for example, several households may come together to cut copra which can then be sold to pay for one student's school fees. Two days of the week are devoted to community work at the village dispensary and the Sandak Primary and Junior Secondary school, in which manual labour such as grass cutting, cement making and so forth are carried out. The school enrols students from as far as the Potovro area. There is a local bank which has around 100 clients both from Matanvat and the surrounding villages. Another community-funded organisation is the Matanvat kindergarten. It has roughly 20 students and although Bislama is the language of instruction, Nese is also taught daily through songs, poems and prayers.

1.2.4 Nese speakers

Nese is moribund and therefore identification of its speakers is a complex matter. Based on data collected in 2002, Crowley (2006c, p. 1) stated that the language is only actively spoken by an extended family in the Matanvat SDA area. While the phrase 'actively spoken' may suggest that all members of the single extended family are dynamically involved in

---

1   The kava plant is a herb grown mostly in the South Pacific and its roots are used to produce a ceremonial drink.

using Nese as the means of communication between themselves, data from my own fieldwork suggests that this is not so. Within this single extended family, consisting of one sister and three brothers, it is only these four people plus two spouses who use Nese on a daily basis. While these four siblings, aged between 50 and 60, employ Nese on a daily basis between themselves and their children, the latter group always respond in Bislama.

Furthermore, my fieldwork data indicates that there are roughly eight other speakers living in Matanvat who speak the language to varying degrees. Similarly, there are other pockets of speakers in Port Vila and Santo who have, more or less, a good understanding of the language, although they do not use it on a daily basis and rarely if ever use it with the other language speakers.

Given that Nese speakers residing in Matanvat speak the language to varying degrees, there is a lot of criticism and contention amongst themselves concerning the 'correct' language to be used; a condition that is perhaps one of the contributing factors to its decline in usage. More specifically, criticism is primarily directed to the single extended family in Matanvat SDA who have been noted by Crowley (2006c, p. 1) as actively speaking the Nese language. They are often derided as speaking a 'baby' version of Nese and are given the label *la compagnie creole* 'the creole company'. The few speakers who speak the language take pride in their knowledge of Nese but rarely use it when communicating with others for fear of censure. Furthermore, for some speakers, knowledge of the language seems to be taken as a feature that defines one as an original Matanvat native with rights to the chiefly title. Therefore, for these sets of speakers, speaking the language may lead to possible leakage of information, which may be used by opposing parties in court regarding the land disputes currently ongoing in Matanvat as well as in legal battles relating to the village chiefly title. The total number of speakers who may be considered fluent is 13. There are roughly 10 other adults who could be labelled as semi speakers, and roughly 20 (adults and children) have a passive knowledge of the language.

Figure 1.6: Three Nese speakers (left to right): Aklyn Silas, Louis Ross and late Chief Gregoire Salyor

Source: The author

Figure 1.7: The late Annie Hymak, one of the last fluent Nese speakers, in her home at Senbokhas

Source: The author

1.2.5 Influence of Bislama

With its mixed population, Bislama is the language that is commonly used in all areas of communication in Matanvat, such as in churches, in meetings and within families. It is even the language of instruction in the Matanvat kindergarten. While the use of Bislama is the primary contributing factor to Nese falling into disuse, there are cases where the use of a local language other than Nese may also be contributing to its decline. In fact, in some Matanvat homes where the female spouse is from the Espiegles Bay community and the male a Nese speaker, the children tend to speak the Espigles Bay language known as Njet rather than Nese. However, women from other islands who have married Nese men tend not to speak their language to their children.

1.2.6 Speakers' attitudes towards their own language

There seems to be a general feeling of deep shame, sadness and regret by the Matanvat community regarding the loss of their language. This is perhaps felt more profoundly by the older generation, those aged from 30 years upwards, regardless of the level of education obtained. It is an issue that brings scorn and contempt from speakers of other neighbouring languages that are not as seriously threatened. The greatest concern for the Nese speakers, as is common in other parts of the world, is that their language is a defining feature of their identity as a Matanvat native. The loss of their language, therefore, means loss of their identity as a Matanvat native.

Furthermore, loss of their language entails the loss of the ability to 'hide' information that should not be disclosed when in the presence of non-Nese-speaking people. Given that the loss of their language is inevitable if measures are not taken to rectify the situation, the Matanvat people are longing for their language to be revived, if possible. Revival of the language is an issue about which they feel deeply and for which they have great concern, to the extent that it is included in prayer petitions. Informal language learning sessions were held by the elderly, in which the children are taught games and basic sentences in Nese. A few families are attempting to speak the language at home and at the church level where the congregation sometimes sings songs in the Nese language. However, this may not necessarily apply to all groups of Matanvat people.

There are a few Matanvat people, in particular those who are educated and working in towns, who question the importance of the Nese language. The fact that nearly all jobs in the two towns of Port Vila and Luganville require potential candidates to be proficient in English and/or French rather than a local language renders the acquiring of Nese a trifling issue. Thus for a working young Nese speaker living in the urban towns, it would be perhaps pointless to invest time and energy in speaking or acquiring a language that does not directly contribute to generating income. The need to retain his or her identity as a Matanvat native does not seem to be on a par with securing a living. For the elderly generation who speak Nese, the usage of Bislama by the younger generation signifies their low opinion of the language compared to Bislama. Bislama is seen as more 'sophisticated' than Nese. When queried why they respond in Bislama rather than Nese they usually give a smile for an answer – a reaction that could be interpreted as either a reflection of shame or one that trivialises the whole issue of language endangerment!

1.2.7 Nese language revival efforts

There have been a number of attempts to revive the Nese language in the Matanvat area in Northwest Malekula. The establishment of the Matanvat kindergarten in 2011 within the Matanvat SDA vicinity provided an avenue through which children may be taught the Nese language. Operated by a committee consisting of local Matanvat natives, the kindergarten is taught by Mrs Aklyn Silas, who is the only language activist in Matanvat. Although the language of instruction is Bislama, Nese is taught for around 20 minutes during class time through the medium of poems, rhymes and songs composed by the teacher. Since no orthography had been developed for the community, learning the Nese language was restricted, until recently, to oral activities, rather than written. Due to the general censure faced by her family from other Nese speakers, the initial phase in which Nese was introduced was met with heavy opposition by some of the villagers.

In 2014 Mrs Silas started using an orthography that I developed in consultation with the speakers and that differs slightly from the one used in this manuscript, as it is aimed at Nese speakers who are categorised as second-language learners. Other literacy resources such as an alphabet chart and copies of three booklets on Nese numerals, Bislama–Nese simple sentences and a custom story were developed by myself and the community with fieldwork funds from the Endangered Languages Documentation Program (ELDP) and these are also now being used in the Matanvat kindergaten.

In early 2014, I obtained a grant from the Foundation for Endangered Languages to initiate a language immersion project in the Nese-speaking community to assist in reviving the language. This again was met with great opposition by some village parties, which delayed its commencement until late 2015. The major aspect of the project involved a one-hour session within the compounds of the Matanvat kindergarten, in which Nese is spoken by the Nese language activist (Mrs Aklyn Silas) to the 21 kindergarten students (aged between three and seven years) in a play-based setting. During this session, some time is also devoted to teaching the Nese alphabet using a phonetic approach. One month into its commencement, it was noted that students were beginning to utter simple sentences in Nese. Upon further request by the Nese speakers to seek additional funding, I obtained another grant from the Christensen Fund to develop literacy materials focused on traditional themes, which were to be used in the local Sandak primary school. The implementation of the project funded by The Christensen Fund was partially successful as we were able to develop and print around 1,000 literacy materials in Nese and carry out a Nese language competition. However, due to the many socio-political divisions within the community, and a lack of community support, the last phase of the project which involved teaching of the language to students was cancelled. Its implementation was difficult due to the many sociopolitical divisions within the community and a lack of community support, which led to its cancellation.

There are also some community members who are attempting to revive the language by simply using it on a daily basis within their homes. This is particularly true of a single nuclear family consisting of seven adults and a three-year-old child, who are located in an area outside of the Matanvat SDA mission compound. This has encouraged other families in Matanvat to converse with one another in Nese within the domestic domain, and also during village programs.

On a more official level, in 2013, the Vanuatu Education Support Program (VESP) was implemented in order to realise the Vanuatu government's favour for the use of a vernacular-based education curriculum for schools in Vanuatu, in which vernacular languages will be used as languages of instruction in the early primary grades. Aimed at improving literacy and numeracy learning for students in kindergarten to grade 2, along with ensuring the sustenance of Vanuatu's linguistic and cultural heritage, the project was funded by the AusAID and NZAID programs through a joint agreement with the Vanuatu government. According to Helen Tamtam, the VESP early vernacular literacy specialist, only 46 vernacular languages were targeted, all of which have 1,000 speakers or more, along with Bislama, which is to be the language of instruction in schools in urban areas (personal communication, 3 March 2016).

Resources in Bislama for grades 1 and 2 have been developed, such as alphabet charts, readers, syllable cards and wordlists to be used in schools within the urban centres where Bislama is the first language of most students. Similar resources were developed in 2016 for the 46 local languages, and trainings were given to teachers of those 46 vernacular languages on how to use the resources.

It is not clear how the Nese-speaking community will benefit from this government initiative given that Nese is not one of the 46 targeted local languages. Furthermore, according to Brian Willietien (personal communication, 17 February 2016), the principal of Sandak primary and junior secondary school in Matanvat, in 2015 the school received teacher instruction manuals on how to teach Bislama in schools, copies of a numeracy book in Bislama for grade 1, and a Bislama alphabet chart, all of which were developed by VESP. The arrival of these Bislama resources also came with instructions to commence using Bislama as the language of instruction for grades 1 and 2, which is proving very difficult for the teachers as they have not received any training to perform such a task. The use of Bislama as the language of instruction in a rural school, located in a village whose language is on the verge of extinction, will quite certainly contribute to further endangerment of Nese's linguistic heritage, given that the already overwhelming presence of Bislama is contributing to the language's falling use.

1.3 The present work

The present study is a synchronic grammatical description of the Nese language and is not firmly embedded in any particular syntactic theory. It is aimed mainly at describing the morphosyntactic properties of the language. This manuscript is divided into seven chapters with the introductory chapter being the present one. Chapter 2 is a description of Nese's phonology, where the cross-linguistically rare apicolabial phonemes are presented and it highlights interesting vowel raising patterns, amongst other themes. Chapter 3 deals with word classes, and although a presentation of the open and closed word classes is given, strict demarcation lines between these categories cannot be easily draw, reflecting flexibility of membership between word classes amongst several lexemes. Chapter 4 is a description of the noun phrase wherein the complex possessive system is presented in conjunction with the interesting discourse role of independent pronouns. Chapter 5 examines the Nese verb complex and its associated prefixes, with a remarkable characteristic being the obligatory use of the irrealis mood in the expression of negation. Chapter 6 is a description of simple sentences and, lastly, Chapter 7 deals with complex sentences.

Example sentences in Chapter 3 and the subsequent chapters are glossed as in (1.1).

1.1 *Je-v'an   lanus.*
    1SG:IRR-go   bush:LOC
    'I went to the bush.'
    (2012_08_27_obnesp01001 00:01:11.734-00:01:12.949, natural text)

The first line in italics is the construction in Nese, while the next line shows the grammatical and lexical glosses. The grammatical glosses are in small caps with the lexical glosses in regular font. Morphological boundaries are indicated by means of a hyphen. However, in cases where a morpheme cannot be morphologically segmented, a colon is used to indicate the different indivisible categories present.

1.3.1 Methodology

The data collection component of this project was made possible through the assistance of a Small Grant from the Endangered Languages Documentation Program, part of the Hans Rausing Endangered Languages Project. The initial field trip covered a period of nine months extending from November 2011 to August 2012. During this period, audio and video recordings were made in which texts from different genres were collected. Since Nese is moribund, this was a challenging task in itself. I initially lived in the village Tontarr Asakh for about a month and then I moved to Matanvat SDA mission grounds. There is a lot of competition amongst the speakers of the language, in particular amongst those aged 40 and above, towards which I tried to maintain a neutral stance. Speakers would tell me not to collect data from certain groups of speakers such as those labelled as *la compagnie creole* because they do not speak the 'correct' language and use a simplified version of the language. I made it clear that I was there to collect data on the language as it was currently used and am not in a position to judge who should be considered a speaker or not, given that it is an issue that is associated with the current land disputes in which the whole village was embroiled. However, I identified older speakers such as Annie Hymak, Louis Ross and Robert Jovi who were proficient in the language and would always verify with older speakers issues relating to word meanings or whether or not a word is a borrowing from another communalect.

I used Bislama to communicate with the Matanvat people and when eliciting and asking questions about the language. If I had used English in any instance, it would have created a barrier between myself and any of the Nese speakers as that would make them feel uncomfortable, and that I was trying to distinguish myself as educated. Note that this, however, would not be the case if a native speaker of English spoke to them in English as they would understand that English is his or her language. As mentioned, Nese is moribund; however, upon my arrival those proficient in the language started using it to each other. The fact that Nese is moribund makes collecting data a time-consuming task, especially when dealing with a single speaker. For most of the 11 fluent speakers, details of the content of a recording session would have to be given to them in Bislama a week in advance or so to allow the speaker time to think about what to say or even to cross-check with other speakers regarding the possible words to use.

Eleven individuals, a group of 10 or so kindergarten students and a choir of about 10 people contributed data, making a total of 31 participants. The analysis presented in this manuscript is based primarily on data given by the 11 individuals, including Aklyn Silas, Louis Ross, Annie Hymak and Robert Jovi. Data given by the kindergarten students is mainly composed of songs and rhymes in Nese which they learnt in school (cf. §1.2.7), but this data is not part of the analysis presented in this manuscript. The choir was composed of Matanvat natives living in Vila and their spouses who were from different islands of Vanuatu but married into Matanvat (cf. §1.2.2).

About eight hours of video recordings and approximately five hours of audio recordings were made. The content of these recordings ranges from gospel songs, custom songs, narratives, procedural texts about how certain traditional dishes are made, names of fish varieties and plant species, a casual conversation on various topics between six speakers, and texts that were a result of stimulus materials. The amount and nature of the data collected is very restricted due to the language being moribund.

Audio recordings were made in WAV files using a solid state recorder and videos were made in MPEG format with a Canon Legria HV40 Digital video camera. Roughly 30 per cent of the recordings were imported to ELAN where they were time-aligned and transcribed and translated into Bislama and English. Fieldwork followed the ethics protocols set out by the University of Newcastle's Human Research Ethics Committee, and written and oral consent was gained from the community as a whole, and everyone participated on a voluntary basis. All the elicitation sessions were carried out in Bislama. Photos were also taken to complement the recordings. All of these were accompanied by full metadata and have been deposited with the Endangered Languages Resource Archive (ELAR).[2]

---

2   The data can be accessed on elar.soas.ac.uk/Collection/MPI931758.

2
Phonology

2.1 Introduction

In this chapter, I describe the phonemic inventory of Nese (§2.2), covering the consonant (§2.2.1) and vowel (§2.2.2) phonemes. This is followed by a description of the phonotactics (§2.3), including a discussion of the syllable structure (§2.3.2) and the way in which consonants (§2.3.2.1) and vowels (§2.3.2.2) are distributed. Section 2.4 is a discussion of stress patterns in Nese. Section 2.5 is a description of morphophonemic processes, namely vowel harmony (§2.5.1), vowel raising (§2.5.2), phonological epenthesis (§2.5.3) and reduplication (§2.5.4). Lastly, Section 2.6 presents the orthographic conventions that will be used in the following chapters; however, all examples in this chapter are presented in an International Phonetic Alphabet (IPA) with phonetic transcriptions given where necessary. It should be noted at the outset that, given the moribund status of the language and the restricted domain in which Nese is used, there are cases where minimal pairs are difficult to establish for consonant phonemes. In these cases, near minimal pairs are used to prove contrastiveness.

2.2 Phonemic inventory

The Nese phonemic inventory consists of 19 consonants[1] and five vowels. Its consonant inventory includes one feature that is somewhat unusual, not only in comparison to other Vanuatu languages, but also cross-linguistically (Maddieson, 1989, p. 350). This contrastive feature is the series of apicolabial phonemes, a voiced stop /b̪/, fricative /ð̪/ and nasal /m̪/. Whilst unusual cross-linguistically, apicolabials are characteristic of languages in the South Santo and Northern Malekula areas such as Tutuba (Naito, 2006, p. 217), Mavea, Aore, Vao, Potovro, V'ënen Taut (Lynch, 2005, p. 389), Tangoa and Araki (François, 2002, p. 12).

2.2.1 Consonants

The 19 consonants in the Nese phonemic inventory are shown in Table 2.1. There are five major places of articulation: labial, apicolabial, alveolar, palatal and velar. There is a lack of voiceless counterparts for the voiced apicolabial stop /b̪/ and the voiced labial stop /b/. There is also a lack of a voiced counterpart for the velar stop /k/. The most distinctive feature of the Nese phonemic inventory is the contrastive apicolabial consonants. The voiced apicolabials /b̪/ and /m̪/ are produced with the tongue pushed out and touching the upper lip while the apicolabial fricative is produced with the apex of the tongue raised and pushed outside of the oral cavity and causing a slight obstruction at the tip of the upper lip. The production of the apicolabial stops /b̪/ and /m̪/ is characteristic of the speech of those aged 40 years and above. Speakers aged below 40 rarely distinguish between apicolabials /m̪/ and /b̪/ and the labials /m/ and /b/. These speakers have commented that they find the apicolabials, in particular /b̪/ and /m̪/, to be 'amusing' and consciously avoid the distinction. Similarly, the apicolabial fricative /ð̪/ is sometimes produced as the labial fricative /v/ by these speakers. In this manuscript, I have opted to use /ð̪/ to represent the apicolabial fricative rather than its alternative representation [β].

---

[1] Crowley's (2006c, p. 38) consonant inventory includes two further phonemes – /g/ and /h/ – whose presence he regards as questionable. Current data shows that these two consonants have no phonemic status and examples given in Crowley (2006c, pp. 39 and 40) to account for the existence of these two phonemes are in fact words from the Naha speech variety, which is spoken in nearby Vovo (§1.2.2, Map 6).

2. PHONOLOGY

Table 2.1: Nese phonemic inventory

	Labial	**Apicolabial**	**Alveolar**	**Palatal**	**Velar**
Voiceless stops			t		k
Voiced stops	ᵐb	ᵐb̪	ⁿd		
Fricatives	v	ð̪	s		ɣ
Affricate				tʃ	
Nasals	m	m̪	n		ŋ
Flap			ɾ		
Trill			r		
Laterals			l		
Glides	w			j	

2.2.1.1 Stops

Voiceless stops

Nese has two voiceless stops – /t/ and /k/ – which are articulated at the alveolar and velar places of articulation respectively. The voiceless alveolar stop /t/ is realised as aspirated [tʰ] word initially[2] and intervocalically. When /t/ occurs word finally and in coda position before a consonant occupying the onset position in the immediately following syllable, it is realised as unreleased [t̚].

- /t/ voiceless alveolar stop
→ [tʰ]/ #_, V_V
→ [t̚] / _#, _$
→ [t]/ elsewhere

/natur/	[natʰur]	'sleep'
/teverik/	[tʰevʷerik]	'oh!' EXCLAM
/nað̪at/	[nað̪at̚]	'money'
/botvon/	[mbot̚vʷon]	'just like that'
/ɾaɣtaɣ/	[ɾaxtax]	'get up'

The voiceless velar stop /k/ is realised with aspiration as [kʰ] word initially and intervocalically and is realised as unreleased word finally.

---

2 A word boundary is determined by a lack of pausing between initial and last syllables that form a word, as well as a regular intonation contour beginning from the initial syllable to the last syllable of the word.

- /k/ voiceless velar stop
→ [kʰ]/ #_, V_V
→ [k̚]/ _#
→ [k] elsewhere

/nakis/	[nakʰis]	'good'
/kanan/	[kʰanan]	'us'
/nuak/	[nuʷak̚]	'boat'
/nekre/	[nekre]	'we (INCL)'

The following examples of minimal pairs and near minimal pairs provide evidence of contrast between the two voiceless stop phonemes /t/ and /k/.

/t/ - /k/

Minimal pairs		Near minimal pairs	
Syllable initial		*Syllable final*	
/tanan/	'his/her father'	/balak/	'like'
/kanan/	'us'	/noroblat/	'paper'
Syllable final		*Intervocalically*	
/sat/	'bad'	/natas/	'sea'
/sak/	'my'	/nakalkal/	'bed'

Voiced stops

All voiced stops are homorganically prenasalised in all environments. The voiced bilabial stop /b/ is realised as a labialised offglide when it occurs word initially in monomorphemic forms before the vowel /e/. The labialised segment cannot be phonemic since there are forms that show free variation between a labialised /b/ and the non-labialised /b/ with no contrast in meaning, for most of the fluent Nese speakers. For example:

/bet/	[bʷet] ~ [bet]	'make'
/belek/	[bʷelek] ~ [belek]	'like'

Similarly, if labialised /b/ was phonemic then it would be expected that labialisation would also consistently occur when the segment occurs before other vowels, as is the case with labialised /v/ (§2.2.1.2). However, the only instance when /b/ is labialised is when it precedes /e/. Although Proto Oceanic is reconstructed with a contrastive labialised bilabial stop /bʷ/ (Lynch et al., 2011, p. 64), evidence shows that in Nese, the segment, which may have been contrastive at one stage, has undergone a loss of labialisation.[3] Loss of Proto Oceanic labialisation in bilabial stops has also been noted in the Atchin language in Malekula (Duhamel, 2010, p. 17).

- /b/ voiced bilabial stop
→ [ᵐbʷ]/ #_, _e
→ [ᵐb]/ elsewhere

/betaribo/	[ᵐbʷetariᵐbo]	'name of area'
/nabaŋbaŋ/	[naᵐbaŋᵐbaŋ]	'a variety of banana'
/nasub/	[nasuᵐb]	'chief'
/bel/	[ᵐbʷel]	'speak'

Nese lacks a non-prenasalised phoneme /b/. This is characteristic of some Malekula languages such as Neve'ei (Lynch, Ross & Crowley, 2002, p. 638). Although Nese speakers do not prenasalise /b/ in the variety of Bislama that is used in the Matanvat area, there is, however, a tendency for prenasalisation in Bislama borrowings containing /b/. Examples are given in Table 2.2.

Table 2.2: Prenasalisation in words borrowed from Bislama

Nese words borrowed from Bislama		Bislama	English
bak	[ᵐbak]	[bak]	'bag'
be[4]	[ᵐbe]	[be]	'but'
bolet	[ᵐbolet]	[bolet]	'bullet'
mobael	[moᵐbael]	[mobael]	'mobile phone'
buluk	[ᵐbuluk]	[buluk]	'bullock'

Prenasalised /b/ is treated as a single phoneme rather than as a phonemic cluster, on the basis that Nese syllable structure allows complex onsets, but not complex codas (cf. §2.3.2.1). More specifically, a consonant cluster in onset position may be composed of two consonants only and the phoneme /b/ can never occupy a C_2 position in the cluster. Therefore,

---

3   Lynch (2019) reinforces the claim that synchronically Nese has lost the distinction between /b/ and /bw/ but that, diachronically, Proto Oceanic *bw is now reflected as /b/. The examples he gives to support this claim are when this consonant occupies word initial position before front low /a/ and back mid /o/. In relation to POc *b, he claims that the consonant is reflected as /b/ when before a POc back vowel and when before a POc non-back vowel the consonant is reflected initially as /b/ then shifting to /d/.

4   Nese also has homophone /be/ 'okay'; however, the occurrence of /be/ in the above example is a different word, meaning 'but', and is a borrowing from Bislama.

the analysis advancing a phonemic cluster would suggest that in words such as /tab/ 'to become lost' ([tamb]), the burden of complexity would be on the coda and that [b] is in C_2 position, violating the phonotactic rules.

The voiced apicolabial stop /ḇ/ is realised with the blade of the tongue protruding out of the mouth and touching the upper lip. As stated above, the presence of this phoneme is more salient in the speech of older speakers, particularly those older than 40 years of age; younger speakers rarely make a distinction between /b/ and /ḇ/. However, even amongst older speakers its presence is very rare. Some older speakers, in particular those who have lost their front teeth, opt for /d/ in coda positions in words that normally contain /ḇ/ in these positions – for example, /laɣad/ for /laɣaḇ/ 'on the fire'. The voiced apicolabial stop is prenasalised in all positions. The following illustrates the environments in which /ḇ/ occurs. Examples show that although the phoneme is rare in today's speech, it does occur in all possible environments: word initially, word finally and intervocalically.

- /ḇ/ voiced apicolabial stop

→ [ᵐḇ]

/ḇyaḇye/	[ᵐḇxa ᵐḇxe]	'short'
/laḇlaḇ/	[laᵐḇlaᵐḇ]	'big'
/naɣaḇ/	[naɣaᵐḇ]	'fire'
/naḇeḇ/	[naᵐḇeᵐḇ]	'butterfly'

Like other voiced stops, the alveolar stop /d/ is homorganically prenasalised in all environments.

- /d/ voiced alveolar stop

→ [ⁿd]

/di/	[ⁿdi]	'already'
/deve/	[ⁿdeve]	'or'
/sider/	[siⁿder]	'cut'
/kudruŋo/	[kuⁿdruŋo]	'be quiet'
/neverad/	[neveraⁿd]	'sow'

2. PHONOLOGY

As is the case with the prenasalised segment /ḅ/, /d/ should be analysed as a phonemic unit rather than a cluster consisting of /n/ and /d/, because Nese does not permit complex codas (cf. §2.3.2.1). It should be noted, however, that Nese speakers do not prenasalise /d/ in words borrowed from Bislama, in contrast with the prenasalisation that occurs in borrowings with /b/. The following are words borrowed from Bislama in which the phoneme /d/ is not prenasalised.

| /nuduls/ | [nuduls] | 'noodles' |
| /rodrik/ | [rodrik] | 'Rodrick' (personal name) |

The following contrastive minimal and near minimal pairs are evidence for the set of consonants presented above:

/d/ - /b/

Minimal pairs		Near minimal pairs	
Intervocalically		*Syllable initial*	
/nabor/	'ear'	/belek/	'like'
/nador/	'horizontal house post'	/deldel/	'horizontally'
/neben/	'by itself, himself, herself'	/nelbe/	'roof timber'
/neden/		/deldel/	'horizontally'

/b/ - /ḅ/

Minimal pairs		Near minimal pairs	
Intervocalically		*Syllable initial*	
/neḅen/ 'its, his, her body'		/naḅak/	'banyan tree'
		/aba/	'right!' EXCLAM
/neben/ 'song.3SG'		/ḅeḅ/	'born'
		/bet/	'make'

/ḅ/ - /d/*

Near minimal pairs	
Syllable initial	
/naḅatav/	'breadfruit'
/nadaɣatʃ/	'coconut leaf mat'
/naḅak/	'banyan tree'
/nadan/	'house post'

37

2.2.1.2 Fricatives

There are four fricative phonemes in Nese: apicolabial /ð̼/, labiodental /v/, alveolar /s/, and velar /ɣ/. The apicolabial fricative /ð̼/ is produced with the blade of the tongue raised and causing a slight obstruction of the airflow at the tip of the upper lip. This is a feature of the speech of those aged 40 and above, in particular those living in Matanvat. With teenagers and children in Matanvat village, and also most of the speakers in Vila, the tongue is raised and causes a slight obstruction of airflow at the upper teeth rather than the upper lip. This phoneme is voiced word initially and intervocalically. However, it is not voiced when it occurs before a voiced consonant and there is no evidence to suggest that it occupies word final position.

- /ð̼/ voiced apicolabial fricative
- → [ð̼]/ #_, V_V,
- → [ð̼]/ _C (+voice)

/ð̼an/	[ð̼an]	'go'
/deð̼e/	[ⁿdeð̼e]	'mother'
/natanð̼at/	[natanð̼at]	'Matanvat (name of area)'
/nað̼ŋe/	[nað̼̊ ŋe]	'hill'

The labiodental fricative /v/ exhibits a somewhat complex set of allophonic variations. It is realised as a voiced labiodental fricative word initially and intervocalically. For example:

/verse/	[verse]	'how'
/nevetable/	[nevetaᵐble]	'a fruit tree of the dracontomelon family'

Word finally in monomorphemic forms and before a voiced consonant, /v/ freely varies between the voiceless labiodental [f] and the voiceless bilabial stop [p]. However, when it occurs before a morphemic boundary, /v/ is invariably voiced, contrasting with its occurrence in word final position where it varies between [f] and [p].

/ᵐbenanev/	[mbenanef] ~ [mbenanep]	'to finish, end'
/lev/	[lef] ~ [lep]	'to carry'
/tevtʃen/	[teftʃen] ~ [leptʃen]	'other side'
/lev-ia/	[lev-ia]	'carry me'

Although [f] and [p] are allophones of the segment /v/, the borrowed words from Bislama in Table 2.3, which contain the contrastive phonemes /f/ and /p/ in Bislama, retain their Bislama phonetic features in Nese. For example, although in Nese there is free variation in word final /v/ between [p] and [f], words borrowed from Bislama that end in /f/ do not freely vary between these two allophones. Similarly, word initially, the segment /v/ is always voiced; however, when a borrowed Bislama word begins with a voiceless labiodental fricative, it retains this feature in that environment in Nese.

Table 2.3: Nese words borrowed from Bislama

Nese words borrowed from Bislama		Bislama	English
/fo/	[fo]* [vo]	[fo]	'four'
/sospen/	[sospen] *[sosvʷen]	[sospen]	'saucepan'
/faef/[5]	[faef] *[vaep] ~ [vaef]	[faef]	'five'
/woʃip/	[woʃip] *[woʃif]	[woʃip]	'worship'
/pas/	[pas] *[vas]	[pas]	'past'

Finally, when /v/ is followed by the vowels /a/, /e/, /i/ and /o/ in words where syllables contain identical vowels and identical reduplicated-like forms, there is a prominent labialised off glide [w]. For example:

/volvol/	[vʷolvʷol]	'sell'
/varvar/	[vʷarvʷar]	'pray'
/velvele/	[vʷelvʷele]	'small'

In non-reduplicated-like forms, labialisation is present when the onset of the immediately following syllable is either /l/, /v/, /s/ or /r/. For example:

/vʷavʷe/	[vʷavʷe]	'aunt'
/vʷala/	[vʷala]	'run'
/vʷaratne/	[vʷaratne]	'really' exclam
/nevʷilᵐbat/	[nevʷilᵐbat]	'hair'

The following near minimal pairs indicate the possibility that the labialised voiced bilabial fricative was once a distinct phoneme, although there is no conclusive evidence of this.

---

5   There was one attested example that proved contrary to this. The word for 'fence' in Bislama varies between [fens] ~ [fanis] and [fenis]. A Nese speaker produced it as [mbanis], therefore opting for the bilabial prenasalised stop rather than /f/ or /v/.

/vise/   [vise] 'how many'   /visi/   [vʷisi] 'squeeze it out (coconut milk)'
/verse/   [verse] 'how'   /ver/   [vʷer] 'say'

The potentially plausible analysis for a contrastive labialised /v/ in Nese will be discarded because, firstly, labialisation is restricted to just 16 word forms in the data, the majority of which resemble 'reduplicated-like' word forms and those forms in which all vowels in the syllables are identical. Although this restricted quantity can be attributed to lack of sufficient data, given that labialised /b/ also occurs in a restricted environment, it can be concluded that what was perhaps once a phonemic labialised labio-dental fricative has now merged with the plain labio-dental fricative /v/, which has a labialised allophone.

• /v/ labio-dental fricative
→ [vʷ]/ _a, _i, _e, _o
→ [p] ~ [f]/ _#, #_C
→ [v] elsewhere

The fricative /s/ is realised as a voiceless alveolar fricative in all environments. There is no allophonic variation.

• /s/ alveolar fricative
/s/→ [s]

/sangav'il/   [saŋaðil]   'ten'
/ɣesve/   [ɣesve]   'nine'
/nasalkal/   [nasalkal]   'narrow'
/ɣos/   [ɣos]   'reach'

The voiced velar fricative /ɣ/ is voiced word initially and intervocalically, but is voiceless word finally and after a stop.

• /ɣ/ voiced velar fricative
→ [x] / _#, Cstop_
→ [ɣ]/ elsewhere

/ɣai /   [ɣai]   's/he, it'
/teɣ/   [tex]   'take'
/ɣro/   [ɣro]   'stay'
/byabɣe/   [ᵐb̪xa ᵐb̪xe]   'short'
/nasɣe/   [nasɣe]   'cooked'

2. PHONOLOGY

Below I present contrastive pairs for the fricative phonemes as evidence of their phonemic status.

/s/ - /ð̞/

Minimal pairs		Near minimal pairs	
Syllable initial		*Syllable initial*	
/sat/	'bad'	/nasal/	'road'
/ð̞at/	'four'	/nað̞au/	'pandanus leaf'
/san/	'hers, his, its'	/nese/	'what'
/ð̞an/	'go'	/deð̞e/	'mother'

/v/ - /ɣ/

Minimal pairs		Near minimal pairs	
Syllable initial		*Syllable initial*	
/ɣe/	'this'	/ɣarav/	'crawl'
/ve/	'say'	/varatne/	'really!' EXCLAM
/ɣise/	'who'		
/vise/	'how many'		
/ɣorɣor/	'scratch'		
/vorvor/	'traditional pudding'		

/s/ - /ɣ/

Minimal pairs		Near minimal pairs	
Syllable initial		*Syllable final*	
/nese/	'what'	/natas/	'sea'
/neɣe/	'wood'	/ataɣ/	'after, behind'
		/tʃeles/	'I see/saw'
		/tʃeleɣ/	'all'
		/asaɣ/	'to the right of'
		/tavaɣ/	'break'

/k/ - /ɣ/

Minimal pairs		Near minimal pairs	
Syllable initial		*Syllable initial*	
/ɣise/	'who'	/ɣotʃɣotʃ/	'proper'
/kise/	'look for'	/kotʃ/	'scratch'
		Syllable finally	
		/nanaloɣ/	'kava'
		/nalok/	'laplap (traditional pudding)'
		/sak/	'my'
		/saɣ/	'point'

2.2.1.3 Affricates

The voiceless affricate /tʃ/ is articulated at the palatal place of articulation. There is no allophonic variation.

- /tʃ/ voiceless palatal affricate
→ [tʃ]

/tʃeleɣ/	[tʃelex]	'all, every'
/nevetʃitʃro/	[nevetʃitʃro]	'lizard'
/naratʃ/	[naratʃ]	'house post'

Although there is no allophonic variation, Takau (2016, pp. 50–51) observes that Nese exhibits an unusual instance where [tʃ] can be described as being an allophone of /s/, specifically occurring in the negative marker -*be*-Verb-*te* in cases where the 1st person subject is prefixed to the verb, an example of which is shown below. This contrasts with the example below where 2nd person subject is prefixed to the verb.

ɣina tʃ-be-rongvuson-i-te
1SG 1SG:IRR-NEG-know-3SGOBJ-NEG2
'I don't know it.'
(2012_08_27_obnesp01003 00:10:00.252-00:10:08.949_natural text)

kani kir-s-mbe-rongvuson-i-te
2SG 2SG-IRR-NEG1-know-3SGOBJ-NEG2
'You people don't know it.'
(2014_01_19_naanhy01001 00:43:57.000-00:44:00.000, natural text)

Other person subject prefixes resort to -*s-be*-Verb-*te* akin to the 2SG form. Crowley (2006c, p. 68) argues that [tʃ] is an allomorph occurring when the 1st person singular subject prefix *ne* occurs before the 1st person singular irrealis form *je*. He also presents evidence for another paradigm of subject prefixes containing [tʃ] occurring simultaneously and alternating freely between the paradigm of subject prefixes containing [s]. In Takau (2016) I argue that this alternative paradigm of subject prefixes may have dropped out of usage shortly after Crowley's documentation, given that [tʃe] is restricted solely to the 1st person singular person when marked for irrealis and is not consistently represented in other persons in the irrealis forms. I posit [tʃ] as a possible allphonic variation over the sequence /t/ + /s/ albeit over a non-morphemic boundary, although this sequence is no longer productive in Nese. As will be explained in §5.5.1.1, negation is closely linked with the irrealis mood, and this explains the use of the 1SG irrealis form [tʃ] (being the phonologically reduced form of [tʃe]) in negated clauses. There is evidence of the alveolar nasal [n] undergoing consonant mutation word initially in certain common nouns when deriving their locational counterparts – for example, [nanus] 'bush' and [lanus] 'in the bush'. Therefore, the usage of [tʃe] in 1SG irrealis form could be treated as a case of consonant mutation where the alveolar nasal occurring prefix initially in the realis form [ne] becomes [tʃe] in the irrealis.

The following pairs prove contrast between the phonemes /s/ and /tʃ/.

Minimal pairs		Near minimal pairs	
Syllable final		*Syllable final*	
/letʃ/	'sit on'	/nevetʃitʃro/	'lizard'
/les/	'see'	/nevesis/	'small shell fish that sticks to rocks'

2.2.1.4 Nasals

The phonemes /m̺/, /m/, /n/ and /ŋ/ are realised as voiced nasals and are pronounced at the apicolabial, labial, alveolar and velar places of articulation respectively. There is no allophonic variation for any of the nasal phonemes. Given the moribund status of the language and its rarity in production, it is very difficult to find contrastive pairs for the apicolabial /m̺/.

- /m̺/ voiced apicolabial nasal

→ [m̺]

/m̺om̺oŋ/	'cough'
/tom̺ot/	'black ground'
/nam̺atʃ/	'fish'

- /m/ voiced bilabial nasal

→ [m]

/moron/	[moron]	'morning'
/namal/	[namal]	'anchorage'
/naram/	[naram]	'yam'

- /n/ voiced alveolar nasal

→ [n]

/naram/   [naram]   'yam'
/nananɣo/   [nananɣo]   'bird'
/natʰan/   [nathan]   'ground'

- /ŋ/ voiced velar nasal

→ [ŋ]

/ŋar/   [ŋar]   'cry'
/ɾeŋen/   [ɾeŋen]   'in'
/naᵐbaŋᵐbaŋ/   [nambaŋmbaŋ]   'a type of banana'

The following pairs are evidence of the contrast between these segments.

/m̪/ - /m/

Minimal pairs		Near minimal pairs	
/nam̪at/	'eye'	/nam̪al/	'a type of eel'
/namat/	'snake'	/nama/	'I come'
/nem̪ere/	'eel'		
/nemere/	'people'		

/n/ - /ŋ/

Minimal pairs		Near minimal pairs	
Syllable final		*Syllable initial*	
/nen/	'its'	/ninin/	'wet'
/neŋ/	'name'	/ŋini/	'to it'
/natan/	'ground'	*Syllable finally*	
/nataŋ/	'basket'		
/nabon/	'napoleon fish'	/naran/	'because'
/naboŋ/	'day'	/naraŋ/	'dry'

/n/ - /m/

Minimal pairs		Near minimal pairs	
Syllable initial		*Syllable initial*	
/navos/	'sore (noun)'	/nanatu/	'right'
/mavos/	'good'	/namat/	'snake'
Syllable finally			
/run/	'with'	/nanarte/	'rope'
/rum/	'wild'	/namartaɣ/	'young man'

2.2.1.5 Trill/Flap

The rhotic consonants /r/ and /ɾ/ are both produced at the alveolar place of articulation. The alveolar trill /r/ is strongly trilled in most environments, although it is weakly trilled word finally in rapid speech. The flap /ɾ/ has a full release intervocalically and word initially. However, it freely varies between a fully released [ɾ] and a less released variant when it occurs before a consonant either over a word boundary or word internally, in particular, in fast speech. For example:

Slow speech	Fast speech	Translation
neɣoɾ nani	neɣoɾ˺ nani	'I grated the coconut'
ne-kuɾkuɾaɣ	ne-kuɾ˺kuɾaɣ	'I am tired'

• /r/ voiced alveolar trill

→ [r]

/ruanen/	[ruʷanen]	'with'
/norul/	[norul]	'egg'
/terter/	[terter]	'strong'

• /ɾ/ voiced alveolar flap

→ [ɾ˺] / _C

→ [ɾ] elsewhere

/ɣɾo/	[ɣɾo]	'stay'
/buɾo/	[ᵐbuɾo]	'only'
/ŋiɾ/	[ŋiɾ˺]	'cry'

Older speakers living in Matanvat generally make a distinction between the flap and the trill, while younger speakers and older speakers who live in Port Vila have lost the distinction in their speech and tend to use /r/ rather than /ɾ/. Therefore, those in the latter group would use [roŋ-o] 'hear it' and [var-i] 'say it' compared to [roŋ-o] and [vaɾ-i].

The following minimal and near miminal pairs is evidence for the two contrastive pairs and with other phonetically similar segments:

/r/ - /ɾ/

Minimal pairs		Near minimal pairs	
Syllable initial		*Syllable initial*	
/ran/	'morning'	/ɾub/	'kill'
/ɾan/	'theirs'	/rum/	'wild'
		/ɾu/	'two'
		/run/	'with'
		/naɾaŋ/	'dry'
		/naram/	'yam'

2.2.1.6 Laterals

The voiced alveolar lateral /l/ exhibits no allophonic variation.

• /l/ voiced alveolar lateral

→ [l]

/leð̃ɣan/	[leð̃ɣan]	'middle'
/tʃeleŋi/	[tʃeleŋi]	'all, every'
/saɣal/	[saɣal]	'one'

The following are contrastive pairs with the phonetically similar segment /r/.

/r/ - /l/

Minimal pairs		Near minimal pairs	
Syllable initial		*Syllable initial*	
/nare/	'blood'	/nalok/	'laplap'
/nale/	'language'	/naror/	'cloud'
/ralok/	'my voice'		
/lalok/	'my heart'		
/niar/	'bow'		
/nial/	'sun'		

2.2.1.7 Glides

The segments /w/ and /j/ are pronounced at the labial and palatal places of articulation respectively. There are only five forms in the data containing /w/ and two stems that contain /j/.

• /w/ bilabial glide

→ [w]

| /wor/ | [wor] | 'eat' |
| /womu/ | [womu] | 'oh' exclam |

2. PHONOLOGY

- /j/ palatal glide

→ [j]

| /jas/ | [jas] | 'go' |
| /jat/ | [jat] | 'sit' |

The following is the only near minimal pair in the data:

Near minimal pairs	
Syllable initially	
/watʃi/	'eat it'
/jas/	'walk'

These two glides may be inserted on the phonetic level, between adjacent falling vowels in particular /i.a/ → [i.ʲa], /i.e/ → [i.ʲe], and /u.a/ → [u.ʷa].

2.2.2 Vowels

Nese's vowel inventory includes the basic five vowel contrast, which is typical of many Vanuatu languages such as South Efate (Thiebeger, 2006, p. 54) and Nahavaq (Dimock, 2009, p. 30). The front and central vowels /e/, /i/ and /a/ are realised with spreading of the lips while the back vowels /u/ and /o/ are realised with rounded lips. There is no evidence for contrastive vowel length or for a contrastive schwa, both of which are features common to many languages of central and northern Malekula such as Naman (Crowley, 2006b, p. 26). The vowel phonemes are given in Table 2.4.

Table 2.4: Vowel phonemes

	Front	Central	Back
High	i		u
Mid	e		o
Low		a	

The segment /i/ is a high front vowel. It has no allophones.

- /i/ high front vowel

→ [i]

/inieɣe/	[iniʲeɣe]	'now'
/navitʃ/	[navitʃ]	'banana'
/kani/	[kʰani]	'you (PL)'

The segment /e/ is a mid front vowel.

- /e/ mid front vowel

→ [e]

/eğan/	[eğan]	'there'
/nasɣe/	[nasɣe]	'cooked'
/tʃeleŋi/	[tʃeleŋi]	'all, every'

Evidence for the contrast is shown by the following near minimal pairs:

/i/ - /e/

Near minimal pairs	
/ɣise/	'who'
/ɣesve/	'seven'
/ŋe/	'this'
/ŋin/	preposition
/nevisi/	'I squeezed it out (the coconut milk)'
/nevesis/	'small shell fish that sticks to rocks'

The segment /a/ is a low central vowel. It has no allophonic variation.

- /a/ low central vowel

→ [a]

/atan/	[atʰan]	'down'
/ğan/	[ğan]	'go'
/ma/	[ma]	'come'

Below I present contrastive pairs for the segments /e/ and /a/ as evidence of their phonemic status.

/e/ - /a/

Minimal pairs		Near minimal pairs	
/natan/	'ground'	/nataŋ/	'basket'
/neten/	'for'	/neteŋe/	'thing'
/ŋer/	'remove pandanus leaves'	/nasal/	'road'
/ŋar/	'cry'	/nese/	'what'

The segment /u/ is a high back vowel and the segment /o/ is a mid back vowel.

- /u/ high back vowel

→ [u]

/use/	[use]	'rain (verb)'
/nause/	[nause]	'rain (noun)'
/nanus/	[nanus]	'bush'
/ɾu/	[ɾu]	'two'

- /o/ mid back vowel

→ [o]

/toɣ/	[toɣ]	'stay'
/maɾo/	[maɾo]	'up'
/noɾoᵐblat/	[noɾoᵐblat]	'paper'

Below are the contrastive pairs for the segments /o/ and /u/.

/o/ - /u/

Minimal pairs		Near minimal pairs	
/ɾov/	'finish'	/noaɾ/	'clean'
/ɾuv/	'plant'	/nua/	'water'
/os/	'different'		
/us/	'ask'		

2.3 Phonotactics

This section describes the way in which Nese phonemes may be combined and the positions they may occupy in a word or syllable. I begin with a discussion of the combination of consonant and vowel phonemes in Nese roots (§2.3.1) followed by a discussion of the Nese syllable (§2.3.2). I then examine the possible consonant (§2.3.2.1) and vowel (§2.3.2.2) distribution.

2.3.1 Consonant and vowel combinations

Roots begin overwhelmingly with consonants rather than vowels, which occur root initially in very low frequency across the word classes. This is particularly true of the back vowels, given that the /u/ vowel is virtually non-existent root initially, only present in the verb root *us-* 'to ask' and the /o/ vowel has merely two occurrences root initially. A somewhat similar statement can be applied to the other two front vowels /i/ and /e/, given that Nese allows /i/ to occur root initially only in the adverb /inieɣe/ and in the demonstrative /ieɣe/. The central vowel /a/ occurs root initially only in the class of directionals in the forms /asaɣ/ 'to the right of', /atan/ 'down' and /asuv/ 'to the left of'.

Any consonant may occupy root initial position. However, the consonants /m̪b̪/, /ð̪/, /m̪/, /w/ and /j/ are not common root initially, although this may be due to lack of data, in particular with the apicolabials. The most common segment to appear root initially is /n/, with nouns comprising the overwhelming majority of roots made up of /n/. The only other word classes that contain roots beginning with /n/ are prepositions and adverbs, although there are roughly less than 10 roots in each of these word classes with root initial /n/. Given that Proto Oceanic employed the *na article to mark the common nonhuman noun (Lynch, 2001), it is no surprise that nouns comprise the majority of roots containing root initial /n/ because virtually all nouns in Nese begin with the segment /n/ and a vowel. The other nasal segments /m/ and /ŋ/ occur in word initial position in less than 10 root forms in the data.

A handful of nouns have root initial /t/ and other word classes that have root initial /t/ are subordinators, adverbs and verbs. Nese does not permit /t/ to be part of a consonant cluster in root initial position since all the roots with /t/ in root initial position can only be followed by any of the five vowels. The voiceless consonant /k/, on the other hand, occurs root initially in only three word classes: pronouns, verbs and adverbs.

Nese also shows a strong preference for consonants to occupy root final position over vowels. The presence of vowels in root final position is very marginal with the vowels /e/ and /a/ being the most common root final vowels. The occurrence of the back vowels /o/ and /u/ in root final position contrasts with their distribution root initially in that Nese has around a handful of roots ending in /o/ and /u/, the majority of these belonging to the class of nouns. All consonants except for the apicolabial fricative /ð̪/ and the glides /w/ and /j/ occur root finally.

2.3.2 Syllable structure

Syllabification may be derived in any language by applying syllabification universals such as the maximal onset principle and language specific syllabification principles. Native speaker intuitions may also be employed to ascertain syllable structure. However, Hayes (1995, p. 253) proposes that the maximal onset principle is perhaps not the ideal method for syllabification cross-linguistically as the syllabification results it sometimes produces do not correspond with the permissible onset clusters in a language. Due to this cautionary note, when attempting to syllabify Nese syllables, I commence by extracting the syllable structure of monosyllabic words and then applying that derived structure to longer polysyllabic words, while taking into consideration the types of permissible onset clusters.

The basic syllable in Nese is:

- $\sigma \rightarrow (C_1)\ (C_2)\ V\ (C_3)$

As shown in Table 2.5, the only syllable patterns allowed in monosyllabic words are:

- $\sigma \rightarrow C_1 V_1$
- $\sigma \rightarrow C_1 V_1 C_2$
- $\sigma \rightarrow C_1 C_2 V_1$
- $\sigma \rightarrow C_1 C_2 V_1 C_3$

Table 2.5: Some examples of monosyllabic words

Some examples of monosyllabic words		
/ma/	'come'	$C_1 V_1$
/te/	subordinator	$C_1 V_1$
/ðan/	'go'	$C_1 V_1 C_2$
/buŋ/	'night'	$C_1 V_1 C_2$
/mre/	'ripe'	$C_1 C_2 V_1$
/vreŋ/[6]	'throw'	$C_1 C_2 V_1 C_3$

There are no words in the data that show that a monosyllabic word can be made up of a single vowel occurring on its own. However, it is in polysyllabic words that we find evidence for having only a vowel in

---

6   Verbs appear in the root form in the 3SG realis form and are pronounceable as a word.

a syllable. As shown in Table 2.6, a syllable may consist of one single nucleus that may stand as the initial syllable in a word; for example, /e.ɖan/ 'there' or /i.ni.e.ɣe/ 'here'. Given that Nese does not show a preference for the high back vowel /u/ to occupy word initial position, it follows that a /u/ cannot form the nucleus of a syllable composed of a single nucleus, lacking codas and onsets (cf. §2.3.2.2).

Table 2.6: Distribution of the vocalic nucleus in the Nese syllable

Vowel forming the nucleus of a syllable	Position of syllable in the word		Position of nucleus in the word	
	Word initial	Word final	Nucleus of first syllable	Nucleus in last syllable
/a/	/a.tan/ 'down'	/ɣi.na/ 'I'	/na.ɣa/ 'tree'	/na.tan/ 'ground'
/e/	/e.ɖan/ 'there'	/ver.se/ 'how'	/ev.laɣ/ 'happy'	/tʃe.leɣ/ 'all, every'
/i/	/i.e.ɣe/ 'here'	/ne.vi.ɾi/ 'dog'	/i.ni.e.ɣe/ 'here'	/ka.ni/ 'you (PL)'
/o/	/os/ 'different'	/no.bo.tol.vo/ 'pillow'	/os/ 'different'	/no.bo.tol.vo/ 'pillow'
/u/		/ne.ɖe.nu/ 'place'	/mu.rol/ 'short'	/no.ɣo.bu/ 'bamboo'

2.3.2.1 Consonant distribution

Nese words that are monomorphemic exhibit the following consonant and vowel patterns shown in Table 2.7.

Table 2.7: Consonant and vowel patterns in monomorphemic words

Pattern	Examples
CV	/ɾu/ 'two'
CVV	/nu.a/ 'water'
CVC	/ɖan/ 'go'
VCVC	/a.tan/ 'down'
CVVCV	/na.u.se/ 'rain'
CVCVCVC	/be.na.nev/ 'yesterday' /ben.an.ev/ /be.nan.ev/
CVCV	/bu.ɾo/ 'only'
CVCVC	/na.nus/ 'bush'
CCV	/mre/ 'ripe'
CVV	/ɣa.i/ 3SG
VVCV	/i.e.ɣe/ 'here'

Pattern	Examples
CVCCV	/nas.ɣe/ 'cooked'
	/na.sɣe/
CCVC	/vreŋ/ 'to throw'

The patterns in Table 2.7 indicate that consonant clusters in the onset and intervocalic positions are limited to two consonant positions. In a Nese syllable, the burden of complexity is on the onset rather than the coda and, therefore, permissible consonant clusters are assigned to onset or word initial positions rather than to coda positions. However, the task of determining an ideal syllabification may be problematic. For example, /tʃotʃomlaɣ/ 'smooth' may be syllabified as /tʃo.tʃom.laɣ/ or /tʃo.tʃo.mlaɣ/ on the grounds that /ml/ is a permissible initial consonant sequence. The presence of two-member consonant clusters in word initial position is quite rare, though, compared to a CV combination.

As shown in Table 2.7, consonant clusters such as CVCCV and CVCVCCV could be syllabified as CVC.CV or CV.CCV depending on the clusters in the word and the phonotactic constraints mentioned previously regarding permissible clusters in onset positions.

Table 2.8 shows the permissible consonant clusters in onset position in initial syllables of monomorphemic words.

Table 2.8: Consonant clusters

Permissible consonant clusters in onset position in initial syllables in monomorphemic words		
C_1	C_2	Example
ɣ velar fricative	ɾ alveolar flap	/ɣɾo/ 'stay'
t alveolar voiceless stop	ɾ alveolar flap	/tɾo/ 'stand'
m labial nasal	r alveolar trill	/mre/ 'ripe'
m labial nasal	l alveolar laterals	/mlerriŋ/ 'desert/leave'
v labial fricative	s alveolar fricative (voiceless)	/vso/ 'white'
b̪ apicolabial voiced stop	ɣ velar fricative	/b̪ɣadɣe/ 'short'
b bilabial voiced stop	r alveolar trill	/bret/ 'thatch'

Permissible consonant clusters in onset position in initial syllables in monomorphemic words

C_1	C_2	Example
v labial fricative	t alveolar voiceless stop	/vtentʃe/ 'thick'
v labial fricative	r alveolar flap	/vreŋ/ 'throw'
b	l	/blablo/ 'a type of basket'

There are no clear-cut generalisations that may be deduced from Table 2.8 regarding possible consonant clusters, since a large number of clusters may be possible. On the whole, both obstruents and sonorants can occur in C_1 and C_2 with a range of possible manners of articulation, although voiced stops cannot occur in C_2 position. Liquids and glides can only occur in C_2 position and never in C_1 position. The nasal /m/ can occur in C_1 position; however, other consonants in C_1 are obstruents.

The following consonants are the only ones that may occupy C_1 position in $C_1C_2V(C_3)$ clusters: fricatives, nasals, stops and affricates. Specific members of these segments that may occur in this position are:

- Fricatives: /ɣ/, /v/ and /s/
- Nasals: /m/
- Stops: /t/, /b̼/ and /b/
- Affricates: /tʃ/

As shown above, all fricative phonemes may occupy C_1 position and the presence of apicolabial phonemes in C_1 position is limited to the phoneme /b̼/. In fact, there is only one word in the data where C_1 is the apicolabial bilabial stop /b̼/ and that is /b̼ɣadʸe/ 'short'.

The majority of consonants that may occupy C_2 position are articulated at the alveolar place of articulation. All liquids and sonorants may occur in this position. The following consonants are the only ones that may occupy C_2 position: alveolar flap/trill, alveolar lateral, alveolar fricatives, alveolar voiceless stop, alveolar nasals and velar fricatives. Specific members of these segments in C_2 positions are:

- Alveolar flap: /ɾ/
- Alveolar lateral: /l/
- Alveolar fricatives: /s/

2. PHONOLOGY

- Alveolar voiceless stops: /t/
- Alveolar nasal: /n/
- Velar fricative: /ɣ/

In connection to permissible combinations of C_1 and C_2 clusters in initial syllables, the following generalisation holds:

- C_1 and C_2 cannot both be voiced segments. The possible combinations are:
  - C_1 is voiced and C_2 is voiceless;
  - C_1 and C_2 are voiceless;
  - C_1 is voiceless and C_2 is voiced;

In Table 2.8, some clusters are shown that are made up of two voiced segments such as /vr/ and /bɣ/. In cases like these, an allophonic variant of one of the fricative phonemes occurs. Therefore, in /vr/ sequence, the voiceless allophone [f] is used instead while in /bɣ/ the voiceless allophone [x] is used. This always and only occurs with fricatives.

While Nese does not permit consonant clusters in word final position, they are acceptable word medially in polysyllabic monomorphemic words. On the basis of phonotactic principles polysyllabic words are syllabified as demonstrated in Table 2.9. The first column of Table 2.9 shows the words and the second column shows the possible options for syllabification.

Table 2.9: Consonant clusters in word medial position

Consonant clusters in word medial position	
/nasɣe/ 'cooked'	nas.ɣe
	na.sɣe
/nenelɣare/ 'cold'	nen.el.ɣar.e
/raɣtaɣ/ 'get up'	raɣ.taɣ
/ɣavɣav/ 'hot'	ɣav.ɣav
/velvele/ 'small'	vel.vel.e
/kurkuraɣ/ 'tired of'	kur.ku.raɣ
	kur.kur.aɣ
/botvon/ 'useless, insignificant'	bot.von
	bo.tvon
/saɣsaɣ/ 'work'	saɣ.saɣ
/noroblat/ 'paper'	no.ro.blat
	nor.ob.lat
/nekre/ 'we'	ne.kre
	nek.re

2.3.2.2 Vowel distribution

All vowels can occupy word initial position, albeit rarely, with the exception of the high back vowel /u/. However, vowel sequences in Nese are relatively uncommon; an overwhelming majority of words begin with consonants rather than vowels. Table 2.10 shows the attested vowel sequences.

Table 2.10: Vowel sequences

	a	e	i	o	u
a			/nial/ 'sun'		/nua/ 'water'
e			/nies/ 'smoke'		/lue/ 'out'
i	/naine/ 'the house'	/tei/ 'cut'			
o					
u	/naute/ 'garden'	/nemeleun/ 'chief'			

The unshaded cells in Table 2.10 represent vowel sequences that appear the most frequently in the Nese data. Grey shaded areas are very rare sequences that may be permitted in borrowed words from Bislama. Unshaded cells are those for which the vowels may co-occur in a sequence while black shaded cells represent impermissible vowel sequences. The table shows that none of the Nese vowels may participate in a V_1+V_1 sequence, and vowel sequences are limited to two member clusters. Apart from prohibiting identical vocalic sequences such as /aa/, other impermissible vocalic clusters include /oa/, /ea/, /iu/, /oe/, /ou/, and /ui/. This is represented by the black shaded cells in Table 2.10. The following generalisations hold regarding the distribution of vocalic clusters:

- If V_1 is a low back vowel /a/ or a mid front vowel /e/, V_2 can only be either a high front vowel /i/ or a high back vowel /u/.
- If V_1 is a high front vowel /i/ or a high back vowel /u/, V_2 can only be a low back vowel /a/, mid front vowel /e/ and a mid back vowel /o/.
- The vocalic sequence that is less favoured than all the others is that which has the mid back vowel /o/ in V_1 position. In the current data, there is only one occurrence of /oi/ and that is in the verb root /ɣoɣoi/ 'to clean'.

Sequences of falling vowels (V_1 is a high vowel and V_2 a low vowel) have an intermediate epenthetic glide. The following vocalic sequences shown in Table 2.11 have intermediate epenthetic glides.

Table 2.11: Sequences of falling vowels

ia	nial	[niʲal] 'sun'
io	io	[iʲo] 'yes'
ua	nua	[nuʷa] 'water'
uo	nevuon	[nevuʷon] 'it's seed'

2.4 Stress

Stress is not contrastive in Nese. As observed by Crowley (2006c, p. 42), Nese generally displays a strong preference for assigning stress to penultimate syllables. A similar stress pattern has been proposed for Proto Oceanic (Lynch et al., 2011, p. 67). However, a few Nese words assign stress on the last syllable, rather than on the penultimate syllable.

The tendency for stress on penultimate syllables is exhibited in most word classes such as nouns, verbs, prepositions, adverbs and numerals. Examples of these are given in Table 2.12.

Table 2.12: Stress placement across word classes

Word classes				
nouns	**verbs**	**prepositions**	**adverbs**	**numerals**
/ˈna.ram/ 'yam'	/ˈsɣas.ɣo/ 'sing'	/ˈre.ŋen/ 'in, on'	/ˈa.taɣ/ 'after, behind'	/ˈsa.ɣal/ 'one'
/ˈna.ɣab̪/ 'fire'	/ˈta.siɣ/ 'fly'	/ˈne.ten/ 'because'	/ˈa.mu/ 'first'	/ˈɣes.ve/ 'nine'
/ˈna.tan/ 'ground'	/ˈva.la/ 'run'			

The examples in Table 2.12 show penultimate stress on disyllabic words, and this pattern also persists in trisyllabic and polysyllabic monomorphemic words as shown in Table 2.13.

Table 2.13: Stress in trisyllabic and polysyllabic words

| /be.ˈna.nev/ 'yesterday' |
| /na.ˈmar.taɣ/ 'last born' |
| /ver.ˈver.ik/ 'small' |
| /na.ˈnar.te/ 'rope' |
| /ne.ˈner.nar/ 'male' |
| /no.ˈro.vitʃ/ 'banana leaf' |
| /sa.ˈŋa.ð̪il/ 'ten' |
| /ne.ve.ˈtʃitʃ.ro/ 'lizard' |
| /ne.me.ˈra.mu/ 'eldest brother' |
| /na.ma.ˈla.kel/ 'young boy' |

The examples in Table 2.12 and Table 2.13 show that stress placement is not based on syllable weight because it generally falls on the penultimate syllable irrespective of the syllable structure. Even though stress is primarily placed on the penultimate syllable, there are a few polysyllabic nouns that deviate from this pattern, along with the class of independent pronouns. Independent pronouns in Nese are either monosyllabic or disyllabic. Some of the disyllabic pronouns have stress on the initial (penultimate) syllable, but three of the pronouns have stress on the final syllable, as shown in Table 2.14. There are also three trisyllabic forms in the data that exhibit stress on the final syllable. As shown in Table 2.14, these are all generic terms referring to animals. This minor variation in stress could reflect earlier stress patterns that may be subject to an ongoing change or internal morphological structure that sees stress being assigned to particular roots rather than to stems of polymorphemic words.

Table 2.14: Polysyllabic words with stress on last syllable

Nouns		Pronouns	
/na.ma.ˈvor/	'clam shell'	/ɣi.ˈna/	'I'
/no.bu.ˈɣas/	'pig'	/ɣu.ˈnoɣ/	'you'
/no.vu.ˈmaɣ/	'bird'	/ka.ˈnan/	'us'

2.5 Morphophonemic processes

Nese exhibits four processes occurring as a result of the interaction between its morphosyntactic and phonological attributes: vowel harmony (§2.5.1), vowel raising (§2.5.2), phonologically conditioned alternation and phonological epenthesis (§2.5.3) and reduplication (§2.5.4).

2.5.1 Vowel harmony

Kramer (2003, p. 3) defines vowel harmony as a phenomenon in which potentially all vowels in adjacent moras or syllables within a domain like the phonological or morphological word (or a smaller morphological domain) systematically agree with each other with regard to one or more articulatory features. This process is a widespread morphophonemic phenomenon in Nese, manifesting itself in the propagation of the feature value [+back] of vowels in initial syllables in verb roots to preceding and following vowels that would otherwise surface as [-back]. In Nese, vowel harmony is bidirectional, applying from right to left and left to right. In the former, the vowels in the verb root affects to the vowel in the immediately

2. PHONOLOGY

preceding morphemes namely, the realis (§2.5.1.1.1) and irrealis subject prefixes (§2.5.1.1.2) and the negative discontinuous markers (§2.5.1.2). When occurring from a right to left direction, the effect of the process is restricted to the 3SG object pro-index (§2.5.1.3).

2.5.1.1 Vowel harmony in subject cross-indexes

As will be discussed in §5.4.1, subject markers prefixed on the verb carry marking for the realis and irrealis moods. Vowel harmony operates via the vowel in the initial syllable of the verb root triggering harmony in the vowel in the subject markers in terms of backness.

2.5.1.1.1 Realis subject prefixes

The realis subject pro-index forms are outlined in Table 2.15 with the corresponding forms that occur as a result of vowel harmony.

Table 2.15: Vowel harmony in realis subject prefixes

Person/ number	Subject prefix	Form of vowel in subject prefix	Form of initial vowel in verb stem with examples
1SG	/ne-/	[ne-]	/a/ e.g. [ne-ᵐbat-e] 'I made it' /i/ e.g. [ne-liɣaɣ] 'I returned' /e/ e.g. [ne-retʃ] 'I spoke'
		[no-]	/o/ e.g. [no-ɣro] 'I stayed' /u/ e.g. [no-sul-u] 'I burnt it'
2SG	/ɣo-/	[ɣo-]	/a/ e.g. [ɣo-ᵐbat-e] 'you made it' /e/ e.g. [ɣo-retʃ] 'you spoke' /i/ e.g. [ɣo-liɣaɣ] 'you returned' /o/ e.g. [ɣo-tʃov] 'you fell' /u/ e.g. [ɣo-sul-u] 'you burnt it'
3SG	Ø-		
1PL INCL	/ri-/	[ri-]	/a/ e.g. [ri-ᵐbat-e] 'we (INCL) did it' /e/ e.g. [ri-ᵐbʷel] 'we (INCL) spoke' /i/ e.g. [ri-liɣaɣ] 'we (INCL) returned'
		[ro-]	/o/ e.g. [ro-ɣro] 'we stayed'
		[ru-]	/u/ e.g. [ru-mul] 'we returned'
1PL EXCL	/ᵐbir-/	[ᵐbir-]	/a/ e.g. [ᵐbir-ᵐbat-e] 'we (EXCL) did it' /e/ e.g. [ᵐbir-tʃnetʃne] 'we (EXCL) fished' /i/ e.g. [ᵐbir-liɣaɣ] 'we (EXCL) returned'
		[ᵐbor-]	/o/ e.g. [ᵐbor-ɣro] 'we (EXCL) stayed'
		[ᵐbur-]	/u/ e.g. [ᵐbur-mul] 'we (EXCL) returned'
2PL	/kir-/	[kir-]	/a/ e.g. [kir-ɠan] 'you (PL) went' /e/ e.g. [kir-tʃnetʃne] 'you (PL) fished' /i/ e.g. [kir-liɣaɣ] 'you (PL) returned'
		[kor-]	/o/ e.g. [kor-ɣro] 'you (PL) stayed'
		[kur-]	/u/ e.g. [sul-u] 'you (PL) burnt it'

Person/ number	Subject prefix	Form of vowel in subject prefix	Form of initial vowel in verb stem with examples
3PL	/ri-/	[ri-]	/a/ e.g. [ri-ǧan] 'they went' /e/ e.g. [ri-tʃnetʃne] 'they fished' /i/ e.g. [ri-liɣaɣ] 'they returned'
		[ro-]	/o/ e.g. [ro-ɣro] 'they stayed'
		[ru-]	/u/ e.g. [ru-mul] 'they returned'

Table 2.15 shows the underlying forms that have the widest distribution under the column titled 'subject prefix', their respective variant forms that have undergone vowel harmony in the 'form of vowel in subject prefix' column, in addition to the environments in which they occur as displayed in the last column. Singular subject cross-indexes, except for the 3SG, which is zero marked, only allow the selection of the high close mid vowel /o/ triggered by [+back close] /u/ vowel and [+back close mid] /o/ vowels in the verb root. This contrasts with plural subject cross-indexes attached to verbs with similar vowels, where the [+back close] /u/ vowel triggers /u/ vowel in the subject cross-index and, on the other hand, the [+back close mid] /o/ vowel triggers the /o/ vowel in the subject cross-index. The vowel in the 2SG form that has undergone vowel raising, however, is invariably /o/ regardless of the backness of the vowel in the initial syllable of the verb root. On the whole, verb roots containing front vowels in their initial syllable trigger harmonising resulting in the high close vowel /i/ in all subject cross-indexes except in the 1SG, where the harmonised form is invariably the high close mid vowel /e/.

The verbal roots in Table 2.15 are mostly monosyllabic with the exception of the intransitive [-tʃnetʃne] and [-liɣaɣ]. This raises a question regarding the operation of vowel harmony in disyllabic forms in which the vowel in the second syllable is high front /i/, high back /u/ or mid front /e/. Evidence from the polysyllabic verb [rongvusoni] 'know' in example (2.1) clearly shows that the initial vowel in the verb root triggers harmony in the 3PL realis subject cross-index.

2.1 *Sᵐbonon ɣar ro-roŋvuson-i.*
some 3PL 3PL:REAL-know-3SGOBJ
'Some they know it.'
(2014_01_19 naanhy01001 00:43:14.000-00:43:16.000, natural text)

2.5.1.1.2 Irrealis subject prefixes

As described in §5.4.1.2, the irrealis mood is marked on the verb via the irrealis marker -*se*- attached to the person and number marker for all persons and numbers with the exception of the 1SG form where there are two variant irrealis forms. These irrealis forms are outlined in the column entitled 'subject prefix' in Table 2.16.

Table 2.16: Forms of subject cross-indexes that have undergone vowel harmony

Person/ number	Subject prefix	Subject prefix (after vowel harmony has occurred)	Environment When the vowel in the verb stem is:
1SG	/ⁿde-/	de-	/a/ e.g. [ⁿde-ᵐbat-e] 'I will do it' /e/ e.g. [ⁿde-ɾetʃ] 'I will speak' /i/ e.g. [ⁿde-liɣaɣ] 'I will return'
		do-	/o/ e.g. [ⁿdo-kol-o] 'I will bring it' /u/ e.g. [ⁿdo-sul-u] 'I will burn it'
	/tʃe-/	tʃe-	/a/ e.g. [tʃe-ᵐbat-e] 'I will do it' /e/ e.g. [tʃe-ɾetʃ] 'I will speak' /i/ e.g. [tʃe-liɣaɣ] 'I will return'
		tʃo-	/o/ e.g. [tʃe-kol-o] 'I will bring it' /u/ e.g. [tʃo-sul-u] 'I will burn it'
2SG	/ɣose-/	ɣo-se-	/a/ e.g. [ɣose-ᵐbat-e] 'you will do it' /e/ e.g. [ɣose-ɾetʃ] 'you will speak' /i/ e.g. [ɣose-liɣaɣ] 'you will return'
		ɣo-so-	/o/ e.g. [ɣoso-ɣɾo] 'you will stay' /u/ e.g. [ɣoso-sul-u] 'you will burn it'
3SG	/se-/	se-	/a/ e.g. [se-ᵐbat-e] 's/he will do it' /e/ e.g. [se-ɾetʃ] 's/he will speak' /i/ e.g. [se-liɣaɣ] 's/he will return'
		so- su-	/o/ e.g. [so-kol-o] 's/he will bring it' /u/ e.g. [su-sul-u] 's/he will burn it'
1PL INCL	/ri-si-/	risi-	/a/ e.g. [risi-ᵐbat-e] 'we will do it' /e/ e.g. [risi-ɾetʃ] 'we will speak' /i/ e.g. [risi-liɣaɣ] 'we will return'
		ru-su-	/u/ e.g. [rusu-mul] 'we will return home'
		ro-so-	/o/ e.g. [roso-ɣɾo] 'we will stay'
1PL EXCL	/ᵐbir-si-/	bir-si	/a/ e.g. [ᵐbirsi-ᵐbat-e] 'we (EXCL) will do it' /e/ e.g. [ᵐbirse-ɾetʃ] 'we (EXCL) will do it' /i/ e.g. [ᵐbiri-liɣaɣ] 'we (EXCL) will return'

Person/ number	Subject prefix	Subject prefix (after vowel harmony has occurred)	Environment When the vowel in the verb stem is:
		bor-so	/o/ e.g. [ᵐborso-ɣɾo] 'we (EXCL) will stay'
		bur-su	/u/ e.g. [ᵐbursu-mul] 'we (EXCL) will return home'
2PL	/kir-si-/	kir-si-	/a/ e.g. [kirsi-ᵐbat-e] 'you (PL) will do it'
			/e/ e.g. [kirsi-ɾetʃ] 'you (PL) will speak'
			/i/ e.g. [kirsi-liɣaɣ] 'you (PL) will return'
		kur-su-	/u/ e.g. [kursu-mul] 'you (PL) will return home'
		kor-so-	/o/ e.g. [korso-kol-o] 'you will bring it'
3PL	/ri-si-/	ri-si-	/a/ e.g. [risi-ᵐbat-e] 'they will do it'
			/e/ e.g. [risi-ɾetʃ] 'they will speak'
			/i/ e.g. [risi-liɣaɣ] 'they will return'
		ru-su-	/u/ e.g. [rusu-mul] 'they will return'
		ro-so-	/o/ e.g. [roso-kol-o] 'they will bring it'

Contrasting with irrealis forms in the 2SG, 3SG, 1PL INCL, 1PL EXCL, 2PL, and 3PL forms that acquire irrealis marking via prefixation of the form *-se-* on the verb with the preceding morpheme bearing person and number marking, the 1SG irrealis forms [ⁿde-] and [tʃe-] are probably derived from /ne/ via some other morphophonological process yet to be ascertained. However, the manner in which vowel harmony operates in the 1SG irrealis forms is analogous to its operation in the 1SG realis form, in that verbs containing [+back +high] and [+back +mid high] vowels in the initial syllable only trigger the occurrence of [+back +mid high] /o/.

Apart from the 1SG and 3SG irrealis forms, which can be referred to as monomorphemic (the 3SG person and number is zero), all other irrealis forms consist of two separate morphemes that are both susceptible to vowel harmony; for example, the 1PL INCL irrealis form /ri-si-/ emerges as /risi-/, /ru-su-/ and /ro-so-/ when under the influence of vowel harmony.

In the 3SG, 1PL INCL, 1PL EXCL, 2PL and 3PL forms, verb roots containing the front vowels /a/, /e/ and /i/ trigger the presence of /i/ in the subject cross-index, while verb roots containing back high and back mid high vowels /u/ and /o/ respectively trigger the presence of identical vowels in the subject cross-index. Therefore, the verbs [-ᵐbat-e] 'make', [-ɾetʃ] 'speak' and [-liɣaɣ] 'return' engender the high front vowel /i/ in the irrealis subject cross-indexes, while [-mul] 'return home' and [kol-] 'bring' distinctly bring about the back high vowel /u/ and the back mid high vowel /o/ respectively.

2.5.1.2 Vowel harmony in the negative discontinuous marker

The second environment in which vowel harmony occurs is in relation to the negative discontinuous markers -*s-be*-Verb-*te* whose functions are described in §5.5.1.1. Given that one of the ways vowel harmony operates is from a right to left position, the final negative discontinuous marker -*te* is excluded in this process. There is deletion of the front mid high vowel in the initial negative marker -*se*- when it occurs before the second discontinuous marker -*be*-, resulting in the phonologically reduced form [s-ᵐbe]. The interaction of vowel harmony with the negative discontinuous markers in all persons and numbers is shown in Table 2.17.

Table 2.17: Subject prefixes and the negative discontinuous marker

Person/ number	Subject prefix and negative discontinuous marker	Form of vowel in subject prefix and negative discontinuous marker	Form of initial vowel in verb stem
1SG	/tʃbe/	[-tʃbe-] [ə], [e]	/a/, /e/ and /i/
		[-tʃbo-] [ə], [o]	/o/ or /u/
2SG	/ɣo-sᵐbe/	[ɣo- sᵐbe-] [ə], [e]	/a/, /e/, /i/
		[ɣo- sᵐbo-] [ə], [o]	/o/ and /u/
3SG	Ø-	[-sᵐbe-]	/a/, /e/ and /i/
		[-sᵐbo-]	/o/ or /u/
1PL INCL	/ri- sᵐbe/	[ri- sᵐbe] [ə], [i]	/a/, /e/, /i/
		[ri- sᵐbo] [ə], [o]	/o/ and /u/
1PL EXCL	/ᵐbir-/	[ᵐbir-sᵐbe] [ə], [i]	/a/, /e/, /i/
2PL	/kir-/	[kir- sᵐbe]	/a/, /e/, /i/
		[kir- sᵐbo]	/o/ and /u/
3PL	/ri-/	[ri- sᵐbe] [ə], [i]	/a/, /e/ and /i/
		[ri- sᵐbo] [ə], [o]	/o/ and /u/

For all persons and numbers, front vowels occurring in initial syllables in verb roots trigger harmonising of the front feature of the vowel in the second discontinuous marker *be*. However, when a back vowel occurs in the first syllable of the verb root, the vowel in the second discontinuous marker is also backed. This is illustrated in examples given in Table 2.18.

Table 2.18: Vowel harmony in negated verb roots

Underlying form of vowel in initial element of negative continuous marker	Verb root containing non-back vowels	
sbe-	/a/, /e/, /i/	
	[s-ᵐbe-tamat-te] 'not calm' [s-ᵐbe-ɾetʃ-te] 'did not talk' [s-ᵐbe-vitai-te] 'did not put'	
	Verb containing back vowels	
	[s-ᵐbo-ɾotʃ-te] 'not sick' [s-ᵐbo-ɾov-te] 'not finished (intr)' [s-ᵐbo-num-te] 'not drink'	

Furthermore, the 1PL INCL, 1PL EXCL, 2PL, and 3PL forms in the column entitled 'Form of vowel in subject prefix and negative discontinuous marker' in Table 2.17 show that vowel harmony does not spread leftwards to the person and number markers, [ri-], [ᵐbir-], [kir-] and [ri-] respectively. This suggests that the presence of the consonant cluster over a morphemic boundary [s-ᵐb] is the prohibiting factor.

2.5.1.3 Vowel harmony in the 3SG object pro-indexes

Vowel harmony in object pro-indexes also involves the propagation of the [+back] feature value of vowels in root syllables; however, it incorporates a right to left direction, given that object pro-indexes occupy the position to the right of the verb root. This contrasts with its operation in the negative discontinuous marker and the subject cross-indexes, where the process propagates from a leftwards direction. Table 2.19 shows the variations of the 3SG object pro-index forms.

Table 2.19: Vowel in monosyllabic verb roots and 3SG object pro-indexes

Vowel in the verb root		Phonological shape of the 3SG object		
[-back] [-low]	/a/	/e/ e.g. /taɣ-e/ 'take it'	[-back] [-low]	/e/
		/i/ e.g. /dar-i/ 'cut it'	[-back] [+high]	/i/
[-back] [+high]	/i/	/i/ e.g. /vis-i/ 'squeeze out milk'	[-back] [+high]	/i/
[+back] [-low]	/o/	/i/ e.g. /vol-i/ 'buy it'	[-back] [+high]	/i/
		/o/ e.g. /kol-o/ 'carry it'	[+back] [-low]	/o/
[-back] [-low]	/e/	/i/ e.g. /vreŋ-i/ 'throw it'	[-back] [+high]	/i/
[+back] [+high]	/u/	/i/ e.g. /suŋun-i/ 'fill it'	[-back] [+high]	/i/
		/u/ e.g. /sul-u/ 'burn it'	[+back] [+high]	/u/

Table 2.19 shows that irrespective of the vowel in the verb root, the [-back] [+high] /i/ is either the 3SG object pro-index as in [vis-] 'squeeze out milk' or an alternative object pro-index as in [taɣ] 'take', which accepts both [-back] [+high] /i/ and [-back] [-low] /e/. The usage of [-back] [+high] /i/ as an object suffix may have been inherited from Proto Oceanic given that the expression of objects is made by adding the short transitive suffix -*i* and the object enclitic to the verb root (Lynch et al., 2011, p. 80). However, the factors contributing to the preference for a particular 3SG pro-index form over another one (e.g. /e/ or /i/ for verb roots with /a/ vowel) for a particular Nese verb are not clear at this stage. The two shaded cells in Table 2.19 clearly show that it is [+back] feature of the vowel in the verb root that causes harmonisation of the vowel in the verb root.

2.5.2 Vowel raising

Nese also exhibits vowel raising, a process that sees the low central vowel /a/ being raised to /e/ under certain conditions. The process is pervasive in the language, with the current data showing transitive verbs, stative and active transitive verbs, nouns, the 3PL pronoun and true prepositions as being susceptible to vowel raising. Given the distinctive peculiarities in relation to its operation in these different forms, each will be discussed separately in the subsequent subsections. Nese distinguishes vowel raising from vowel harmony by the fact that the former is triggered solely by morphosyntactic influences while the latter is caused by morphophonological factors. Although I adopt the term 'vowel raising' here and in Takau (2016), previous work on Nese relating to this similar phenomena have used the term 'ablaut' (Crowley, 2006c) and 'low vowel dissimilation' (Lynch, 2000).

2.5.2.1 Vowel raising in transitive verbs

Transitive verbs that attract vowel raising in which the low front vowel /a/ is raised to the mid front vowel /e/ are limited to six monosyllabic roots: /taɣ-/ 'take', /bat-/ 'make', /bal-/ 'speak', /bwel/ 'to light (a fire)', /var-/ 'say', and to the disyllabic extended transitive /vitai/ 'put'. Diverging slightly from this raising pattern, is the monosyllabic verb root /waj-/ in which the /a/ vowel in the verb root is not only raised but is also backed to /o/.

In monosyllabic transitive verb roots, the /a/ vowel is raised to /e/ when the verb takes a lexical noun phrase as its object as shown in (2.3) and (2.5). However, when the transitive verb takes an object suffix the /a/ vowel in the verb stem is not raised as shown in (2.2) and (2.4).

2.2 /tua bir-**bat**-e/
    before 1PLEXCL:REAL-make-3SGOBJ
    'In the past we did it.'
    (2012_08_27 obnesp 01003 00:12:54.472-00:13:03.018, natural text)

2.3 /kiɾ-**bet** norian ɾa-r/
    2PL:REAL-make food CLED-POSS:3PL
    'You guys make their food.'
    (2012_06_11 obrojo 01005 00:00:49.283-00:00:53.080, natural text)

2.4 /ale ɾe-ŏan ɾe-**taɣ**-e ɾeŋen namba
    CONJ 3PL:REAL-go 3PL:REAL-take-3SGOBJ LOC number
    'Then they went and brought it on the

    wan/
    one
    first.'
    (2014_01_19 naanhy01001 00:48:18.000-00:48:21.000, natural text)

2.5 /ɣai Ø-ŏan teɣ nanat-ne/
    3SG 3SG:REAL-go take child-3SG:POSS
    'She went and took her child.'
    (2014_01_19 naanhy01001 00:55:22.000-00:55:25.000, natural text)

In relation to the disyllabic extended transitive verb /vitai/ 'put' the presence of the noun phrase (NP) object /norojal/ 'coconut leaf' triggers the raising from /a/ to /e/; however, it is difficult to determine whether /i/ in (2.6) is the object pro-index, given that for transitive verb roots containing front vowels, the object pro-indexes are either the mid front /e/ vowel or the high front /i/ vowel.

2. PHONOLOGY

2.6   /Ne-**vitai**   ðan   laɣad/
      1SG:REAL-put   go   fire:LOC
      'I put it on the fire.'
      (2012_05_16 obanhy01001 00:00:59.500-00:01:01.000, natural text)

2.7   /ɣina   ne-**vitei**   noɾojal   buɾo/
      1SG   1SG:REAL-put   coconut.leaf   GENMOD
      'I put coconut leaves only.'
      (2014_01_19 naanhy01001 00:47:34.000-00:47:36.000, natural text)

Although the criterion relying on the presence or absence of an NP object in order to determine the raising of /a/ also applies to the monosyllabic transitive verb root /waj-/, there is an evident addition of the backing feature where /a/ vowel transitions to /o/, as shown in (2.8) and (2.9). In (2.8) the presence of the NP object /norul nasasaɣ/ 'rice' triggers the raising and backing of the /a/ vowel in /waj-/ 'eat' in (2.9).

2.8   /kanan   bor-so-**wotʃ**   norul nasasaɣ/
      1PLEXCL   1PLEXCL-IRR-eat   rice
      'We will eat the rice.'
      (2014_01_19 naanhy01001 00:02:34.000-00:02:37.000, natural text)

2.9   /ɣai   ɣe,   ri-si-**watʃ**-i   ri-si-wun   ɣe/
      3SG   DEM   3PL:IRR-eat-3SGOBJ   3PL:IRR-full
      'That one, we'll eat it, we will be full.' (as opposed to not being full)
      (2014_01_19 naanhy01001 00:02:51.000-00:02:52.000, natural text)

2.5.2.2 Vowel raising in intransitive verbs

Contrasting with transitive verbs where the presence of the NP object determines the raising, intransitive verbs lack objects and, obviously, the factors triggering the raising ought to be solicited elsewhere. The monosyllabic intransitive active verb root /nas/ 'die' and the intransitive stative verb root /ralral/ 'crazily, crazy' are the only two verb roots that are susceptible to vowel raising.

The front low /a/ vowel in monosyllabic *nas* 'die' accepts raising to /e/ when the verb root is prefixed with the aspectual marker /-ti-/ and simultaneously followed by an adverb irrespective of whether there is a front or back vowel in the adverb root. The aspectual /-ti-/ is affixed to the verb root *nas* in (2.10) and to the raised variant /nes/ in (2.11). Although the latter is modified by the adjunct phrase /latas ɣe/, the presence of the adjunct, which is lacking in (2.12) cannot be used as a factor determining the raising.

2.10 /Ø-**ti-nas**   ale   nau-ne   Ø-ti-jat
      3SG:REAL-ASP-die   CONJ   spouse-3SG:POSS   3SG:REAL-ASP-sit
      'He died and his spouse, sitting

      maro   laine…/
      up   house:LOC
      up in the house…'
      (2012_05_16 obanhy01005 00:04:14.000-00:05:17.000, natural text)

2.11 /Ø-**ti-nes**   di   vele   latas   ɣe/
      3SG:REAL-ASP-die   already   so.sad   sea:LOC   DEM
      'He's died already in the sea, that's so sad.'
      (2012_05_16 obanhy01005 00:05:37.000-00:05:40.000, natural text)

This is due to the fact that *nas* can be modified by adjuncts as demonstrated in (2.12).

2.12 /nenet-ni   ɣe   ɣar   re-se-**nas**   latas/
      child-   dem   3PL   3PL-IRR-die   sea:LOC
      'Those children of you, as for them, they're going to die in the sea.'
      (2014_01_19 naanhy01001 01:04:08.000-01:04:13.000, natural text)

In (2.11) /nes/ is modified by the adverb /di/, which contains the high front vowel /i/ and this is one out of the three instances in which aspectual /-ti-/ is suffixed to the verb root variant /nes/, therefore implying that an immediately following element, more specifically an adverb containing a high front vowel, could trigger raising. Example (2.14) disqualifies this assumption given that the adverb [botvʷon] 'fruitlessly' contains a mid back vowel and the vowel in the verb root is raised, even with the presence of aspectual /-ti-/.

2.13 /merte   ɣe   Ø-ti-**nes**   **botvon**/
      man   dem   3SG:REAL-ASP-die   fruitlessly
      'That man died fruitlessly (nothing came out from him).'
      (2014_01_19 naanhy01001 00:46:06.000-00:46:08.000, natural text)

Therefore, it can be concluded that the presence of aspectual /ti/ simultaneously occurring with an immediately following adverb modifying the verb root *nas* are the factors triggering vowel raising in the intransitive verb root /nas/.

In relation to the disyllabic intransitive stative verb /ralral/ 'crazily, crazy', the low front vowel in both syllables are affected and raising is triggered by the presence of an NP subject occurring after the instrumental prepositional verb /ɣin/ (cf. §6.6.1.1) when the stative verb is the second verb (V₂) of a serial verb construction. Compare (2.15) where /relrel/ is the second verb in a serial verb construction and (2.16) where the verbal preposition *ɣin* with an instrumental denotation follows /relrel/.

2.14 /ɣai   Ø-sungun   **relrel**   **ɣin**   taŋatar/
     3SG:real 3SG:REAL-fill crazily PREP things
     'It's being filled crazily with things.'
     (2014_01_19 naanhy01001 01:08:23.000-01:08:26.000, natural text)

2.15 /ɣota   ɣo-sungun   **ralral**   **ɣin**-i/
     DEHORT 2SG:REAL-fill crazily PREP-3SGOBJ
     'Don't you fill it up crazily with it.'
     (2014_01_19 naanhy01001 01:07:59.000-01:08:00.000, natural text)

Nese permits the stative verb /ralral/ to occur as the main verb in a non-serialising construction as shown in (2.17).

2.16 /ɣai   Ø-**ralral**   buro/
     3SG   3SG:REAL-be.crazy   GENMOD
     'He's just being crazy.'
     (2014_01_19 naanhy01001 01:07:59.000-01:08:00.000, natural text)

In such cases, its argument structure can be extended by the addition of the verbal preposition /ɣin/ with the meaning 'about' (cf. §6.6.1.1) and taking complements in the form of a noun phrase (2.18) or an object pro-index (2.19).

2.17 /kir- ralral   ɣin   **nanaloɣ**/
     2PL:REAL-be.crazy   PREP   kava
     'You guys are crazy about kava.'
     (2014_01_19 naanhy01001 01:07:59.000-01:08:00.000, natural text)

A GRAMMAR OF NESE

2.18 /Ø-**ralral**   buɾo   ɣin-i/
      3SG:REAL-be.crazy   GENMOD   PREP-3SGOBJ
      'He's just crazy about it.'
      (2014_01_19 naanhy01001 00:40:11.000-00:40:13.000, natural text)

Construction (2.17) shows that there is no vowel raising when /ɣin/ takes a noun phrase as its complement, contrasting with the scenario in (2.14) where /ralral/ is the second verb in a serialising construction and /ɣin/ has an instrumental function. It can, therefore, be concluded that vowel raising in intransitive /ralral/ is restricted to when the intransitive root is V₂ in a serialising construction followed by the verbal preposition /ɣin/ taking a lexical noun phrase as its complement. There is no evidence in the data suggesting that raising occurs when arguments of intransitive verbs are extended via the use of /ɣin/ when it has a dative function.

Lastly, when /ralral/ is modifying a noun phrase, the /a/ vowel is raised to /e/ as shown in (2.20).

2.19 /kir-ba-num   teŋe   **relrel**   ɣe/
      2PL:POT-drink   thing   crazy   DEM
      'You guys are going to drink this crazy thing.'
      (2014_01_19 naanhy01001 00:53:31.000-00:53:33.000, natural text)

2.5.2.3 Vowel raising in nouns

Non-compound nouns, directly possessed nouns, indirectly possessed nouns with constructions involving the associative /nan/ and nominalised verbs come under the influence of vowel raising. Factors triggering raising differ in each of these elements, ranging from the presence of demonstratives, modification by stative intransitive verbs, stress shift, the presence of a lexical noun phrase possessor and plurality, therefore, each will be dealt with individually.

2.5.2.3.1 Vowel raising in non-compound nouns

To begin with, there are nine common noun stems that undergo vowel raising without being in a compound noun construction. These are outlined in Table 2.20.

2. PHONOLOGY

Table 2.20: Vowel raising in common noun stems

Noun stems	After vowel raising	
[tʰaðat]	[tʰeðet]	'woman'
[tʰaɲatʰaɾ]	[tʰeɲetʰeɾ]	'things'
[nani]	[neni]	'coconut'
[nanarte]	[nenerte]	'rope'
[naine]	[neine]	'house'
[nanatʃ]	[nenetʃ]	'fish'
[nale]	[nele]	'language'
[nasɣe]	[nesɣe]	'owl'
[naðanu]	[neðenu]	'place, area'

Table 2.20 shows that all the low front vowel /a/ in all noun roots are raised to mid high /e/ vowel regardless of whether the noun roots are disyllabic or trisyllabic. The factor triggering the raising is the presence of the demonstratives /ɣe/ or /ɲe/ modifying the noun root, as illustrated in the following examples.

In (2.20), there is no raising of the vowel in the noun root /taðat/; however, this nominal root undergoes raising when it is modified by the demonstrative /ɣe/, as shown in (2.21).

2.20 /kanan til **taðat**/
  1PLEXCL three women
  'Three of us are women.'
  (2012_05_22 obcero01001 00:00:26.000-00:00:29.000, natural text)

2.21 /ru-su-ɾub-u   Ø-sa-nas neten **teðet** **ɣe**/
  1PLEXCL-IRR-kill-3SGOBJ 3SG-IRR-die PURP2 woman DEM
  'Let's kill him because of that woman.'
  (2012_05_16 obanhy01005 00:04:09.000-00:04:12.000, natural text)

However, in (2.22), the presence of the demonstrative /ɣe/ does not trigger the raising and this is explained by the fact that /ɣe/ has an emphatic function rather than modifying function. In this context it is not modifying the preceding noun /taðat/ so as to give further clarification about that particular woman, but it is making a contrast about the action denoted by the verb.

2.22 /ɣai   ɣe   ro-so-kron-i   min   **taḏat**   ɣe/
     3SG   DEM   1PLINC-IRR:give-3SGOBJ   PREP2   woman   DEM
     'That one, we're going to give it to the woman.' (as opposed to doing something else with it)
     (2014_01_19 naanhy01001 00:31:40.000-00:31:45.000, natural text)

The noun root /taḏat/ may be also be modified by /ŋe/ and, consequently, there is raising of the /a/ vowel to /e/ as shown in (2.23).

2.23 /re-les   te   **teḏet**   **ŋe**   Ø-ti-jat/
     3PL:REAL-see   SUB   woman   DEM   3SG:REAL-ASP-sit
     'They saw that the woman was sitting.'
     (2012_05-16 obanhy01005 00:01:18.000-00:01:20.000, natural text)

In (2.24) the low front vowel /a/ in the common noun /taŋatar/ 'things' is raised to /e/ when it is modified by the demonstrative /ɣe/. When the demonstrative is not present, there is no raising, as shown in (2.25).

2.24 /ɣota   nemere   Ø-bet   **teŋeter**   **ɣe/**
     DEHORT   man   3SG:REAL-make   thing   DEM
     'One mustn't do this thing.'
     (2014_01_19 naanhy01001 00:37:09.000-00:37:11.000, natural text)

2.25 /Ø-bet   **taŋatar**   ḏan   ḏan.../
     3SG:REAL-make   things   go   go
     'He's been working on things for a while…,
     (2014_01_19 naanhy01001 00:46:09.000-00:46:12.000, natural text)

Out of all these nine common nouns that undergo vowel raising due to the presence of the demonstratives /ɣe/ and /ŋe/, the common noun /naḏanu/ 'place' also undergoes raising when modified by elements such as the stative intransitive verb /nanas/ 'dry' (2.26) and /os/ 'different' (2.27). The eligibility of the latter in triggering raising suggests that the presence of back vowels in stative intransitive verbs has no effect on allowing raising since the central motivating factor is its modifying property.

2.26 /neḏenu   ieɣe   **neḏenu**   **nanas**   saɣal./
     place   DEM   place   dry   one
     'The place here is one dry place.'
     (2012_08_22 anhy012 00:42:35.000-00:42:38.000, elicited text)

2.27 /tʃe-ǧan   tʃe-kisa   ɾeɲen   **neǧenu   os**/
     1SG:IRR-go   1SG:IRR-look for   PREP   place   different
     'I am going to go and look for it in a different place.'
     (2014_01_19 naanhy01001 00:41:24.000-00:41:27.000, elicited text)

2.5.2.3.2 Vowel raising in directly possessed nouns

Vowel raising in directly possessed nouns is more complex. While the processes in the previously described word classes and in non-compound nominal structures show that morphosyntactic influences external to the affected root are triggering raising, in directly possessed nouns, influences internal to the affected stem seem to be provoking raising. Furthermore, in attempting to explain the operation of vowel raising in directly possessed nouns, one cannot avoid alluding to other concomitant phonological processes that are lacking in other word classes.

As will be shown in Chapter 3, directly possessed nouns may be subdivided into three separate subclasses with the distinguishing factor being the types of pronominal possessive suffixes they may take. The discussion of vowel raising applies to the subclass that takes the *-aC* pronominal possessive suffixes shown in Table 2.21.

Table 2.21: *-aC* pronominal possessive suffixes

Person/number	Noun
1SG	/nanat-**ak**/ 'my eye'
2SG	/nanat-**am**/ 'your eye'
3SG	/nanat-**an**/ 'his/her eye'
3SG (possessor is expressed as a noun phrase)	/nenet-**en** navos/ 'the sore's eye'
1PL INCL	/nenet-**ar**/ 'our (PL) eye'
1PL EXCL	/nenet-**anan**/ 'our eye (INCL)'
2PL EXCL	/nenet-**am'i**/nenet-**ani**/ 'your eye'
3PL	/nenet-**ar**/ 'their garden'

2.5.2.3.3 Vowel raising in *-aC* directly possessed nouns

Nouns that are in this subclass of directly possessed nouns appear in two forms from a synchronic viewpoint.[7] There are those that present themselves as free roots in their unpossessed form such as /naine/ 'house'

---

7 I hesitate to invoke related diachronic forms to assist in explaining the operation of vowel raising since its operation in forms in the other word classes can be explained synchronically rather than diachronically. Although /naine/ 'house' includes morphologically POc article *na, I do not consider these as two separate morphemes but one single root synchronically.

and /naute/ 'garden', which are considered words when used in isolation. Then there are those that appear as bound roots in their unpossessed forms such as /nanat-/ 'eye' and /tam-/ 'father' where their unpossessed forms cannot be used as words in isolation without the possessor being marked on the noun via the possessive suffix. Free forms that can be used as words in isolation typically end with a vowel or consist of an open final syllable, contrasting with the bound roots that always contain a closed final syllable. The process of vowel raising in these two unpossessed forms will be discussed separately.

Free roots in their unpossessed forms bearing open final syllables ending in the high front vowel /e/ may have vowel final /e/ either undergoing deletion or retention when the -aC possessive suffix is added. The basis for deletion lies in the fact that stress falls primarily on the penultimate syllable; therefore, a final open syllable is more prone to being unstressed, eventually becoming a candidate for deletion. The suffixation of the possessive -aC closed syllable engenders a stress shift from the penultimate syllable to the last syllable, triggering raising of the low back /a/ vowel in the preceding syllable or syllables. Therefore:

Free roots in unpossessed form	Weakening of unstressed vowel	Vowel deletion	Addition of -aC possessive suffix	Output
[nauˈte̥] 'garden'	[nauˈtᵉ̥]	[nauˈt]	[nauˈt-ak]	[neut-akˈ] 'my garden'
[nauˈte̥] 'garden'	[nauˈtᵉ̥]	[nauˈt]	[nauˈt-am]	[neut-amˈ] 'your garden'

It appears that only front high vowels /e/ and /i/ are susceptible to deletion regardless of whether they occur in a stressed syllable or whether they occur in an initial or final syllable. Consider the free root [naine] 'house' whose attested possessed forms in the 1SG and 2SG are [nem-ak] 'my house' and [nem-am] 'your house' respectively. Apart from the weakening of an unstressed vowel syllable finally, vowel deletion and addition of the -aC possessive suffix causing shift in stress resulting in vowel raising in the preceding syllables, there is also a change from alveolar nasal /n/ to the bilabial nasal /m/. Therefore:

2. PHONOLOGY

Free roots in unpossessed form	Weakening of unstressed vowel	Vowel deletion	Change from /n/ to /m/	Addition of -aC possessive suffix	Output
[naiˈneˌ] 'garden'	[naiˈnᵉˌ]	[nanˈ]	[namˈ]	[nam-akˈ]	[nem-akˈ] 'my house'
[naiˈneˌ] 'garden'	[naiˈnᵉˌ]	[nanˈ]	[namˈ]	[nam-amˈ]	[nem-amˈ] 'your house'

Back vowels do not undergo deletion, regardless of whether they occur in a stressed or unstressed syllable, or whether they are part of a diphthong or are the only vowel in a syllable as shown in [nauˈteˌ] 'garden' and in [naɣaˈnuˌ] 'place' respectively. Therefore:

Free roots in unpossessed form	Weakening of unstressed vowel	Vowel deletion	Change from /n/ to /m/	Addition of -aC possessive suffix	Output
[naɣaˈnuˌ]	-	-	-	[naɣanu-akˈ]	[neɣenu-akˈ]
[naɣaˈnuˌ]	-	-	-	[naɣanu-amˈ]	[neɣenu-amˈ]

As mentioned at the beginning of this subsection, word final /e/ may be either deleted or retained, and this is reflected in [naˈleˌ] 'language, word'. In current Nese, this noun may be directly possessed and indirectly possessed. When it is directly possessed, we get the forms [neliʲ-ek] 'my language/words' [neliʲ-em], 'your language/words' [neliʲ-en], 'his/her language/words'. A possible explanation for deriving these three directly possessed forms is that there is weakening of the /e/ in the final open syllable, in conjunction with the addition of the *-aC* possessive suffix, which shifts stress to the final syllable, causing raising of /a/ in the preceding syllable to /e/.

Free roots in unpossessed form	Weakening of unstressed vowel	Addition of -aC possessive suffix	Stress shift to final syllable	Unstressed vowel + Glide	Output
[naˈleˌ]	[naˈlᵉˌ]	[nalᵉ-ʲakˈ]	[nelᵉ-ʲakˈ]	[nelᵉ-ʲekˈ]	[neli-ʲekˈ]

Roots that are considered free in their unpossessed form exhibit raising of the /a/ vowels in the noun root for all persons and numbers as shown in Table 2.22 for the free noun *naute* 'garden'.

A GRAMMAR OF NESE

Table 2.22: Possessive forms for *naute* 'garden'

Person/number	Form	
1SG	/neut-ak/	'my garden'
2SG	/neut-am/	'your garden'
3SG	/neut-an/	'his/her garden'
1PL INCL	/neut-ar/	'our garden'
1PL EXCL	/neut-anan/	'our (EXCL) garden'
2PL	/neut-am'i/-ani/	'your (PL) garden'
3PL	/neut-ar/	'their garden'

Vowel raising in noun roots that are inherently bound in their unpossessed forms such as /nanat-/ 'eye' and /ral-/ 'voice' conversely take a different approach. The three suffixes used to express possession in inherently bound roots appear in the form *-oC*, *-aC* and *-uC*. At this stage, there is no clear indication regarding the motivations for the choice of one over the other.

Table 2.23: Possessive suffixes

Type of possessive suffix		Noun	Person/number	Possessed forms	
Type 1	-aC	/nanat-/	1SG	/nanat-ak/	'my eye'
			2SG	/nanat-am/	'your eye'
			3SG	/nanat-an/	'his/her eye'
				/nenet-en tʃon/	'John's eye'
Type 2	-oC	/ral-/	1SG	/ral-ok/	'my voice'
			2SG	/ral-om/	'your voice'
			3SG	/ral-on/	'his/her voice'
				ral-on tʃon/	'John's voice'
Type 3	-uC	/nat-/	1SG	/nat-uk/	'my child'
			2SG	/nat-um/	'your child'
			3SG	/nat-ne/	'his/her child'
				/netin nato/	'the fowl's child' (chicken)

In cases where the possession relationship is expressed by means of the *-aC* and *-uC* suffixes, there is raising when the possessor is expressed as a lexical noun phrase as shown in [nenet-en tʃon] 'John's eye', whereas possession relationships encoded by the *-oC* suffix do not exhibit raising when the possessor is conveyed via a lexical noun phrase as illustrated in [ral-on tʃon] 'John's voice'.[8] This may be due to the fact that the back vowel [o] prevents raising. Interestingly, with noun roots attached to 3SG pronominal -*aC* suffix where the possessor is indicated by a lexical noun phrase, all the low front vowels in the noun root as well as the possessive suffix are raised as shown in [nenet-en tʃon] 'John's eye'.

As illustrated in Table 2.23, repeated here for convenience, all low front vowels in the noun root attached to plural pronominal possessive forms are susceptible to raising, suggesting that raising may be induced by plurality. More data, however, may point to other possible sources of raising rather than plurality.

Person/number	Noun
1SG	/nanat-**ak**/ 'my eye'
2SG	/nanat-**am**/ 'your eye'
3SG	/nanat-**an**/ 'his/her eye'
3SG (possessor is expressed as a noun phrase)	/nenet-**en**/ navos 'the sore's eye'
1PL INCL	/nenet-**ar**/ 'our (PL) eye'
1PL EXCL	/nenet-**anan**/ 'our eye (INCL)'
2PL EXCL	/nenet-**am'i**/nenet-**ani**/ 'your eye'
3PL	/nenet-**ar**/ 'their garden'

A comparison of the operation of vowel raising in noun roots that are free in their unpossessed form and those that are bound in their unpossessed form clearly shows that the former allow raising in noun roots attached to all pronominal possessive suffixes as well as in cases where the possessor is expressed via a lexical noun phrase. On the other hand, the latter restrict raising to noun forms attached to plural possessive suffixes and when the possessor is expressed via a lexical noun phrase. Due to lack of data on noun roots taking the plural -*oC* suffix, it is not clear whether plurality induces vowel raising. However, the fact that the back vowel blocks raising when the possessor is a lexical noun phrase suggests a possible parallel scenario in relation to plural possessor suffixes.

---

8   Takau (2016, pp. 82–83) describes nominal compound structures as undergoing vowel raising, stating that there are no clear reasons for the raising. However, the examples of nominal compound structures given to support this are in fact directly possessed nouns with lexical noun phrase possessors with the exception of one example /nav'at nanaki/ 'namangi stone'.

2.5.2.3.4 Vowel raising in 3SG indirect possession

The operation of vowel raising in indirect possession is comparatively very restricted, demonstrating productivity only in the 3SG pronominal possessive form resulting in the raising of the /a/ vowel in [s-an] 'his/hers' to [s-en] with the latter brought into use when the possessor is expressed as a lexical noun phrase. Therefore, compare example (2.28), where the general possessive classifier is used with the 3SG pronominal possessive suffix, with (2.29), where the possessor is expressed via the lexical noun phrase /taɣar/ 'whiteman'.

2.28 /Ø-se-teɣ   ral-ok   reŋen   taŋatar   **s-an**   ɣe/
     3SG-IRR-take   voice-1SG:POSS   PREP   things   CLGEN-3SG:POSS   DEM
     'She's going to take my voice with those things of hers.'
     (2012_05_16 obanhy01001 00:00:29.000-00:00:33.000, natural text)

2.29 /navɾo   **s-en**   taɣar/
     war   CLGEN-3SG:POSS   whiteman
     'The whiteman's war.'
     (2012_06_19 obfaha01001 00:00:07.000-00:00:09.000, natural text)

2.5.2.3.5 Vowel raising in the associative /nan/

The associative marker /nan/ is also susceptible to vowel raising, in which the low front vowel /a/ in this monosyllabic form transitions to the mid front /e/ in two specific environments. The first is the presence of the possessor noun phrase immediately following the associative marker. The second is when the demonstrative /ɣe/ occupies the slot immediately following the associative marker and /nen/ is co-referential with a lexical noun phrase that has already been established in a previous clause.

In (2.30), /nan/ is co-referential with the noun phrase /pilen/ 'plane' in the previous clause.

2.30 /pilen   Ø-ti-ma   Ø-ti-anke   ɣe
     Plane   3SG:REAL-ASP-come   3SG:REAL-ASP-anchor   DEM
     'The plane came and landed down there just towards the sea

     vila   buɾo   nasale   eɠan   vila
     down seawards   GENMOD   anchorage   there   down seawards
     at the anchorage there down towards the sea, you see

ɣe,	ɣo-les	netʃor	**nan**…/
DEM	2SG:REAL-see	rifle	ASSOC

you see its rifle…

(2012_06_19 obfaha01001 00:01:13.000-00:01:22.000, natural text)

In (2.31), the presence of the possessee noun phrase /nuak ɣe/ 'that boat' in the slot immediately after /nan/ triggers the raising to /nen/.

2.31
/boss	**nen**	nuak	ɣe	sa-ma./
boss	ASSOC	boat	DEM	3SG:IRR-come

'The boss of that boat will come.'

(2014_01_19 naanhy01001 00:18:53.000-00:18:55.000, natural text)

However, when the possessee noun phrase is in an antecedent clause, the demonstrative /ɣe/ is present, as shown in (2.32).

2.32
/ne-ve	kir-wotʃ	tʃeleŋi	nebet naɣav	ɣe
1SG:REAL-say	2PL:REAL-eat	all	bread	DEM

'I said you people have eaten all that bread

ale	sana	ɣe	kir-se-wotʃ	teŋe	**nen**	ɣe/
CONJ	today	DEM	2PL-IRR-eat	thing	ASSOC	DEM

so today you're going to eat its thing.'

(2014_01_19 naanhy01001 00:03:05.000-00:03:09.000, natural text)

In (2.32), associative /nen/ is coreferential with the lexical noun phrase /nebet naɣav ɣe/ 'that bread' in the previous clause and the presence of the demonstrative /ɣe/ triggers the raising of /a/ to /e/ in the associative /nan/.

2.5.2.3.6 Vowel raising in nominalised verbs

There are scattered examples of nominalised verbs that emerge with /e/ vowels in their nominalised forms, although they contain /a/ vowels prior to undergoing nominalisation. These are /varvar/ 'to pray', /natur/ 'to sleep' and /nas/ 'to die'. Nominalisation entails optional reduplication of the verb root and affixation of the Proto Oceanic noun phrase prefix *na and the Proto Oceanic general nominaliser *-ian on the verb (cf. §4.7). The three nominalised forms given are, however, not susceptible to reduplication and their nominalised forms are /neververian/ 'the praying', /neneturian/ 'the sleeping' and /nenesian/ 'the dying'. It is possible that the high vowel in the nominalising suffix -*ian* is the triggering factor inducing raising not only in the verb root but also in the noun phrase prefix -*na*.

2.5.2.4 Vowel raising in 3PL *yar*

The /a/ vowel in the 3SG independent pronoun *yar* 'they' undergoes vowel raising when the pronoun is used as a modifier of a lexical noun phrase to express plurality (cf. §4.5.4) and when it is modified by the demonstrative /ɣe/ 'this, these'. All the instances showing a raising from /a/ to /e/ simultaneously show the affected 3PL pronoun followed by the demonstrative /ɣe/. This is illustrated in (2.33) and (2.34), where the nouns are modified by /ɣer/ with the demonstrative /ɣe/ occurring after the plural /ɣer/.

2.33 /no- roŋo   siɣa   min   norian   **ɣer**   ɣe/
      1SG:REAL-want   NEG   PREP   food   PL   DEM
      'I am sick of these foods.'
      (2014_01_10 naanhy01001 00:00:32.000-00:00:33.000, natural text)

2.34 /ɣai   Ø-se-ma   neten   noroblat   **ɣer**   ɣe/
      3SG   3SG-IRR-come   PURP2   paper   PL   DEM
      'She will come because of these papers.'
      (2014_01_19 naanhy01001 00:06:22.000-00:06:23.000, natural text)

2.5.2.5 Vowel raising in the prepositions *balak* 'as' and *raŋan* 'in/into it'

The disyllabic true prepositions /balak/ 'like, as' and /raŋan/ 'in/into it' also exhibit vowel raising in which both low front vowels in both syllables are raised to /e/. The only factor that causes the raising is when /belek/ takes its object either in the form of a lexical noun phrase (2.36), or a complement clause introduced by /te/ (2.37), there is raising of the /a/ vowel in /balak/ (2.35) whose object is topicalised and appearing in an antecedent.

2.35 /ne-bat-e   **balak**   ɣe   neten   te   ri-mertʃe/   O!
      1SG:REAL-do-make   like   DEM   PURP2   SUB   1PLINCL:REAL-old   O!
      'I just did it like this because oh we're old!'
      (2014_01_19 naanhy01001 00:59:23.000-00:59:27.000, natural text)

2.36 /ne-les   **belek**   Edwin/
      1SG:REAL-see   like   Edwin
      'That looks like Edwin.' (literally, 'I see as if it's Edwin.')
      (2014_01_19 naanhy01001 00:38:07.000-00:38:10.000, natural text)

2. PHONOLOGY

2.37 /ɣunoɣ   yo-so-kot-o   **belek** te   ɣo-roŋvuson-i/
     2SG   2SG:IRR-do-3SGOBJ   like   SUB   2SG:REAL-know-3SGOBJ
     'You'll do it how you know how.'
     (2014_01_19 naanhy01001 00:04:15.000-00:04:17.000, natural text)

In relation to the preposition /reŋen/, the raising is caused by either topicalisation of the noun phrase functioning as the complement or when the referent noun phrase has already been referred to in previous discourse. Noun phrase complements of the preposition typically occur after the preposition as shown in (2.38); however, when these noun phrases are topicalised, there is raising of both /a/ vowels in the disyllabic preposition, resulting in /raŋan/ as illustrated in (2.39).

2.38 /ɣina   no- rongo   siɣa   de- ǧan   **reŋen**   sto/
     1SG   1SG:REAL-want NEG   1SG:IRR-go   PREP   store
     'I don't want to go to the shop.'
     (2014_01_19 naanhy01001 00:04:24.000-00:04:26.000, natural text)

2.39 **/nause lab̲lab̲   ɣe,**   re- ǧan   re-tʃnetʃne   **raŋan/**
     rain   big   DEM   3PL:REAL-go   3PL:REAL-fishing   PREP
     'This heavy rain, they went fishing in it.'
     (2014_01_19 naanhy01001 00:25:08.000-00:25:11.000, natural text)

2.5.3 Phonological epenthesis

Vowel raising also occurs concurrently with phonological epenthesis. Nese exhibits phonological epenthesis in direct possessive relationships involving a 3SG pronominal possessor or a lexical noun phrase possessor. Examples in the current data point to nouns identifying with the *-uC* possessive suffix with 3SG pronominal possessor expressed via the suffix *-ne* or having a lexical noun phrase possessor as candidates for phonological epenthesis.

	Types of possessive suffixes		
	-uC	*-oC*	*-aC*
3SG pronominal possessor	/nat-**ne**/ 'his/her/its child'	/nevu**l-on**/ 'his/her/it's skin'	/nanat-**an**/ 'his/her/its eye'
3SG lexical noun phrase possessor	/ne**t-in** nato/ 'the hen's child'	/nevu**l-on** nani/ 'the coconut's skin'	/nene**t-en** navos/ 'the sore's eye'

The examples in the second row entitled '3SG lexical noun phrase possessor' show that in possessive relationships involving a possessor expressed as a lexical noun phrase, there is a preference for the phonological form of the possessor to be composed of a final closed syllable. In cases where the 3SG pronominal possessor is composed of a closed syllable, the forms are simply juxtaposed with the possessor noun such as /nevulon nani/ 'the coconut's skin' and /neneten navos/ 'the sore's eye'. However, when the 3SG pronominal possessor is composed of an open final syllable such as /natne/ 'his/her child', there is deletion of the word final /e/ when a lexical noun phrase is expressed, generating a consonant cluster /nat-n nato/ over a morphemic boundary. Therefore, the high front vowel /i/ is inserted in order to break up an otherwise impermissible consonant cluster. Insertion of the high front /i/ is restricted to this type of environment, given that possessed nouns such as /nau-ne/ 'his/her spouse' that contain an open syllable in the noun root do not require insertion of /i/ when a lexical noun phrase possessor is added, as shown in /nou-n taɖat/ 'wife's spouse'. Possessive suffixes (§2.5.2.3.3), which are inherently consonant final such as *-on* and *-an*, are by nature insensitive to phonological epenthesis.

2.5.4 Reduplication

Verb stems in Nese can undergo a reduplication process aligning with either a CVC or a CV template. There are roughly 15 single verb roots and two serial verbs that are susceptible to reduplication. Out of the 15 single verb roots, five are inherently intransitive roots, while the other 10 are transitive verb roots. These are outlined in Table 2.24. The serial verb *viteikhor* 'to block' is also listed in the column for transitive verb roots.

Table 2.24: Transitive and intransitive verb roots susceptible to reduplication

Intransitive verb roots susceptible to reduplication	Transitive verb roots susceptible to reduplication
/nas/ 'die'	/wak-/ 'to plant'
/natur/ 'sleep'	/khij-/ 'to serve'
/mul/ 'return'	/sob-/ 'to tell a story'
/wun/ 'fill up'	/siɣa/ negative verb
/vala/ 'run'	/vol-/ 'to buy'
/vanaɣ/ 'to steal'	/kot-/ 'to do'
/retʃ/ 'to speak'	
	/tun-/ 'to roast'
	/rongvuson-/ 'to understand'

Intransitive verb roots susceptible to reduplication	Transitive verb roots susceptible to reduplication
	/viteiɣor-/ 'to block'
	/vis-/ 'to squeeze'
	/ras-/ 'to grate'
	/num-/ 'to drink'

2.5.4.1 CVC reduplication

There are four verb roots that undergo reduplication in association with the nominalisation process: /wak/ 'to plant', /ɣij/ 'to serve', /nas/ 'to die' and /natur/ 'to sleep'. Out of these four verb roots, only the two former roots may undergo reduplication without being subject to the nominalisation process. It may be that the other verb roots also align with this; however, given the restricted nature of the data, this cannot be verified.

Furthermore, the current data shows that there are no strict phonological or morphological criteria to distinguish which verbs may undergo CV and which ones are susceptible to the CVC reduplication patterns. When a verb stem is reduplicated, the subject cross-index is affixed to the reduplicated form while the verb stem does not carry any subject marking.

Verb roots reduplicated following the CVC pattern include both transitive and intransitive monosyllabic and polysyllabic roots. A monosyllabic verb stem may be composed of a closed syllable (CVC) and in such cases the whole syllable template may undergo reduplication. This is illustrated in (2.40), where the closed monosyllabic verb /wak/ 'to plant' encodes a habitual meaning, which means that the action of planting was carried out recurrently as opposed to being a one-off event or occurring for a particular season and eventually permanently ceasing. In reduplication, the reduplicated forms precede the verb root.

2.40 /ale   bir-ma   ale   bir-**wak**-**wak**/
     CONJ   1PLEXCL:REAL-come   CONJ   1PLEXCL:REAL-REDUP-plant
     'And then we came and we planted.'
     (2012_06_19 obfaha01003 00:04:43.000-00:04:46.000, natural text)

Other transitive closed syllable verbs that are subject to a CVC reduplication process include /vis/ 'to squeeze out milk', /sob/ 'to relate a story', /ɣitʃ/ 'to serve', /vol/ 'to buy', /kot/ 'to do' whose reduplicated forms are /visvis/, /sobsob/, /ɣitʃɣitʃ/, /volvol/ and /kotkot/ respectively.

Closed monosyllabic verb stems that are subject to reduplication may be negated by the negative discontinuous markers. To negate these verb stems, the negative discontinuous markers enclose both the reduplicated verb form and the original verb stem. This is shown in example (2.41), where the closed monosyllabic verb stem and its reduplicated form are both enclosed by the negative discontinuous markers -*be*-Verb-*te*.

2.41 /nekre   ri-s-bo-**wotʃ**-**wotʃ**-te   naram/
      1PLINCL   1PL-IRR-NEG1-REDUP-eat-NEG2   yam
      'We do not eat yams.'
      (2012_05_16 obanhy01003 00:10:06.000-00:10:08.000, natural text)

Polysyllabic verb stems may also undergo a CVC reduplication pattern, in which the second consonant forms the onset of the following syllable. This is exemplified in (2.42), where the reduplication of the polysyllabic negative existential stem /siɣa/ is characterised by a CVC reduplication pattern involving the onset of the following syllable.

2.42 /naram   O   siɣ-siɣa/
      Yam   Oh!   REDUP-NEG
      'Oh there is no yam!'
      (2012_05_16 oanhy01010 00:08:26.000-00:08:27.000, natural text)

Another example of a polysyllabic verb root reduplicated by way of the CVC pattern is given in (2.43).

2.43 /vave   ɣai   nuɣunɣan   neten   te   Ø-ti-van-vanaɣ/
      aunty   3SG   ashamed   PURP2   SUB   3SG:REAL-ASP-REDUP-steal
      'Aunty is ashamed because she steals.'
      (2012_08_19 elanhy01004 00:11:52.000-00:11:57.000, elicitation)

In (2.43), the transitive verb /vanaɣ/ is reduplicated via a CVC pattern in which the consonant following the vocalic nucleus forms the onset of the following syllable. Here, the object is omitted and a habitual meaning is conveyed through reduplication. Lastly, the trisyllabic verb root /roŋvuson/ 'to know, understand' also has the initial closed syllable as its reduplicated form, giving /roŋroŋvusoni/. The serial verb /viteiɣoro/ 'to block', however, has /viteiɣorɣoro/ as its reduplicated form, in which the initial and only syllable of the V$_2$ is reduplicated.

2.5.4.2 CV reduplication

Reduplication in Nese is also based on a CV template, whereby the reduplicated form is made up of a consonant and vowel combination occurring word initially. There are two types of patterns exhibited in this CV template. In the first case, Nese permits only closed monosyllabic verb stems to be reduplicated via this manner. The second case relates only to two intransitive verbs stems that have undergone nominalisation, transforming them into nouns. These are /nas/ 'to die' and /natur/ 'to sleep' becoming /nenesian/ and /neneturian/ respectively. In both cases, the low front vowel /a/ in the initial syllable is raised and this syllable is reduplicated.

Verbs that belong to the former group are /mul/ 'return', /wun/ 'full' and /tun/ 'to roast'. Example (2.44) shows the closed monosyllabic transitive verb /tun/ when reduplicated.

2.44 ne-ve ale kur-tu-tun.

1SG:REAL-say okay 2PL:real-REDUP-roast.

'I said okay you guys do the roasting.'

(2014_01_19 naanhy01001 00:03:22.000-00:03:23.000, natural text)

2.5.4.3 Object omission

Reduplication of transitive verbs in Nese is characterised, for the most part, by omission of the object argument, which is, in transitive clauses, realised either by way of an object suffix or a lexical noun phrase object. Consequently, transitive verbs undergoing reduplication become intransitive. This is illustrated in (2.45), where the object of the transitive verb root /tun/ 'roast' is not present, although it is present in (2.46) where the verb is not reduplicated.

2.45 /ne-**tun-u**/

1SG:REAL-roast-3SGOBJ

'I roasted it.'

(2012_06)12 obaksi01001 00:01:23.000, natural text)

In (2.45), the object of the transitive verb /tun/ 'to roast' is omitted and a habitual meaning is conveyed via reduplication, which is characterised by the CV pattern. Other transitive verbs aligning with the CVC pattern whose objects are omitted on undergoing reduplication are /sob/,

/kot/ and /vol/. Examples of these are given in (2.46), (2.49) and (2.50) respectively, along with their non-reduplicated forms in (2.47), (2.48) and (2.51) respectively; the objects are realised as the 3SG object pro-indexes.

2.46 /ru-**sob-sob** sat/
1PLINCL:REAL-REDUP-to.relate.a.story bad
'We are telling stories badly.'
(2012_01_19 naanhy01001 00:42:58.000, natural text)

2.47 /ru-su-**sob-o**/
1PLINCL-IRR-to.relate.a.story-3SGOBJ
'We're going to tell stories about it.'
(2104_01_19 naanhy01001 00:10:20.000-00:10:21.000, natural text)

2.48 /ne-ve ale kani kir-**kot-o**/
1SG:REAL-to.say ale 2PL 2PL:REAL-to.make-3SGOBJ
'I said ok you guys do it.'
(2014_01_19 naanhy01001 00:10:20.000-00:02:55.000, natural text)

2.49 /...ɣar ɾo-**kot-kot** teŋe ɣer ɣe/
3PL 3PL:REAL-REDUP-do thing 3PL DEM
'...They are doing these things.'
(2014_01_19 naanhy01001 00:22:23.000-00:22:26.000, natural text)

2.50 /ɣai ɣe, nat-ne ɾo-**vol-vol** ɣin melen/
3SG DEM child-3SG:POSS 3PL:REAL-REDUP-buy PREPI melons
'That one, his child, they sell melons.'
(2014_01_19 naanhy01001 00:11:53.000-00:11:55.000, natural text)

2.51 /ɣar ɾo-**vol-i** buɾo ɾo-num-u/
3PL 3PL:REAL-buy-3SGOBJ GENMOD 3PL:REAL-drink-3SGOBJ
'They just buy it and drink it.'
(2014_01_19 naanhy01001 00:48:06.000-00:48:08.000, natural text)

Evidently, object omission occurs irrespective of the reduplication pattern with which the affected verb root aligns.

2.6 Orthography

The Nese data presented in the following chapters commencing from Chapter 3 are presented in orthographic representations rather than in IPA. The orthographic representations used for consonant and vowel phonemes in Nese are outlined in Table 2.25.

Table 2.25: Orthographic representation of Nese phonemes

Consonant phonemes	Orthographic representation	Vowel phonemes	Orthographic representation
/t/	t	/a/	a
/d/	d	/e/	e
/s/	s	/i/	i
/m̪/	m'	/o/	o
/b̪/	b'	/u/	u
/ð̪/	v'		
/b/	b		
/v/	v		
/m/	m		
/n/	n		
/w/	w		
/tʃ/	j		
/j/	y		
/k/	k		
/ɣ/	kh		
/ŋ/	ng		
/l/	l		
/ɾ/	r		
/r/	rr		

3
Word classes

3.1 Introduction

In assigning lexemes to word classes in Nese, I consider their grammatical properties, in particular the distributional properties of the lexemes and the range of morphosyntactic functions they have. This follows Schachter's (1985, p. 6) argument that 'parts-of-speech classes must be distinguished from one another on the basis of a cluster of properties, none of which by itself can be claimed to be a necessary and sufficient condition for assignment to a particular class'. Nese has two open word classes: nouns (§3.2) and verbs (§3.3). The latter includes a subclass of stative intransitive verbs, given that there is no distinct adjective class in the language. These two open word classes are distinguished on the basis of several grammatical properties. Other forms belong to the following closed word classes: pronouns (§3.4), prepositions (§3.5), adverbs (§3.6), quantifiers (§3.7), conjunctions and subordinators (§3.8), relational classifiers (§3.9), directionals (§3.10), demonstratives (§3.11), negative particles (§3.12), verbal particles (§3.13), greetings and leavetakings (§3.14) and interjections (§3.15). Although greetings and leave takings are discussed together in §3.14, they do not form a word class. Some lexemes are members of more than one word class and this issue of flexibility of class membership is discussed in §3.16.

3.2 Nouns

Nouns are distinguished on the basis of their ability to function as heads of noun phrases. Apart from this, there are no strong morphosyntactic criteria to distinguish all members of the class of nouns from other word classes. The primary distinction when classifying nouns in Nese is between those that can be the head of a noun phrase – which is an argument in the clause – and those that cannot be heads of noun phrases, i.e. arguments. Further subdivisions within the class of nouns are made on the basis of the morphological forms of the nouns and the syntactic functions associated with the adjacent elements such as the type of modifiers that usually occupy the position immediately after the noun. From this, other subdivisions within the class of nouns that have been deduced are common nouns, proper nouns, locational nouns and temporal nouns. These various subclasses are shown in Table 3.1. Common and proper nouns can also be further subdivided.

Table 3.1: Noun subclasses

Nouns				
Common nouns		**Proper nouns**		**Locational nouns**
Bound	Free	Kinship terms	Non-kinship terms	

The following are the criteria used to distinguish different subclasses of nouns:

- whether or not nominal compound forms may take the accreted nV-article
- whether or not they can be modified by a numeral
- whether or not they can be modified by a demonstrative determiner
- the kind of possessive marking they can have
- whether they can be modified by a relative clause
- whether they can be the head of a locative noun phrase
- whether they are bound or free roots
- whether or not they may be conjoined by the conjunction *rrun*.

Although the classification in Table 3.1 generally reflects that which is given for Proto Oceanic noun sub classifications, Nese deviates in a few respects concerning the criteria used to establish the different noun classes (Lynch et al., 2011, p. 69). To begin with, the criteria for initial subdivision in Proto Oceanic noun classes is based on possession. This means that nouns that are indirectly possessed form one category and nouns that are directly possessed form another category. In Nese, the initial subdivision of nouns is based on the distinction between a common noun and a proper noun. In spite of this, a similarity is shown whereby indirect possession in Nese is manifested by four classifiers, while Proto Oceanic employed three or more relational classifiers. The second subdivision of Proto Oceanic nouns is formed on the basis of the types of articles and prepositions that are found in construction with the nouns and from these criteria three other subdivisions are made: personal nouns, common nouns and local nouns. Nese, on the other hand, has bound and free nouns as another subdivision within the subclass of common nouns. Lastly, Table 3.1 indicates a third subdivision of nouns whose members are locational nouns. Members of this subdivision are equivalent to local nouns in Proto Oceanic, and in Nese they include both bound and free common nouns. Lynch et al. (2011, p. 69) argue that they form a separate subclass to that of common nouns in Proto Oceanic, even though they may function like common nouns in some instances.

3.2.1 Common nouns

Common nouns are defined semantically as animate and inanimate entities, body parts and abstract entities. They are distinguished on the basis of the following criteria shown in Table 3.2 along with examples for each criteria.

Table 3.2: **Distinguishing criteria of common nouns and examples**

Criteria	Examples
May be modified by an intransitive stative verb	3.1 *nuak* ***velvele*** boat small 'small boat'
May be modified by a demonstrative determiner	3.2 *nebetnakhav* ***khe*** bread DEM 'this bread'
May be modified by a relative clause	3.3 *nuak* ***te*** ***nemerjian*** ***nas*** boat REL old people die 'The boat the old people died in.'

Criteria	Examples

Are able to take possessive marking (indirect or direct)	Indirect possessive marking
	3.4 *nesde* **sa-k**
	   knife CLGEN-1SG:POSS
	   'my knife'
	Direct possessive marking
	3.5 *nanata-k*
	   eye-1SG:POSS
	   'my eye'

The noun phrase headed by the noun may be an argument of a verbal clause	3.6 *Khai* Ø-*les* **nemerrte**.
	   1SG 3SG:REAL-go man
	   'She saw the man.'

The noun phrase headed by the common noun may be an argument of a prepositional phrase in which either a true preposition or a verbal preposition is the head	3.7 *Khar* *rri-lelngaro* **min** **Nasub**
	   3PL 3PL:REAL-listen PREP2 chief
	   'They listened to the chief.'
	True preposition
	3.8 *Khai* Ø-*suwo* **rengen** **wel**
	   3SG 3SG:REAL-swim LOC well
	   'She swam in the well.'

Generally, common nouns differ from proper nouns in two respects: by the type of modification that is allowed and whether they may enter into a possessive construction. While common nouns may be modified by an intransitive stative verb, a demonstrative determiner, a numeral and a relative clause, proper nouns do not take these modifiers; apart from the demonstrative determiner when it has an emphatic function (§3.11).

On the basis of morphosyntactic criteria, common nouns are further subdivided into free and bound nouns. Free nouns are those that enter into an indirect possessive relationship contrasting with bound nouns that enter into a direct possessive relationship. Indirect possessive constructions are marked in Nese by classifiers to which a possessor suffix is attached (§3.9), while direct possessive relationships are marked by possessor suffixes affixed directly to the nouns (§4.5.8).

3.2.1.1 Free nouns

The nouns in this class constitute the largest subclass of nouns, and indirect possession is marked by the relational classifiers *s*, *ji*, *rr* and *m* (§4.5.8). Takau (2016) analyses relational classifiers as occurring in the forms *sa-*, *jin-*, *rra-* and *ma-*; however, I now discard this analysis given that the pronominal possessive forms *-ak* (1SG), *-am* (2SG) and so forth resemble equivalent forms in direct possessive relationships where they are suffixed directly onto the noun stems, as shown in Table 3.3 for the possession of *norrurr* 'clothes' and *nev'enu-* 'place'.

Table 3.3: Possessive pronominals in indirect and direct possession

Indirect possession		Direct possession
norrurr	*s-**ak***	*nev'enu-**ak***
clothes	CLGEN-1SG:POSS	place:1SG:POSS
'my clothes'		'my place'

The class of free nouns includes all nouns that are not body parts, institutionalised place names or names of individuals. Even though there is no strict division concerning the kinds of nouns whose possessive relationship is indicated on the general relational classifiers *s* and *jin-* (cf. §4.5.8), there is a clear distinction regarding the types of nouns whose possessive relationships are indicated on the relational classifiers *rr* and *m*. More specifically, items that are edible are indicated on *rr* and those that are drinkable are indicated on *m*. The possessive relationship of an edible common noun that is not intended for eating or drinking may be indicated on either of the two general relational classifiers *s* and *jin-*. For example, a coconut that is not for drinking or eating may have its possessive relationship expressed on the relational classifiers *s* or *jin-*. Table 3.4 shows examples of nouns that may be indirectly possessed through the four relational classifiers.

Table 3.4: Indirectly possessed nouns

	Relational classifiers			
Person/number	s	jin-	rr	m
1SG	*nani s-ak* 'my coconut'	*norrurr jin-a* 'my clothes'	*narram rr-ak* 'my yam'	*nua m-ak* 'my water'
2SG	*nani s-am* 'your coconut'	*norrurr jin-okh* 'your clothes'	*narram rr-am* 'your yam'	*nua m-am* 'your water'
3SG	*nani s-an* 'his/her coconut'	*norrurr jin-i* 'his/her clothes'	*narram rr-an* 'his/her yam'	*nua m-an* 'his/her water'
1PL INCL	*nani s-arr* 'our coconut'	*norrurr jin-krre* 'our clothes'	*narram rr-arr* 'our yam'	*nua m-arr* 'our water'
1PL EXCL	*nani s-anan* 'our coconut'	*norrurr jin kanan* 'our clothes'	*narram rr-anan* 'our yam'	*nua m-anan* 'our water'

Relational classifiers				
Person/number	s	jin-	rr	m
2PL	*nani s-am'i* 'your (PL) coconut'	*norrurr jin kani* 'your clothes'	*narram rr-am'i* 'your (PL) yam'	*nua m-am'i* 'your water'
3PL	*nani s-arr* 'their coconut'	*norrurr jin-err* 'their clothes'	*narram rr-arr* 'their yam'	*nua m-arr* 'their water'

3.2.1.2 Bound nouns

Bound common nouns are those that take direct possessive marking. Unlike free common nouns that take indirect possessive marking, possession in bound nouns is marked by way of possessor suffixation of the possessum noun. Nese employs three types of possessive suffixes, labelled here as *-aC* (Type 1), *-oC* (Type 2) and *-uC* (Type 3). Takau (2016) does not make this distinction; however, Crowley (2006c, p. 55) recognises two types of direct possession patterns expressing 'close inalienable' relationship, on the one hand, and 'distant alienable relationship', on the other hand. The latter corresponds to Type 1 in the current analysis and nouns in the Type 2 group are analysed by Crowley as a subtype of the 'close inalienable relationship' pattern. Nouns currently in Type 3 are another subtype of this same pattern (Crowley, 2006c, p. 57). This is illustrated in Table 3.5.

Table 3.5: Types of direct possession suffixes

Type of possessive suffix	Noun		Person/number	Possessed forms	
Type 1 Distant inalienable possession	*-aC*	*nanat-*	1SG	*nanat-ak*	'my eye'
			2SG	*nanat-am*	'your eye'
			3SG	*nanat-an*	'his/her eye'
				nenet-en John	'John's eye'
Type 2 Close inalienable possession subtype	*-oC*	*ral-*	1SG	*ral-ok*	'my voice'
			2SG	*ral-om*	'your voice'
			3SG	*ral-on*	'his/her voice'
				ral-on John	'John's voice'
Type 3 Close inalienable possession subtype	*-uC*	*nat-*	1SG	*nat-uk*	'my child'
			2SG	*nat-me*	'your child'
			3SG	*nat-ne*	'his/her child'
				netin nato	'the fowl's child' (chicken)

The structural division between direct and indirect possession generally reflects that of the semantic division between inalienable and alienable categories. Therefore, it is common that bound nouns include body parts and kin terms. The subclass of bound nouns is a closed class. Table 3.6 shows some examples of common nouns that take the three direct possessive markings, and Table 3.7 gives the possessive suffixes attached to nouns in these three categories, albeit some forms missing for certain persons and numbers.

Table 3.6: Directly possessed nouns

Type 1 -aC	Type 2 -oC	Type 3 -uC
navar- 'hand'	ral- 'voice'	tas- 'younger same-sex sibling'
mer- 'mother'	jokh- 'uncle'	nat- 'child'
neut- 'garden'		nabat- 'head'
nev'enu- 'place'		sokhos- 'sister'
nem- 'house'		nabalak- 'leg'

Table 3.7: Possessive suffixes for each possessive types

Person/ number	Type 1	Type 2	Type 3
1SG	neut-ak 'my garden'	ral-ok 'my voice'	nabat-uk 'my head'
2SG	neut-am 'your garden'	ral-om 'your voice'	nabat-me 'your head'
3SG	neut-an 'his/her garden'	ral-on 'his/her voice'	nabat-ne 'his/her head'
1PL INCL	neut-arr 'our garden' (INCL)		
1PL EXCL	neut-anan 'our garden' (EXCL)		
2PL	neut-am'i/ni 'your (PL) garden		
3PL	neut-arr 'their garden'		nabat-rre 'their head'

Further discussion of directly possessed nouns is in §4.5.8.

3.2.2 Proper nouns

Proper nouns are those that associate an individual or place with a name. They are distinguished by the following characteristics:

- they cannot be modified by the demonstrative determiner *khe* 'this/ that' (however, they can be modified by *khe* when it is functioning as a pragmatic particle or emphatic marker (§3.11))
- they function like locational nouns in that they are not complements of prepositions in prepositional phrases indicating 'on' or 'at' a location

- they cannot be modified by a relative clause
- they cannot be modified by a numeral
- there are both free and bound distinctions
- nominal compound forms of place names may take the *nV-* article
- they cannot take possessive marking.

Kinship terms are considered to be a subclass of proper nouns on the basis of their inability to be modified by a relative clause. They may, however, be modified by an intransitive stative verb and they may be an argument of a verbal clause as well as functioning as the predicate of a non-verbal clause. Kinship terms are also used as address terms and do not take the accreted *nV-* article. However, not all kinship terms are used as both reference and address terms. They are used in speech situations where a speaker is addressing a relative or family member or referring to himself or herself with the relevant kin term that his or her addressees would use. Table 3.8 shows these address terms and their corresponding equivalents that are not used as address terms. Words for older sibling *tu-*, younger sibling *tas-*, uncle *jokh-* and aunt *vave* do not have separate address and reference terms. The address terms are indirectly possessed while the reference terms are directly possessed.

Table 3.8: Address and reference terms

Address terms	Reference terms
tete 'dad'	*tana-/tete s-* 'father'
dev'e/ mama 'mum'	*mer-a* 'mother'
pupu 'grandparent' *pupu nasub* 'grandfather' *pupu lekhterr* 'grandmother'	*teb-* 'grandparent'
tu- 'older sibling'	
tasu- 'younger sibling'	
vave 'aunt'	
jokh-o 'uncle'	

The class of proper nouns also includes traditional names. The current data indicates that there is a small subset of traditional names that are given to males and females. Female names commonly begin with *le* while male names are based on the roots *lele, mal* and *meltekh*. Each of the male name roots is associated with the different customary ranks into which males are initiated at various specified times in their lives, with *meltekh* placed at the highest customary ranking system. It is also common to find male and female name roots forming compounds with verbal modifiers. Table 3.9 shows the attested closed set of traditional names.

Table 3.9: Traditional names

Male	Female
meltekh-rej 'high person who talks'	*le-sal* 'a woman who is lost'
meltekh-sob 'high person who is a speaker'	*le-sale* 'a woman who welcomes'
meltekh-jovi 'high person who cannot be beaten'	*le-yat-yat* 'a woman who sits'
meltekh-rovon 'high person who is heavy'	
meltekh-kila 'high person who seeks/looks'	
rejtutun 'person whose speech roasts'	

Further discussion of proper nouns and examples are given in Chapter 4.

3.2.3 Locational nouns

Locational nouns form a third, closed, subdivision within the category of nouns. In fact, there are merely eight locational nouns in this restricted class, as shown in Table 3.10. They are evidently derived from their corresponding common noun equivalent with the simple replacement of the initial *n* consonant with *l*. These locational nouns indicate familiar place names that are culturally significant in the lives of the Nese-speaking people, such as the garden. They are distinguished from other common nouns in that they can only be the head of a noun phrase that is functioning as an adjunct in a clause. The only situation in which they may be the head of a noun phrase functioning as a core argument is in relation to the extended transitive verb *vitai* 'put'. Other evidence that indicates locational nouns form a separate subdivision within the noun class is that, although the conjunction *rrun* can conjoin both animate and inanimate common nouns (cf. §3.2.1, example (3.45)) and proper nouns, it cannot conjoin locational nouns. Furthermore, while common nouns may be modified by numerals (cf. §4.5.6, example (4.52)), locational nouns are not susceptible to modification by numerals.

Generally, the locational nouns in the first column of Table 3.10 resemble proper noun place names in that proper noun place names cannot be complements of prepositions in prepositional phrases indicating 'on' or 'at' a location (§3.2.1). Other common nouns that are not members of this closed subset may occur as heads of noun phrases functioning as core arguments in a clause and as objects of prepositions and verbal prepositions that function as clausal adjuncts.

Table 3.10: Locational nouns and their equivalent common nouns

Locational nouns	Common nouns with an initial *n* that are replaced by an initial *l* to form locational nouns
laute 'at the garden'	*naute* 'garden'
lasal 'at/on the road'	*nasal* 'road'
latas 'at/in the sea'	*natas* 'sea'
lemak 'at/in my house'	*nemak* 'my house'
leutak 'at my garden'	*neutak* 'my garden'
latan 'on the ground'	*natan* 'ground'
lanus 'at/in the bush'	*nanus* 'bush'
laine 'at/in the house'	*naine* 'house'

The following example sentences serve to illustrate the distinction between the locational noun *lanus* 'in, at the garden', which does not require a true preposition or a verbal preposition (3.9–3.11), and a non-locational noun, which can take a true preposition or a verbal preposition (3.12). Example (3.13) illustrates the common noun *nial* 'sun' as the complement of the prepositional phrase, which is headed by the locational preposition *rengen* 'in, at'. Here, *nokhobu* indicates the 'goal' of the action expressed by the extended transitive verb *vitai* 'put'. Example (3.14) contains the proper place noun *Natanv'at* 'Matanvat' as the object of the intransitive verb, resembling the locational noun phrases that are not complements of prepositional phrases.

3.9   *Khina,*   *ne-likhakh*   ***lanus***   *khe.*
     1SG   1SG:REAL-return   bush:LOC   DEM
     'I have really returned from the bush.'
     (2012_05_16 obanhy01003 00:07:36.000-00:07:38.000, natural text)

3.10   **Khina,*   *ne-likhakh*   *rengen*   ***lanus***   *khe.*
     1SG   1SG:REAL-return   LOC   bush:LOC   DEM

3.11 *Khina,   ne-likhakh   rengen   **nanus**   khe.
      1SG   1SG:REAL-return   LOC   bush   DEM

3.12 Majis   khai   Ø-tokh   **rengen**   nere-n   **nejal**.
      matches 3SG   3SG:REAL-stay   LOC   end-3SG:POSS mat
      'The match is at the end of the mat.'
      (2012_08_22 anhy012 00:29:41.000-00:29:46.000, natural text)

3.13 Khai   Ø-tekh   nat-ne   khe   rengen
      3SG   3SG:REAL-take   child-3SG:POSS DEM   LOC
      'She took that child of hers in

      nial   khe.
      sun   DEM
      this sun.'
      (2014_01_19 naanhy01001 00:35:04.000-00:36:07.000 natural text)

3.14 Nev'enua-k,   khai   Ø-khro   **Natanv'at**.
      place-1SG:POSS   3SG   3SG:REAL-exist   Matanvat
      'My place is in Matanvat.'
      (2012_05_16 obanhy01001 00:00:19.500-00:00:22.500, natural text)

3.3 Verbs

Verbs are characterised by their ability to function as the head of a verb complex. A verb is identified as a form that is marked with an obligatory subject prefix and, in the case of transitive verbs, an object suffix. The subject prefix encodes both person and mood. Adjectival verbs functioning as noun modifiers, however, do not take the obligatory subject prefixes. Another indication of the verbal status of an element is the existence of an optional aspectual prefix *-ti-* (cf. §5.5.9, which occurs between the subject prefix and the verb root). Examples of an intransitive verb marked with a subject prefix, a transitive verb marked with both a subject and object prefix and an intransitive verb with the *-ti-* prefix are shown in (3.15), (3.16) and (3.17) respectively.

3.15 *Khina*   **ne-yat**   *khe.*
     1SG   1SG:REAL-sit   DEM
     'I live here.'
     (2012_05_16 obanhy01001 00:00:09.500-00:00:11.500, natural text)

3.16 *Ne-khor*   *nani,*   **ne-vis-i**   *ne-vita-i*
     1SG:REAL-grate   coconut   1SG:REAL-squeeze out   1SG:REAL-put-
                                  milk-3SGOBJ   3SGOBJ

   v'an   *lakhab*
   DIR   LOC:fire
   'I grate the coconut, I squeeze out the milk, I put it on the fire.'
   (2012_05_16 obanhy01001 00:00:57.000-00:01:01.000, natural text)

3.17 *Ne-les*   *nemerrte* *sakhal* *Ø-**ti-v'an***   *lauta-k*
     1SG:REAL-see   man   one   3SG:REAL-ASP-go   LOC:garden-1SG:POSS
     'I saw a man go to my garden.'
     (2012_05_16 obanhy01003 00:01:06.000-00:01:08.000, natural text)

The primary classification of verbs in Nese is based on transitivity. Verbs that are transitive take object arguments when they are underived, while those that are intransitive cannot take an object. Transitive verbs are divided into three subclasses and intransitive verbs are further subdivided into two subclasses, as shown in Table 3.11. There are no ditransitive verbs in Nese – that is, there are no verbs that can take two noun phrases following the verb in object position. However, there are extended transitive verbs and these form a closed subclass of the transitive verb.

Table 3.11: Subclasses of verbs

Verbs	
Intransitive	Stative intransitive verbs (adjectival verbs)
	Active intransitive verbs
Transitive	Reduplicated to form intransitive
	No intransitive form
	Extended transitive verbs

The two subclasses of intransitive verbs are stative and active intransitive verbs. The difference between stative and active verbs is that stative verbs can be both the head of a predicate and a modifier in an NP, whereas active verbs cannot modify an NP head. As there is no distinct adjective class in Nese, and intransitive stative verbs have a modifying function, similar to adjectives, they are also referred to here as adjectival verbs. The latter label is employed in keeping with Ross (1998, p. 91), who defines adjectival verbs as those stative verbs that can modify a noun as well as being the head of a predicate. Table 3.12 shows some examples of intransitive stative verbs.

Table 3.12: Intransitive stative verbs

sat	'be bad'
ninin	'be wet'
narang	'be dry'
velvele	'be small'
lab'lab'	'be big'

Examples (3.18) and (3.19) respectively illustrate the intransitive stative verb *velvele* 'small' functioning as a modifier of the noun *tev'et* 'woman' and as head of a predicate.

3.18 *Mak   khai   Ø-jujmu   tev'et   **velvele**   khe.*
      Mark   3SG   3SG:REAL-kiss   woman   small   DEM
      'Mark kissed that small woman.'
      (2012_08_22 elanhy01011 00:22:17.000-00:22:20.000, elicitation)

3.19 *Tua   naine   khai   Ø-velvele.*
      before   house   3SG   3SG:REAL-small
      'In the past, houses were small.'
      (2012_08_17 obnesp01001 00:14:41.000-00:14:46.000, natural text)

As shown in Table 3.13, transitive verbs are further subdivided into two subclasses depending on whether or not they can be derived to form an intransitive. One subclass may be reduplicated to form an intransitive verb, whereas the other subclass does not have a derived intransitive form. Table 3.13 shows some examples of intransitive verbs derived from transitive verb roots via reduplication and some transitive verbs with no intransitive counterparts by way of reduplication.

Table 3.13: Transitive verbs

Transitive verb	Intransitive verb
sob-o 'relate a story'	*sobsob* 'relate a story'
khij-i 'serve it'	*khijkhij* 'serve'
sul-u 'burn it'	*sulsul* 'burn'
Transitive verbs that cannot be reduplicated to form intransitive	
bat-e 'make it'	**batbat*
takh-e 'take it'	**takhtakh*
vreng-e 'throw it'	**vrengvreng*

Examples (3.20) and (3.21) show the transitive verb *sob* and its intransitive form *sobsob*, which is derived via reduplication. As illustrated in (3.21), reduplication transforms the transitive verb into an intransitive verb that does not require an object argument to be expressed either by way of an object suffix or an object NP.

3.20 *Kho-se-**sob**-o,   kho-var-i,   lakhm'al   khai*
     2SG-IRR-relate a story-3SGOBJ   2SG:REAL-say-3SGOBJ   nakamal   3SG
     'You'll relate it, say that the nakamal it

   belek   naine   buro.
   like   house   GENMOD
   is just like a house.'
   (2012_08_27 nsesp01002 00:00:10.000-00:00:17.000, natural text)

3.21 *Ne-ve   de-**sobsob**,   khai   khe   ne-sobsob.*
     1SG:REAL-say   1SG:IRR-relate a story   3SG   DEM   1SG:REAL-relate a story
     'I said I will relate a story, there you go, I just did.'
     (2012_08_22 anhy01005 00:03:53.000-00:03:55.000, natural text)

There are no ditransitive verbs in Nese – that is, Nese lacks verbs that can take two noun phrases following the verb in object position. There are, however, extended transitive verbs following Dixon's (2010, p. 120) terminology, which can take an object argument and an oblique argument that is marked by a preposition. The extended transitive verbs in Nese are *rej* 'talk', *var* 'tell', *kron* 'give', *vervis* 'reveal', *vitai* 'put' and *us* 'ask'. In general, with the exception of the extended transitive verb *vitai* 'put', the verbal prepositions *min* and *khin* are employed to add a third core argument, which usually bears the semantic role of recipient, to all the extended transitive verbs above, and bearing the semantic role of source for the verb *us* 'ask'. The verb *vitai* 'put', on the other hand, requires a third argument that indicates a location or has a spatial directional meaning. The third argument of *vitai* may be either introduced by the true preposition *rengen*, which generally bears a locative denotation, or it may be in the form of a locational noun phrase.

Chapter 6 presents a more detailed explanation of intransitive and transitive verbs.

3.4 Pronouns

Nese has one set of independent pronouns, which can occur as the head of a noun phrase, and four sets of dependent, bound pronominal forms. Table 3.14 outlines the independent pronouns.

Table 3.14: Independent pronouns

Person/number	Pronoun
1SG	*khina*
2SG	*khunokh*
3SG	*khai*
1PL INCL	*nekrre*
1PL EXCL	*kanan*
2PL	*kam'i/kani*
3PL	*khar*

Pronouns generally function as heads of noun phrases and this is illustrated in (3.22) and (3.23) with the pronouns *khar* and *kanan* respectively.

3.22 **Khar**　　ri-vitei　　　　　　kava

　　　3PL　　　3PL:REAL-put　　meat-3SG:POSS

　　　'They put the iron roofing.'

　　　(2014_01_19 naanhy01001 00:47:39.000-00:47:40.000, natural text)

3.23　Ale　**kanan**　bir-khro,　　　　　　bir-yat　　　　　　ev'an　lasal

　　　CONJ　1PLEXCL　1PLEXCL:REAL-stay　1PLEXCL:REAL-sit　there　LOC:road

　　　'Then we stayed, we sat there on the road

　　　v'an　v'an　bung.

　　　go　　go　　night

　　　until nightfall.'

　　　(2012_05_16 obanhy01002 00:00:32.000-00:00:37.000, natural text)

3.24	*Khai*	*ver*	*nelie-n*	*nasumb*	*maro*	*khin*	***kanan***.
	3SG	say	word-3SG:POSS	chief	up	PREP1	

'He told God's message to us.'
(2014_01_19 naanhy01001 00:09:36.000-00:09:39.000 natural text)

A comparison of the phonological shape of the independent pronouns, in particular the 1PL INCL, 1PL EXCL, 2PL and 3PL forms, with that of the counterpart forms of the suffixes attached to the relational classifiers (§3.9), reveals that the suffixes of the possessive forms are perhaps reduced forms of the independent pronouns. For example, the latter portion of the independent 1PL EXCL pronoun *kanan* is akin to the 1PL EXCL possessive suffix attached to the edible and drinkable relational classifiers such as *-anan*. Furthermore, it is evident from Table 3.14 that Nese pronouns generally begin with either *kh* or *k* with the exception of the 1PL INCL form, which begins with *n*. This pronominal system would fall into the second of two sets of pronouns reconstructed by Lynch et al. (2011, p. 68) as commencing with *k(a), which is a courtesy marker in Proto Malayo Polynesian (PMP).

There are six types of bound pronominal forms: two sets of subject prefixes, a set of object suffixes and three sets of possessive suffixes. In Haspelmath's terms (2013, p. 9), the subject prefixes are cross-indexes, whereas the object suffixes should be classified as pro-indexes. In essence, subject prefixes, which are obligatory, can co-occur with a subject NP while object suffixes cannot co-occur with an NP representing the object argument. It is always the case that either the object suffix or an object NP can occur in a transitive clause,[1] but they cannot both occur concurrently.

The two sets of subject prefixes distinguish realis and irrealis mood. Table 3.15 shows the realis and irrealis forms. Note that all realis and irrealis subject prefixes except the second and third person singular forms are subject to vowel harmony (cf. §2.5.1) and the irrealis suffix is essentially *-sV-*, which is attached to the default realis markers for all persons and numbers except in the first person singular and number.

---

1   Note that they may also occur as objects of verbal prepositions where they have a different behaviour.

Table 3.15: Realis and irrealis subject prefixes

Person/number	Realis subject prefixes	Irrealis subject prefixes
1SG	nV-	jV, dV-
2SG	khV-	kho-sV-
3SG	Ø-	-sV-
1PL INCL	rrV-	rrV-sV-
1PL EXCL	bVrr-	bVrr-sV-
2PL	kVrr-	kVrr-sV-
3PL	rrV-	rrV-sV-

In relation to the two forms of the 1st person singular irrealis prefix, *jV-* and *dV-*, the latter is used in negative complement clauses, which are of the form *no-rong-o sikha de-* 'do not want to…' and in complement clause involving *no-rong te* and *ne-ve* (cf. §7.5.1), while the former is never used in these contexts. There is further discussion of the realis and irrealis forms in §5.4.1.

Table 3.16: Object suffixes

Person/number	Object suffixes
1SG	-ia, -a
2SG	-okh
3SG	-i
1PL INCL	-krre
1PL EXCL	-
2PL	-
3PL	-err

It should be noted from Table 3.16 that the 1PL and 2PL forms are not represented in the object suffix paradigm. Nese employs the independent pronouns for these proforms.

The three other sets of bound pronominal forms are the possessive suffixes that attach either to relational classifiers or bound nouns. Table 3.17 lists the possessive suffixes associated with direct possession. Contrasting with object suffixes, which do not have suffixes in the 1PL EXCL and 2PL forms, the 1PL EXCL and 2PL forms have possessive suffixes.

Table 3.17: Possessive suffixes

Person/number	Type of possessive suffix				
	Indirect possession		Direct possession		
	m, s, rr	*jin-*	Type 1 *-aC*	Type 2 *-oC*	Type 3 *-uC*
1SG	-ak	-a	-ak	-ok	-uk
2SG	-am	-okh	-am	-om	-me
3SG	-an	-i	-an	-on	-ne
1PL INCL	-arr	-krre	-arr		
1PL EXCL	-anan				-inan
2PL	-am'i/ani		-am'i/ani		
3PL	-arr				-rre

3.5 Prepositions

There are two classes of prepositions that are differentiated on the basis of the types of complements they can take. One class is labelled verbal prepositions, based on the fact that they can take either object suffixes or an NP as their complement. The other class may be called true prepositions due to the fact that they cannot take object suffixes but can only take an NP as complement. The verbal prepositions are presented in Table 3.18 and the true prepositions are given in Table 3.19.

Table 3.18: Verbal prepositions

Verbal preposition	Function
min	dative 'to' (used interchangeably with *khin*)
	comitative 'with'
	allative 'towards'
khin	instrumental 'with'
	purposive 'for'
	dative 'to' (used interchangeably with *min*)
sur	purposive 'for'
ngin	purposive 'for'

Each of the verbal prepositions has a number of different meanings and functions, which are discussed in more detail in Chapter 4. However, examples are given below showing the preposition *min* with NP as complement (3.25 and 3.27) and with object suffix as complement (3.26).

- Allative *min*

3.25 *Ne-najnge*   *te*   *kho-se-lev*   *ralo-k*   *v'an*
1SG:REAL-agree   SUB   2SG-IRR-take   voice-1SG:POSS   go
'I agree that you will take my voice (record)

min   **akaev**.
PREP2   archive
for archiving.'
(2012_07_05 obaksi01001 00:00:37.000-00:00:46.000, natural text)

- Comitative *min*

3.26 *No-kol-o*   *lue*   *ma*   *jalin,*   *kanan*
1SG:REAL-carry-3SGOBJ   out   come   outside   1PLEXCL

min-er   *bir-waj-i.*
PREP2-3PLOBJ   1PLEXCL:REAL-eat-3SGOBJ
'I brought it hither outside and us with them we ate it.'
(2012_05_16 obanhy01001 00:01:03.000-00:01:09.500, natural text)

- Ablative *min*

3.27 *Rri-rrurri*   *norroyat*   *rri-vitai*   *v'an*
1PL INCL:REAL-tie   palm leaf   1PLINCL:REAL-put   go
'We tie the palm leaf and put it thither

    ale   *rri-si-milj-i*   *terrterr,*   *Ø-se-vitei*   *khoro*   *kanan*
    CONJ   1PLINCL-IRR-fasten-3SGOBJ   strong   3SG-IRR-block   1PLINCL

then we fasten it tightly, it will block us

min   **nause**,   *nial*   *neren*   *te*   *rrisi-naturr*   *laine.*
PREP2   rain   sun   when   SUB   1PLINCL:IRR-sleep   house:LOC
from the rain, sun when we sleep in the house.'
(2012_07_12 obaksi01001 00:00:53.000-00:01:00:000, natural text)

Table 3.19: True prepositions

rengen	locative 'in', 'at'; instrumental 'with'
neten	purposive
belek	similitive

The preposition *rengen* is the preposition with the widest distribution, with a number of locative meanings, 'into', 'to', 'in', as well as an instrumental.

The following are some examples in which *rengen* has a locative meaning (3.28) and an instrumental meaning (3.29).

3.28 Kani   kirr-v'an   **rengen**   sukul.
     2PL   2PL:REAL-go   LOC   school
     'You (PL) go to school.'
     (2014_01_19 naanhy01001 00:03:36.000-00:03:38.000, natural text)

3.29 *Je-serteng*   **rengen**   nale   nev'enu   iekhe.
     1SG:IRR-count   LOC   language   place   DEM
     'I will count in the language of this place.'
     (2012_08_05 obloro01001 00:00:02.000-00:00:07.000, natural text)

A more in-depth discussion of *rengen* is presented in §5.4.1.

- *neten* (purposive)

3.30 *Ne-v'an*   **neten**   navij   sakhal.
     3SG   PURP2   banana   one
     'I went for a banana.'
     (2012_05_16 obanhy01003 00:01:43.000-00:01:46.000 natural text)

In (3.30), the preposition *neten* serves a purposive function, encoding the reason for the occurrence of the action of going expressed by the intransitive verb *van* 'go'. Further discussion of *neten,* along with examples, is given in §6.6.2. Similarly, the preposition *belek* 'like' is discussed in §6.6.2.

3.6 Adverbs

Adverbs are a closed class, having two subclasses that are distinguished on the basis of their ability to modify either the head of a verb complex or a clause. Adverbs that modify verbs always occur immediately after the verb, while clausal adverbs may occupy a clause initial position or occur after the verb. Verb complex adverbs include those that have aspectual, intensification and manner meanings, some examples of which are given in Table 3.20. Clause-level adverbs are composed primarily of adverbs with temporal meanings, functioning as temporal adjuncts, as highlighted in the examples given in Table 3.21.

Table 3.20: Verb complex adverbs

Manner		Intensification		Aspectual	
monoi	'careless'	*je*	'very'	*v'an*	'until such point'
skheskhalekh	'each, one by one'	*jaru*	'too'	*di*	'already'
sirsir	'quickly'	*kele*	'again'	*buro*	'yet, still'
navon	'aimlessly'	*lemje*	'a lot'	*wor*	'yet, still'
ververik	'slowly'				
ralral	'crazily, crazy'				

Examples (3.31) and (3.33) respectively show a manner adverb *sirsir* 'quickly' modifying the verb and the adverb *lemje* 'a lot' adding intensity to the verb *use* 'to rain'. It is ungrammatical for the adverbs to occupy post verbal position as shown in (3.32) and (3.34).

3.31 *John,*   *khai*   *Ø-vala*   ***sirsir***.
      John   3SG   3SG:REAL-run   quickly
      'John ran quickly.'
      (2012_08_08 elanhy01003 00:00:04.000-00:00:05.000 elicitation)

3.32 **John*   *khai*   *sirsir*   *Ø-vala*.
      John   3SG   quickly   3SG:REAL-run
      (Fieldnotes, elicitation)

3.33 *Nause*   *khai*   *Ø-se-use*   ***lemje***.
      rain   3SG   3SG-IRR-rain   a.lot
      'The rain will pour down heavily.'
      (2012_05_16 obanhy01003 00:03:30.000-00:03:34.000, natural text)

3.34 ****lemje***   *nause*   *Ø-se-use*.
      a.lot   rain   3SG-IRR-rain
      (Fieldnotes, elicitation)

Table 3.21: Clause adverbs

Clause adverbs	
tua	'before'
renran	'everyday'
naleng	'maybe'
dokh	'first of all'
benanev	'yesterday'

The following are example sentences in which the temporal adverbs *tua* and *benanev* are modifying the clauses. The fact that clause adverbs may occupy both clause initial and clause final positions is illustrated in (3.35) and (3.36) and (3.37) and (3.38) with respect to these two temporal adverbs.

3.35 **Tua**   naine   khai   Ø-velvele
     before   house   3SG   3SG:REAL-small
     'Before, houses were small.'
     (2012_08_27 obnesp01001 00:14:41.000-00:14:46.000, natural text)

3.36 *Kanan*   *bir-tutur*   *khin-i*   ***tua*…**
     1PLEXCL   1PLEXCL:REAL-prepare   PREP1-3SGOBJ   coconut
     'We prepared for it before….'
     (2012_08_19 elanhy01006 00:01:29.000-00:01:34.000 elicitation)

3.37 **Benanev**   *ne-les*   *nemerrte*   *sakhal.*
     yesterday   1SG:REAL-see   man   one
     'Yesterday I saw someone.'
     (2012_07_29 elloro01001 00:25:57.000-00:25:58.000, elicitation)

3.38 *Khai*   *Ø-ma*   *benanev.*
     3SG   3SG:REAL-come   yesterday
     'S/he came yesterday.'
     (2012_08_19 elanhy01003 00:00:07.000-00"00"09.000 elicitation)

Further discussion of adverbs is given in §5.5.7.

3.7 Quantifiers and numerals

Quantifiers are classified on the basis of their ability to occur both as modifiers in NPs and as heads of NPs. The forms in the initial subdivision of this word class are quantifiers, which are shown in Table 3.22, and ordinal numbers outlined in Table 3.23. These are classed together on the basis of their ability to occur in the same post-head modifying position in NPs and semantically refer to quantity. The ordinal numbers outlined in Table 3.23 form a subclass of the quantifier and numeral word class on the basis of the morphological derivation, which transforms cardinal numbers to ordinal numbers.

3. WORD CLASSES

The distribution of the quantifiers outlined in Table 3.22, however, differs slightly given that while *sobonon* and *jelengi* can be heads of NPs, *jelekh* cannot be the head of an NP.

Table 3.22: Quantifiers

Quantifier	Syntactic function
sobonon 'some'	• modifier of NP • head of NP
jelengi 'all'	• head of NP
jelekh 'every'	• modifier of NP

Examples (3.39) and (3.40) illustrate *sobonon* functioning as a modifier of an NP and as the head of an NP respectively. While *sobonon* has a dual function, the quantifier *jelengi* can only function as the head of an NP, as illustrated in (3.41). *Jelekh* is also included in this closed class of quantifiers because it modifies the head of an NP as shown in (3.42). However, unlike the other two quantifiers, *jelekh* exhibits other grammatical functions that suggest it belongs to other word classes as well. This and other similar phenomena are dealt with in §3.16.

3.39 *Rri-si-ver   nale   **sobonon**   lalon.*
     1PLINCL-IRR-say   language   some   inside
     'We're going to say some language words inside it.'
     (2014_01_19 naanhy01001 00:08:22.000-00:08:24.000 natural text)

3.40 ***Sobonon**,   khar,   ri-rongvuson-i,   sobonon,   khar,*
     some   3PL   3PL:REAL-understand-3SGOBJ   some   3PL
     'Some, they understand it, some, they

  rri-s-be-rongvuson-i-te.
  3PL-IRR-NEG1-understand-3SGOBJ-NEG2
  don't understand it.'
  (2014_01_19 nanhy01001 00:43:14.000-00:43:17.000, natural text)

3.41 *Ne-vrre   **jelengi**   khe   ne-vitai   tokh.*
     1SG:REAL-remove inner bit   all   DEM   1SG:REAL-put   stay
     'I remove all of those inner bits and I left it there.'
     (2012_06_21 obmame01001 00:00:19.000-00:00:21.000 natural text)

111

3.42 *Nuak khe, nemere **jelekh** re-ve   nuak sakhal khe,*
     boat DEM   people   all   3PL:REAL-say boat one   DEM
     'This boat, everyone says that this one boat

   khai   Ø-vala   belek   plen.
   3SG   3SG:REAL-run   like   plane
   runs like the plane.'
   (2014_01_19 naanhy01001 01:06:24.000-01:06:30.000 natural text)

These quantifiers are discussed further in §4.5.5.

3.7.1 Ordinal numerals

Like quantifiers, numerals occur both as NP heads and as modifiers in NPs. While cardinal numbers belong to the initial subdivision of the quantifier word class, ordinal numbers are a subclass of this word class on the basis of the morphological derivation, which transforms cardinal numbers to ordinal numbers.

Nese has a numeral system that resembles one described by Lynch (2009, p. 8) as having the numerals six to nine morphologically marked while one to five are morphologically unmarked. This numerical system is somewhat similar to the patterns found in the imperfect decimal systems in which numbers below five are treated differently from six to nine. Table 3.23 shows that numbers one to 10 (in the third column) are reflexes of the Proto Oceanic forms. The numbers six to nine in Nese have an initial *khV-* attached to their equivalent POc bases, resulting in *kho/n* 'six', *kho/dit* 'seven', *kho/al* 'eight' and *khe/sve* 'nine'. Lynch (2009, p. 13) suggests that the prefix *kh-* may be derived from the PNCV verb *lakau 'cross over', which means that when one reaches the number five then one crosses over the hands to begin counting the number six.

Nese employs the prefix *vakha-*, which is affixed to the cardinal numerals two to seven to produce equivalent ordinal numerals; and the prefix *to-* to derive ordinal numbers eight to ten from their cardinal counterparts. The prefix *vakha-* is perhaps a reflex of the Proto Oceanic causative *paka-* (Lynch, Ross & Crowley, 2011, p. 83). It is unclear why two different prefixes *vakha* and *to* are used to derive the ordinal numbers two to seven and eight to ten respectively.

3. WORD CLASSES

Table 3.23: Cardinal numbers and ordinal numbers

Numbers	Cardinal	Ordinal	POc forms (Lynch et al., 2011, p. 72)
1	sakhal	sakhal	Various including *ta *sa *tai *kai
2	ru	vakharu	*rua
3	til	vakhatil	*tolu
4	v'at	vakhav'at	*pat(i)
5	line	vakhaline	*lima
6	khon	vakhakhon	*onom
7	khodit	vakhakhodit	*pitu[2]
8	khoal	tokhoal	*walu
9	khesve	tokhesve	*siwa
10	sangav'il	tosangav'il	*sa-[na]-puluq
11	sangav'il ram sakhal	sangav'il ram sakhal	*rua-na-puluq
12	sangav'il ramaru	sangav'il ramaru	

Examples (3.43) and (3.44) illustrate the numeral *sakhal* 'one' modifying the noun head *nemerte* 'man' and functioning as the head noun respectively. In (3.44), *sakhal* is functioning as an indefinite pronoun.

3.43 *Nemerrte* **sakhal**, *khai Ø-se-ma   lem-ak   khe.*
     man   one   3SG 3SG-REAL-come LOC:house-1SG:POSS DEM
     'Someone is coming to my house.'
     (2014_01_19 naanhy01001 00:09:57.000-00:10:00.000 natural text)

3.44 *Kanan   line,   **sakhal**   Ø-nas.*
     1PLEXCL   five   one   3SG:REAL-die
     'There's five of us and one died.'
     (2012_05_22 obcero01001 00:00:11.000-00:00:14.000 natural text)

There is evidence to suggest that the numeral *sakhal* 'one' may be verbal and this is discussed in §3.16.

---

[2] Lynch (2019, p. 64) reconstructs *bitu for Proto North Central Vanuatu (PNCV) proposing that PNCV */b/ underwent a shift from */b/ to apicolabial /b'/ and finally to alveolar /d/ when before a non-back vowel.

113

3.8 Conjunctions and subordinators

3.8.1 Conjunctions

Nese has two subclasses of conjunctions that are differentiated on the basis of their ability to link noun phrases, verb complexes and clauses, as outlined in Table 3.24. The conjunctions that link noun phrases are further divided into two subclasses, one of which consists of conjunctions that coordinate noun phrases in a manner in which the coordinated nominal elements are juxtaposed immediately preceding and following the conjunction. The other subgroup of nominal conjunctions consists of a coordination pattern in which the second coordinated element has been mentioned in a previous clause and it does not occur immediately after the conjunction. This subclass of noun phrase conjunctions includes the comitative verbal preposition *min*.

Table 3.24: Conjunctions

Conjunctions	Noun phrase conjunctions	Immediate conjunction	*rrun* 'and' *min* 'and' (comitative verbal preposition) *deve* 'or'
		Distant conjunction	*rruanen* 'with'
	Clause-level conjunctions	*be* 'but' *deve* 'or' *din* 'and/then' *ale* 'and/then'	

The subcategory of clause-level coordinators contains the conjunctions *be* 'but', *deve* 'or', *din* 'and/then' and *ale* 'and/then.' The contrast between the positions occupied by a nominal conjunction and a clausal conjunction is illustrated in (3.45) and (3.46), where the nominal phrase conjunction *rrun* 'and' joins two noun phrases *bin* 'bean' and *norrulnasasakh* 'rice', while the clausal conjunction *deve* 'or' joins two verb complexes. As shown, *rrun* occurs between two noun phrases while *deve* can occur between two verb clauses.

3.45	*Rri-si-woj*	*na,*	*bin*	*iekhe*	***rrun***
1PLINCL-IRR-eat	HESIT	bean	DEM:LOC	CONJ

'We will eat um, those beans here with

na,	*norrulnasasakh.*
HESIT	rice

um, rice.'
(2014_01_19 naanhy01001 00:04:56.000-00:04:58.000, natural text)

3.46	*Kho-sid-e*	***deve***	*kho-darr-i*
2SG:REAL-cut -3SGOBJ	or	2SG:REAL- split-3SGOBJ

'Do you cut it or you split it?'
(2014_01_19 naanhy01001 00:04:56.000-00:04:58.000 natural text)

As mentioned above, the comitative verbal preposition *min* also has a linking function that, therefore, warrants its inclusion in the list of conjunctions. The fact that a verbal preposition with a comitative denotation can also function as a conjunction has also been noted in Longgu, an Oceanic language of Guadalcanal, Solomon Islands (Hill, 2011, p. 545). In Nese, this conjunction *min* differs starkly from *rrun* in that the two nouns it is joining can only be animate nouns, such as a proper noun, the 1PL INCL and 3PL independent pronouns or the object suffixes with animate references. In contrast, the conjunction *rrun* can join any animate and inanimate non-locative bound and free common nouns. Another interesting property of comitative *min* is that the initial noun phrase occurring before the conjunction always contains a superset free pronoun, namely the 1PL EXCL and 3PL independent pronouns, and the noun phrase occurring after the conjunction refers to individuals who could be added to individuals referred to by the independent pronoun. This is illustrated in (3.47).

3.47	*Ri-v'an*	*ri-jnejne,*	***khar***	***min***	*sorsilin*
3PL:REAL-go	3PL:REAL-to.fish	3PL	CONJ	Sorsilin

'They went finishing, them and Sorsilin,

ri-v'an	*rengen*	*nause.*
3PL:REAL-go	LOC	rain

they went in the rain.'
(2014_01_19 naanhy01001 00:24:59.000-00:25:07.000 natural text)

It has been observed that many Oceanic languages have the comitative conjunction expressed by the form *mV*, and it has further been proposed that the phonological shape of that form may be derived from a Proto Oceanic comitative verb reconstructed as *ma-i* or *ma-ni* meaning 'to be with' (Bril, 2011, p. 259). Nese comitative *min* could, therefore, be a reflex of the latter.

As illustrated in Table 3.24, there are two subdivisions within the category of noun phrase conjunctions: immediate conjunction and distant conjunction, the latter expressed by way of the conjunction *rruanen*. The difference between the two conjunctions is that *rruanen* joins two noun phrases, both of which are expressed earlier and not juxtaposed by the conjunction *rruanen*. The difference between the position in which the conjoined noun phrases occur in *rrun* and *rruanen* is shown in (3.48) and (3.49) respectively.

3.48 *Iyo   protesten   **rrun**   presbyterien.*
     Yes   Protestant   CONJ   Presbyterian
     'Yes, Protestant and Presbyterian.'
     (2014_01_19 naanhy01001 00:11:08.000-00:11:11.000 natural text)

3.49 *Ne-ve   'Gregory   v'an   vol   tin   nanaj*
     1SG:REAL-say   Gregory   go   buy   tin   fish
     'I said, "Gregory go and buy one canned fish

   ba-sakhal,   tekh   makroni   khe   ba-ru   ma,   jo-kuk-u
   POT-one   take   noodles   DEM   POT-two   come   1SG:IRR-cook-3SGOBJ

   take those two noodles hither, I will cook it

   ***rruanen**.'*
   CONJ
   with it (i.e. the two things together)".'
   (2014_01_19 naanhy01001 00:00:59.000-00:01:11.000 natural text)

The other subgroup of conjunctions include *din* 'and/then', *ale* 'and/then', *deve* 'or', *seve* 'if' and *be* 'but', and these coordinating conjunctions may join sentences or clauses. The clausal conjunction *din* 'and' is a form that is rarely used and is largely replaced by *ale* 'and', which is a borrowing from Bislama.

Below are examples of the usage of the conjunction *din* (3.50), *deve* (3.51–3.52) and *seve* (3.53).

3.50 *Je-sul neut-ak, Ø-se-rov, ale je-kron, sori,*
1SG:IRR-burn garden:POSS:1SG 3SG-IRR-finish CONJ 1SG:IRR-leave sorry

'I will burn my garden, when that is finished then I will leave it, sorry,

din *je-kron neuta-k Ø-se-tokh.*
CONJ 1SG:IRR-leave garden:POSS:1SG 3SG-IRR-stay

then I will leave my garden, it's going to stay like that.'
(2012_08_27 obnesp01003 00:08:01.000-00:08:14.000 natural text)

In (3.50), *din* is employed to link two verbal clauses and it indicates the events occurring in a sequential order. The conjunction *deve* 'or', on the other hand, may conjoin noun phrases and verbal clauses as shown in (3.51) and (3.52) respectively. When *deve* conjoins noun phrases and verbal clauses, it is proposing two alternative possibilities.

3.51 *Naleng haf pas fo **deve** haf pas faev bur-khos laine.*
ADV half past four CONJ half past five 1PLEXCL:REAL-reach LOC:house

'We reached the house at around half past four or half past five.'
(2011_12_21 obrojo01003 00:00:22.000-00:00:25.000 natural text)

3.52 *Jo-kol-o lue **deve** Ø-so-tokh buro?*
1SG:IRR-3SGOBJ CONJ 3SG-IRR-stay GENMOD

'Should I remove it or should I just leave it?'
(2012_06_12 obaksi01001 00:06:59.000-00:07:02.000 natural text)

3.53 ***Seve** line be line*
CONJ five

'If five, but (let it be) five.'
(naanhy01001 00:48:44.000 natural text)

Examples of the Bislama borrowed conjunctions *ale* and *be* are shown in (3.54) and (3.55). *Ale* is used to conjoin clauses and sentences in which the events expressed occur in a sequential order, while *be* conjoins clauses and sentences.

3.54 *Je-bat-e   jelengi* **ale**   *Ø-se-takh-e   Ø-se-mul   lilakh.*
      1SG:IRR-3SGOBJ all   CONJ 3SG-IRR-3SGOBJ 3SG-IRR-return   back
      'I did all of it then she will take it and will return back.'
      (2014_01_19 naanhy01001 00:16:34.000-00:16:38.000 natural text)

3.55 *Nalang   Ø-rub*   **be**   *khai   s-be-rubvej-te   naine.*
      wind   3SG:IRR-kill CONJ 3SG   IRR-NEG1-blow.down-NEG2   house
      'The wind howled but it did not blow down the house.'
      (2012_08_22 anhy01007 00:04:50.000-00:04:55.000 natural text)

3.8.2 Subordinators

Subordinators are distinguished from other word classes on the basis of their ability to mark a variety of subordinate relationships by linking a subordinate clause to the main clause. In Nese, relative and complement clauses are introduced by the general subordinator *te*. This general subordinator also co-occurs with the subordinators *neten* 'because' and *neren* 'when', which are used to introduce different types of adverbial clauses. The subordinators in Table 3.25 introduce subordinate clauses.

Table 3.25: Subordinators and functions

te	introduces a complement clause
	introduces a relative clause
neten te	'because', introduces an adverbial clause of reason
neren te	'when', introduces a temporal adverbial clause
seve	'if'

The following are examples of subordinators introducing a complement clause (3.56) and a relative clause (3.57). In (3.56), the complement clause is introduced by the free form subordinator *te* and a similar pattern is seen in (3.57) in which the relative clause is introduced by *te*, functioning as a modifier of the noun phrase *nuak* 'ship'. In this case, the relative clause has a descriptive functioning, describing the type of ship in question.

3.56 *Re-les*   **te**   *tev'et   nge   Ø-ti-yat.*
      3PL:REAL   SUB   woman   DEM   3SG:REAL-ASP-sit
      'They say that the woman was sitting.'
      (2012-05_16 obanhy01005 00:01:18.000-00:01:20.000 natural text)

3. WORD CLASSES

3.57 | *Te-jiblakh* | *ri-yat* | *rengen* | *nuak* | ***te*** | *belek* | *Big sista.*
|---|---|---|---|---|---|---|
| PL-child | 3PL:REAL | LOC | boat | SUB | like | Big sista |

'The children sat in the boat which is like Big Sister.'
(2014_01_19 naanhy01001 00:05:16.000-00:05:20.000 natural text)

The other two subordinators co-occur with the nouns *neten* 'because' and *neren* 'when' in order to denote reason and the time in which an event occurs respectively. In (3.58), *neten te* introduces the reason clause that expresses the reason why the action expressed in the main clause occurred. Finally, example (3.59) illustrates *neren te* introducing a subordinate clause, which gives the time setting of the event described in the main clause.

3.58 | *No-rongo* | *sikha* | ***neten*** | ***te*** | *nause* | *Ø-ti-use* | *je.*
|---|---|---|---|---|---|---|
| 1SG:REAL-feel | NEG | PURP2 | SUB | rain | 3SG:REAL-ASP-rain | ADV |

'I don't want to because it is raining a lot.'
(2014_01_19 naanhy01001 00:14:29.000-00:14:32.000 natural text)

3.59 | *Kanan* | *iekhetan* | ***neren*** | ***te*** | *skul* | *Ø-se-tebekh*
|---|---|---|---|---|---|
| 1PLEXCL | DEM:LOC | when | SUB | school | 3SG-IRR-start |

'As for us down here, when school starts,

nemerre *jelekh,* *kavra.*
people copra

everyone makes copra.'
(2014_02_18 naaksi01001 00:12:14.000-00:12:20.000 natural text)

The subordinating conjunction *seve* occurs sentence or clause initially, introducing a conditional clause that ends with a pause followed by another clause whose fulfilment depends on the realisation of the initial clause. This is illustrated in (3.60).

3.60 | ***Seve*** | *nev'khe* | *Ø-ma,* | *Ø-se-us-i* | *min-a.*
|---|---|---|---|---|
| CONJ | tomorrow | 3SG:REAL-come | 3SG-IRR-ask-3SGOBJ | PREP2-1SGOBJ |

'If tomorrow comes, she will ask me about it.'
(2014_01_19 naanhy01001 00:42:29.000-00:42:32.000 natural text)

A more detailed discussion of these conjunctions and subordinators is given in Chapter 7.

3.9 Relational classifiers

Indirect possession is indicated in Nese by means of possessive suffixes attached to relational classifiers. As mentioned in §3.2.1.1, there are four different classifiers, which indicate the type of possession between the possessed noun and the possessor. Table 3.26 shows the relational classifiers (cf. §4.5.8).

Table 3.26: Relational classifiers

| jin- | general possession | rr- | possession of food items meant for eating |
| s- | general possession | m- | possession of liquids intended for drinking |

Relational classifiers attach to possessive suffixes and they are distinguished from other word classes on the basis of their inability to be modified. In addition to this, they can only modify noun roots functioning as the head of the noun phrase. As shown in Table 3.26, the classifiers *rr-* and *m-* strictly apply to possession of food items that are meant to be eaten and to liquids meant for drinking respectively. On the other hand, *jin-* and *sa-* are associated with possession of general items. The function of the relational classifiers is discussed with examples in §4.5.8.

3.10 Directionals

Directionals (cf. §5.5.4) are distinguished on the basis of their ability to modify head verbs and head nouns by indicating the spatial direction to which the verbs refer or the location of a particular noun phrase referent. They differ from adverbs in that they cannot modify clauses. Nese directionals are listed in Table 3.27. This is a closed class of directionals that occupy post-verbal position and may be further divided into two different subcategories depending on the kinds of elements they may modify. One subclass consists of the intransitive verbs *ma* 'come' and *v'an* 'go', which function as directionals meaning 'hither/toward the speaker' and 'thither/away from the speaker' respectively, when they occur as the final verb in a serial verb construction. These two directionals cannot modify noun phrases. The other subclass consists of directionals that do not occur as part of a serial verb construction and can modify noun phrases. Within this subclass are *lokhsa* 'there' and *ev'an* 'there', which distinguish between a location that is in close proximity to the speaker or hearer and that which is further away from where the speaker or hearer is located. The directionals that mark the axes of the geographic system *vila* 'down towards the sea' and *vokhte* 'inland' also belong to this subclass.

Table 3.27: Directionals

atan	'down'
maro	'up'
ev'an	'there' (proximal)
lokhsa	'there' (distant)
vila	'down seawards'
vitan	'down'
asakh	'to the right of'
asuv	'to the left of'
vokhte	'in land'

In (3.61), the directional *v'an* indicates a movement away from the speaker. It is not functioning in this context as the independent verb *ma* 'come' since, if it had, the corresponding 1PL EXCL irrealis subject prefix would be affixed to the verb *ma* and the meaning 'hither' would not be present.

3.61 *Bur-su-mul* **v'an** *Santo.*
1PLEXCL-IRR-return hither Santo
'We returned hither to Santo.'
(2014_01_19 naanhy01001 00:18:58.000-00:18:59.000 natural text)

The other subcategory of directionals differ from *ma* and *v'an* in that they cannot function as independent verbs. They may also modify nouns as shown in (3.62), where the directional *maro* modifies a common noun phrase, although its status as a verbal modifier is undisputable as shown in (3.63).

3.62 *Khai Ø-ver nele-n nasub* **maro** *khin*
3SG 3SG:REAL-say message-3SG:POSS chief up PREP1
'She said God's (the chief up there) message to

kanan.
1PLINCL
us.'
(2014_01_19 naanhy01001 00:09:35.000-00:09:39.000 natural text)

3.63 *Naskhe   Ø-ti-yat   **maro** rengen nenibor   sakhal.*
      kingfisher 3SG:REAL-ASP-sit   up   LOC   nenibor tree one
      'The kingfisher sat up, on the nenibor tree.'
      (2012_05_16 obanhy01004 00:00:10.000-00:00:14.000 natural text)

Other directionals that modify proper noun place names are *asakh* 'to the right of' (3.64) and *asuv* 'to the left of' (3.65). These are the only two place names in the data that have these directionals incorporated as part of place names.

3.64 *Ri-v'an   v'an v'an Tontar **asakh**.*
      3PL:REAL-go   go   go   Tontar to the right of
      'They went until Tontar that is at the right.'
      (2012_08_22 anhy01005 00:02:01.000-00:02:03.000 natural text)

3.65 *Je-sob-sob   Tontar **asuv**.*
      1SG:IRR-REDUP-talk about   Tontar to the left of
      'I am going to talk about Tontar that is on the left.'
      (2012_08_22 anhy01005 00:00:01.000-00:00:05.000 natural text)

The directionals *atan* 'down', *maro* 'up', *vila* 'down towards the sea', *vitan* 'down' and *vokhte* 'in land' have a fixed reference, while *ev'an* 'there (proximal)', *lokhsa* 'there (distant)' and *asakh* 'to the right of' and *asuv* 'to the left of' are employed to express spatial distance that is relative to the speaker and or the hearer. Example (3.66) illustrates *ev'an* indicating the spatial location that is visible to the speaker and hearer.

3.66 *Nato   khai   Ø-wov   **ev'an**.*
      fowl   3SG   3SG:REAL-lay egg there
      'The fowl laid its eggs there.'
      (2012_08_22 elanhy01011 00:13:38.000-00:13:40.000 elicitation)

3.11 Demonstratives

There is no single class of demonstratives that can be defined on the basis of their morphosyntactic characteristics. However, I categorise nominal and adverbial demonstrative forms together here on the basis of their shared function as deictic forms, which are used to locate and refer to items and events. The nominal demonstratives *khe* and *nge* share properties as heads and modifiers in NPs, as indicated in Table 3.28. The adverbial demonstratives *iekhe* and *iekhetan* are verbal and clause-level modifiers. These four demonstratives in Nese are listed in Table 3.28.

Table 3.28: Demonstratives

Demonstratives			
Nominal		**Local adverbial**	
khe	<ul><li>modifies the head noun in noun phrases</li><li>functions as the complement of the preposition *belek* 'like'</li><li>modifies whole clauses</li><li>is the subject in a non-verbal clause</li><li>modifies the subject of a non-verbal clause</li><li>modifies temporal nouns and verbs</li></ul>	*iekhe*	<ul><li>functions as a locative adverb</li></ul>
nge	<ul><li>modifies the head noun in noun phrases</li></ul>	*iekhetan*	<ul><li>functions as a locative adverb</li></ul>

Dixon (2003, p. 62) defines a nominal demonstrative as one which may co-occur with a noun or a pronoun in a noun phrase or can be the only constituent in the noun phrase. This contrasts with a local adverbial demonstrative which may occur by itself or with a noun which takes a local marking with the meaning 'here'. The demonstrative forms in Nese reflect this broad distinction; *khe* and *nge* are nominal demonstratives, while *iekhe* and *iekhetan* are local adverbial demonstratives.

While I classify *khe* as a nominal demonstrative, it has the broadest distribution and can also modify verb complex heads. Note that the adverbial demonstratives are derived from the root *khe*. This morphological derivation has been observed as being typical by Dixon (2003, p. 62), who states that local adverbial demonstratives tend to be morphologically derived from nominal demonstratives in languages in which nominal demonstratives also function as modifiers to verbs. The form *iekhetan* is derived from *khe* and the directional *atan* 'down'.

The two nominal demonstratives *khe* and *nge* differ in their functions. The former has anaphoric, spatial deictic and emphatic uses, while the latter only has anaphoric functions. In addition to modifying noun heads, the demonstrative *khe* also functions as a clause final demonstrative modifying propositions or events. The following are examples that show demonstrative *khe* modifying different types of noun heads.

3.67 *Rri-si-woj   nebetnakhav   **khe**   buro.*
      1PLINCL-IRR-eat   bread   DEM   GENMOD
      'We will only eat this bread.'
      (2014_01_19 naanhy01001 00:00:29.000-00:00:31.000 natural text)

3.68 *Khai **khe** rri-si-waj-i   rri-si-won   khe.*
      3SG   DEM   1PLINCL-IRR-eat-3SGOBJ   1PLINCL-IRR-full   DEM
      'That one, we'll eat it we will be full.'
      (2014_01_19 naanhy01001 00:02:50.000-00:02:52.000 natural text)

3.69 ***Lana   khe**   *khai*   *Ø-se-ma*   ***khe**   sana   **khe**.*
      Lana   DEM   3SG   3SG-IRR-come   DEM   today DEM
      'That Lana (the one we've been talking about), she will come here, today.'
      (2014_01_19 naanhy01001 00:02:50.000-00:09:48.000 natural text)

In (3.67), (3.68) and (3.69), the nominal demonstrative is deictic in nature in that the speaker is referring to the bread, the referent of the 3SG pronoun and the person (Lana) who was previously mentioned.

In (3.69), *khe* also modifies the verb *ma* 'come' and the temporal noun *sana* 'today'. When it is modifying the verb *ma*, it is functioning as a local adverbial demonstrative. In (3.70), the nominal demonstrative *khe* is the complete noun phrase functioning as the complement of the preposition *belek* 'like'.

3.70 *Ne-var-i   khin-er   belek   **khe**.*
      1SG:REAL-tell-3SGOBJ   PREP-3PLOBJ   like   DEM
      'I said it to them like this.'
      (2014_01_19 naanhy01001 00:09:46.000-00:09:48.000 natural text)

In (3.71) and (3.72), demonstrative *khe* is modifying the locational noun phrase *latan* and the intransitive verb *v'an* 'go' functioning as a clausal adjunct.

3.71 *No-kol-o   ma   khe   ne-yat   **latan**   **khe**.*
      1SG:REAL-carry-   come   DEM   1SG:IRR-sit   ground:LOC   DEM
      3SGOBJ
      'I brought it hither, here I sat down here.'
      (2012_06_21 obmame01001 00:00:15.000-00:00:10.000 natural text)

3. WORD CLASSES

3.72 | *Yvon* | *khai* | *Ø-ma* | *re-ve* | *dev'e* | *khina*
| Yvonne | 3SG | 3SG:REAL-come | 3PL:REAL-say | 'mother' | 1SG

'Yvonne she came and they said, "Mum, I

| *ne-v'an* | ***khe***, | *j-be-les-te* | *nobolokv'at* | *s-ak* | *ev'an*
| 1SG:REAL-go | DEM | IRR-NEG1-see-NEG2 | cow | CLGEN-1SG:POSS | DIR

went there but I did not see my cow at

latas.
sea:LOC

the sea".'

(2014_01_19 naanhy01001 00:06:29.000-00:06:35.000 natural text)

Example (3.73) shows that the morpheme *khe* can co-occur with the local adverbial demonstrative *iekhe*, and therefore in this context the former cannot be considered as either a local adverbial demonstrative or a nominal demonstrative, but rather as a deictic marker.

3.73 | *No-rong-o* | *sikha* | *ne-ve* | *'no* | *khina* | *tenge*
| 1SG:REAL-want-3SGOBJ | NEG | 1SG:REAL-say | no | 1SG | thing

'I did not want to, I said, "No as for me, this

| *iekhe* | ***khe*** | *Ø-sat* | *khe.*
| DEM:LOC | DEM | 3SG:REAL-bad | DEM

thing here is bad".'

(2019_01_19 naanhy01001 00:06:29.000-00:06:35.000 natural text)

Other contexts where *khe* is best described as a deictic marker are when it occurs with a noun taking local marking such as in (3.74) and when it occurs as part of a verb complex (3.75). This morpheme has the same discourse function that has been described by Crowley in relation to the Bislama morpheme *ia* as a pragmatic particle, which also has a demonstrative function (Crowley, 2004, p. 196).

3.74 | *No-kol-o* | | *ma* | *khe* | *ne-yat* | ***latan*** | ***khe***.
| 1SG:REAL-carry-3SGOBJ | | come | DEM | 1SG:IRR-sit | ground:LOC | DEM

'I brought it hither, here I sat down on the ground here.'

(2012_06_21 obmame01001 00:00:16.000-00:00:19.000 natural text)

3.75 | Yvon | khai | Ø-ma | re-ve | 'dev'e | khina
Yvonne | 3SG | 3SG:REAL-come | 3PL:REAL-say | mother | 1SG

'Yvonne she came and they said, "Mum I

ne-v'an | **khe** | j-be-les-te | nobolokv'at
1SG:REAL-go | DEM | IRR-1SG:REAL-NEG1-see-NEG2 | bullock

went there but I did not see my bullock

s-ak | ev'an | latas.
CLGEN-1SG:POSS | DIR | sea:LOC

there at the sea".'
(2014_01_19 naanhy01001 00:06:29.000-00:06:35.000 natural text)

The local adverbial demonstratives *iekhe* and *iekhetan* signal spatial proximity and mean 'here' and 'down here' respectively. With these two demonstratives, the speaker is the deictic centre and the referents are located spatially on a distance scale relative to the deictic centre. *Iekhe* indicates entities that are proximal to the speaker and *iekhetan* indicates entities that are proximal but at a downward direction. The two demonstratives may be used with pointing gestures.

3.76 | No-rong-o | sikha | ne-ve | 'no | khina | tenge
1SG:REAL-want-3SGOBJ | NEG | 1SG:REAL-say | no | 1SG | thing

'I did not want to, I said, "No as for me, this

iekhe | **khe**, | Ø-sat | khe.
DEM:LOC | DEM | 3SG:REAL-bad | DEM

thing is bad".'
(2014_01_19 naanhy01001 00:41:29.000-00:41:34.000 natural text)

The demonstrative *iekhe* contrasts with *khe* in that the former is a local adverbial demonstrative that has spatial deictic meaning. It may be uttered with a gesture indicating the location of an event or an action. In (3.76), the speaker is referring to her knee (a location on her body), which is in clear visibility and although she did not point to it, it is possible for speakers to indicate it by pointing. *Iekhe* can also refer to a spatial location rather than a bodily location as illustrated in (3.77).

3.77   *Kanan*   *bir-khro*   ***iekhe***.
       1PLEXCL   1PLEXCL:real-stay   DEM:LOC
       'We stay here.'
       (2014_01_19 naanhy01001 00:00:17.000-00:00:19.000 natural text)

The demonstrative *khe* also occurs in the position also occupied by *iekhe* (3.78); however, it does not have the meaning 'here' in this context. In this context, it is a pragmatic marker.

3.78   *Kirr-se-ma*   *khota*   *kirr-s-be-worr-te*   *sana*   *neten*   *te*
       2PL-IRR-come   DEHORT   2PL-IRR-NEG1-eat-NEG2   today   PURP2   SUB
       'You guys will come and you won't eat today because

       khina   *ne-rong-o*   *sikha*   *de-tu-tun*   ***khe***.
       1SG   1SG:REAL-want-3SGOBJ   NEG   1SG:IRR-REDUP-roast   DEM
       I don't want to roast.'
       (2014_01_19 naanhy01001 00:01:41.000-00:01:44.000 natural text)

The demonstrative *nge* in the vast majority of cases modifies inanimate nominal heads of noun phrases, as shown in example (3.79), while the demonstrative *khe* modifies both animate and inanimate nominal heads of noun phrases.

3.79   *Khai*   *vol-i*   *ji-n*   *severine*   *ale*   *Ø-v'an*
       3SG   buy-3SGOBJ   CLGEN-3SG:POSS   severine   CONJ   3SG:REAL-go
       'She bought it from Severine and she went and

       Ø-kol   *bin*   ***nge***.
       3SG:REAL-carry   bean   DEM
       brought those beans.'
       (2014_01_19 naanhy01001 00:04:04.000-00:04:10.000 natural text)

Both demonstratives *khe* and *nge* may modify the interrogative *nese* 'what', as shown in examples (3.80) and (3.81), and in these cases they are functioning as pragmatic particles rather than demonstratives.

3.80 *No,*   *kho-sob-o*   *nese*   **nge**, *norrotvon*
      No   2SG:IRR-talk about-3SGOBJ what   DEM   face of the canoe
      'No you talk about that thing, the face of the canoe.'
      (2012_08_27 obnesp01001 00:11:08.000-00:11:19.000 natural text)

3.81 *Rro-sob*   *nese*   **khe**, *naine?*
      1PLINCL:REAL-talk about   what   DEM   house
      'What's that we're talking about, houses?'
      (2012_08_27 obnesp01001 00:01:33.000-00:01:42.000 natural text)

In (3.79), the use of *nge* is anaphoric; that is, the beans have already been previously mentioned. Example (3.79) may also have a deictic denotation if it is accompanied by a gesture, in which case it would mean that the beans may be referred to as being 'here'. In constructions (3.80) and (3.81), *khe* and *nge* are being used as discourse particles forming part of the expression *nese nge/khe*, which is only used when the speaker is trying to remember something.

3.12 Negative particles

Nese has two negative particles to express negation. Firstly, it uses a discontinuous negative particle *sbe*-Verb-*te* to express negation in all verbal clauses except for verbal clauses where the head of the clause is *rong-* with the meaning 'want/like/prefer' (cf. §5.5.1.1). This particle does not negate nominal elements. The other type of negative particle is *sikha*. This negative particle negates clauses in which the head verb is *rong-* 'want/like/prefer' and it also negates non-verbal clauses with the meaning 'there is no X'. Negation of verbal clauses via *sbe*-Verb-*te* are discussed in §5.5.1.1 and the role of *sikha* in the negation of non-verbal existential predicates is discussed in §5.5.1.2 and §7.5.1.

3.13 Verbal affixes

In addition to the bound subject and object pro-indexes described in §3.4, Nese has two other preverbal affixes: *-ti-* and *-ba-*. The former, which functions as a generic aspectual marker, may co-occur with certain bound subject pro-indexes (§5.5.9), although its presence is not obligatory.

The latter affix *ba-*, on the other hand, is prefixed to verbs and in these instances it indicates the potential mood. It only co-occurs with the 1PL EXCL form. The functions and distribution of these two affixes are further described in §5.5.9 and §5.5.10 respectively.

3.14 Greetings and leavetakings

The following phrases constitute a small closed class of greetings used when a speaker meets someone or is about to leave.

nakis tumorrorran	'good morning'
nakis tubung	'good night'
nakis tirevrav	'good afternoon'
ale	'goodbye'
khunokh	'goodbye/see you later'
verse?	'how are you?'
loko	'that's fine'

The expression *khunokh* is no longer used and is being replaced with the expression *ale*, which is a borrowing from Bislama via French. The reason for including the greetings *nakis tumorrorran* and *nakis tubung* here in this word class is that, in these contexts, they are not functioning as nominal arguments of verb clauses. Being an argument of a verb clause is a criterion for membership in the noun class. Similarly, they are different in that, with nouns in the noun class, the modifying intransitive stative verb occurs post-nominally whereas in the context where they are used as greetings the intransitive stative verb modifying the noun occurs before the noun (cf. §4.5.3).

3.15 Lexical interjections

The following are some interjections that are used as pro sentences, which means they may be substituted for whole sentences.

sikha	'no'
iyo	'yes'
ale	'okay'

Hesitation markers and exclamations are two other small subclasses of interjections. The following are hesitation markers used in Nese.

na   'um'
netenge 'thingummy'

Netenge is used when the speaker is trying to think of a name (either of an animate or inanimate thing).

The following are some examples of exclamatory particles in Nese:

Wolei   exclamation of surprise
Teverik exclamatory expression used when one is surprised or exhausted
O!   this is used for emphatic purposes
Varatne! exclamation of surprise which may be translated as 'really?'

These are different from the interjections because they cannot be used as pro sentences.

3.16 Flexibility of word class membership

The discussions in the previous subsections of this chapter have revealed that some Nese lexemes have morphosyntactic properties and functions that enable them to be a member of more than one word class. These lexemes are listed in Table 3.29, which also shows the word classes they are compatible with, co-referenced to either their relevant examples or sections in which they are discussed.

Table 3.29 shows that, in general, verb complex adverbs may also function as modifiers of noun phrases. Only one verb complex adverb *lemje* 'a lot' exhibits verbal properties that are demonstrated by its ability to take verbal negation and subject prefixes as illustrated in example (3.82). Its ability to modify a head noun is illustrated by example (3.83). The other lexeme that exhibits flexible membership is the quantifier *jelekh* 'all', which also functions as a verb complex adverb and a noun modifier. The verbal preposition *min* also has properties that make it eligible for it to be included in the conjunction word class.

3. WORD CLASSES

Table 3.29: Flexible lexemes

Lexeme	Word class membership						
	Quantifier	Verbal preposition/ True preposition	Adverb	Verb	Conjunction	Other functions
lemje 'a lot'			verb complex adverb (cf. §3.6)	takes negation, the potential and aspectual marker and subject prefixes (example 3.82)		modifies heads of noun phrases (example 3.82)
wor 'yet, still'			verb complex adverb (cf. §4.5.10)			modifies heads of noun phrases (cf. §4.5.10)
buro 'just'			verb complex adverb (example 3.84 and 3.85)			modifies heads of noun phrases (example 3.83)
jelekb 'every'	quantifier					modifies heads of noun phrases (§4.5.5)
min 'with, to, towards'		verbal preposition (cf. §6.6.1.2)			noun phrase conjunction (cf. §3.2.1)	
belek 'like'		true preposition (cf. §6.6.2)		takes aspectual *ti* and may be negated via the negative discontinuous markers (cf. §6.6.2)		
row 'finish'				Stative verb		Modifies common nouns and independent pronouns

131

3.82   Iyo,   Protesten   rrun   Presbyterien   neten   te
       yes   Protestant   CONJ   Presbyterian   PURP2   SUB
       'Yes, Protestant and Presbyterian churches because

       kanan   bir-s-be-**lemje**-te.
       1PLEXCL   1PLEXCL-IRR-NEG1-a.lot-NEG2
       we were not many.'
       (2014_01_19 naanhy01001 00:11:08.000-00:11:14.000 natural text)

3.83   Rri-bet   norrian   **lemje**   je,   khise
       3PL:REAL-make   food   a.lot   ADV   who
       'We made lots of food, who

       nemerrte   nen,   khise   Ø-se-ma   Ø-so-worr?
       man   ASSOC   who   3SG-IRR-come   3SG-IRR-eat
       are the people who will eat it, who will come and eat it?'
       (2014_01_19 naanhy01001 00:15:00.000-00:15:04.000 natural text)

The verb complex adverbs with aspectual meanings, *wor* 'yet, still' and *buro* 'just' also modify nouns. Examples (3.84) and (3.85) illustrate *buro* modifying a verb and a noun respectively. Given that these two lexemes may modify both heads of verb complexes and NP heads, they are referred to as general modifiers.

3.84   Ø-So-tokh   **buro**.
       3SG-IRR-stay   GENMOD
       'Just let it stay there.'
       (2014_01_19 naanhy01001 00:34:30.000-00:34:32.000 natural text)

3.85   No,   sikha,   nobukhas   sikha,   nav'at   **buro**.
       no   NEG   pig   NEG   money   GENMOD
       'No, no, no pigs, just money.'
       (2014_01_19 naanhy01001 00:29:00.000-00:29:04.000 natural text)

The flexibility of these lexemes in Nese could be attributed to their functions these lexemes have in Proto Oceanic and the paths of grammaticalisation they have taken. For example, as mentioned in §3.2.1, conjunctive *min* could have possibly originated from Proto Oceanic comitative verb reconstructed as *ma-i* or *ma-ni* 'to be with' (Bril, 2011,

p. 259). At this stage in Nese, it has retained both its inherited verbal property, that is its ability to take object suffixes, and also the semantic property of 'accompaniment', which is a characteristic that is attributed to conjunctions. Given that the lexeme *min* also carries other functions (cf. §3.16), it is evident that *min* has undergone an extension of its functions to accommodate for functions for which the language lacks a lexeme to express, although this may also be partly due to contact with other nearby related communalects.

The flexibility of the members of the adverb word class outlined above is probably a reflection of a grammaticalisation process in which Nese is undergoing. Lynch et al. (2011, p. 63) proposed that Proto Oceanic may have had a small word class of underived adverbs. Since there are no adverbs reconstructed for Proto Oceanic, it may be safe to assume that the lexemes in question originated from Proto Oceanic verbs, since the verb word class existed in Proto Oceanic. The adverbs in question have an aspectual function and given that aspectual verbal morphemes such as *rov* 'finish, end' occur post-verbally, this accords with aspectual *buro* and *wor* also occuring post-verbally, similar to other adverbs.

The occurrences of these two morphemes as noun phrase modifiers could be attributed to contact with Bislama. The adverbial form *nomo* 'only, just' in Bislama (Crowley, 2004, p. 113), whose equivalent form in Nese is both *buro* and *wor,* can also be seen as modifying noun phrases in Bislama (Crowley, 2004, pp. 144–45). Therefore, given the overwhelming presence of Bislama in the Nese speaking area, it is very likely that the functions of *wor* and *buro* as nominal modifiers are derived from Bislama.

4
The noun phrase

4.1 Introduction

In this chapter, I describe the structure of the Nese noun phrase (NP). Section 4.2 delineates the order of the noun phrase constituents. Section 4.3 discusses the functions of noun phrases and §4.4 identifies the words that can function as heads of noun phrases. Section 4.5 centres on the elements that may modify the noun phrase head, with a discussion of the discourse role of pronouns presented in §4.6. Lastly, §4.7 is a description of nominalisation.

4.2 Order of noun phrase constituents

A noun phrase in Nese may contain a head noun by itself or a head noun with modifying elements, as shown in Figure 4.1.

The head noun may be modified by nouns (including locational nouns), bound personal pronouns, numerals, demonstratives, nominalised verbs, possessive markers (relational classifiers), stative intransitive verbs (adjectival verbs), general modifiers and relative clauses.

A GRAMMAR OF NESE

NP head		Modifiers											
Noun subclasses				Noun		Bound personal pronouns	Numeral	Number	Demonstrative	Nominalised verb	Possessive	Intransitive stative verb	Relative clause	Locational nouns	General modifiers
				Proper noun (place name)	Common noun										
Common nouns	Bound	✗	✓	✗	✓	✗	✓	✓	✓	✓	✓	✗	✓
	Free	✓	✓	✓	✓	✓	✓	✓	✓	✗	✗	✗	✓
	Locational	✗	✗	✗	✗	✗	✓	✗	✗	✗	✗	✗	✓
Proper nouns		✗	✗	✗	✗	✗	✗	✗	✗	✗	✗	✗	✓
Kinship terms		✗	✗	✗	✗	✗	✓	✗	✓	✓	✗	✗	✓
Independent pronouns		✗	✗	✓	✓	✗	✓	✗	✗	✗	✗	✗	✓

Figure 4.1: NP heads and modifiers

There are restrictions on the types of modifiers that may co-occur with a head noun depending on the type of noun functioning as the head noun as well as its semantic properties. The extent to which modifiers may co-occur with one another is largely determined by the semantic properties of the head noun they are modifying as well as those of the modifiers. As illustrated in Figure 4.2, the only obligatory element is the head noun, with most of the modifiers, being optional elements, occurring in the slots after the head noun. The only modifying element that may occur before the head noun is the quantifier *jelengi* 'all'.

Even though modifiers are optional by nature, there are some relationships that manifest strict ordering patterns. Specific cases are the position of numerals in between possessive classifiers and demonstratives, demonstratives having a tendency to occur after stative intransitive verbs or demonstratives and nominalised verbs occurring immediately after the head noun. In general, there is a strong preference for relative clauses or general modifiers to occupy phrase final position.

(quantifier) **HEAD...**
(noun) (nominalised verb) (stative intransitive verb) (bound personal pronoun) (possessive relational classifier) (numeral) (quantifier) (demonstrative) (general modifier) (relative clause)

Figure 4.2: Constituents of a noun phrase

As shown in Figure 4.2, a noun phrase may simply consist of a head noun only. This is illustrated in (4.1).

4.1 *Ne-bet* **nalok**.
1SG:REAL-make laplap
'I made laplap.'
(2014_01_19 naanhy01001 00:25:16.000-00:25:17.000 natural text)

A head noun may be a common noun as shown in (4.1) or it may be an independent pronoun as illustrated by (4.2).

4.2 **Khar** *ro-khro* *ev'an*.
3PL 3PL:REAL-stay DIR
'They stayed there.'
(2014_01_19 naanhy01001 00:12:01.000-00:12:03.000 natural text)

A head noun may be modified by another noun. This is illustrated in (4.3) where the head noun *nuak* 'boat' is modified by another common noun *natan* 'land/ground' indicating what type of boat it is.

4.3 *Ale* *ne-les* *te* **nuak** *natan* *Ø-ti-vala...*
CONJ 1SG:REAL-see SUB boat land 3SG:REAL-ASP-run
'Then I saw that the land boat (truck) went...'
(2012_01_19 naanhy01001 00:32:17.000-00:32:20.000 natural text)

Independent pronouns, however, that are head nouns cannot be modified by another noun.

A head noun may also be modified by a bound personal pronoun. This is illustrated in (4.4), which shows the 3SG bound personal pronoun modifying a head noun expressed by a common noun.

4.4 **Takharr   sed-en   khai   Ø-yas.**
    whiteman   PERS.PRON-3SG   3SG   3SG:REAL-go
    'The whiteman went by himself.'
    (Fieldnotes, elicitation)

A pronoun functioning as the head noun may also be modified by a bound personal pronoun, as illustrated in (4.5).

4.5 **Khai sed-en**   buro   khai s-be-num-te   nanalokh.
    3SG PERS.PRON-3SG   GENMOD   3SG IRR-NEG1-drink-NEG2   kava
    'It is only he himself who does not drink kava.'
    (2014_01_19 naanhy01001 00:51:14.000-00:51:18.000 natural text)

A head noun may also be modified by the demonstrative *nge*, as illustrated in (4.6).

4.6 *Na-ma,*   *no-kuk-u*   *rrun*   **norrulnasasakh**   ***nge***.
    1SG:REAL-come-eat   1SG:REAL-cook-   DEM   rice   DEM
                          3SGOBJ
    'I came, I cooked it with that rice.'
    (2014_01_19 naanhy01001 00:01:12.000-00:01:16.000 natural text)

Although the demonstrative *nge* may modify a common noun functioning as the head of a noun phrase, it cannot modify a pronoun functioning as the head of a noun phrase. This contrasts with the demonstrative *khe*, which may modify both common nouns and pronouns (cf. §3.11 examples (3.66) and (3.67)).

Relational classifiers that are used to express indirect possessive relationships may also modify noun heads as shown in (4.7).

4.7 *Ø-se-woj*   **nalok**   **rr-ak**   ***nge***.
    3SG-IRR-eat   laplap   CLED-1SG:POSS   DEM
    'S/he will eat this/that bread of mine.'
    (Fieldnotes, elicitation)

When they co-occur with a demonstrative, they precede the demonstrative. An independent pronoun functioning as a head noun cannot be modified by a relational classifier.

A head noun may be modified by a possessive relational classifier, a numeral and the demonstrative *nge*. This is illustrated in (4.8).

4.8   Ø-se-woj   **nalok**   **rr-ak**   **ru**   **nge.**
     3SG-IRR-eat   laplap   CLED-1SG:POSS   TWO   DEM
     'S/he will eat these two laplap of mine.'
     (Fieldnotes, elicitation)

As shown in (4.8), in addition to possessive relational classifiers and demonstratives functioning as modifiers, numerals may also function as modifiers of noun heads. When numerals occur in conjunction with possessive relational classifiers and demonstratives, they can only occupy the slot in between these two other modifiers, as illustrated in (4.8).

A head noun may be modified by a possessive relational classifier, a numeral, demonstrative and the general modifier *buro* 'only'. Example (4.9) illustrates that when occurring in conjunction with the other modifiers, *buro* occupies phrase final position.

4.9   Ø-se-woj   **nalok**   **r-ak**   **rru**   nge   buro.
     3SG-IRR-eat   laplap   CLED-3SG:POSS   TWO   DEM   GENMOD
     'S/he will eat these two laplap of mine only.'
     (Fieldnotes, elicitation)

Similarly, a head noun may be modified by a quantifier such as *sobonon* 'some', which occupies the slot after the head noun as shown in (4.10).

4.10   Khar   re-ve   'nemere   **sobonon**   rengen   nuak
     3PL   3PL:REAL-say   people   some   LOC   boat
     'They said

     natan   khe.'
     land   DEM
     there are some peopne in that land boat (truck).'
     (2014_01_19 naanhy01001 00:32:34.000-00:32:39.000 natural text)

Relative clauses introduced by the subordinator *te* may also modify a head noun as shown in (4.11).

4.11   Ø-se-woj   **[nebetnakhav [te   ri-bat-e   benanev.]]**
     3SG-IRR-eat   bread   SUB   3PL:REAL-make 3SGOBJ   yesterday
     'S/he will eat the bread that they made yesterday.'
     (Ficldnotes, elicitation)

In (4.11), the relative clause gives information about the date on which the head noun 'bread' was baked. Example (4.12) illustrates the position in which a relative clause may occur in conjunction with an intransitive stative verb and a demonstrative when they function as modifiers of a head noun.

4.12　Ø-*se-woj*　　[*nebetnakhav*　*velvele*　*khe*　[*te*　*ri-bat-e*
　　　3SG-IRR-eat　bread　　　　small　　DEM　SUB　3PL:REAL-make-3SGOBJ
　　　'S/he will eat this/that small bread that they made

　　　benanev.]]
　　　yesterday
　　　yesterday.'
　　　(Fieldnotes, elicitation)

4.13　Ø-*se-woj*　　[*nebetnakhav*　*velvele*　*r-ak*　　　　*rru*　*nge*
　　　3SG-IRR-eat　bread　　　　small　　CLED-1SG:POSS　two　DEM
　　　'S/he will just eat those two small breads of mine

　　　buro　　　*te*　　*ri-bat-e*　　　　　　　　*benanev.*]
　　　GENMOD　SUB　3PL:REAL-make-3SGOBJ　yesterday
　　　which they made yesterday.'
　　　(Fieldnotes, elicitation)

The elicited maximally long noun phrase in (4.13) contains most of the modifiers indicated in Table 4.1. In relation to the ordering of the modifiers, there are certain generalisations that must hold. Firstly, numerals cannot precede possessive relational classifiers. Furthermore, possessive relational classifiers cannot precede intransitive stative verbs. Lastly, there is a strong preference for demonstratives, general modifiers such as *buro* and relative clauses to occupy phrase final position, if occurring in conjunction with the other modifiers.

4.3 Functions of noun phrases

Noun phrases have different intra- and extra-clausal syntactic functions. A noun phrase may function as:

- a subject argument of a verbal clause
- a subject argument of a non-verbal clause

- an object argument of a verbal clause
- a complement of a true preposition or a verbal preposition
- a locative adjunct
- a predicate of a non-verbal clause.

When a noun phrase occurs as a subject argument of a verb clause, it occupies a preverbal position. This is illustrated in (4.14) and (4.15), where a noun and a pronoun respectively may function as the subject of a clause.

4.14 **Tawu** Ø-ti-natur latas.
coneshell 3SG:REAL-ASP-sleep sea-LOC
'The coneshell slept in the sea.'
(2012_05_16 obanhy01004 00:00:07.000-00:00:09.000 natural text)

4.15 **Kanan** bir-khro iekhe buro.
1PLEXCL 1PLEXCL:REAL-stay DEM:LOC GENMOD
'We stayed here only.'
(2014_01_19 naanhy01001 00:00:17.000-00:00:19.000 natural text)

A noun phrase may also be a subject argument of a non-verbal clause, as illustrated in (4.16).

4.16 **Khai** iekhe.
3SG DEM:LOC
'It's here.'
(2012_06_12 obaksi01001 00:07:18.000-00:07:20.000 natural text)

In (4.17), an independent pronoun modified by the demonstrative *khe* is functioning as a subject argument of the non-verbal clause.

4.17 **Khai** khe norojian.
3SG DEM sick
'This one is a sickness.'
(Fieldnotes, elicitation)

A noun phrase may function as an object argument in a verbal clause, as illustrated in (4.18).

4.18   khai   Ø-se-woj   **nebetnakhav**   nge   wor.
      3SG   3SG-IRR-eat   bread   DEM   still
      'She's still going to eat that bread.'
      (2014_01_19 naanhy01001 00:02:25.000-00:02:27.000 natural text)

Object arguments are not merely restricted to full lexical noun phrases as pronouns may also function as object arguments. This is illustrated in (4.19).

4.19   Nakhab'   Ø-ti-sul   **kanan**.
      fire   3SG:REAL-ASP-burn   1PLEXCL
      'The fire burnt us.'
      (2014_02_18 elaksi01002 00:02:39.000-00:02:40.000 natural text)

As noted in §3.4, Nese does not have the 1PL EXCL and 2PL object suffixes, employing their corresponding independent pronouns instead.

A noun phrase may also function as an object of a true preposition, as illustrated in (4.20).

4.20   Kirr-ma   kirr-sev   nua   iekhe   buro
      2PL:REAL-come   2PL:REAL-collect   water   DEM:LOC   GENMOD
      'You (PL) come and collect the water

      rengen   tank.
      LOC   tank
      in the tank here.'
      (2012_03_01 obloro01001 00:00:59.000-00:01:03.000 natural text)

In (4.20), the noun *tank* 'tank' is functioning as the object of the true preposition *rengen* 'in'. True prepositions do not take independent pronouns as objects. Similarly, a noun phrase may function as an object of a verbal preposition, as shown in (4.21).

4.21   J-be-vervis-te   khin   **nelekhterr**   khe.
      1SG:IRR-NEG1-reveal-NEG2   PREP1   woman   dem
      'I did not reveal (it) to that woman.'
      (2014_01_19 naanhy01001 00:09:49.000-00:09:51.000 natural text)

Apart from full noun phrases functioning as object arguments as in (4.21), pronominal suffixes may also function as object arguments of verbal prepositions, as shown in (4.22).

4.22 *Rri-si-jnejne*   *khin-**i***   *khe.*
1PLINCL-IRR-to fish   PREP1-3OBJ   DEM
'We will go fishing in it.'
(2014_01_19 naanhy01001 00:09:49.000-00:28:28.000 natural text)

Lastly, noun phrases with a locational head noun (cf. §3.2.3) may function as adjuncts, as shown in (4.23).

4.23 *Benanev*   *no-khro*   *buro*   ***laine.***
yesterday   1SG:REAL-stay   GENMOD   house:LOC
'Yesterday I just stayed at home.'
(2014_01_19 naanhy01001 00:00:03.000-00:00:05.000 natural text)

Heads of noun phrases composed of locative noun phrases may only occupy a post-verbal adjunct position.

4.4 Words and bound pro-indexes functioning as heads of noun phrases

Nese allows free common nouns, bound common nouns, proper nouns, locational nouns and pronouns to function as heads of noun phrases. In (4.24), a free common noun is functioning as the head of the subject noun phrase.

4.24 ***Nial***   *Ø-ti-terrterr.*
sun   3SG:REAL-ASP-be.strong
'The sun was strong.'
(2012_08_27 00:05:44.000-00:05:45.000 natural text)

Bound common nouns may also function as heads of noun phrases, as shown in (4.25).

4.25 *Ne-yat*   *rengen*   ***nev'enu-ak****.*
1SG:REAL-sit   LOC   place-1SG:POSS
'I sit in my place.'
(2012_05_16 obanhy01001 00:00:14.000-00:00:17.000 natural text)

A proper noun indicating the name of a person may also function as the head of a noun phrase, as shown in (4.26).

4.26 **Yvon** khai Ø-rong-o sikha neten te
Yvonne 3SG 3SG:REAL-want-3SGOBJ NEG PURP2 SUB
'As for Yvonne, she does not want to because

re-ve khai Ø-se-woj nebetnakhav nge wor.
3PL:REAL-say 3SG 3SG-IRR-eat bread DEM just
they said she's going to just eat this bread.'
(2014_01_19 naanhy01001 00:02:23.000-00:02:27.000 natural text)

Similarly, a proper noun indicating the name of a place may function as the head of a noun phrase, as shown in (4.27).

4.27 ...Mista Norman Wiles Ø-ma Ø-lol **Matanvat**.
...Mr Norman Wiles 3SG:REAL-come 3SG:REAL-live Matanvat
'Mr Norman Wiles came and lived in Matanvat.'
(2012_03_01 obloro01001 00:00:25.000-00:00:27.000 natural text)

Kinship nouns may also function as head nouns. This is illustrated in (4.28).

4.28 **Jokh-ok** Ø-se-ma.
uncle-1SG:POSS 3SG-IRR-come
'My uncle is going to come.'
(Fieldnotes, elicitation)

Locational nouns may also be heads of noun phrases; however, this is possible only when they function as clausal adjuncts, as shown in (4.29).

4.29 Tawu Ø-ti-natur **latas**.
cone shell 3SG:REAL-ASP-sleep sea:LOC
'The cone shell slept in the sea.'
(2012_05_16 obanhy01004 00:00:07.000-00:00:08.000 natural text)

Independent pronouns may also function as heads of noun phrases, functioning as subject of a verbal clause (4.30) or as object of verbal clauses in cases where object suffixes are not used (4.31).

4.30 **Khina** ne-likhakh lanus khe.
1SG 1SG:REAL-return bush:LOC DEM
'I have just returned from the bush.'
(2012_05_16 onbanhy01001 00:07:36.000-00:07:38.000 natural text)

4.31 Kho-ba-terev **kanan.**
2SG:REAL-POT-wait 1PLEXCL
'You will await us.'
(2012_05_16 obanhy01003 00:02:34.000-00:02:36.000 natural text)

The example given in (4.31) has the 1PL EXCL independent pronoun as the head of the noun phrase functioning as the object of clause. As highlighted in Table 3.14 (§3.4), while Nese employs independent pronouns functioning as objects in the 1PL EXCL and 2PL forms, it uses bound pro-indexes to express object arguments in other proforms. This raises the question of whether these other bound pro-indexes ought to be considered as heads of noun phrases and, in effect, arguments in a clause, like the 1PL EXCL and 2PL independent forms.

The issue of whether or not a bound pronominal form is an argument has been the subject of some debate. Jelinek (1984, p. 44) postulates that these forms are arguments and asserts that when they co-occur with independent pronouns, the pronoun is an adjunct. In contrast, Bresnan and Mchombo (1987, p. 741) argue that bound forms ought to be viewed as agreement markers. Haspelmath (2013, p. 3) does not see the usefulness of viewing these bound forms as either 'agreement markers' or 'bound pronouns' and suggests that they should rather be analysed as argument indexes.

The discussion in §4.4 demonstrates that free common nouns, bound common nouns, proper nouns and kinship terms may function as heads of noun phrases. In the absence of a lexical noun phrase object, Nese permits the indexing of the bound pronominal on the verb. Given that an object lexical noun phrase cannot co-occur with a pro-index, it may be tempting to view the latter as the object argument in the clause. However, unlike noun heads that can be modified by a range of elements such as intransitive stative verbs, numerals, demonstratives, relative clauses and general modifiers, modification of object pro-indexes is restricted to the demonstrative *khe* as shown in example (4.22), repeated here as (4.32).

4.32 *Rri-si-jnejne*   *khin-**i***   ***khe**.*
      1PL INCL-IRR-to fish   PREP1-3OBJ   DEM
      'We will really go fishing in it.'
      (2014_01_19 naanhy01001 00:28:26.000-00:28:28.000 natural text)

Therefore, they cannot be considered as heads of noun phrases or as genuine arguments, but rather as argument indexes in line with Haspelmath's (2013) definition.

Quantifiers may also function as heads of noun phrases. Out of the three quantifiers in Nese *sobonon* 'some', *jelekh* 'every' and *jelengi* 'all', *sobonon* and *jelengi* are the only ones that can function as heads of noun phrases, along with their nominal modifying function. In (4.33), the quantifier *sobonon* is the head of the noun phrase functioning as the object argument of the clause. Its ability to function also as the head of a noun phrase in subject position was illustrated in Chapter 3, example (3.40), where *sobonon* is the head of a noun phrase functioning as a topicalised subject argument. Therefore, it can function as both subject or object argument in a clause.

4.33 *Ne-kron*   ***sobonon***   *min*   *vingote*   *ji-n*   *Stewart.*
      1SG:REAL-give   some   PREP2   in law   CLGEN-3SG:POSS   Stewart
      'I gave some to my in-law who is Stewart's wife.'
      (2012_05_16 obanhy01003 00:03:16.000-00:03:26.000 natural text)

The quantifier *jelengi* 'all', on the other hand, can only form the head of a noun phrase functioning as an object argument, as shown in (4.34). The element can also function as a nominal modifier, as illustrated in §4.5.

4.34 *No-kuk*   ***jelengi**,*   *Ø-naskhe…*
      1PL SG:REAL-cook   all
      'I cooked all of it, it is cooked…'
      (2014_01_19 naanhy01001 00:01:17.000-00:01:18.000 natural text)

Numerals may also function as heads of noun phrases. As illustrated in (4.35), the numeral *line* 'five' is functioning as the head of a noun phrase in a non-verbal equational clause. The numeral *sakhal* 'one' forms the head of the noun phrase, which is functioning as a subject argument of the second verbal clause.

4.35 *Kanan   line,   sakhal   Ø-nas.*
      1PLEXCL   five   one   3SG:REAL-die
      'There's five of us, one died.'
      (2012_05_22 obcero01001 00:00:11.000-00:00:14.000 natural text)

Nominalised verbs may also be heads of noun phrases. Example (4.36) shows a nominalised verb functioning as the head of a noun phrase that is in topic position.

4.36 *Letang!*   **vis-vis-ian**   *khai*   *Ø-ti-rov.*
      Sister!   REDUP-squeeze milk-NOM   3SG   3SG:REAL-ASP-finish
      'Sister! The squeezing of the milk is over.'
      (2012_06_12 obaksi01001 00:10:36.000-00:10:38.000 natural text)

The corresponding verb stem of the nominalised verb in (4.36) is *vis-* 'squeeze milk' and the whole verb stem is reduplicated. Another illustration of a nominalised verb is given in (4.37) where *novojokhian* 'gathering/feast' is the head of the noun phrase functioning as the complement in a prepositional phrase, which is a locative adjunct. The nominalised verb is derived from the verb *vojokh* 'to get/gather together'. In contrast with example (4.36), the verb stem in example (4.37) is not reduplicated.

4.37 *Nekrre   rri-si-v'an   rengen   **no-vojokh-ian.***
      1PLINCL   1PL-IRR-go   LOC   ART-gather-NOM
      'We will go to the gathering.'
      (Fieldnotes, elicitation)

Further discussion of the nominalisation process is in §4.7.

4.5 Modification of the head

Heads of noun phrases may be modified by nouns (§4.5.1), bound personal pronouns (§4.5.2), intransitive stative verbs (§4.5.3), numbers (§4.5.4), quantifiers (§4.5.5), numerals (§4.5.6), demonstratives (§4.5.7), possessive constructions (§4.5.8), relative clauses (§4.5.9) and general modifiers (§4.5.10). As observed in §3.16, some elements may function both as heads of noun phrases and as nominal modifiers. The expression of number in a noun phrase is discussed in (§4.5.4).

4.5.1 Nominal modifiers

Nominal modifiers in Nese are common nouns, proper nouns, locational nouns and nominalised verbs, generally occupying the slot after the noun they are modifying. When a proper noun modifies a common noun as in (4.38), the modifying proper noun indicates the place from which the common head noun originates.

4.38   *Ne-les*   **tev'et**   **Neneluam.**
       1SG:REAL-see   woman   Neneluam
       'I saw a woman from Neneluam.'
       (Fieldnotes, elicitation)

A similar effect is seen when a common noun is modified by locational noun, as shown in (4.39).

4.39   *Nekrre*   *kele*   *rri-v'an*   *rru-num,*   *netenge,*   *naleb',*
       1PLINCL   again   1PL:REAL-go   1PL:REAL-drink   thingummy   pool
       'Again we went and drank, that thingummy, pool,

    nua   **lanus**   *khe.*
    water   bush:LOC   DEM
    the water from the bush.'
    (Fieldnotes, natural text)

A common noun may be modified by another common noun, as shown in (4.40). In this example, the modifying common noun indicates the specific type of the preceding common noun.

4.40   *Ne-jil-e*   *Ø-v'an*   *rengen*   **nokhobrok**   **norrian.**
       1SG:REAL-serve-3SGOBJ   3SG:REAL-go   LOC   plate   food
       'I served it on the food plate.'
       (2012_05_16 obanhy01001 00:01:17.000-00:01:11.500 natural text)

As is the case with the preceding examples, when a common noun is modified by a nominalised verb, the latter occurs in the slot after the common noun. This is illustrated in (4.41), where the modifying nominalised verb *nenesian* 'death' modifies the common noun *tenge* 'thing'. In this case, the nominalised verb denotes a state.

4.41 *Tenge   kher   khe,   **tenge   nenesian**   jelekh.*
     Thing   PL   DEM   thing   death   all
     'These things, they are all deadly things.'
     (2014_01_19 naanhy01001 01:07:36.000-01:07:39.000 natural text)

A modifying nominalised verb can also give further information about the age of the referent. This is illustrated in (4.42) where the nominalised verb *nemerjian* 'old' indicates the maturity of the noun *tav'at* 'woman'.

4.42 ***Tav'at   nemerjian***   *sakhal   khar   rrun   nokhod-ne*
     Woman   old   one   3PL   CONJ   grandchild-3SG:POSS
     'An old woman with her grandchild

   ro-khro.
   3PL:REAL-stay
   stayed.'
   (2012_05_16 obanhy01005 00:00:22.000-00:00:26.000 natural text)

4.5.2 Bound personal pronouns

Nouns may be modified by bound personal pronouns, which are formed with the directly possessed roots *sed-* and *ned-*, both having the meaning 'by oneself'. These two different stems showing homogenous inflectional paradigms of bound personal pronouns are presented in Table 4.2. In both columns, the bound personal pronoun root indicates a personal relationship while the bound suffix expresses the person and number of the co-referential head noun. Generally, bound personal forms occur in the slot after the nouns they are modifying. Noun heads that may be modified by bound personal pronouns are restricted to proper nouns, common nouns and pronouns.

Table 4.2: Bound personal pronouns

	sed-	*ned-*
1SG	sed-okh	ned-okh
2SG	sod-om	ned-om
3SG	sed-en	ned-en
1PL INCL	sed-err	ned-err
1PL EXCL	sed-enan	ned-enan
2PL	sed-ani	ned-ani
3PL	sed-err	ned-err

The two bound personal pronoun paradigms exhibit the following similarities. To begin with, they both have identical suffixes for each of the different persons and numbers that are affixed to the two different personal roots *sed-* and *ned-*. Similarly, both have a somewhat uniform phonological shape for the personal roots for all persons and numbers, with the exception of the 1SG and 2SG forms, which differ from the other persons and numbers in each paradigm.

More specifically, the *sed-* based personal pronoun form for the 2SG person differs from the other persons and numbers in that paradigm. These suffixes are somewhat akin to those employed in direct and indirect possession in Table 3.15 (§3.4). The current data suggests that both the bound personal pronouns may be used interchangeably and there are no criteria that exclude employing one from the other. This is illustrated in (4.43) and (4.44), where the 3SG bound personal forms from the two sets may be used interchangeably with no difference in meaning.

4.43   *Khunokh*   **sod-om**   *kho-se-v'an?*
       2SG   PERS.PRON-2SG   2SG-IRR-go?
       'You're going to go by yourself?'
       (Fieldnotes, elicitation)

4.44   *Khunokh*   **ned-om**   *kho-se-v'an?*
       2SG   PERS.PRON-2SG   2SG-IRR-go?
       'You're going to go by yourself?'
       (Fieldnotes, elicitation)

However, further data may prove that perhaps there was once a distinction in usage between the two paradigms that may be based on the types of verbs used. The current data also shows some disparity as the examples obtained contain bound personal pronouns that modify heads of noun phrases in preverbal position. Therefore, it is not clear whether bound personal pronouns can also modify heads of noun phrases that occur post-verbally as object arguments or whether the use of corresponding independent pronouns is sufficient.

Bound personal pronouns may modify heads of noun phrases composed of a single common noun. This is illustrated in (4.45).

4.45 | *Takharr* | ***sed**-en* | | *Ø-yas.* |
| whiteman | PERS.PRON-3SG | | 3SG:REAL-depart |

'The white man went by himself.'
(Fieldnotes, elicitation)

Similarly, a bound personal pronoun may modify coordinated pronouns functioning as preverbal subject arguments. This is illustrated in (4.46) where the bound personal pronoun root *sed-* indicates a relationship in which the co-referential noun phrase is composed of two coordinated proper nouns in preverbal position. The suffix that is affixed to the bound personal pronoun base co-references both proper noun phrases in (4.46).

4.46 | *Lana* | *rrun* | *Aklyn* | ***sed**-err* | *risi-yas.* |
| Lana | CONJ | Aklyn | PERS.PRON-3PL | 3PL:IRR-depart |

'Lana and Aklyn will go by themselves.'
(Fieldnotes, elicitation)

A bound personal pronoun may also modify a pronoun functioning as a subject argument in preverbal position. This is illustrated in (4.47).

4.47 | *Kani* | ***sed**-ani* | *kirr-se-v'an?* |
| 2PL | PERS.PRON-2PL | 2PL-IRR-go |

'Will you people go by yourselves.'
(Fieldnotes, elicitation)

4.5.3 Intransitive stative verb modifiers

Intransitive stative verbs may function as attributive modifiers of the head noun. When an intransitive stative verb is the head of a predicate, it takes the subject cross-index, as in (4.48); however, when it occurs as a modifier of a head NP, it does not take the subject cross-index (4.49).

4.48 | *Rru* | ***Ø-se-velvele.*** |
| two | 3SG-IRR-be.small |

'Two will be small.'
(2012_81_27 obnesp01001 00:06:42.000-00:06:10.000 natural text)

4.49 **Nuak**　　**velvele**　　khe,　　rri-si-takh-e
　　　boat　　　small　　　DEM　　1PLINCL-IRR-take-3SGOBJ
　　　'That small boat, we're going to take it

　　　rri-si-yas　　khin-i.
　　　1PLINCL-IRR-depart　　PREP1-3SGOBJ
　　　and use it to depart.'
　　　(2014_01_19 naanhy01001 00:18:31.000-00:18:34.000 natural text)

Intransitive stative verbs with an attributive function may modify common nouns and kinship nouns functioning as heads of noun phrases. Example (4.50) illustrates the intransitive stative verb *velvele* 'small' modifying the head of the noun phrase composed of a common noun.

4.50 *Nause*　　khai　　Ø-se-use　　lemje　　neten　　**naror**
　　　rain　　　3SG　　3SG-IRR-to.rain　　a.lot　　PURP2　　dark cloud
　　　'It will rain because of the

　　　velvele　　sakhal.
　　　small　　　　one
　　　one small cloud.'
　　　(2012_05_16 obanhy01003 00:03:34.000-00:03:38.000 natural text)

When the intransitive stative verb *velvele* modifies a 3SG nominal subject, it may be difficult to distinguish whether the intransitive stative verb is the head of a predicate (given that the 3SG realis subject cross-index is not overt) or whether it is functioning as a modifier. However, this may be resolved by testing whether a numeral modifier can occur after the stative intransitive verb. If the construction allows a numeral to occur after an intransitive stative verb, such as in (4.50), the intransitive stative verb is functioning attributively.

When the intransitive stative verb *sat* 'bad' modifies a common noun functioning as the head of a noun phrase, it is adding further information about the head noun in terms of its quality, as illustrated in (4.51).

4.51 Khina **nemerre** sat.
      1SG   man   bad.
      'I am a bad person.'
      (2014_04_26 obmach01001 00:00:50.000-00:00:54.000 natural text)

An intransitive stative verb such as *os* 'different' may also be used to provide contrast, as illustrated in (4.52).

4.52 Ale   **neren** **os**   Ø-ma,   ale   bir-v'an
      CONJ   time   different   3SG:REAL-come CONJ   1PLEXCL:REAL-go
      'Then at a different time, we go

      bir-wak-e.
      1PL:REAL-plant-3SGOBJ
      and plant.'
      (2012_06_19 obfaha01003 00:04:26.000-00:04:29.000 natural text)

Example (4.53) shows that an intransitive stative verb may also modify kinship nouns functioning as the head noun of a noun phrase in an attributive manner.

4.53 Dev'e   **lab'lab**   Ø-ti-v'an   maro.
      mother   big   3SG:REAL-ASP-go   up
      'The big (older) aunty went up.'
      (Fieldnotes, elicitation)

4.5.4 Number

Nese does not productively encode number on the head noun through morphological means. There are only two nouns that show some kind of morphological plural marking. The first is the noun *jiblakh* 'child', which takes the prefix *te-* to form the plural *tejiblakh* 'children'. The second is the noun *nemerte* 'man' where the /t/ in the final syllable is deleted to form the plural *nemere* 'men'. Otherwise, for other common nouns the most common way in which Nese expresses plurality is through the use of the plural marker *kher* (cf. §2.5.2.4), which occurs after the noun in the noun phrase. This is illustrated in (4.54). There are no examples in the data showing *kher* occurring relative to the other modifiers except in between a common noun and the demonstrative *khe*.

4.54 No-rong-o   sikha   min   norrian   **kher**
     1SG:REAL-like-3SGOBJ   NEG   PREP2   food   PL
     'I am sick of these

     khe.
     DEM
     foods.'
     (2014_01_19 naanhy01001 00:00:32.000-00:00:34.000 natural text)

As will be seen in §4.6, Nese employs independent pronouns for emphatic purposes and this is illustrated in example (4.112) in §4.6 where *khar* is employed for this purpose. This suggests that *kher* in (4.54) may also be used to emphasise the lexical noun phrase *norrian* in addition to indicating its plurality.

In the absence of the plural morpheme *kher* and where number is not marked in the NP, the determination of whether a lexical noun phrase subject is plural or not is based on the subject cross-index on the verb. For example, the subject noun *nani* 'coconuts' (4.55) is clearly singular given that the cross-index on the verb is 3SG singular. However, with lexical noun phrase objects, where number is not encoded within the object noun phrase, the object noun phrase may be interpreted as either singular or plural, as shown in (4.56) and (4.57).

4.55 **Nani**   s-ak   Ø-se-ninin.
     Coconut   CLGEN-1SG:POSS   3SG-IRR-be.wet
     'My coconut will be wet.'
     (2014_01_19 obanhy01003 00:00:58.000-00:01:01.000 natural text)

4.56 Ne-tekh   **nani**.
     1SG:REAL-take   coconut
     'I took the coconut/coconuts.'
     (Fieldnotes, elicitation)

4.57 Khai   Ø-les   **nanankho.**
     3SG   3SG:real-see   bird
     'She saw the bird/birds.'
     (Fieldnotes, elicitation)

Plurality and singularity are encoded by the subject cross-indexes and object pro-indexes. For example, when the subject cross-index encodes a plural number as shown in (4.58), the preceding co-referential lexical noun phrase is treated as a plural noun phrase. However, when there is no overt subject cross-index, a case that is applicable only to the non-overt 3SG subject cross-index that the preceding lexical noun phrase to which it is co-referential is treated as a singular noun phrase. This is illustrated in (4.59).

4.58 *Nobukhas* **ri**-*v'an*.
pig 3PL:REAL-go
'The pigs went.'
(Fieldnotes, elicitation)

4.59 *Nobukhas* **Ø**-*v'an* *laute*.
pig 3SG:REAL-go garden:LOC
'The pig went to the garden.'
(Fieldnotes, elicitation)

4.5.5 Quantifiers

The quantifiers *sobonon* 'some', *jelekh* 'every' and *jelengi* 'all' may modify heads of noun phrases. In (4.60), the quantifier *sobonon* occurs after the head noun *nakha* 'wood' and the intransitive stative verb modifier *velvele* 'small'.

4.60 *Je-tei* **nakha** *velvele* **sobonon,** *je-vita-i*
1SG:IRR-cut wood small some 1SG:IRR-put-3SGOBJ
'I will cut some small pieces of wood and I will put it

rengen *nem-ak*.
LOC house-1SG:POSS
in my house.'
(2012_08_27 obnesp01001 00:01:08:000-00:01:13.000 natural text)

The quantifier *jelekh* 'every' may modify heads of noun phrases that are common nouns. It may modify a singular common noun, as shown in (4.61), and it may also modify a plural head noun, as shown in (4.62).

4.61 Ne-ver   **tenge**   **jelekh**   di.
      1SG:REAL-say   thing   every   already
      'I have said everything.'
      (2012_07_12 obaksi01001 00:25:42.000-00:25:49.000 natural text)

4.62 Nuak   khe, **nemere** **jelekh**   re-ve   'nuak
      boat   DEM   people   every   3PL:REAL-say   boat
      'That boat, all the people say that "that boat

      sakhal   khe,   khai   Ø-vala   belek   plen.
      one   DEM   3SG   3SG:REAL-RUN   like   plane
      it runs like the plane".'
      (2014_01_19 naanhy01001 01:06:24.000-01:06:30.000 natural text)

Nese exhibits an interesting situation where the quantifier *jelekh* may combine with the quantifier *rov* 'to finish, end' to modify the 1PL inclusive, 3PL pronouns and plural common nouns. Example (4.63) shows *rov jelekh* modifying the 1PL inclusive pronoun in which case the 1PL inclusive pronoun is emphasised as 'every single one of us' while this emphasis is not present when *rov* is not present, as shown in (4.64).

4.63 Khai   Ø-be-ve   nale   ba-tokh,   **nekrre**   rrov¹
      3SG   3SG:REAL-POT-say   language   POT-exist   1PLINCL   fully
      'She said that the language will stay, every single

      jelekh   rri-be-rej-rej   min-i.
      every   1PLINCL:REAL-POT-REDUP-speak   PREP-3SGOBJ
      one of us will speak it.'
      (2014_01_19 naanhy01001 00:07:16.000-00:07:20.000 natural text)

---

1   It is only in these cases that *rov* serves as a modifier of a head noun; elsewhere, it functions as an intransitive verb and a completive marker modifying the head of a VP (cf. §5.5.8).

4.64 Seve   kho-tuturr   min   tenge jelekh, kho-tei
      COND   2SG:REAL-to.prepare   PREP2   thing every   2SG:REAL-cut
      'If you prepare everything, you cut

      norroyat   **nekrre**   **jelekh**   rri-ma   rri-yat
      pandanus leaves 1PLEXCL   every   1PLEXCL:REAL-come   1PLEXCL:REAL-sit
      the palm leaves all of us come and sit

      rri-si-tentan-i.
      1PLEXCL-IRR-remove veins-3SGOBJ
      and we'll remove its veins.'
      (2012_07_12 obaksi01001 00:12:20.000-00:12:27.000 natural text)

Lastly, the quantifier *jelengi* 'all' may modify heads of noun phrases that are expressed by means of lexical noun phrases as well as object pro-indexes. This is illustrated in (4.65) and (4.66) respectively.

4.65 Mary   khai   Ø-woj   jelengi   kumala   ale   Ø-tun   novusbuak
      Mary   all   laplap   all   kumala   CONJ   3SG:REAL-roast   taro
      'Mary ate all the kumala (sweet potato) and roasted the taro.'
      (2012_08_08 elanhy01005 00:01:08.000-00:01:12.000 elicitation)

4.66 Kanan   bir-khro   iekhe   laine   v'an   v'an
      1PLEXCL   1PLEXCL:REAL-stay   DEM   LOC:HOUSE   go   go
      'We just stayed here at home for a while

      ale   ne-bet   nebetnakhav   sakhal,   no-kuk-**u**   **jelengi**.
      CONJ   1SG:REAL-make   bread   one   1SG:REAL-cook-3SGOBJ all
      then I made a bread and cooked it all.'
      (2014_01_19 naanhy01001 00:00:23.000-00:00:25.000 natural text)

Jelengi differs from *jelekh* in that it may precede the noun it is modifying, as shown in (4.65). In example (4.65), *jelengi* is functioning as the head of a noun phrase forming a compound noun with *nalok*. In (4.66), *jelengi* is modifying a singular object pro-index but the head noun being modified does not undergo any increase in numerical value. In this example, *jelengi* is used to mean all the different parts of that single bread were thoroughly cooked.

4.5.6 Numerals

Numerals may modify common nouns (4.67) and independent pronouns (4.68). Modification in both cases simply involves adding a numerical value to the common noun and independent pronoun.

4.67 *Ne-sob   na   te-jiblakh,   **namalakel   sangav'il.***
       1SG:REAL-relate story   HESIT   PL-child   young men   ten
       'I will tell a story about children, about ten young men.'
       (2012_05_16 obanhy01005 00:00:04.000-00:00:09.000 natural text)

4.68 *Kanan   **til**   bir-se-v'an   rengen   plantesen   nani*
       1PLEXCL   three   1PLEXCL-IRR-go   LOC   plantation   coconut
       'The three of us will go to the coconut plantation.'
       (2012_06_22 elrojo01003 00:02:50.000-00:02:57.000 elicitation)

4.5.7 Demonstratives

As stated in §3.11, Nese has four demonstratives – *khe, nge, iekhe* and *iekhetan* – all of which occupy a post-nominal position. *Khe* and *nge* are nominal demonstratives, whereas *iekhe* and *iekhetan* are locative adverbial demonstratives. The latter two, however, are both based on the root *khe*. Of these four demonstratives, *khe* is the most commonly used demonstrative and also has spatial reference.

The demonstrative *khe* modifies nominal heads that are common nouns, proper nouns, independent pronouns or the interrogative *nese*, which itself is a member of the class of nouns. Example (4.69) shows *khe* modifying a nominal head, which is a common noun, having anaphoric reference, in that it refers to a bread that has already been mentioned in previous clauses.

4.69 *Ne-ve   iyo   khai   Ø-nakis   kirr-se-woj*
       1SG:REAL-say   yes   3SG   3SG:REAL-be.good   2PL:IRR-eat
       'I said, "okay, that's fine, you people will eat

       nebetnakhav   khe   *buro.
       bread   DEM   GENMOD
       this bread only".'
       (2014_01_19 naanhy01001 00:00:37.000-00:00:41.000 natural text)

Example (4.70) shows modification of a proper noun by *khe* in which the demonstrative has an emphatic function, bringing into focus the head noun it is modifying.

4.70 Ale **Gregory khe,** khai re-ve natas
CONJ Gregory DEM 3SG 3PL:REAL-say sea
'And that Gregory, he said that the sea

s-be-tamat-te kanan bir-si-yas khe.
IRR-NEG1-peace-NEG2 1PLEXCL 1PLEXCL-IRR-depart DEM
is not calm, we are leaving.'
(2014_01_19 naanhy01001 00:18:14.000-00:18:20.000 natural text)

Pronouns functioning as heads of noun phrases may be modified by the demonstrative *khe* as illustrated in (4.71).

4.71 Kava, ri-vitei maro. **Khai khe,** khina
Iron sheet 3PL:REAL-put up 3SG DEM 1SG
'The iron sheets, they put it up. That one, I've

ne-vitei norojal buro.
1SG:REAL-put coconut leaves GENMOD
just put coconut leaves.'
(2014_01_19 naanhy01001 00:47:31.000-00:47:37.000 natural text)

In a similar manner as in (4.70), demonstrative *khe* also has an emphatic function in (4.71), bringing into focus the 3SG pronoun it is modifying.

The interrogative *nese* 'what', which is a member of the class of nouns, may occupy subject position in a non-verbal clause in conjunction with the demonstrative *khe* occurring in the predicate slot as shown in (4.72).

4.72 Nese **khe?**
What DEM
'What is this?'
(2012_08_27 nsesp01002 00:03:39.000-00:03:44.000 natural text)

The demonstrative also has the meaning 'here' and 'there' when it is used to make spatial reference. This is illustrated in (4.73), where the speaker is referring to two different adjacent locations using *khe*.

4.73 Khai   Ø-ti-tokh   **khe**,   sobonon   Ø-ti-tokh   **khe**.
      3SG   3SG:REAL-ASP-stay DEM   some   3SG:REAL-ASP-stay DEM
      'It stayed here, some stayed there.'
      (2012_07_12 obaksi01001 00:06:12:000-00:06:27.000 natural text)

In (4.73), both instances of *khe* are functioning as locative adverbial demonstratives akin to *iekhe* and *iekhetan*, a fact that further gives weight to the assumption that the latter two locative adverbial demonstratives are derived from *khe*.

The demonstrative *nge*, on the other hand, can only modify heads of noun phrases that are common nouns. This is illustrated in (4.74).

4.74 Ale   ro-kol   **nua**   **nge**,   nua   nokhobu   nge
      CONJ 3PL:REAL-carry water   DEM   water   bamboo   DEM
      'Then they carried that water, that water in the bamboo

      ro-mul   v'an.
      3PL:REAL-return home   DIR
      and they returned home.'
      (2012_01_18 obrolo01001 00:02:15.000-00:02:19.000 natural text)

In (4.74), the noun head being modified *nua* 'water' was already mentioned previously in the discourse and demonstrative *nge* is used to refer to that water, therefore, *nge* is used for anaphoric reference.

It may also be used for emphasis as shown in (4.75), where the temporal common noun *bensev* 'five days ago' is in a clause initial topic position with *nge* occupying the following slot and functioning as a modifier, adding more emphasis to the temporal noun.

4.75 **Bensev**   **nge**   khar   re-v'an.
      Five days ago   DEM   3PL   3PL:REAL-go
      'Five days ago they went.'
      (2014_01_19 naanhy01001 00:30:17.000-00:30:18.000 natural text)

Demonstrative *nge* differs from *khe* in that *khe* can modify NP heads that are common nouns, proper nouns and independent pronouns, while *nge* can only modify heads of noun phrases that are common nouns. Furthermore, *khe* also has a locative function; a function that is not performed by *nge*. Thus *nge* cannot be used to express a position proximal or distal to the speaker.

As mentioned in §3.11, *iekhe* and *iekhetan* are locative adverbial demonstratives in that they express spatial distance. *Iekhetan* is derived from *iekhe* and the preposition *atan* 'down'. *Iekhe* indicates a location that is near to or visible to the speaker, while *iekhetan* expresses a location that is simultaneously within the speaker's proximity and is at a downward direction. These two demonstratives may be accompanied by gestures.

Iekhe may modify a common noun functioning as the head noun. This is illustrated in (4.76). When the local adverbial demonstrative *iekhe* modifies a noun head, it specifies the location of the head noun. The same applies to *iekhetan*, as shown in (4.77), in which there is the added meaning of a downward direction.

4.76 Navara-k **iekhe**, khai Ø-khuskhus belek khe.
Hand-1SG:POSS DEM:LOC 3SG 3SG:REAL-move like DEM
'My hand, here, it moves like this.'
(2014_01_19 naanhy01001 00:39:09.000-00:39:12.000 natural text)

In (4.76), *iekhe* is not only modifying a common noun that is the head noun, but the common noun is also a directly possessed noun. The locative adverbial demonstrative *iekhetan* 'down here' may modify heads of noun phrases that are common nouns and pronouns. These are shown in (4.77) and (4.78) respectively.

4.77 Kavra, **nemere iekhetan** rri-kot kavra.
Copra people DEM 3PL:REAL-make copra
'As for copra, people down here they make copra.'
(2014_02_18 naaksi01001 00:10:45.000-00:10:47.000 natural text)

4.78 *Sobonon,   khar   ri-bet   nalok   vorrvorr   khe*
      some   3PL   3PL:REAL-make   laplap   sosor   DEM
      'Some people, when making the sosor laplap,

   ri-vnas-i   buro,   netenge,   norob'e   deve
   3PL:REAL-leave open-3SGOBJ   GENMOD   thingummy   bay leaves CONJ
   they just leave it open, um, that thing, the bay leaves or the cabbage

   *nokhmok   ale   nedikh   norrian   Ø-v'an,   be   **nekrre***
   cabbage   CONJ   meat   food   3SG:REAL-go   CONJ   1PLINCL
   then in goes the meat, but as for us

   ***iekhetan**   ri-si-viteikhor-o.*
   DEM   3PL-IRR-block-3SGOBJ
   down here, we will have it blocked.'
   (Fieldnotes, natural text)

4.5.8 Possessive constructions

The expression of possession in Nese is a complex issue. Nese exhibits both direct and indirect patterns of possession, patterns that are characteristic of Oceanic languages (Lichtenberk, 1985). Direct possession is marked by a possessor suffixed directly on the possessum head noun, whereas indirect possession is exhibited via relational classifiers postposed after the possessum head noun. The category of indirectly possessed nouns is further divided into three different types of possessive relationships. Nese makes a distinction between possession of items for drinking, those for eating, and possession of other non-edible and non-drinkable items. In addition to these relational classifiers, Nese employs the associative *nan* to express a possessive relationship in which the possessor is generic or non-specific.

4.5.8.1 Directly possessed nouns

The formal division between direct and indirect possession roughly corresponds to the semantic distinction between alienable and inalienable possession. Generally, nouns that are inalienably possessed in Nese are body parts, kinship terms and nouns, denoting locations that are central to the traditional way of life, such as house and garden. Table 4.3 gives a list of some inalienable nouns.

4. THE NOUN PHRASE

Table 4.3: Inalienably possessed nouns

Body parts			
lal-	'heart'	*nabat-*	'head'
navar-	'hand'	*nakhab'-*	'wing'
nam'at-	'eye'	*nakh-*	'face'
nokus-	'nose'	*nalaso-*	'testicles'
nojung-	'mouth'	*nanak-*	'thigh'
naba-	'knee'	*nejin-*	'bone'
Kin terms			
natas-	youngest	*tavai-*	'friend, brother'
nosokos-	female sibling	*tua-*	'older same-sex sibling'
nanat-	'child'	*takh-*	'brother-in-law'
nokhod-	'grandchild'	*tas-*	'younger same-sex sibling'
nau-	'spouse'		
Locations			
nev'enu-	'place'	*nul-*	'hole'
nem-	'house'		
neut-	'garden'		
lakhnal-	'nakamal'		
ton-	'ground'		
Products of humans and animals			
ral-	'voice'	*nanngas*	'urine'
navarvar-	'promise'	*nele-*	'language'
naj-	'excrement'	*nere-*	'blood'
lulu-	'vomit'	*nesuv-*	'breath'

In discussing direct possession, Crowley (2006c) makes a distinction between distant alienable possession and close inalienable possession, with the former marked by one possessive suffix paradigm and the latter involving two different paradigms, each with unpredictable irregularities. Takau (2016), on the other hand, does not make this distinction and only gives one paradigm of possessive suffixes for directly possessed nouns. However, re-examination of the data shows that there appear to be three paradigms of possessive suffixes relating to direct possession, as mentioned in §3.4. These three paradigms are outlined in Table 4.4, where some suffixes related to certain pronominal categories are missing.

Table 4.4: Possessive suffixes in direct possession

Person/number	Direct possession		
	Type 1 (*-aC*)	Type 2 (*-oC*)	Type 3 (*-uC*)
1SG	*-ak*	*-ok*	*-uk*
2SG	*-am*	*-om*	*-me*
3SG	*-an*	*-on*	*-ne*
1PL INCL	*-arr*		
1PL EXCL			*-inan*
1PL TRIAL	*-arr nekrre til*		
2PL INCL	*-am'i/ani*		
2PL EXCL	*-am'iru/-eniru*		
2PL TRIAL	*-am kani til*		
3PL	*-ar*		*-rre*

I have chosen to use the labels *-aC*, *-oC* and *-uC*, for want of better terms, since they correspond to the forms for the 1SG, 2SG and 3SG forms for the different possessive paradigms. Table 4.5 shows examples of these possessive forms with the full paradigm given just for Type 1 (*-aC*) suffixes, while data for some pronominal categories in the Type 2 (*-oC*) and Type 3 (*-uC*) suffixes are missing.

Table 4.5: Examples of direct possession

	Type 1 (*-aC*) possession	Type 2 (*-oC*)	Type 3 (*-uC*)
1SG	*nanat-ak* 'my eye'	*ral-ok* 'my voice'	*nokhod-uk* 'my grandchild'
2SG	*nanat-am* 'your eye'	*ral-om* 'your voice'	*nokhod-me* 'your grandchild'
3SG	*nanat-an* 'his/her eye'	*ral-on* 'his/her voice'	*nokhod-ne* 'his/her grandchild'
1PL INCL	*nanat-ar* 'our eyes'		*nokhod-inan* 'our grandchild'
1PL EXCL	*nanat-anan* 'our eyes'		
1PL TRIAL (INCL)	*nanat-arr nekrre til* 'our (trial) eyes'		
2PL INCL	*nanat-am'i/ nenet-eni* 'your eyes'		
2PL EXCL	*nanat-am'iru / nenet-eniru* 'your (dual) eyes'		
2PL TRIAL (EXCL)	*nanat-am kani til* 'your (trial) eyes'		
3PL	*nenet-arr* 'their eyes'		

As mentioned in §3.2.1, nouns in the Type 2 subgroup emerge in two forms synchronically. There are those I label as 'free roots' in their unpossessed forms and those that are considered as bound roots in their unpossessed forms. It is not clear whether nouns based on Type 2 and Type 3 direct possessive relationships also exhibit this property. There are no clear defining criteria for membership in one possessive type given that some nouns that cannot be physically removed from a person, such as body parts like *nanat-* 'eye', may accept the *-aC* suffix while *nabalak-* 'leg' enters into the *-oC* possessive type. Kinship terms such as *jokh-* 'uncle' accepts the *-oC* suffix type while *mer-* 'mother' takes the *-ak* suffix type and *nokhod-* 'grandchild' accepts the *-uk* suffix type. Nouns that are physically disconnected from a person's body, such as *natan* 'land', take the *-oC* possessive suffix, while *naute* 'garden' takes the *-aC* possessive suffix type. Given these idiosyncrasies and limited data, it is difficult to ascertain the grounds for membership within one suffix type.

Evidently, the structure of direct possessive relationships is based on possessum + possessor order whereby the possessor is affixed onto the possessum noun. The referent of the possessor suffix is already established previously in the discourse or is retrievable from context due to its high saliency. This is shown in example (4.79) where the possessed common noun, which is a body part, has the possessor indicated by the 1SG possessive suffix *-ak,* whose referent has already been established previously in the discourse.

4.79　***Nam'at-ak***　　*Ø-ti-nial.*
　　　eye-1SG:POSS　　3SG:REAL-ASP-red
　　　'My eye was red.'
　　　(Fieldnotes, elicitation)

A locative common noun may also be directly possessed, as shown in (4.80). Here, the possessor is expressed via the proper noun *Bernar,* occupying the slot directly after the possessed locational noun *lemen.* As shown in §2.5.2.3.3, the /a/ vowel in the second syllable of a directly possessed noun in the third person is raised to /e/ when the possessor is expressed as a lexical noun phrase object. In this respect, example (4.80) contrasts with (4.81) where the possessor is expressed via the 3SG possessive suffix *-n* whose referent is co-referential with that of the 3SG pronoun *khai* functioning as the subject of the clause. In example (4.80), the 3SG possessive suffix is co-referential with the proper noun *Bernar.*

4.80 *Rri-ma,*   *ma*   *Senbokhas*   *khe,*   *nasal*   *Ø-van*
3PL:REAL-come   DIR   Senbokhas   DEM   road   3SG:REAL-go
'We come till we reach Senbokhas, a road

maro,   *v'an*   **lem-en**   **Bernar**.
up   DIR   house:LOC-3SGPOSS   Bernar.
goes up, it goes to Bernard's house.'
(2012_08_22 anhy01005 00:00:24.000-00:00:30.000 natural text)

4.81 **Khai**   *Ø-khro*   *buro*   **lem-an**.
3SG   3SG:REAL-stay   GENMOD   LOC:house-3SG:POSS
'He just stayed at his house.'
(2014_01_19 naanhy01001 00:12:52.000-00:12:56.000 natural text)

A bound possessive suffix may also be directly attached to a head noun, which may be a kinship term. This is illustrated in (4.82) where the referent of the possessor, expressed via the 1SG possessive suffix, is co-referential with that of the 1SG independent pronoun *khina*.

4.82 *Khina*   **na-uk**   *Ø-ti-nas*   *di.*
1SG   husband-1SG:POSS   3SG:REAL-ASP-die   already
'As for me, my husband has died already.'
(2012_05_16 obanhy01005 00:05:30.000-00:05:32.000 natural text)

Possessive suffixes are also attached to head nouns that refer to things produced by a human. This is illustrated in (4.83), where the noun *nale* 'language' is directly possessed. The possessor, indicated by the 3PL possessive suffix, is co-referential with the referent of the 1PL independent pronoun, which is functioning as the subject of the clause.

4.83 | *Rri-ba-rej-rej* | *khin* | *nale* | *renran* | *ma*
3PL:REAL-POT-REDUP-speak | PREP1 | language | always | DIR

'We should speak the language always up till now,

khai *ba-nakis,* *be* *nekrre* *rri-s-be-rej-te*
3SG POT-good CONJ 1PLINCL 1PLINCL-IRR-NEG1-NEG2

that would be better, but as for us, we do not speak

nelie-rr.
language-1PL:POSS
our language.'
(Fieldnotes, natural text)

4.5.8.2 Indirectly possessed nouns

As stated at the beginning of this subsection, indirect possessive relationships are expressed by means of relational classifiers that occur post-nominally. Contrasting with direct possessive relationships where possessive suffixes are attached to the head noun, indirect possession has the possessive suffixes attaching to the relational classifiers. Indirect possessive relationships are, therefore, expressed by way of POSSESSUM + RELATIONAL CLASSIFIER + POSSESSOR. These relational classifiers indicate whether the noun being possessed is edible, drinkable or none of the two, while the possessive suffix indicates the owner(s) of the noun(s) being possessed.

Nese makes the distinction between four relational classifiers that are based on the roots, *rr-, m-, jin-* and *s-*. The latter two roots are used for possession of general items while *rr-* is used for possession of food items meant for eating and *m-* is used for liquids meant for drinking. The forms of these relational classifiers slightly contrast, albeit having similar functions, with those proposed in Takau (2016) where they appear in the forms *rra-, ma-* and *sa-*, while Crowley (2006c) proposes two paradigms of indirect possessive suffixes based on the roots *sa-* and *jin-*, which can be used interchangeably. The set of possessive suffixes that are attached to these roots and the relational classifiers are presented in Table 4.6.

Table 4.6: Relational classifiers

Person/ number	Relational classifier			
	General possession		Possession of liquids intended for drinking	Possession of food intended for eating
	jin-	*s-*	*m-*	*rr-*
1SG	*jin-a*	*s-ak*	*m-ak*	*rr-ak*
2SG	*jin-okh*	*s-am*	*m-am*	*rr-am*
3SG	*jin-i*	*s-an*	*m-an,*	*rr-an*
1PL INCL	*jin-krre*	*s-arr*	*m-arr*	*rr-arr, rrin-krre*
1PL EXCL	*jin kanan*	*s-anan*	*m-anan*	*rr-anan*
2PL	*jin kam'i*	*s-am'i, sa-ni*	*m-ani*	*rr-am'i/ r-ani*
3PL	*jin-err*	*s-arr*	*min-err*	*rr-arr*

Table 4.6 shows that there is a uniform pattern running through the possessive suffix paradigms in all persons and numbers for the relational classifiers *s-*, *m-* and *rr-*, with the exception of *jin-*. The paradigm for *jin-* differs from the other three paradigms in a few respects. Firstly, the 1SG possessive suffix is *-a*, instead of *-ak*. Similarly, the 2SG possessive suffix is *-okh* rather than *-am*. In the 1PL EXCL form, *jin-* utilises the 1PL EXCL independent pronoun instead of any possessive suffixes, while the other three relational classifiers employ possessive suffixes, whose phonological shapes are identical and they resemble part of the 1PL EXCL independent pronoun *-anan* (cf. §3.4 Table 3.17).

4.5.8.2.1 Relational classifier *rr-*

The use of *rr-* to indicate possession of an item meant for eating is illustrated in (4.84).

4.84 Ø-Ti-ve   ale   khunokh   ma   tekh   nobungon
     3SG:REAL-ASP-say CONJ   2SG   come   take   half
     'She said, "Ok you come and take this left over bit

     nabov   **rr-ak**   **khe**   waj-i.
     Chinese.yam   CLED-1SG:POSS   DEM   eat-3SGOBJ
     of my Chinese yam and eat it".'
     (2012_05_16 obanhy01005 00:02:30.000-00:02:45.000 natural text)

In Nese, *rr-* is strictly used as a classifier associated with edible items that are meant for eating since it is possible that some food items, such as coconut, may be used for other purposes apart from eating. This is illustrated in (4.85), where the classifier for possession of general items is used to indicate possession of a food item.

4.85 | *Nobukhas* | *khai* | *Ø-ti-v'an* | *Ø-woj* | *maniok*
| pig | 3SG | 3SG:REAL-ASP-go | 3SG:REAL-eat | manioc

'The pig went and ate all our

s-anan.

CLGEN:1PLEXCL:POSS

manioc.'

(2012_05_16 obanhy01003 00:05:57.000-00:06:02.000 natural text)

In (4.85), the classifier for general items that is based on the root *s-* is used instead of the classifier that is used for edible items because that particular food item is still in the garden and there is no clear indication yet whether it is meant for eating.

In terms of the syntax of this particular possessive construction, the possessum occurs in the slot before the classifier *rr-* to which the possessor, expressed in the form of an affix, is attached. The possessum and classifier combination is tightly bound, making no allowances for any intervening entity. As shown in example (4.84), the possessum may be a compound noun phrase *nobungon nabov* or it may be a single noun phrase such as *maniok* in (4.85). In (4.85), the referent of the possessor, expressed via the 1SG possessor suffix *-ak* is co-referential with that of the 3PL subject pro-index affixed to the verb *ve* in the main clause. The possessor may also be expressed via a lexical noun phrase as in *tejiblakh* in (4.86). In such cases, the 3SG possessor suffix is obligatorily attached to the possessive classifier and, interestingly, there is a mismatch with the number feature of possessor suffix and the plural noun phrase *tejiblakh*.

4.86 *Ne-ve*   *Ø-se-v'an*   *vele*   *Ø-se-woj*
      3SG:REAL-say   3SG-IRR-go   sadly   3SG-IRR-eat
      'I said he's sadly going to eat

      norrian   **rr-in**   **tejiblakh**.
      food   CLED-3SG:POSS   children
      the children's food.'
      (2014_01_19 naanhy01001 00:37:56.000-00:37:59.000 natural text)

4.5.8.2.2 Relational classifiers *s-* and *jin-*

As stated earlier in this subsection, the relational classifiers *s-* and *jin-* can be used interchangeably. This flexibility is illustrated in (4.87) where the possession of coconuts is expressed with the relational classifier *jin-*, which is the relational classifier used for possession of general items.

4.87 *Benanev*   *bir-ma,*   *bir-ma*   *Lerrongrrong.*
      yesterday   1PLEXCL:REAL-come   1PLEXCL:REAL-come   Lerrongrrong
      'Yesterday, we came, we came to Lerrongrrong.

      Bir-v'an   *bir-kij*
      1PLEXCL:REAL-go   1PLEXCL:REAL-remove inner part of coconut
      We went and we removed the inner flesh of

      nani   **jin**   *Mosli.*
      coconut   POSS   Mosli
      the coconuts which belong to Mosli.'
      (2011_12_21 obro01003 00:00:00.000-00:00:10.000 natural text)

Even though coconut is an edible item, the relational classifier used for possession of general items is used instead in (4.87). This is because the coconuts are intended for copra and not for eating. As shown in (4.87), when a possessor is expressed as a full lexical noun phrase, the possessor suffix is not used. In (4.88), the coconuts referred to here are those in the coconut plantations that will be used for copra and the general classifier *s-* is used.

4.88	*Khina*	*naleng*	*je-kliaik*	*kele*	*nani*	**s-ak**
	1SG	maybe	1SG:IRR-look for	again	coconut	CLGEN-1SG:POSS

'As for me, maybe I'll go look for my coconuts again

ev'an   *vila.*
there   down towards the sea
there down towards the sea.'
(2014_01_19 naanhy01001 00:58:12.000-00:58:16.000 natural text)

A comparison of examples (4.87) and (4.88) clearly show that *s-* and *jin-* are used interchangeably for edible items not meant for eating, since although references were made to edible plant items in both examples, the possessive root *jin-* is used in one example while *s-* is used in the other.

The relational classifiers used for possession of general items are *jin-* and *sa-*, their forms having been presented in Table 4.6. The difference between the distributions of these two classifiers is not clear at this stage. To begin with, both classifiers may be used to express possession of inanimate items. This is illustrated in (4.89) and (4.90).

4.89	*Bir-v'an*	*rengen*	**nuak**	*velvele*	**jin**	*tojan*	*sakhal.*
	1PLEXCL:REAL-go	LOC	boat	small	POSS	Atchin	one

'We went in a small boat belonging to a man from Atchin.'
(2014_01_19 naanhy01001 01:03:15.000-00:03:19.000 natural text)

4.90	*Khar*	*re-ve,*	**mobael**	**s-ak**		*khe*
	3PL	3PL:REAL-say	mobile	CLGEN-1SG:POSS		DEM

'They said, "that mobile of mine

Ø-sat.   *khe*
3SG:REAL-be.bad   DEM
is really bad".'
(2014_01_19 naanhy01001 00:33:08.000-00:33:11.000 natural text)

In examples (4.89) and (4.90), both nouns are inanimate and are introduced items of foreign origin. Animacy cannot be used as a distinguishing criterion between the two relational classifiers *jin-* and *s-* since, as illustrated in (4.91) and (4.92), both can be used to express possession of animate items.

In example (4.89), the possessor is expressed as a singular lexical noun phrase *tojan sakhal* and there is no suffix attached to the relational classifier *jin-*, whose referent is co-referential with the noun phrase *tojan sakhal*. This contrasts with lexical noun phrases occurring in complement positions to other relational classifiers such as *m-*, *rr-* and *s-* where the 3SG possessive suffix obligatorily attaches to the relational classifier.

4.91	*Khina*	*ne-v'an*	*khe,*	*j-be-les-te*		***nobolokv'at***
	1SG	1SG:REAL-go	DEM	1SG:IRR-NEG1-see-NEG2		cow

'I went but did not see my cow

s-ak	*ev'an.*
CLGEN-1SG:POSS	there

there.'
(2014_01_19 naanhy01001 00:06:31.000-00:06:35.000 natural text)

4.92	*No-kol*	***tev'et***	***velvele***	*khe*	***jin***	*Patrik.*
	1SG:REAL-carry	woman	small	DEM	POSS	Patrick

'I carried that little girl, who is Patrick's.'
(2014_01_19 naanhy01001 00:40:16.000-00:40:20.000 natural text)

In (4.91), the possession of the animate item 'cow' is expressed by the general relational classifier *sa-*. In (4.92), the possessed item is expressed by the animate common noun phrase *tev'et* 'woman'.

Under the possessive paradigm based on the *s-* root, when a third person referent is the possessor the form *s-an* or *s-en* is used (cf. §2.5.2.3.4). When the former is used, the possessor is implied, given that it may have already occurred in an antecedent clause or is highly salient in discourse. This is shown in (4.93).

4.93	*Bubu*	***s-an,***	*nenerrnarr*	*Ø-nas.*
	Grandfather	CLGEN-3SG:POSS	male	3SG:REAL-die

'His grandfather, the male one, he died.'
(2014_01_19 00:35:26.000-00:35:28.000 natural text)

However, when *s-en* is used, the possessor is explicitly expressed via a lexical noun phrase, which occupies the position immediately after the classifier, as shown in (4.94).

4.94 *Ale*   *kanan*   *bir-ti-lol*   *iekhe,*
      CONJ   1PLEXCL   1PLEXCL:EXCL-ASP-stay   DEM:LOC
      'And we stayed here,

      navro,   *navro*   **s-en**   **takharr**   *Ø-ti-ma*
      war   war   CLGEN-3SG:POSS   whiteman   3SG:REAL-ASP-come
      the war, the whiteman's war came.'
      (2012_06_19 obfaha01001 00:00:03.000-00:00:10.000 natural text)

In (4.94), the referent of the 3SG possessive suffix *-en* is the same as that of the noun *takharr* 'whiteman' and it is only in this context that the possessor is required to be explicitly stated in the position after the possessive classifier.

It is highly probable that the relational classifier based on the root *s-* is a reflex of either Proto Oceanic general classifier **sa* (Ross, 1988, p. 185) or the Proto Oceanic **ta*, a morpheme that functioned as a locative and possessive preposition, although it was the only POc preposition that took possessive suffixes (Lynch et al., 2011, p. 79). Lynch et al. further argue that in present Oceanic languages, reflexes of **ta* are used either as 'the only marker of indirect possessive classifiers, or it is used as **an alternative to the language's possessive classifier**' (p. 79, emphasis added). Given that in Nese items meant for eating and drinking have possessive relational classifiers to which they are assigned, the relational classifier *s-* is perhaps the alternative classifier used for possession of items that are not covered by *rr-* and *m-*. This, however, does not explain the fact that *s-* may be used interchangeably with *jin-*.

The status of *jin-* as solely a relational classifier in Nese is debatable. Firstly, as illustrated in (4.95) and (4.96), *jin-* has a preposition-like function with the meaning 'from' or 'to'.

4.95 *Khai*   *vol-i*   **jin**   *Severine.*
      3SG   buy-3SGOBJ   POSS   Severine
      'She bought it from Severine.'
      (2014_01_19 naanhy01001 00:04:04.000-00:04:06.000 natural text)

4.96   *Ne-v'an*   *v'an*   **jin**   *Pasta*   *Roy.*
1SG:REAL-go   DIR   POSS   Pastor   Roy
'I went to Pastor Roy.'
(2014_01_19 naanhy01001 00:04:34.000-00:04:35.000 natural text)

Given that *jin*- cannot be a reflex of Proto Oceanic *ta, it is probable that it originated as a verbal preposition with benefactive and dative functions (amongst other plausible functions) and these functions were later extended to include possessive relationships in Nese, in particular involving possession of general items.

The examples used thus far in relation to *jin*- are those in which the possessor is a full noun phrase and the possessed item is also a full noun phrase.

4.97   *Nekrre*   *rru*   *rri-si-v'an*   *rri-si-lev*   *netenge*   *mandarin*
1PLEXCL   two   1PLEXCL-IRR-go   1PLEXCL-IRR-take   thing   mandarines
'The two of us, we'll go and take, what's that, our

jin-krre.
CLGEN-1PLEXCL:POSS
mandarins.'
(2012_07_05 naaksi01001 00:04:34.000-00:04:35.000 natural text)

In example (4.97), the possessed noun is the mandarins and the possessor is expressed by the 1PL EXCL possessor suffix, which is affixed to the relational classifier *jin*-. The reason why *rr*- is not used in this context is because the immediate purpose of collecting the mandarins is for selling rather than for eating.

4.5.8.2.3 Relational classifier *m*-

The relational classifier used for items meant for drinking is based on the root *m*-. This is illustrated in (4.98) where water meant for drinking is used in connection with the relational classifier *m*-.

4.98   *Ma*   *num*   *nua*   **m-am**.
come   drink   water   CLLIQ-2SG:POSS
'Come drink your water.'
(Fieldnotes, elicitation)

4. THE NOUN PHRASE

This relationship in which food items meant for eating are distinguished from food items not meant for eating is also evident in the possessive divide between liquids that are meant for drinking and those not used for drinking. If water is fetched for washing clothes, the general relational classifier *jin-* is used; however, if it is fetched for drinking the classifier *m-* is employed.

In (4.98), the referent of the 2SG possessive suffix is not present within the clause and has already been established in discourse. In (4.99), the possessor is expressed via the 3SG possessive suffix *-an* and it is co-referential with the referent of the 3SG possessive suffix *-ne* in the noun phrase *meren natne*, both of which are co-referential with the proper noun *Rodrik*, which has been established prior in discourse.

4.99	*Mer-en*	*nat-**ne***	*khai*	*Ø-vol*	*nua*	***m-an***
	mother-3SG:POSS	child-3SG:POSS	3SG	3SG:REAL-buy	water	CLLIQ-3SG:POSS

'His child's mother she bought his alcohol.'

(2014_01_19 naanhy01001 00:55:41.000-00:55:44.000 natural text)

When the possessor is a lexical noun phrase, it occupies the position after the relational classifier, as shown in (4.100), and it is co-referential with the referent of the 3SG possessive suffix attached to the relational classifier.

4.100	*Nua*	***m-in***	*lekhterr*	*khe*.
	Water	CLLIQ-3SG:POSS	woman	DEM

'That woman's water.'

(2012_08_22 elanhy01001 00:05:01.000-00:05:07.000 elicitation)

4.5.8.3 Associative *nan*

Lastly, Nese uses the associative *nan* for possessive-like relationships in which both the possessor and possessee are lexical noun phrases. When *nan* is used, the possessee lexical noun phrase has already been mentioned in a previous clause; however, the usage of its raised variant *nen* is triggered by the presence of the possessor noun phrase occurring immediately after associative *nan*. This is illustrated in (4.101).

4.101 *Ru-tu-jor* *khin* ***nejor*** ***jin-er,***
3PLEXCL:REAL-ASP-shoot PREP I rifle CLGEN-3PL:POSS
'They were shooting with their rifles,

kho-les *nies nakhab'* ***nan***,...
2SG:REAL-see smoke ASSOC
you see the smoke of the rifles...'
(2012_06_19 obfaha01001 00:00:22.000-00:00:32.000 natural text)

In (4.101), the referent in associative *nan* is co-referential with that of the lexical noun phrase *nejor jinerr* 'their rifles' in the previous clause. There are only two instances in the data of *nan* occurring in this context. In this case, it is clear that the use of the associative semantically denotes a relationship of 'ownership', the possessor being a generic or non-specific noun phrase.

When the *nen* variant of the associative marker is used, the possessor noun phrase occurs immediately after the associative marker, as illustrated in (4.102).

4.102 *Ale* *bir-v'an* *maro,* *re-bet* *norrian* ***nen***
CONJ 1PLEXCL:REAL-go up 3PL:REAL-make food ASSOC
'Then we went up and they made food for the

dakho.
circumcision
circumcision.'
(2014_01_19 naanhy01001 00:30:56.000-00:31:00.000 natural text)

The non-specific possessor noun phrase *dakho* 'circumcision' modifies the referent noun phrase *norrian*, specifying the type of food being prepared. There is an additional purposive meaning that can be inferred from the associative construction in (4.102) in that the food has the purpose of being used in circumcision. This purposive denotation is perhaps more evident in (4.103), where the Bislama-borrowed noun phrase *yis* 'yeast' that is kept specifically for bread making has been used for making home-made brew instead.

4.103 *Yis*   **nen**   *bred*   *khe*   *khar*   *ro-num-u.*
       Yeast   ASSOC   bread   DEM   3PL   3PL:REAL-drink-3SGOBJ
       'That yeast for the bread, they drank it.'
       (2014_01_19 naanhy01001 00:51:54.000-00:51:48.000 natural text)

The form *nan* is perhaps a reflex of the Proto Oceanic morpheme *ni*, which is used to express possessive relationships where the possessor was non-specific (Lynch et al., 2011, p. 77).

The patterning of the constituents within an associative construction contrasts with that exhibited by possessive relationships expressed by the general relational classifier *jin-*, in that the lexical noun phrase preceding the relational classifier-suffix sequence is the possessed noun and the possessor occurs after the possessive relational classifier-suffix sequence (cf. example 4.92).

4.5.9 Relative clauses

Heads of noun phrases in Nese may also be modified by a relative clause introduced by the subordinator *te*. Further discussion of relative clauses is presented in §7.5.2. Common nouns are the only types of heads of noun phrases that may be modified by relative clauses. This is shown in examples (4.104) and (4.105).

4.104 *So*   *tete*   *min*   **norrian**   *te*   *khai*   *Ø-ti-tokh.*
       Thanks   father   PREP2   food   SUB   3SG   3SG:REAL-ASP-exist
       'Thank you father for the food which is here.'
       (2012_06_12 obaksi01001 00:11:19.000-00:11:22.000 natural text)

4.105 *Rri-ti-tekh*   **norrurr**   *te*   **Merika**
       3PL:REAL-ASP-take   clothes   SUB   America
       'We took the clothes that the Americans

       Ø-ti-vreng-i.
       3SG:REAL-ASP-throw-3SGOBJ
       threw.'
       (2012_06_09 obfaha01003 00:00:06.000-00:00:11.000 natural text)

4.5.10 General modifiers

The lexemes classed as general modifiers are *buro* and *wor*. As stated in §3.16, these two lexemes may function both as modifiers of the verb complex and the noun phrase. When *wor* modifies a head noun, it denotes 'alone' and *buro* signifies 'only', 'just' or 'alone'. Both modifiers occupy a post-nominal position.

The general modifier *wor* may modify a proper noun functioning as the head of a noun phrase in topic position, as illustrated in (4.106).

4.106 *Lana* **wor** *khai* *Ø-se-rongvuson-i*
Lana GENMOD 3SG 3SG-IRR-understand-3SGOBJ
'Only Lana she knows it.'
(2014_01_19 naanhy01001 00:07:47.000-00:07:49.000 natural text)

Wor may also modify a common noun functioning as head of a noun phrase, as shown in (4.107), where it occupies a post-nominal position and is modifying the common noun *lokvusbuak* functioning as the subject of the verbal predicate.

4.107 *Lokvusbuak* **wor** *Ø-nakis* *Ø-nakis* *Ø-nakis!*
Laplap taro GENMOD 3SG:REAL-good 3SG:REAL-good 3SG:REAL-good
'Laplap taro alone is good, good, good!'
(2014_01_19 naanhy01001 00:22:04.000-00:22:07.000 natural text)

The general modifier *buro* may modify heads of noun phrases that are common nouns in object position, as illustrated in (4.108).

4.108 *Khai* *Ø-rong* *te* *ba-num* *nanalokh* **buro**.
3SG 3SG:REAL-want SUB POT-drink kava GENMOD
'He wants to drink kava only.'
(2014_01_19 naanhy01001 00:11:23.000-00:11:26.000 natural text)

It may also modify a noun phrase composed of an independent pronoun conjoined with an object pro-index, as exemplified in (4.109), where the noun phrase in subject position is modified by *buro*.

4.109 *Kanan* *min-i* **buro** *bur-worr.*
1PLEXCL PREP2-3SGOBJ GENMOD 1PLEXCL:REAL-eat
'It was just us and him who ate.'
(2014_01_19 naanhy01001 00:02:21.000-00:02:22.000 natural text)

Similarly, *buro* may modify a proper noun phrase functioning as the topic of a verbal clause as illustrated in (4.110).

4.110	*Yvon*	***buro***	*khai*	*Ø-v'an*	*bentaru.*
	Yvonne	GENMOD	3SG	3SG:REAL-go	two days ago

'It was just Yvonne who went yesterday.'

(2014_01_19 naanhy01001 00:24:51.000-00:24:53.000 natural text)

4.6 Discourse role of pronouns

Independent pronouns play a prominent discourse role, maintaining anaphoric reference with either lexical noun phrases, bound subject cross-indexes or object pro-indexes or entities that are highly salient in the context of the communicative setting. When a pronoun occurs in preverbal position in conjunction with the cross-index, the pronoun serves a contrastive function. This contrastive function is exhibited in two contexts. Firstly, when a new participant is introduced into the discourse and it is important to differentiate this new participant and, secondly, when a previously mentioned participant, which is no longer the focus in the discourse, needs to be retrieved in order to differentiate it from other participants. The first context is illustrated in (4.111).

4.111	***Kani***	***kirr**-v'an*	***kirr**-num*	*nanalokh be*	***kirr-se**-ma*
	2PL	2PL:REAL-go	2PL:REAL-drink	kava CONJ	2PL-IRR-come

'You guys go and drink kava but when you return,

	khota	***kirr**-s-be-worr-te*	*sana*	*neten*	*te*	***khina***	***no**-rongo*
	PROHIB	2PL:IRR-NEG1-eat-NEG2	today	PURP2	SUB	1SG	1SG:REAL-want

you won't eat today because I am really

	sikha	***de**-tu-tun.*	*khe.*
	NEG	1SG:IRR-REDUP-roast	DEM

tired of roasting (cooking).'

(2014_01_19 naanhy01001 00:01:39.000-00:01:47.000 natural text)

In (4.111), the speaker uses the 2PL independent pronoun to introduce a new participant. Reference to the 2PL referent is made by way of the corresponding subject cross-indexes up to the point where another participant is introduced, expressed by the 1SG independent pronoun. The 1SG referent is then again expressed by the corresponding subject cross-indexes. In the discourse text, the 1SG independent pronoun has previously been employed; however, since it has not been a participant in the immediately previous discourse, it is imperative that the independent pronoun be used in order to establish its re-entry in the discourse. Example (4.111) also shows that when there is no need to make a contrast between the participants, the subject cross-indexes are used; however, when contrast is needed, the independent pronouns are used to establish the contrast.

In addition to these two preverbal nominal elements, a full lexical noun phrase can co-occur in conjunction with an independent pronoun and a subject cross-index as shown in *teverik* 'men' in (4.112).

4.112 *Ale* **teverik khe khar** *re-v'an   re-ve   ru-su-num*
      CONJ men   DEM 3PL   3PL:REAL-go 3PL:REAL-say 3PL-IRR-drink
      'Then these men they went and they said, "we will drink
      nanalokh.
      kava
      kava".'
      (2014_01_19 naanhy01001 00:01:35.000-00:01:38.000 natural text)

In (4.112), the left dislocated full noun phrase *teverik khe* 'these men' establishes the participant as the topic, co-occurring with both the 3PL independent pronoun, which is the subject NP, and the obligatory 3PL subject cross-index. In this context, the 3PL independent pronoun is used for emphatic purposes. Its absence would have rendered the construction less emphatic and this, therefore, implies that independent pronouns have a more prominent discourse role.

The lexical noun phrase *teverik khe* occupies a clause external position that is typically reserved for topics. It cannot be analysed as the subject because this position is also the landing spot for dislocated objects whose trace is expressed in the clause by way of an object pro-index. This is illustrated in (4.113), where the clause external *nanalokh khe* has the same referent as the clause internal 3SG object pro-index rather than the 3SG subject pronoun *khai*.

4.113 **Nanalokh khe** khai Ø-num-**u** benanev.
Kava DEM 3SG 3SG:REAL-drink-3SGOBJ yesterday
'This kava, he drank it yesterday.'
(Fieldnotes, elicitation)

In Nese this discourse role is not restricted to reference tracking but also extends to the tracking of a meaning encoded in a particular verb in a previous clause, as is evident in (4.114). This example highlights this extended discourse function in the use of the 1SG independent pronoun.

4.114 [**Khina ne**-najnge te Ø-ma akaev Ø-ma
1SG 1SG:REAL-agree SUB 3SG:REAL-come archive 3SG:REAL-come
'I agree for it to come, the archive is coming

Ø-se-tekh ral-ok.]^a1 [**Khina ne**-yat khe.]^b1
3SG-IRR-take voice-1SG:POSS 1SG 1SG:REAL-stay DEM
it's going to take my voice (my voice will be recorded). I stay here.

[**Khina** neng s-ak Annie Hymak.]^c1 [**Ne**-yat
1SG name CLGEN-1SG:POSS Annie Hymak 1SG:REAL-sit
My name is Annie Hymak. I stay

rengen nev'enu-ak Senbokhas...]^b2 [**ne**-najnge te
LOC place-1SG:POSS Senbokhas 1SG:REAL-agree SUB
my place Senbokhas. I agree that

Ø-se-tekh ral-ok...]^a2
3SG-IRR-take voice-1SG:POSS
it's going to take my voice (record my voice).'
(2012_05_16 obanhy01001 00:00:00.000-00:00:33.500 natural text)

The construction bracketed as (a1) has both the 1SG independent pronoun and its counterpart 1SG subject cross-index and the verb in the main clause encodes the meaning of 'agreeing'. The next intransitive clause (b1) has the intransitive verb '*yat*' as the head verb meaning 'stay' or 'live' and in this clause the speaker is now talking about living in that particular location and, again, the independent pronoun and its counterpart subject cross-index co-occur. Given that Ariel (2009, p. 25) has proposed that the presence of reduced pronominal forms, such as the 1SG subject cross-index in Nese, corresponds to a higher degree of accessibility, compared to a full pronoun, which corresponds to a lower degree of accessibility (4.114), as it is present during conversation time, the repeated use of the independent 1SG pronoun (a1), (b1) and (c1) seems overly redundant. However, it is probable that the presence of the two noun phrases *akaev* 'archive' functioning as the subject of the subordinate clause in (a1) and *ralok* 'voice', which functions as the object of *tekh* 'take', have rendered the 1SG pronominal entity less accessible, and reference to the entity has to be made by the full pronoun as well as its corresponding subject cross-index.

The presence of the intervening full noun phrases cannot, however, be used to explain the re-occurrence of the 1SG independent pronoun given that there is no intervening full noun phrase in the intransitive clause labelled (b1) and the following clause labelled as (c1). Thus an explanation of the continuous use of the 1SG independent pronoun and its corresponding subject cross-index must be sought elsewhere.

As can be seen in example (4.114), the speaker tends to use the 1SG subject cross-index singly when the verb to which the subject cross-index is attached has occurred in a previous antecedent main clause. For example, in (a2) the speaker picks up again on the issue of agreeing to be recorded and only the 1SG subject cross-index is used. Similarly, in (b2) where the place of residence is mentioned again, it is only the subject cross-index that is used. This shows that the co-occurrence of the 1SG independent pronoun and its counterpart 1SG subject cross-index signal the introduction or emphasis of new information and the retrieval or development of this information further in the discourse is signalled by the occurrence of the 1SG subject cross-index occurring without its counterpart independent pronoun. This pattern is in fact pervasive throughout the text in which example (4.114) is taken. However, there is a need for further investigation in relation to the factors that trigger the presence of independent pronouns versus full noun phrases in discourse.

I have stated in §3.2 and §3.4 that nouns and independent pronouns function as heads of noun phrases. Therefore, the common nouns co-occurring with the 3PL independent pronoun in example (4.112) are considered as topicalised elements and the independent pronoun is analysed as the subject of the clause. This implies that Nese allocates clause initial position to topicalised elements, which could be noun phrases employed for emphatic or contrastive purposes. This analysis conforms to that of the Proto Oceanic verb complex structure of which it has been claimed that topicalised arguments or adjuncts occupy preverbal position (Lynch et al., 2011, p. 86).

4.7 Nominalisation

Nouns may be derived from verbs by means of the nominalisation suffix attached to the verb stem. Nese employs the suffix *-ian* to nominalise a verb root. Figure 4.3 shows the position that the nominalising suffix occupies in relation to a verb stem.

> *nV*-(reduplicated form of verb)-Verb root-*ian*

Figure 4.3: Nominalisation

All verbs require the presence of the residual Proto Oceanic common noun phrase prefix *na and the Proto Oceanic general nominaliser *-an (Lynch et al., 2011, pp. 70–71) in order to derive a nominalised noun phrase from a verb. Table 4.7 contains a list of some nominalised verbs.

Table 4.7: Examples of nominalised verbs

Nominalised verbs	Root verbs
norojian 'sickness'	*roj* 'to be sick'
nemerjian 'old person'	*merje* 'to grow old'
nowakwakian 'the planting'	*wak* 'to plant'
neververian 'prayer'	*varvar* 'to pray'
neneturian 'the sleep'	*natur* 'to sleep'
novojokhian 'the gathering'	*vojokh* 'to gather together'
nenesian 'death'	*nas* 'to die'
nonorvoan 'life'	*norvo* 'to live'
nosobsobian 'the relating of a story'	*sob* 'to relate a story'
nosakhsakhian 'work'	*sakhsakh* 'to work'

As shown in Table 4.7, both transitive verbs and intransitive verbs may be nominalised by the *nV-* prefix and *-ian* suffix. For example, intransitive *roj* 'to be sick' and transitive *wak* 'to plant' both employ *-ian* to derived their counterpart nominalised forms. The two transitive verbs *wak* 'to plant' and *sob* 'to relate a story' are both reduplicated. Since reduplication eliminates the object argument, it is perhaps necessary for such forms to undergo reduplication as part of the nominalisation process. It is also evident from Table 4.7 that forms that are nominalised are susceptible to vowel raising as shown in *nenesian* 'death' (cf. §2.5.2.3.6).

There is evidence that the nominalised verbs may be indirectly possessed, as shown in (4.115) where the nominalised verb *norrorrovokhian* 'a play' is indirectly possessed and occurring as a complement of the preposition *rengen* 'in, at'.

4.115 *Tejiblakh* *khar* *ro-rrorrovokh* *rengen* **norrorrovokhian**
children 3PL 3PL:REAL-play LOC play
'The children were playing

s-arr *sakhal*.
CLGEN:3PL:POSS one
one of their games.'
(2014_01_24 elanhy01001 00:09:04.000-00:09:09.000 natural text)

There is no evidence in the data to suggest that nominalised verbs can be directly possessed. As illustrated in (4.115), they may be the head of a noun phrase functioning as the complement of the true preposition *rengen*. Nominalised verbs may also be the heads of noun phrases functioning as the subject of an intransitive verb (4.116).

4.116 **Nemerjian** *re-nes* *jelekh*.
Old people 3PL:REAL-die all
'The old people died, all of them.'
(2012_08_22 anhy01005 00:03:28.000-00:03:30.000 natural text)

They may be modified by demonstrative *khe* and forming a left dislocated noun phrase, such as *nemerjian khe* 'that old man' in (4.117), where the noun phrase is co-referential with the 3SG pronominal object functioning as the complement of the verbal preposition *min*.

4.117 **Nemerjian** *khe,* *kanan* *min-i* *bir-sukul*.
Old person DEM 1PL:EXCL PREP2-3SGOBJ PREP2:REAL-school
'That old person, us and him we went to school.'
(2014_01_19 naanhy01001 00:12:14.000-00:12:19.000 natural text)

They may also function as objects of transitive verbs such as in (4.118), where not only is the noun phrase *norrian* 'food' the object of transitive *bat-* 'to make', but it can also be modified by the nominal modifier *lemje* 'a lot'.

4.118 *Ri-bet*   **norrian**   *lemje.*
       3PL:EXCL-make   food   a.lot
       'They made a lot of food.'
       (2014_01_10 naanhy01001 00:15.00.000-00:15.00.000 natural text)

Moreover, they may occur in a compound noun phrase in a modifying position, ascribing some kind of quality to the noun they are modifying. This is illustrated in (4.119) where the nominalised verb *neneturian* 'sleeping' modifies *neren* 'time' resulting in 'sleeping time' or 'time for sleeping'.

4.119 *Re-ve*   **neren neneturian**   *ale*   *Ø-natur*   *buro.*
       3PL:REAL-say   time   sleeping   CONJ   3SG:REAL-sleep GENMOD
       'They said it's sleeping time and so she just slept.'
       (2014_01_19 naanhy01001 00:13:49.000-00:13:53.000 natural text)

Lastly, nominalised verbs may participate in an associative construction in which they assume the possessor role, encoding a non-specific and generic quality. The noun phrase formed by the associative construction *tenge nen nenesian jelekh* has the non-specific and generic noun *nenesian* 'death' modifying the noun phrase *tenge* 'things'.

4.120 *Tenge*   *kher*   *khe*   *tenge*   *nen*   **nenesian**   *jelekh.*
       thing   3PL   DEM   thing   ASSOC   death   all
       'These things, they're all things for death/dying.'
       (2014_01_19 naanhy01001 00:07:36.000-01:07:39.000 natural text)

In (4.120), the nominalised verb *nenesian* assigns the character or quality of 'death/dying' to the common noun *tenge* 'thing'. There is no evidence in the data to suggest that a nominalised verb may be in the possessor role in an associative construction.

5
The verb complex

5.1 Introduction

In this chapter, I discuss the order of elements in the Nese verb complex (§5.2), the kinds of verbs that may be heads of verb complexes (§5.3), argument indexes (§5.4), elements that may modify the head verb (§5.5), serial verb constructions (§5.6) and valency (§5.7). Descriptions of Oceanic languages have applied the term 'verb phrase' to represent either a verb head, its associated particles and subject and object markers (Hyslop, 2001, p. 23; Dimock, 2009, p. 121) or to just the associated particles excluding the nominal arguments associated to the verb (Crowley, 1982, p. 118). Lynch (1998) replaces the term 'verb phrase' with the term 'verb complex' to signify the head verb and its auxiliary particles excluding the object. I use the term 'verb complex' in this grammar in line with Lynch's (1998) definition, fully cognisant that while the label is seemingly appropriate for Oceanic languages, it poses serious questions in generative grammatical theory, given that it dispenses with the object NP in the verb phrase (McGinn, 2001). Another central issue is whether the object pro-indexes within the verb complex can be defined as noun phrase arguments of the verb, when the lexical NP object is not present. If they are arguments then the verb complex notion becomes redundant because the object is in fact inside the verb complex and the entity is, therefore, a verb phrase. As demonstrated in §4.4, object pro-indexes cannot be considered as heads of noun phrases because of their inability to host modifiers that typically modify a lexical noun phrase head. Overall, the notion of a verb complex is widely used and understood in the descriptive literature on Oceanic languages. I follow that practice and use it here.

5.2 Order of elements in the Nese verb complex

The minimal verb complex in Nese consists of the head and its obligatory subject cross-index, in intransitive clauses, and object pro-index, if the verb head is transitive. In Figure 5.1, the obligatory elements are highlighted in bold.

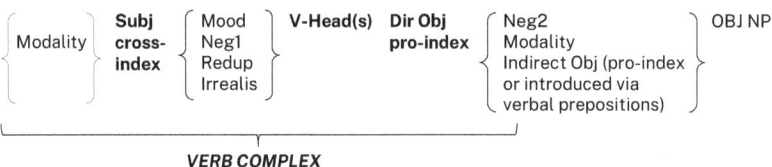

Figure 5.1: Verb complex constituents

The only obligatory elements in the verb complex are the verb or serial verb compound forming the nucleus of the phrase, along with the subject cross-indexes and object pro-indexes, which occur in a rigid order with respect to the verb. Optional preverbal elements are the dehortative, the preverbal negative discontinuous and reduplicative markers that occur in the preposed periphery. Optional post-verbal elements are the second part of the negative discontinuous marker, adverbs, demonstrative *khe*, multiplicatives and directional occurring in the postposed periphery. The only obligatory post-verbal element is the object pro-index, which is always attached directly to the head of the verb complex. As with preverbal elements, the order of post-verbal elements, whether obligatory or optional, is also rigid. Figure 5.1 demonstrates the optional NEG2 occupying a post-verbal position within the verb complex and, when the elements within the verb complex conjoin with the lexical object NP, the structure fits the standard definition of the verb phrase.

5.3 Heads of verb complex

The head of a verb complex can be a transitive verb (including extended transitive verbs), an intransitive active verb, an intransitive stative verb, or a nuclear serial verb. These are illustrated in (5.1), (5.2), (5.3) and (5.4) respectively. In (5.3), the stative intransitive verb head *lemje* 'a lot' takes the 1PL EXCL subject cross-index. There are, however, certain stative intransitive verbs that do not take subject cross-indexes (cf. §5.5.1.2).

5.1   *[Ne-tun-u   jelekh.]*_{VC}
      1SG:REAL-roast-3SGOBJ   all
      'I roasted it all.'
      (2012_06_12 obaksi01001 00:01:22-000-00:01:23.000 natural text)

5.2   *[Ne-ma   khe.]*_{VC}
      1SG:REAL-come   DEM
      'I am coming/on my way.'
      (2012_05_16 obanhy01003 00:00:04.000-00:00:06.000 natural text)

5.3   *[Bir-s-be-lemje-te.]*_{VC}
      1PLEXCL-IRR-NEG1-a.lot-NEG2
      'There are not a lot of us.'
      (2014_01_19 naanhy01001 00:11:13.000-00:11:14.000 natural text)

5.4   *Ale*   *ri-si-v'an*   *[ri-si-bet*   *khojkhoj]*_{VC}   *nuak.*
      CONJ   3PL-IRR-go   3PL-IRR-make   be.proper   boat
      'Then they went and prepared the boat.'
      (2014_01_19 naanhy01001 00:27:24.000-00:27:26.000 natural text)

Nese exhibits transitive verbs such as *tun* 'roast' in example (5.1), which may take two core arguments: a subject (A) and an object (O). While the overwhelming majority of transitive verbs fall under this category, three transitive Nese verbs are categorised as extended transitive verbs. An extended transitive verb is defined by Dixon (2010, p. 335) as a transitive verb taking three core arguments rather than two and, in Nese, the verbs that can do this are *vitai* 'put', *kron* 'give' and *us* 'ask'. The verb *vitai* 'put' requires a subject, object and an extended locational argument that expresses the place at which the action expressed by the verb occurs. *Kron* 'give' and *us* 'ask' both have an extended core argument that expresses the person to which an action is directed upon. Example (5.5) illustrates *kron-* 'to give' with its three core arguments, the subject expressed by the 1PL inclusive subject cross-index 'we', the object represented by the noun phrase *navij* 'bananas' and, finally, the third argument expressed by the 3SG object pro-index 'him'.

5.5 [Rro-so-kron]_VC   navij   min-i.
     1PLINCL-IRR-give   banana   PREP2-3SGOBJ
     'We will give the bananas to him.'
     (2014_01_19 naanhy01001 00:37:48.000-00:37:50.000 natural text)

5.4 Argument indexing

5.4.1 Subject cross-indexes

Apart from the verb head, the only other obligatory preverbal elements in the Nese verb complex are the preverbal subject cross-indexes, which occur as portmanteau prefixes combine person and number marking and mood marking. Nese presents an interesting scenario in terms of the morphosyntactic devices it employs to distinguish realis from irrealis mood marking. While the former is zero marked, being inherently encoded in the person and number categories, the latter is marked via *-se-*, which remains uniform for all persons and numbers with the exception of the 1SG form where two variant forms emerge: *dV-* and *-jV-*. It is interesting to note that person, number and the realis mood are equally unmarked in the 3SG, which is the only aberrant form in this regard. These realis and irrealis forms have been outlined in §3.4 but are repeated here in Table 5.1 for convenience.

Table 5.1: Subject cross-indexes

Person/number	Cross-indexes	
	realis	irrealis
1SG	*nV-*	*dV-, jV-*
2SG	*kho-*	*kho-sV-*
3SG	Ø-	Ø-*sV-*
1PL INCL	*rrV-*	*rrV-sV-*
1PL EXCL	*bVrr-*	*bVrr-sV-*
2PL	*kirr-*	*kirr-sV-*
3PL	*rrV-*Ø	*-sV-*

Elliot (2000, p. 56) distinguishes the realis from the irrealis by proposing that the realis is semantically linked with 'the status of an event as being grounded in perceived reality' and the irrealis as a status of event 'existing only as a conceptual idea, thought, or hypothetical notion'. Given that Nese does not formally mark tense, the specification of the temporal location of a particular event in relation to the time of speech is embedded in the realis and irrealis moods, with further indication provided by other modality particles.

5.4.1.1 Realis subject cross-indexes

As mentioned above, lack of formal marking for the category of tense in Nese means non-future denotations are encoded in the realis mood. The non-future setting is linked to events perceived by the speaker as being real and factual. A real event is compatible with actions set in the past or in the present. Example (5.6) indicates how a realis marked clause can be used to refer to an event that is set in the past or present.

5.6 ***Ne**-ma.*
1SG:REAL-come
'I came.'/ 'I am coming.'/ 'I come.'
(2012_05_16 obanhy01003 00:00:04.000-00:00:06.000 natural text)

In a realis clause, the presence of time adverbials can assist in distinguishing whether past or present time reference is being expressed as shown in (5.7).

5.7 ***Benanev***   *no-khro*   *buro*   *laine.*
Yesterday   1SG:REAL-stay   GENMOD   house:LOC
'Yesterday I just stayed at home.'
(2014_01_19 naanhy01001 00:00:02.000-00:00:05.000 natural text)

In narratives, the realis mood is always employed to refer to both actions currently occurring and those that have occurred in the past. The difference between these two time frames is context dependent. This is illustrated in (5.8) where the narrator first uses the realis to indicate the action of telling a story that is occurring at the present time and then to indicate that the story was set in the past.

5.8 ***Ne-sob***   *te-jiblakh*   *namalakel*   *sangav'il,*   *khar*
1SG:REAL-relate.story   PL-child   young men   ten   3PL
'I am telling the story of ten young men, they

   ***ro-khro**,*   *re-bet*   *novso*   *ververik.*
   3PL:REAL-stay   3PL:REAL-make   arrow   small
   stayed, they made little arrows.'
   (2012_05_16 obanhy01005 00:00:04.000-00:00:13.000 natural text)

The realis interacts with dehortative *khota* in affirmative constructions to express the imperative, contrasting with its use in a similar environment in negated constructions where it conveys the unlikelihood that an event will happen. Example (5.9) shows a command being given to the addressee not to talk to the speaker, with the verbs 'come' and 'talk' being marked for realis. The reason why the realis is used is because the event of coming and talking has already occurred in the past right up to the time of speech.

5.9 *Khota*   **kho-Ø-ma**   **kho-Ø-rej**   *min-a.*
     DEHORT   2SG-REAL-come 2SG-REAL-talk
     'Don't come and talk to me!'
     (2014_01_19 naanhy01001 00:06:39.000-00:06:41.000 natural text)

5.4.1.2 Irrealis subject cross-indexes

In Nese, the irrealis is linked to events or states set in the hypothetical or imaginary realm from the speaker's perspective in a particular temporal setting. Although it more generally attracts constructions that express events or states set in a future time frame, the irrealis is also linked to desiderative and negated constructions. To begin with, the most typical constructions that encode irrealis mood are those in which the events or states are deemed as having the potential or possibility to occur. As illustrated in (5.10), the action of coming is described as being a potential event that may happen, and it also encodes the meaning 'S/he may come'.

5.10 *Khai*   *Ø-se-ma.*
     3SG   3SG-IRR-come
     'S/he will come.'
     (2014_01_19 naanhy01001 00:10:12.000-00:10:13.000 natural text)

On a broader scale, the overall context of the narrative may be grounded in the past; however, the irrealis may be used in such contexts to refer to events happening in the future within the context of the narrative, as illustrated in (5.11).

5.11 *Rre-ve*   *'kho-so-khro*   *iekhe*   *lema-rr'.*
     3PL:REAL-say   2SG-IRR-stay   DEM:LOC   house-3PL:POSS
     'They said, "You will stay here at our house".'
     (2012_05_16 obanhy01005 00:00:51.000-00:00:52.000 natural text)

5. THE VERB COMPLEX

5.12   *Ne-ve*   *rro-mul*   *v'an*   *neten*   *te*
       1SG:REAL-say   1PL:REAL-go back   go   PURP2   SUB
       'I said, "Let's go back because

       je-lijkhor   ***nenet-in***   ***nato***   *be*   *seve*   *sikha*
       1SG:IRR-block   child-3SG:POSS   hen   CONJ   COND   NEG
       I have to close the chickens in because if not

       ri-si-natur   *jalin*   *sana,*   *neviri*   *Ø-**so**-waj-er*
       3PL-IRR-sleep   outside   today   dog   3SG-IRR-eat-3PLOBJ
       they'll be sleeping outside today, the dog will probably/may eat them

       deve   ***nese.***
       CONJ   what
       them or what".'
       (2014_01_19 naanhy01001 00:33:29.000-00:33:38.000 natural text)

In (5.12), while the verb in the subordinate clause is marked for irrealis having the possible meaning of 'I will/may close…', it is the serious nature of the proposition in the apodosis of the negated conditional clause that suggests the closing in of the chickens is a necessity or obligation. The apodosis contains two propositions whose likelihood of occurring is considered to be different. In the initial event clause, the speaker is certain that the chickens will be sleeping outside, but the event of the dogs eating the chickens is uttered with the conjunction *deve* at the end, implying that it is just one out of the many other possible consequences of having the chickens sleep outside.

Lexical cues or contextual information can assist in determining whether irrealis marking on a verb means 'necessity' or 'potentiality', and if leaning towards 'potentiality' whether the event under discussion is certain to occur or *may* happen.

5.13   *Ale*   *seve*   *re-bet*   *nanalokh*   *khai*   *Ø-**se-num**-u.*
       CONJ   COND   3PL:REAL-make   kava   3SG   3SG-IRR-drink-3SGOBJ
       'And if they make kava, he'll drink it.'
       (2014_01_19 naanhy01001 00:50:08.000-00:50:11.000 natural text)

In (5.13), the speaker had previously been admonishing her children's daily habit of drinking kava and comparing it to their father who only drinks it once in a while when kava is made. On these occasions he is not obligated to consume the grog but rather that he will do so out of his own free will. Here, the apodosis incorporates no element of doubt, therefore, it cannot be translated as '… he may drink it'.

Although the propositions in the apodoses in (5.12) and (5.13) are marked for irrealis, Nese does not necessarily restrict these structures to the irrealis mood as shown in (5.14), where both the protasis and apdosis are in realis mood.

5.14 *Seve kor-kron-i balak khe, khai **Ø-nenelkharre** khe.*
cond 2PL-REAL-take-3SGOBJ like this 3SG 3SG-REAL-cold EMP
'If you (PL) are taking it like this, it's cold.'
(2014_01_19 naanhy01001 00:44:20.000-00:44:23.000 natural text)

There are two forms of the 1SG irrealis subject cross-index given in Table 5.1: *de-* and *je-*. *Je-* is used in verb complexes in main clauses, as in (5.15), whereas the irrealis form *de-* would be ungrammatical here (5.16). The latter is only used in verb complexes that are functioning as complements of the desiderative verb *rong-* 'want', in which case the situation or event being described is not real or has not happened yet, as illustrated by (5.17).

5.15 ***Je**-v'an.*
1SG:IRR-go
'I will go.'
(2014_01_19 naanhy01001 00:05:05.000 natural text)

5.16 **De-v'an*
1SG:IRR-go
(Fieldnotes, elicited)

5.17 *No-rong te **de**-waj-i buro khise khai*
1SG:REAL-want SUB 1SG:IRR-eat-3SGOBJ GENMOD who 3SG
'I intended to eat it, but who

ba-tekh min-a
POT-take PREP2-1SGOBJ
will bring it to me.'
(2014_01_19 naanhy01001 00:22:17.000-00:22:20.000 natural text)

In examples such as (5.17), the form *je-* would be ungrammatical when occurring in verb complexes functioning as the complement of the verb *rong*, as shown by ungrammatical (5.16). If the latter was grammatical, its intended translation would be as the grammatical translation given for example (5.18).

5.18   *No-rong   te   ***je****-waj-i*   *buro*   *khise*
       1SG:REAL-want   SUB   1SG:IRR-eat-3SGOBJ   GENMOD   who
       'I really do want to eat it, but who

       khai   *ba-tekh*   *min-a.*
       3SG   POT-take   PREP2-1SGOBJ
       will bring it to me.'
       (Fieldnotes, elicitation)

De- is also used in negative desiderative complement structures as shown in (5.19).

5.19   *No-rong-o*   *sikha*   ***do****-woj*   *norrulnasasakh*   *khe.*
       1SG:REAL-want-3SGOBJ   NEG   1SG:IRR-eat   rice   DEM
       'I don't want to eat this rice.'
       (Fieldnotes, elicitation)

It is only in the 1SG irrealis that a distinction is made regarding which form (*de-, je-*) is used. With other irrealis subject cross-indexes, the irrealis forms are used in complement constructions, as shown in (5.20) for the 3SG form.

5.20   *Kho-les*   *te*   *Aklyn*   *Ø-rong-o*   *Ø-se-ma*
       2SG:REAL-see   SUB   Aklyn   3SG:REAL-want-3SGOBJ   3SG:IRR-come
       'You see that Aklyn wants to come,

       Ø-se-rong   *te*   *rri-si-rej-rej*   *min-i.*
       3SG:IRR-want   SUB   1PLINCL-IRR-REDUP-speak   PREP2-3SGOBJ
       she wants to come so we will speak to her.'
       (2014_01_19 naanhy01001 00:08:16.000-00:08:21.000 natural text)

5.4.2 Object pro-indexes

Nese has a set of object pro-indexes that are affixed directly to the verb root. This set of object pro-indexes is outlined in §3.4 and are repeated in Table 5.2.

Table 5.2: Object pro-indexes

Person	Number	
	Singular	Plural
1	-ia	INCL -krre
		EXCL (kanan)
2	-okh, (khunokh)	(kani)
3	-i,-u, -e, -o, (khai)	-er, (khar)

As indicated in Table 5.2, the object suffix paradigm is not symmetrical, with the absence of object pro-indexes for the 1PL EXCL and 2PL forms, in which case their corresponding independent pronouns are used. Although first singular objects require the object suffix, the object suffix may be used interchangeably with the corresponding independent pronouns for the second singular, third singular and third plural forms. Furthermore, as shown in Table 5.2, there is no uniform pattern for 3SG forms.

In general, the lexical noun phrase object and the object pro-index cannot co-occur. Constructions (5.21), (5.22) and (5.23) illustrate this. Example (5.23), with both an object noun phrase and the object cross-referenced with a suffix on the verb, is ungrammatical.

5.21   Re-v'an   re-ve   ru-su-**num**   **nanalokh**
       3PL:REAL-go   3PL:REAL-say   1PLINCL-IRR-drink   kava
       'They said they will drink kava.'
       (2014_01_19 naanhy01001 00:01:36.000-00:01:38.000 natural text)

5.22   Re-v'an   re-**num-u**   ev'an.
       3PL:REAL-go   3PL:REAL-drink-3SGOBJ   there
       'They went and drank it there.'
       (2014_01_19 naanhy01001 00:48:20.000 natural text)

5.23   *Re-v'an   re-**num-u**   **nanalokh**   ev'an.
       3PL:REAL-go   3PL:REAL-drink-3SGOBJ   kava   DIR
       'We went and drank it the kava there.'
       (Fieldnotes, elicitation)

In example (5.24), the referent of the object pro-index *-i* is co-referential with the lexical noun phrase *khai khe* and the subject of the stative intransitive verb *sat* 'be bad'.

5.24   *Khai*   *khe*   *je-var-**i***   *Ø-se-sat.*
       3SG   DEM   1SG:IRR-tell-3SGOBJ   3SG-IRR-be.bad
       'That one, I am going to tell it and it will be bad.'
       (2012_08_22 anhy012 00:40:48.000-00:40:45.000 natural text)

The lexical noun phrase *khai khe* is in fact the direct object NP, which has been left dislocated for emphatic or focus purposes.

In addition to the direct object expressed via the *-i* affix, the verb *var-* may also take another object suffix indicating the beneficiary or beneficiaries of the action. This is illustrated in (5.25), in which the beneficiary is expressed by means of direct suffixation of the 1PL EXCL suffix *krre,* to the 3SG object pro-index.

5.25   *Namalvar*   *var-i-**krre***.
       High person   tell-3SGOBJ-1PLINCLOBJ
       'The high person told us.'
       (2012_04_26 obmach01001 00:01:25.000-00:01:30.000 song)

Interestingly, the beneficiary argument of the verb *var-* may also be expressed via the prepositional verbs *khin* and *min*. A comparison of examples (5.25) and (5.26) suggests that if the beneficiary is to be realised by an object pro-index, one that is to be directly affixed to the 3SG direct object, then it must not begin with a vowel. If the beneficiary concerned commences with a vowel, then one of the two prepositional verbs *khin* 'with, for, to' or *min* 'to, with, towards' is employed.

5.26   *Na-var-i*   ***khin**-er*   *belek*   *khe.*
       1SG:REAL-tell-3SGOBJ   PREPI-3PLOBJ   like   DEM
       'I told it to them like this.'
       (2014_01_19 naanhy01001 00:10:07.000-00:10:09.000 natural text)

Transitive verbs containing /o/ portray a somewhat different picture in relation to the phonological shape of the 3SG object pro-index. To begin with, unlike verb roots containing a single vowel /u/, in which case the 3SG object pro-index can only be realised as /u/, verb roots containing a single /o/ can have their 3SG object pro-indexes realised as /i/ or /o/.

This is illustrated in (5.27) and (5.28). In (5.27), the referent of the 3SG object suffix is co-referential with the *vave* 'aunt' and not with the 3SG independent pronoun *khai*, which is functioning as the subject. In (5.28), however, the 3SG object pro-index attached to the verb *woj* 'to pound' is not co-referential with the referent of the subject cross-indexes of the two verbs in this construction.

5.27 *Khai*   **Ø-se-tov-i**   *vave.*
3SG   3SG-IRR-call-3SGOBJ   aunty
'She will call her 'aunty'.'
(2012_05_16 oanhy01010 00:09:24.000-00:09:25.000 natural text)

5.28 *Iniekhe   no-rong-o   te   bir-se-**woj-o**.*
now   1PLEXCL:REAL-want-3SGOBJ   SUB   1PLEXCL-IRR-pound-3SGOBJ
'Now I want us to pound it.'
(2012_06_12 obaksi01001 00:01:24.000-00:01:27.000 natural text)

Although monosyllabic verbs with a single /o/ vowel tend to follow the generalisation given above regarding the incompatible co-occurrence of a lexical noun phrase object and an object pro-index, verbs ending with a diphthong do not present a clear picture. This is illustrated in (5.29) with the verb *khokhoi* 'to clean'.

5.29 *Ne-tekh   nokhmak   ma,   **ne-khokhoi**   jelengi*.
1SG:REAL-take   cabbage   come   1SG:REAL-clean   all
'I took the cabbage hither and I washed all of it.'
(2012_05_16 obanhy01001 00:00:45.000-00:00:48.000 natural text)

As we have seen in §4.4 and §4.5.5, *jelengi* can function both as the head of a noun phrase and as a modifier of a head noun phrase. It is not clear whether the /i/ vowel in the verb is the 3SG object suffix, in which case *jelengi* is functioning as a modifier or whether it is part of the verb root, implying that *jelengi* is functioning as the object noun phrase. A similar opacity is present with the verb *vitai* 'to put' in which the /i/ vowel can be treated as part of the verb root as shown in (5.30), where there is a distinct expression of the object argument by means of the lexical noun phrase or it can be treated as representing the 3SG object pro-index, as illustrated in (5.31), where there is a lack of a distinct lexical noun phrase object.

5.30　*Je-**vitai**　**tenge**　iekhetan　iekhe,　je-v'an　je-kisai*
　　　1SG:IRR-put　thing　DIR　DEM:LOC　1SG:IRR-go　1SG:IRR-search
　　　'I'll put something down here, then I'll go and search for it

　　　rengen　nev'enu　wos.
　　　LOC　place　different
　　　in a different place.'
　　　(2014_01_19 naanhy01001 00:41:21.000-00:41:27.000 natural text)

5.31　*Khai　Ø-kuk-u　Ø-naskhe,　Ø-kol-o　v'an*
　　　3SG　3SG:REAL-cook-3SGOBJ　3SG:REAL-cooked　carry-3SGOBJ　DIR
　　　'She cooked it and it was cooked, then she took it

　　　***vita-i**　laine.*
　　　put-3SGOBJ　house:LOC
　　　into the house.'
　　　(2014_01_19 naanhy01001 00:41:21.000-00:41:27.000 natural text)

It is clear that there is an asymmetrical relationship between vowel final transitive verbs or, more specifically, between verbs with a singular final vowel and those that end with a diphthong. In the former group, the final singular vowel has affix status representing the 3SG object pro-index, while in the latter, the status of the final vowel in the diphthong is less clear as it can function as the 3SG object pro-index as well as occurring simultaneously with a lexical noun phrase object.

5.5 Modification of the head verb

Heads of verb complexes may be modified by elements occurring in post- and preverbal positions. Preverbal elements are composed of the initial negative discontinuous marker, which is discussed in §5.5.1.1, the negative *sikha* (§5.5.1.2), the preverbal dehortative marker *khota* (§5.5.2), the prohibitative *orro* (§5.5.3), directional (§5.5.4), multiplicatives (§5.5.5), the aspectual *-ti-* (§5.5.9) and the potential marker *ba-* (§5.5.10). Post-verbal modifiers in Nese are directionals (§5.5.4), the emphatic *khe* (§5.5.6), the free form adverbs that are discussed in §5.5.7 and completive *rov* (§5.5.8).

5.5.1 Negation

There are two forms of negation in Nese. The discontinuous marker *-be*-Verb-*te* negates verbal clauses, and there is also a negative predicate verb *sikha*. The former is analagous to two of the negative discontinous markers attested in Crowley's (2006c, p. 70) analysis, which are *-be*-Verb-*te* and the affixation of negative *-be-* with another negative discontinuous marker *-se-* forming *-se-be*-Verb-*te*. The negative predicate verb is primarily used to predicate the non-existence of a noun phrase and its use as a verbal clause negator is restricted to a verb clause headed by the verb *rong* 'want'.

5.5.1.1 Negative discontinuous marker *-be*-Verb-*te*

Takau (2016) proposes *sbe*-Verb-*te* as the negative discontinus marker, bearing a striking resemblance to the form *-se-be*-Verb-*te* proposed initially in Crowley (2006c, p. 70). Re-examination of the data suggests that there is a close link between the irrealis mood and negation. I propose here that negation in Nese is expressed via the juxtaposition of the irrealis affix *-se-* with the negative discontinous markers *-be-* and *-te*, manifesting itself in the form *-se-be*-Verb-*te*. When the open monosyllabic morpheme *-se-* occurs before the intial negative discontinous marker *-be-*, which contains the phonemic consonant cluster [-mbe] as well as an identical vowel, there is deletion of the front close- mid /e/ vowel in the irrealis prefix. Therefore, contrary to the fused initial discontinuous morpheme *sbe-* proposed in Takau (2016), we get the separate phonologically reduced irrealis morpheme *-s-* attached to the initial discontinuous marker *be*, forming *-s-be*-Verb-*te*. On the other hand, *-s-* could be treated as the initial negative marker, as a consequence, insinuating that negation in Nese is tripartite. Proposing a tripartite negation pattern in Nese is not a far-fetched hypothesis, given that this pattern persists in Vanuatu languages such as Bierebo (Budd, 2010) and Lewo (Early 1994), (although it is marked in Bierebo). However, as shown in Table 5.3, there is a very close interaction between the irrealis and negation: all negated clauses irrespective of their temporal setting are obligatorily marked for the irrealis mood. From a semantic point of view, an event not occurring either in the past or future setting corresponds to non-actual facts. Given this close association between negation and irrealis-related events, I will discard the tripartite negation pattern, proposing instead that the phonologically reduced irrealis marker *-s-* combines with the negative discontinuous markers *-be-* and *-te* to express negation in Nese.

5. THE VERB COMPLEX

Table 5.3: Negated realis and irrealis subject cross-index forms

Person/number	Cross-indexes			
	Realis	Negated realis forms	Irrealis	Negated irrealis forms
1SG	nV-	j-be-Verb-te	dV-, jV-	j-be-Verb-te
2SG	kho-	kho-s-be-Verb-te	kho-s-	kho-s-be-Verb-te
3SG	Ø	Ø-s-be-Verb-te	Ø-s-, ba-	Ø-s-be-Verb-te
1PL INCL	rrV-	rrV-s-be-Verb-te	rrV-sV-	rrV-s-be-Verb-te
1PL EXCL	bVrr	bVrr-s-be-Verb-te	bVrr-sV-	bVrr-s-be-Verb-te
2PL	kirr	kirr-s-be-Verb-te	kVrr-sV-	kirr-s-be-Verb-te
3PL	rrV	rrV-s-be-Verb-te	rrV-sV-	rrV-s-be-Verb-te

In example (5.32), it is from the time adverbial *benanev* 'yesterday' in the previous clause that the temporal setting of the event is deduced. The intransitive verb *v'an* 'go' is negated and simultaneously marked for the irrealis mood in the 1SG person.

5.32   *Benanev   no-khro   buro   laine.*   **J-be-v'en-te**

yesterday   1SG:REAL-stay   GENMOD   house:LOC   1SG:IRR-NEG1-go-NEG2

'Yesterday I just stayed at home. I did not go

lanus.

bush:LOC

to the bush.'

(2014_01_19 naanhy01001 00:00:03.000-00:00:07.000 natural text)

Semantically speaking, the event of going to the bush had not occurred in the real world at a point in time prior to the time of utterance and is, therefore, compatible with non-factual events. The interaction between the irrealis and negation in negated statements has been observed in Caddo, the Northern Iroquoian language of North America where all negative propositions are marked for irrealis (Mithun, 1995, p. 382).

In (5.33), the stative verb *lemje* 'a lot' is also marked for irrealis when negated even though the state expressed was manifested in a past time frame.

5.33   *Kanan   bir-s-be-lemje-te.*

1PLEXCL   1PLEXCL-IRR-NEG1-a.lot-NEG2

'There weren't a lot of us.'

(2014_01_19 naanhy01001 00:11:12.000-00:11:14.000 natural text)

201

In relation to the operation of the negative discontinuous marker *s-be-*Verb-*te* in verb clauses that have object pro-indexes and those that have full noun phrase objects, there is a specified ordering of the negative and object suffixes on the verb stem. When the object is realised by means of the object pro-index, the pro-index is suffixed directly to the verb root and the negative marker *-te* occurs in the slot after the object pro-index, as shown in (5.34) and in ungrammatical (5.35). Often the object pro-index is elided. However, when the object is a full noun phrase, the negative marker is suffixed directly to the verb root and the object noun phrase occupies the position after the second negative discontinuous marker, as illustrated in (5.36).

5.34 *No-rong-o*   *sikha*   *do-num-u,*   *khai*
1SG:REAL-want-3SGOBJ   NEG   1SG:IRR-drink-3SGOBJ   3SG
'I don't like to drink it, he

*s-bo-**num-u**-te.*
IRR-NEG1-drink-3SGOBJ-NEG2
does not drink it.'
(2014_01_19 naanhy01001 00:52:35.000-00:52:37.000 natural text)

5.35 **No-rong-o*   *sikha*   *do-num-u,*   *khai*
1SG:REAL-want-3SGOBJ   NEG   1SG:IRR-drink-3SGOBJ   3SG
'I don't like to drink it, he

s-be-num-te-u.
IRR-NEG1-drink-NEG2-3SGOBJ
does not drink it.'
(Fieldnotes, elicitation)

5.36 *Khai*   *send-en*   *buro,*   *khai*   ***s-be-**num-**te***
3SG   PERS.PRON-3SG   GEN.MOD   3SG   IRR-NEG1-drink-NEG2
'Only he himself, he does not drink

nanalokh.
kava
kava.'
(2014_01_19 naanhy01001 00:51:14.000-00:51:18.000 natural text)

If the object is an independent pronoun, the negation relationship that holds for full noun phrases applies, as shown in (5.37).

5.37 *Tan-an* **Ø-s-be-*les*-*te*** *khai.*
father-3SG:POSS 3SG-IRR-NEG1-see-NEG2 3SG
'His father did not see him.'
(2012_07_05 obaksi01001 00:00:47.000-00:00:49.000 natural text)

When verbs are reduplicated, the verb stem and the reduplicated form are both enclosed by the negative discontinuous markers (5.38).

5.38 *Kirr-**s-be**-rej-rej-**te***.
2PL-IRR-NEG1-REDUP-speak-NEG2
'You (PL) are not talking.'
(Fieldnotes, elicitation)

The negative discontinuous marker operates in a similar manner in relation to nuclear layer serial verbs, where the discontinuous marker encloses both verbs as shown in (5.39).

5.39 *Gregory khai* **Ø-s-be**-*jnejne* *vusokh-**te**.*
Gregory 3SG 3SG-IRR-NEG1-go.fishing be.able-NEG2
'Gregory cannot fish.'
(2014_01_19 naanhy01001 00:25:41.000-00:25:43.000 natural text)

5.5.1.2 Negative verb *sikha*

Nese employs the negative verb *sikha* to negate the existence of something and also in connection with desiderative *rong-* 'want' when it has a complement. The reason for treating *sikha* as a verb is that it may take the aspectual marker *ti*, as illustrated in (5.40), and it may undergo reduplication, a process that mainly affects verbs, as shown in (5.41).

5.40 *Jokh-ok* *neng* *sen* *navle* *khai* **Ø-*ti*-*sikha***
uncle-1SG:POSS name 3SG:POSS month 3SG 3SG:REAL-ASP-NEG
'My uncle, there is no name for months.'
(2012_08_27 obnesp01003 00:06:03.000-00:06:08.000 natural text)

5.41 *Nemerrte* **sikh-sikha**
man REDUP-NEG
'There is no one.'
(2014_01_19 naanhy01001 00:10:49.000-00:10:50.000 natural text)

The only verb that may be negated by *sikha* is *rong-* when it has the meaning of 'want'. As mentioned earlier on, the verb *rong-* may mean 'want', 'like' (5.42) and 'hear' (5.43).

5.42 *Khina* **no-rong** *novusbuak.*
 1SG 1SG:REAL-like taro
 'I like taro.'
 (2012_07_29 elloro01001a 00:00:19.000-00:00:21.000 elicitation)

When the verb has the meaning 'hear', it is negated with the negative discontinuous marker (5.43).

5.43 *Khina* **j-be**-*rong-o*-**te**.
 1SG 1SG:IRR-NEG1-hear-3SGOBJ-NEG2
 'I did not hear it.'
 (Fieldnotes elicitation)

However, when it means 'want' or 'like', it cannot be negated by the negative discontinuous marker but can only be negated with the negative predicate *sikha*, as illustrated in examples (5.44) to (5.46). Ungrammatical constructions are given with their intended meanings.

5.44 *Khina* *no-rong-o* **sikha** *de-v'an.*
 1SG 1SG:REAL-want-3SGOBJ NEG 1SG:IRR-go
 'I do not want to go.'
 (2014_01_19 naanhy01001 00:04:29.000-00:04:30.000 natural text)

5.45 *Khina *jbe-rong-o* *sikha* *de-v'an.*
 1SG 1SG:IRR-want-3SGOBJ NEG 1SG:IRR-go
 'I will not want to go.'
 (Fieldnotes, elicitation)

5.46 *No-rong-o* **sikha** *novusbuak.*
 1SG:REAL-like-3SGOBJ NEG taro
 'I do not like taro.'
 (2012_06_22 elrojo01002 00:00:21.000-00:00:22.000 natural text)

While it is primarily treated as verbal, negative *sikha* has a couple of properties that render it non-verbal. Although cases such as example (5.46) may be interpreted as involving zero subject cross-indexes, Nese does not permit *sikha* to take any of the subject cross-indexes, or indeed the potential mood marker *-ba-*.

5.5.2 Dehortative mood marker *khota*

Nese employs a preposed dehortative mood marker *khota* to express, firstly, the unlikelihood of an event to happen and, secondly, the imperative mood that also includes giving warning. Expression of the former is characterised by the dehortative marker occurring in conjunction with the negative discontinuous marker. The possibility that an event will not happen encodes the meaning of 'may not', 'is not likely' and 'won't' or 'will not'. Therefore, it is not surprising that negation, which inherently involves the irrealis mood, is employed in conjunction with *khota*.

In (5.47) and (5.48), *khota* occupies the position preceding NEG1 and may also have the meaning 'may not come' and 'be full' respectively.

5.47   *Re-ve*   *'no, lana*   **khota**   *Ø-se-be-me-te*
       3PL:REAL-say   No Lana   DEHORT   3SG-IRR-NEG1-come-NEG2
       'They said, "No Lana won't come

       khe.'
       DEM
       here".'
       (2014_01_19 naanhy01001 00:06:11.000-00:06:14.000 natural text)

5.48   *…seve*   *sikha*   **khota**   *s-bo-won-te*   *khe.*
       if   NEG   DEHORT   IRR-NEG1-be.full-NEG2   DEM
       '…if not one really won't be full.'
       (2014_01_19 naanhy01001 00:02:41.000-00:02:43.000 natural text)

In contrast when *khota* is used with non-negated verbs, it encodes the imperative mood, expressing the giving of an order or command. The imperative mood captures meanings such as 'must not', 'should not'. In these constructions, *khota* still occupies a preverbal position; however, interestingly, the verb occurring after the particle can only be marked for realis mood and not for the irrealis mood. This is illustrated in (5.49).

5.49 *Re-ve*   '*mama*   **khota**   *kho-naturr.*'
3PL:REAL-say   Mum   DEHORT   2SG:REAL-sleep
'They said, "Mum don't sleep!"'/ 'They said, "Mum you mustn't sleep!"'.
(2014_01_19 naanhy01001 00:15:51.000-00:15:52.000 natural text)

Evidence suggests that in constructions containing verbs in sequences, the dehortative marker has scope over all the verbs in sequence and, although it is obligatory for the initial verb to be marked for realis only, this requirement does not hold for the following verbs. Contrast examples (5.50) and (5.51).

5.50 **Khota**   **kho-ma**   **kho-rej**   *min-a.*
DEHORT   2SG:REAL-come   2SG:REAL-talk   PREP-1SGOBJ
'Don't you come and talk to me!'
(2014_01_19 naanhy01001 00:06:39.000-00:06:41.000 natural text)

5.51 **Khota**   **kho-bat**-*e*   **ri-si**-*ma*   **ri-si**-*terev*
DEHORT   2SG:REAL-make-3SGOBJ   3PL-IRR-come   3PL-IRR-wait
'Don't you make them come and wait

khunokh.
you

for you!' (literally, 'Don't you make it so they'll come and wait for you.')
(2014_01_19 naanhy01001 00:16:06.000-00:16:08.000 natural text)

5.5.3 Prohibitive *orro*

Nese employs the prohibitive *orro* to signal a prohibition. It may be used in conjunction with a verb that is marked for realis and irrealis mood, as illustrated in (5.52) and (5.53) respectively.

5.52 *Kani*   **orro**   *kirr-worr*   *sana.*
2PL   PROHIB   2PL:REAL-eat   today
'Today you guys are forbidden to eat.'
(Fieldnotes, elicitation)

As shown in (5.52), prohibitive *orro* occupies the position immediately before the subject cross-index, a property that is also characteristic of the dehortative marker. If an independent pronoun is present in preverbal position, it occupies the slot before prohibitive *orro*.

Orro may also be used to express the prohibition of events happening in the future. This is illustrated in (5.53) where the time adverbial *nev'khe* 'tomorrow' and the 2PL irrealis cross-index indicate a future time reference.

5.53	Kani	**orro**	kirr-se-worr	nev'khe.
	2PL	PROHIB	2PL-IRR-eat	tomorrow

'Tomorrow you guys will not eat.'
(Fieldnotes, elicitation)

At this stage, there is not enough data to account for why two different moods may be used with the prohibitive marker. However, a plausible analysis is that in example (5.52) the time frame associated with the adverb 'today' has already begun and, therefore, the prohibition has begun at the time of speech. When the whole event is set in the future, as shown in example (5.53), the irrealis mood is used instead. In contrast with the dehortative marker, the prohibitive marker is never used with negated verbs as shown in (5.54), in which the translation given is the intended meaning had the construction been grammatical.

5.54	*Kani	**orro**	kirr-s-be-worr-te	nev'khe.
	2PL	PROHIB	2PL-IRR-NEG1-eat-NEG2	tomorrow

'Tomorrow you guys won't eat.'
(Fieldnotes, elicitation)

5.5.4 Directionals

Directionals modify verbs by adding spatial meaning. There are two subclasses of directionals as described in §3.10 and these consist of the subclass containing the transitive verbs *ma* 'come' and *v'an* 'go', which add a directional meaning when occurring as the second verb in a serial verb construction. The other subclass consists of spatial deictics, which give directional meaning to a verb but which do not occur as part of a serial verb construction. The former is discussed in §5.6.1.3 while those in the latter subclass are discussed below.

Generally, the directional *atan* 'down' indicates a physical location that is at a downward direction relative to the speaker's position or a position that is at a downward direction. This is illustrated in (5.55).

5.55 *Ne-vita-i* **atan**.
1SG:REAL-put-3SGOBJ down
'I put it down.'
(Fieldnotes, elicitation)

The directional *atan* also signifies a decrease in intensity or strength as illustrated in (5.56).

5.56 *Nakhad khai Ø-ti-v'an* **atan**, *ne-lev*
fire 3SG:REAL-go 3SG:REAL-ASP-go down 1SG:REAL-take
'The fire has gone down, I am taking

nadatav…'
breadfruit
the breadfruit…'
(2012_06_12 obaksi01001 00:01:19.000-00:01:21.000 natural text)

In (5.56), while *atan* encodes a downward physical direction in relation to the initial height of the fire, it also encodes a decrease in the intensity or strength of the fire.

The directional *maro* means 'up'. This is illustrated in (5.57).

5.57 *Ø-v'an* **maro**
3SG:REAL-go up
'He went up.'
(2014_01_19 naanhy01001 00:09:31.000 natural text)

Vila indicates a seaward direction, as illustrated in (5.58).

5.58 *Khina naleng je-klaik nani s-ak ev'an*
1SG maybe 1SG:IRR-look for coconut CLGEN-1SG:POSS DIR
'As for me, maybe I will go and look for my coconuts there down

vila.
DIR
at the sea.'
(2014_01_19 naanhy01001 00:58:12.000-00:58:16.000 natural text)

The directional *vokhte* means 'inland', and this is illustrated in (5.59).

5.59 Khar   ri-vial   **vokhte**.
     3PL   3PL:REAL-walk   inland
     'They walked inland.'
     (Fieldnotes, elicitation)

5.5.5 Multiplicatives

Nese uses two derivational prefixes *vakha* and *to* in association with numerals to indicate that an event has occurred a specific number of times. The prefix *vakha* is used with numerals two to six, as illustrated in (5.60), and *to* is used on numbers seven to 10, as illustrated in example (5.61). No other numerals carry any multiplicative prefix.

5.60 Ne-v'an   **vakha**-ru,   j-be-les-i.
     1SG:REAL-go   MULT-two   1SG:REAL-see-3SGOBJ
     'I went twice but I did not see it.'
     (Fieldnotes, elicitation)

5.61 Ne-v'an   **to**-sangav'il.
     1SG:REAL-go   MULT-ten
     'I went ten times.'
     (Fieldnotes elicitation)

5.5.6 Emphatic *khe*

The demonstrative *khe* can modify heads of verb complexes. When it modifies head verbs, *khe* functions as an emphatic particle rather than as a demonstrative indicating spatial direction or location. In (5.62), *khe* adds emphasis to the proposition that the person spoken about will really come; whereas, in (5.63), where modifying *khe* is absent, an emphatic reading cannot be deduced.

5.62 Khai   Ø-ve   Ø-se-ma   **khe**.
     3SG   3SG:REAL-say   3SG-IRR-come   DEM
     'She said that she will really come.'
     (2014_01_19 naanhy01001 00:06:16.000-00:06:18.000 natural text)

5.63 *Khai*   *Ø-ve*   *Ø-se-ma.*
3SG   3SG:REAL-say   3SG-IRR-come
'She said that she will come.'
(Fieldnotes, elicitation)

In intransitive clauses, *khe* may be the right-most delimiter, as shown in (5.64).

5.64 *Khai*   *Ø-khro*   **navon**   **buro**   **khe**.
3SG   3SG:REAL-stay   aimless   GENMOD   EMP
'She really just stayed aimlessly.'
(2014_01_19 naanhy01001 00:17:04.000-00:17:06.000 natural text)

5.65 *Ne-yat*   *khe*   **buro**.
1SG:REAL-sit   SPAT   just
'I just sat there.'
(2014_01_19 naanhy01001 00:32:27.000-00:32:29.000 natural text)

A difference in meaning can be deduced when *khe* occurs in conjunction with other modifiers, delimiting the right-most position, and when it occupies the position immediately after the verb head. As shown in (5.64), *khe* has an emphatic meaning contrasting with its position in (5.65) where a spatial interpretation is deduced.

Determining the status of *khe* in a transitive clause containing an object pro-index modified by *khe* is quite tricky, given that both the verb and object pro-index are within the scope of modification. However, a possible test to verify whether *khe* modification in such constructions (5.66) is a genuine modification of the verb head rather than the object pro-index lies in the order of modifying elements that can modify an object noun phrase.

5.66 *Teb'-ne*   *khai*   *Ø-rongvuson-i*   **khe**.
Grandfather-3SG:POSS   3SG   3SG:REAL-understand-3SGOBJ   DEM
'Her grandfather, he does understand it.'
(2014_01_19 00:13:26.000-00:13:29.000 natural text)

For comparison, modification of an object NP by *khe* is characterised by its position immediately after the object NP with other modifying elements occurring after, as shown in (5.67). In these cases, there is a rigid and tight relationship between the object NP and *khe* as there are no examples in such constructions where *khe* occupies the right-most delimiter position with other modifying elements intervening between itself and the verb.

5.67 *Rri-si-woj*   *nebet nakhav* **khe**   **buro**   *rri-natur.*
      1PLINCL-IRR-eat bread   DEM   GENMOD   1PLINCL:REAL-sleep
      'We'll just eat this bread and then sleep.'
      (2014_01_19 naanhy01001 00:00:29.000-00:00:31.000 natural text)

Unfortunately, none of the examples in the data where *khe* occurs after an object pro-index display any other modifying elements such as *buro* occupying a position after *khe,* the presence of which would be in strong favour of an analysis supporting *khe* modifying the object pro-index.

5.5.7 Adverbs

As stated in §3.6, Nese has manner adverbs, aspectual adverbs and adverbs of intensification that modify heads of verb complexes. These were outlined in Table 3.20 but are repeated here in Table 5.4 for convenience.

Table 5.4: Verb complex adverbs

Manner		Degree		Aspectual	
monoi	'careless'	*je*	'very'	*di*	'already'
skheskhalekh	'each, one by one'	*jaru*	'too'	*buro*	'yet, still'
khojkhoj	'properly'	*kele*	'again'	*wor*	'yet, still'
sirsir	'quickly'	*lemje*	'a lot'		
navon	'aimless'				
ververik	'slowly'				
ralral	'crazily, crazy'				
jelengi	'completely'				

5.5.7.1 Manner adverbs

Some of the lexemes classed as manner adverbs can function as stative intransitive verbs; therefore, they will be discussed in §5.6.1.1 and §5.6.2. These include *khojkhoj* 'proper', *sirsir* 'quickly' and *ralral* 'crazily, crazy'. A manner adverb, occupying a post-verbal position, describes the way in which an action is carried out. This is illustrated in (5.68), in which the adverb *monoi* 'carelessly' indicates that the action expressed by the verb was done carelessly.

5.68	Khai	Ø-bat-e		***monoi***.
	3SG	3SG:REAL-make-3SGOBJ		ADV

'She did it carelessly.'
(Fieldnotes, elicitation)

The manner adverb *skheskhalekh* means 'one by one', as shown in (5.69).

5.69	Khar	re-ma	buro	nekrre	lemje	rru-su-mul
	3PL	3PL:REAL-come	GENMOD	1PLINCL	a.lot	3PL-IRR-return

'When they come, then there's lots of us, they'll be leaving

	skheskhalekh	v'an	v'an	Ø-se-rov.
	ADV	go	go	3SG-IRR-finish

one by one until it will be finished.'
(2014_01_19 naanhy01001 00:32:27.000-00:32:29.000 natural text)

The adverb *navon* means 'aimlessly' and it appears after a verb to indicate that an action is performed unnecessarily or to no good effect. This is illustrated in (5.70).

5.70	Khai	Ø-khro	***navon***	buro	khe.
	3SG	3SG:REAL-stay	aimlessly	just	EMP

'He's really just staying aimlessly.'
(2014_01_19 naanhy01001 00:17:04.000-00:17:06.000 natural text)

The adverb *ververik* modifies a verb by adding the meaning of 'in small parts', as shown in (5.71).

5.71	Nekrre	buro	rri-worr	***ververik***	buro.
	1PL	GENMOD	1PL:REAL-eat	small parts	GENMOD

'It was just us, we ate in small parts.'
(2014_01_19 naanhy01001 00:15:04.000-00:15:07.000 natural text)

5.5.7.2 Degree adverbs

In general, degree adverbs express the intensity of an emotion or action and these are listed in Table 5.4 as *je* 'very', *jaru* 'too', *kele* 'again' and *lemje* 'a lot'.

In (5.72), the degree adverb *je* modifies the stative intransitive verb *sat* 'be sad', indicating the degree to which the subject feels sad.

5.72 | Khai | Ø-ti-rongo-o | | sat | ***je.***
 | 3SG | 3SG:REAL-ASP-feel-3SGOBJ | | be.sad | very

'She feels really sad.'

(Fieldnotes, elicitation)

When it modifies a transitive verb whose object is expressed by a lexical noun phrase, the degree adverb *je* occurs immediately after the verb and before the lexical noun phrase object, as illustrated in (5.73).

5.73 | Khina | no-rong-o | | sikha | te | kirr-bo-khro
 | 1SG | 1SG:REAL-want-3SGOBJ | | NEG | SUB | 2PL:REAL-POT-stay

'I don't want you guys to stay

neten | te | kirr-kot | ***je*** | nanalokh.
PURP2 | SUB | 2PL:REAL-do | very | kava

because you do a lot of kava.'

(2014_01_19 naanhy01001 00:21:00.000-00:21:05.000 natural text)

The degree adverb *jaru* 'too' is also used to express the intensity of a state and it is always used in conjunction with the degree adverb *je*. This is illustrated in (5.74).

5.74 | Seve | khina | khe | khota | j-be-ve-te | | tejiblakh
 | COND | 1SG | DEM | DEHORT | 1SG-IRR:NEG1-be-NEG2 | | children

'If it was me, I would not tell the children

ma | rengen | nuak | neten | te | nuak | khe | Ø-ti-velvele
come | LOC | boat | because | SUB | boat | DEM | 3SG:REAL-ASP-be.small

to come in the boat because it is small

jaru je.
too very

so very small.'

(2014_01_19 naanhy01001 01:05:04.000-00:05:12.000 natural text)

The adverb *lemje* 'a lot' behaves in a similar manner as *jaru* in that it only modifies intransitive stative verbs and is used in conjunction with the degree adverb *je*. This is illustrated in (5.75).

5.75 *Nav'anu*   *Ø-ti-vavang*   ***lemje***   ***je***.
place   3SG:REAL-ASP-open   a.lot   very
'The place is so very open.'
(2014_01_19 naanhy01001 01:05:04.000-00:23:36.000 natural text)

The adverb *kele* 'again' indicates another occurrence of the action expressed by the verb. This is illustrated in (5.76).

5.76 *Nat-uk*   *Ø-se-volvol*   ***kele***   *khin*   *nuak*   *khe*.
Child-1SG:POSS   3SG-IRR-sell   again   PREP1   boat   DEM
'My child will sell this boat again.'
(2014_01_2014 naanhy01001 00:20:34.000-00:20:36.000 natural text)

5.5.7.3 Aspectual adverbs

Aspectual adverbs in Nese are *wor* 'yet, still', *di* 'already' and *buro* 'just'. As stated in §3.16, the lexemes *wor* and *buro* also function as modifiers of NP heads; therefore, they are glossed as general modifiers.

The continuative *wor* indicates that an ongoing action is still continuing, as illustrated in (5.77).

5.77 *Khai*   *Ø-khuskhus*   ***wor***.
3SG   3SG:REAL-move   still
'It is still moving.'
(2014_01_19 naanhy01001 00:39:55.000-00:39:58.000 natural text)

When *wor* occurs with the discontinuous negative markers, it has a 'not yet' meaning, indicating that an action has still not happened. This is illustrated in (5.78).

5.78 *Khai*   *Ø-s-be-sukul-te*   ***wor***.
3SG   3SG-IRR-NEG1-school-NEG2   still
'He still has not gone to school still.'
(2014_01_19 naanhy01001 00:37:40.000-00:37:43.000 natural text)

In (5.78), the verb *sukul* is intransitive and it is enclosed by both negative discontinuous markers with the adverbial general modifier *wor* occupying the slot after NEG2. Lexical NP objects occupy the position in between NEG2 and *wor*, as shown in (5.79).

5.79 *John   khai   Ø-se-be-num-te   nanalokh   wor.*
      John   3SG   3SG-IRR-NEG1-drink-NEG2   kava   yet
      'John has not drank kava yet.'
      (Fieldnotes, elicitation)

The aspectual *di* indicates that an action has already taken place. This is illustrated in (5.80) where *di* occurs in a post-verbal position after the object pro-index.

5.80 *Ri-var-i   **di**   bentaru.*
      3PL:REAL-tell-3SGOBJ   already   two days ago
      'They already said it two days ago.'
      (2014_01_19 naanhy01001 00:58:52.000-00:58:57.000 natural text)

When an object is expressed by means of a lexical noun phrase, the adverb *di* also occurs after the lexical noun phrase object. This is shown in (5.81).

5.81 *Ne-ver   tenge   jelekh   **di**.*
      1SG:REAL-say   thing   all   already
      'I've already said everything.'
      (2012_07_12 obaksi01001 00:25:42.000-00:25:43.000 natural text)

The adverbial general modifier *buro* 'just' may modify active intransitive verbs, as shown in (5.82).

5.82 *Nemere   khar   ro-khro   **buro**   ro-rong-o.   sikha…*
      people   3PL   3PL:REAL-stay   just   3PL:REAL-3SGOBJ   NEG
      'The people are just there but they don't want to.'
      (2014_01_19 naanhy01001 00:11:19.000-00:11:22.000 natural text)

The adverbial general modifier may also modify heads of verb complexes that are stative intransitive verbs, as shown in (5.83).

5.83 *Natas   Ø-ti-tamat   **buro**,   be   Ø-ti-naralon.*
      sea   3SG:REAL-ASP-be.calm   just   CONJ   3SG:REAL-ASP-drown
      'The sea was just calm but it drowned.'
      (2014_01_10 naanhy01001 00:06:18.000-01:06:22.000 natural text)

When *buro* modifies a transitive verb head whose object is expressed by means of the object pro-index, the adverb occurs after the object pro-index. This is illustrated in (5.84).

5.84	*Ro-kol-o*	*ma*	*ru-sul-u*	***buro***	*laine.*
3PL:REAL-bring-3SGOBJ	come	3PL:REAL-burn-3SGOBJ	just	house:LOC

'They brought it over and they just burnt it at home.'
(2012_08_22 anhy01005 00:02:24.000-00:02:27.000 natural text)

This also applies to transitive verb heads, which have lexical noun phrase objects, as illustrated in (5.85).

5.85	*Rri-woj*	*nebetnakhav*	*khe*	***buro***.
1PLINCL:REAL-eat	bread	DEM	just

'We'll just eat this bread.'
(2014_01_19 naanhy01001 00:00:29.000-00:00:31.000 natural text)

The fact that the adverb *buro* is placed after the noun phrase suggests that it is modifying the lexical noun phrase object only, rather than modifying the verb head. In fact, this would be a more appropriate analysis given that *buro* adds the meaning of singling out 'bread' as the item for eating as opposed to any other food items, rather than stating that they should eat as opposed to doing anything else, such as baking the bread. When *buro* modifies an intransitive active and a stative verb (examples (5.82) and (5.83) respectively), it is clear that it has within its scope the head verb; however, this clarity is not evident with transitive verbs functioning as the head verb with lexical noun phrase objects.

5.5.7.4 *Mu* 'no longer'

The form *mu* is only attested in negative contexts to mean 'no longer'. It is used to indicate the cessation and discontinuing of a habitual action or event that a subject has been performing or used to perform. This is illustrated in examples (5.86), (5.87) and (5.88) where actions performed by the subject on a habitual basis have ceased and are no longer continuing.

5.86	*Khai*	*Ø-se-be-num-te*	***nanalokh***	***mu***.
3SG	3SG-IRR-NEG1-drink-NEG2	kava	no.longer

'He no longer drinks kava.'
(Fieldnotes, elicitation)

In (5.86), the lexical noun phrase object occurs after NEG2 when *mu* co-occurs with the negative discontinuous markers. However, when the object is expressed via the object pro-index, it occupies a VC internal position before NEG2, as illustrated in (5.88).

5.87 Nalang khai Ø-se-be-sirsir-**ia**-te   **mu**   terrterr.
      wind   3SG 3SG-IRR-NEG1-blow-1SGOBJ-NEG2   no.longer strong
      'The wind is not blowing me strongly anymore.'
      (2012_08_22 anhy012 00:17:28.000-00:17:31.000 natural text)

In (5.88), the head verb modified by *mu* is composed of a transitive verb and an intransitive stative verb in serial formation.

5.88 Ø-bet   tangatarr v'an v'an Ø-se-**bet-khojkhoj**-te
      3SG:REAL-make thing   go   go   3SG-IRR-mek-be.proper-NEG2
      'He made all things for some time but he did not do it properly

   mu...
   no.longer
   anymore...'
   (2014_01_19 naanhy01001 00:46:09.000-00:46:14.000 natural text)

5.5.8 Completive *rov*

The marker *rov* expresses a completive meaning. It can be used with verbs marked for the irrealis mood, as in (5.89), and those marked for the realis mood, as shown in (5.90).

5.89 Rri-si-vita-i   khojkhoj   v'an   **rov**   ale
      1PLINCL-IRR-put-3SGOBJ be proper   go   COMPL   CONJ
      'We'll put it properly (once that is done) then

   rri-si-bing-i.
   1PLINCL-IRR-fasten-3SGOBJ
   we'll fasten it.'
   (2012_07_12 obaksi01001 00:16:11.000-00:16:15.000 natural text)

5.90 Ri-ma   **rov**   ale   iniekhe   je-lav-i,
      3PL:REAL-come   COMPL   CONJ   now   1SG:REAL-pull-3SGOBJ
      'They came then now I will pull

   neveng.
   thatch
   the thatch.'
   (2012_07_12 obaksi01001 00:02:33.000-00:02:41.000 natural text)

The completive marker is usually followed by the conjunction *ale* and this indicates the commencement of the next action, upon completion of the current one.

5.5.9 Aspectual -*ti*-

The generic aspectual marker -*ti*- is a preverbal prefix, expressing a couple of perfective meanings and a broad range of aspectual distinctions, which are strictly associated with a non-future temporal setting. Furthermore, the prefix bears a conjunction-like property, denoting sequentiality of events in main clauses, with a further unexplained obligatory role in subordinate clauses. Only occurring with the 3SG, 3PL and 2PL subject cross-index, if data on the two latter persons and numbers was absent, its position in the 3SG would be debatable given the nullity of the 3SG subject cross-index, as shown in (5.91) and (5.92).

5.91 *Tavu* ***ti**-Ø-natur* *latas.*
coneshell ASP-3SG:REAL-sleep sea:LOC
'The coneshell slept in the sea.'
(2012_05_16 obanhy01004 00:00:07.000-00:00:09.000 natural text)

5.92 *Tavu* *Ø-**ti**-natur* *latas.*
coneshell 3SG:REAL-ASP-sleep sea:LOC
'The coneshell slept in the sea.'
(2012_05_16 obanhy01004 00:00:07.000-00:00:09.000, natural text)

However, as shown in (5.93), the 3PL realis subject cross-index is affixed onto -*ti*-, which means that in cases where the 3SG realis subject cross-index is Ø, Nese prefers the pattern in which -*ti*- occurs after the 3SG subject cross-index.

5.93 *Khai* *khe,* ***rri-ti**-ver* *Gregory* *khe,* ***kirr-ti**-ve*
3SG DEM 3PL:REAL-ASP-say Gregory DEM 2PL:REAL-ASP-say
'That one, they said that Gregory, you people say that

khai *Ø-jnejne?*
3SG 3SG:REAL-fish
he fishes?'
(2014_01_19 naanhy01001 00:47:04.000-00:47:08.000 natural text)

5.94 *Mama   mama   khota   kho-natur   Lana   Ø-**ti**-ma.*
mother mother DEHORT   2SG:REAL-sleep Lana   3SG:REAL-ASP-come
'Mother, mother, don't sleep, Lana has come.'
(2014_01_19 naanhy01001 00:15:51.000-00:15:54.000 natural text)

With respect to the aspectual distinctions, *-ti-* expresses a resultative perfect meaning making reference to a present state that is a result of some past event. Such instantiations are referred to as the perfect of result (Comrie, 1976). Thus *-ti-ma* in (5.94) has the meaning 'has come', which means that Lana is now here and, therefore, there is an inherent notion of current relevance at the time the speech was uttered. Furthermore, it expresses a perfect of persistent situation as defined in Comrie (1976, p. 60) in which a described event occurred in the past and still obtains in the present. This is illustrated in (5.95) where the *-ti-vitai* refers to the act of 'putting the paper', which occurred in the past and at the time of the speech the paper was still present at that location where it had been placed. This construction could also be translated as 'She'll come for the paper which she had left here'.

5.95 *Ø-se-ma   khin   noroblat   sa-n   te*
3SG-IRR-come   PREP I   paper   CLGEN-3SG:POSS   SUB
'She'll come for her paper which

*Ø-**ti**-vita-i   iekhe.*
3SG:REAL-ASP-put-3SGOBJ   DEM, LOC
she left here.'
(2013_01_19 naanhy01001 00:16:23.000-00:16:26.000 natural text)

Apart from these two perfective distinctions, *-ti-* also expresses the progressive aspect associated with events or actions that have occurred in the past and also in the present. In (5.96), the event of the sun going down is occurring at the time of speech; that is, in the present tense.

5.96 *Khai   khe,   ne-les-i   neten   te   nial   Ø-**ti**-v'an*
3SG   DEM   1SG:REAL-see-3SGOBJ   PURP2   SUB   sun   3SG:REAL-ASP-go
'That one, I saw him because the sun is going

atan.
dir
down.'
(2014_01_19 naanhy01001 00:38:22.000-00:38:26.000 natural text)

Furthermore, it is used to denote actions set in the past. This is illustrated in (5.97).

5.97 *Wolei! sori merte nge **Ø-ti**-nes botvon.*
Oh sorry man DEM 3SG:REAL-ASP-die fruitlessly
'Oh, that's sad! That man died fruitlessly.'
(2014_01_19 naanhy01001 00:46:03.000-00:46:08.000 natural text)

Lastly, it may denote actions set in the present, as shown in (5.98).

5.98 *Khar re-se-v'an rengen nuak velvele khe*
3PL 3PL-IRR-go LOC boat small DEM
'They will go in that small boat

***Ø-ti-khro** Tontar khe.*
3SG:REAL-ASP-exist Tontar EMP
it's really at Tontar.'
(2014_01_19 naanhy01001 00:18:26.000-00:18:29.000 natural text)

Aspectual *-ti-* also has a conjunction-like use, as shown in (5.99), where it is employed to express a sequence of actions expressed by the verb. This conjunction-like property is the basis for Takau's (2016) position for a possible origin from the extinct Nese conjunction *din*.

5.99 *Naskhe sakhal rrun tavu sakhal ro-khro Lewor,*
kingfisher one CONJ coneshell one 3PL:REAL-stay Lewor
'There was once a kingfisher and a coneshell who lived at Lewor,

*rengen nasale. Tavu Ø-**ti**-natur latas, naskhe*
LOC anchorage coneshell 3SG:REAL-ASP-sleep sea:LOC kingfisher
at the anchorage. The coneshell slept in the sea, the kingfisher

*Ø-**ti**-yat maro rengen nekhere-n nenibor sakhal,*
3SG:REAL-ASP-sit DIR LOC branch-3SG:POSS Nenibor one

was up on a dry branch of a Nenimbor tree,

*Ø-**ti**-narang. Tavu Ø-**ti**-natur latas*
3SG:REAL-ASP-be.dry coneshell 3SG:REAL-ASP-sleep sea:LOC
it was dry. The coneshell sleeping in the sea,

*Ø-**ti**-rong...*
3SG:REAL-ASP -hear
heard...
(2012_05_16 obanahy01004 00:00:01.000-00:00:22.000 natural text)

In (5.99), *-ti-* is used in the second and subsequent clauses, a property that is also characteristic of the conjunction *din*, given that it never fills the slot preceding the predicate of initial clauses.

The data also demonstrate the use of *-ti-* in clauses where the relationship between the propositions is not sequential but rather when one of the clauses enters into a subordinate relationship with the matrix clause. This is illustrated in example (5.100) where *-ti-* is affixed to a verb root in the subordinate clause. Its absence would render the construction ungrammatical, as shown in example (5.101).

5.100 | *Khai* | *Ø-ve* | *tenge* | *khokhorr* | *sakhal* | *khe,* |
|---|---|---|---|---|---|
| 3SG | 3SG:REAL-say | thing | hard | one | DEM |

'It is one difficult work

neten	*te*	*nale*	*Ø-**ti**-rov*	*di.*
PURP2	SUB	language	3SG:REAL-ASP-finish	already

because the language is already finished.'
(2014_01_19 naanhy01001 00:07:11.000-00:07:16.000 natural text)

5.101 | **Khai* | *Ø-ve* | *tenge* | *khokhorr* | *sakhal* | *khe,* |
|---|---|---|---|---|---|
| 3SG | 3SG:REAL-say | thing | hard | one | DEM |

'It is one difficult work

neten	*te*	*nale*	*Ø-rov*	*di.*
PURP2	SUB	language	3SG:REAL-finish	already

because the language is already finished.'
(Fieldnotes, elicitation)

The scenario is far more complex as evidence suggests that when the subject noun phrase in the subordinate clause is a focused constituent, involving the co-occurrence of the lexical noun phrase with its corresponding independent pronoun as in (5.102), and the aspectual *-ti-* is not present, the construction is ungrammatical. However, when aspectual *-ti-* is present, the construction is grammatical, as shown in (5.103).

5.102 *... | neten | te | **nause** | khai | Ø-use.
| PURP2 | SUB | rain | 3SG | 3SG:REAL-rain.

(Fieldnotes, elicitation)

5.103 ... | neten | te | **nause** | Ø-**ti**-use | | je.
| PURP2 | SUB | rain | 3SG:REAL-ASP-to.rain | | very

'...because it rained heavily.'
(2014_naanhy01001 00:14:29.000-00:14:31.000 natural text)

Conversely, with respect to subordinate clauses containing the intransitive stative verb *velvele* 'small', the presence or absence of *-ti-* has no bearing on whether or not the subject noun phrase is focused or not, the constructions are still grammatical, as shown in (5.104) and (5.105) respectively.

5.104 ... | neten | te | **nuak** | **khe** | Ø-**velvele** | jaru | je.
| PURP2 | SUB | boat | DEM | 3SG:REAL-small | too | very

'...because the boat was way too small.'
(2014_01_19 naanhy01001 01:04:13.000-01:04:18.000 natural text)

5.105 ... | neten | te | **nuak** | Ø-**ti-velvele** | jaru | je.
| PURP2 | SUB | boat | 3SG:REAL-ASP-small | too | very

'...because the boat was way too small.'
(2014_01_19 naanhy01001 01:05:10.000-01:05:12.000 natural text)

In complement clauses, the presence of *-ti-* is obligatory, as shown in the grammatical example (5.106) and ungrammatical example (5.107).

5.106 *Kho-les* | te | Ø-**ti**-*v'an* | maro | na | bolet | nen.
2SG:REAL-see | SUB | 3SG:REAL-ASP-go | DIR | um | bullet | POSS

'You saw that it went up, um its bullet.'
(2012_06_19 obfaha01001 00:00:32.000-00:00:38.000 natural text)

5.107 **Kho-les* | te | Ø-*v'an* | maro | na | bolet | nen.
2SG:REAL-see | SUB | 3SG:REAL-go | DIR | um | bullet | POSS

(Fieldnotes elicitation)

Crowley (2006c, p. 68) treats aspectual *-ti-* as an alternative 3SG realis subject prefix, which simultaneously performs an unidentified function in the 3PL person. Takau (2016, p. 245) reinforces its status as a subject prefix or subject cross-index, but in attempting to account for its restricted occurrences, suggests that it probably belonged to another extinct paradigm of subject prefixes rather than belonging to the one set of inflectional subject prefixes in Nese. Takau's (2016) attempt to explain its possible origin out of the already extinct clausal coordinator *din* is problematic on several fronts. To begin with, the loss of *din* as a clausal coordinator is a recent phenomenon,[1] and, therefore, an explanation must be sought to account for how its existence as a preverbal free form can undergo gradual loss and eventually end up as a prefix occupying the slot between the subject cross-index and the verb. In addition, *din* is replaced by the Bislama *ale*, and there are instances in the current data where *ale* is used as a conjunction with the immediately following clause containing the preverbal prefix *-ti-*, for example (5.108).

5.108 *Ø-ti-nas*   **ale**   *nau-ne*   *Ø-ti-yat*   *maro*
       3SG:REAL-ASP-die   CONJ   spouse-3SG:POSS   3SG:REAL-ASP-sit   up
       'He died and his wife was sitting up

       laine
       house:LOC
       in the house.'
       (2012_05_16 obanhy01005 00:05:13.000-00:05:8.000 natural text)

This cancels out any assumptions regarding *din* undergoing phonological reduction resulting in *-ti-*. The discussion in this subsection showed evidence of two perfective meanings derived from the usage of *-ti-* along with a broad range of other aspectual denotations associated with events set in the past and present tense. The presence of limited perfective denotations suggests that perhaps *-ti-* is a residue of a set of inflectional affixes denoting perfective, deriving from the PMP perfective infix *<in> but whose functional load in Nese has undergone extension to incorporate the progressive aspect. Neighbouring Vënen Taut has a similar perfective prefix *t(ë)*, which is never used with verbs marked for the irrealis but denotes action that has been carried out in the past (Dodd, 2015, p. 103).

---

1   The reason why I propose that loss of *din* is a recent phenomenon is because the oldest Nese speakers remember clearly that it was used before and prior to one particular recording session in 2012, they discussed and purposed amongst themselves to use *din* instead of *ale* during the recording.

5.5.10 Potential -*ba*-

Nese employs the prefix -*ba*- to express the potential mood. Like aspectual -*ti*-, it is primarily associated with 3SG subjects; however, it is also attested with subjects in 2SG person (35 times in the corpus), 2PL person (36 times) and 1PL inclusive person (35 times). There are no examples in the data in which -*ba*- co-occurs with the 1SG forms. In example (5.109), -*ba*- is shown as co-occurring with the 1PL, 3SG and 2SG persons.

5.109 *Nekrre   rov   jelekh   **rri-be**-rej-rej   min-i,*
      1PL   COMP   all   1PL-POT-REDUP-speak   PREP-3SGOBJ
      'All of us, the whole lot, would speak it,

   *khai   Ø-ba-nakis   bel**ek**   te   khunokh   **kho-ba**-v'an*
   3SG   3SG-POT-be.good   like   SUB   2SG   2SG-POT-go
   it would be good,

   ***kho-ba**-bal-e.*
   2SG-POT-talk-3SGOBJ
   you will go and speak it.'
   (2014_01_19 naanhy01001 00:07:18.000-00:07:24.000 natural text)

It is clear from example (5.109) that not only does potential -*ba*- fill the same structural slot as the irrealis mood marker, but also it does not encode number. More importantly, the irrealis markers and -*ba*- do not co-occur, inferring a possible contrast in function. A potential or irrealis meaning would be highly in favour of the proposition that -*ba*- is a reflex of the bilabial stop initial Proto Oceanic conjunction *be, which was employed to express subordinating or irrealis conjunction (Moyse-Faurie & Lynch, 2004, p. 487).

At this stage, it is difficult to draw a line distinguishing the functions of -*ba*- and the irrealis mood markers. Generally, -*ba*- asserts a hypothetical situation. A hypothetical situation may be one that has not happened but is desired. This is illustrated by the use of -*ba*- in (5.109), where it is the speaker's wish for the language to be spoken again. In (5.110), a clause taken from (5.109), the POT mood on the verb indicates that the proposition is perceived as a wish or a desired outcome. This desiderative meaning is lacking in (5.111) where the irrealis is used.

5.110 Kho-**ba**-bal-e.
    2SG-POT-speak-3SGOBJ
    'You would speak it.'
    (2014_01_19 naanhy01001 00:07:24.000 natural text)

5.111 Kho-**se**-bal-e.
    2SG-IRR-speak-3SGOBJ
    'You will speak it.'
    (Fieldnotes, elicitation)

The potential mood may also mark a situation that is accepted and acknowledged as not occurring in the real world. This is illustrated in (5.112) where the speaker is questioning who will risk going to the sea to catch fish for her to eat because, in reality, no one is doing that for her.

5.112 Khina   ne-rong   te   de-waj-i   buro,   khise
    1SG   1SG:REAL-want SUB   1SG:IRR-eat-3SGOBJ GENMOD   who
    'As for me, I do want to eat it, who

    ba-suwo   khin-i.
    POT-swim   PREPI-3SGOBJ
    will go and swim for it.'
    (2014_01_19 naanhy01001 00:22:17.000-00:22:23.000 natural text)

Potential *ba-* is not only prefixed to verb roots but is also prefixed to numerals, as shown in (5.113).

5.113 Ne-ve   'Gregory   van   vol   tin   nanaj   **ba**-sakhal,
    1SG:REAL-say Gregory   go   buy   tin   fish   POT-one
    'I said, "Gregory go and buy a can of fish, make it one,

    tekh   na   netenge   makroni   **ba**-ru.
    take   um   thingumy   noodles   POT-two
    take a, thingummy, noodles and make it two".'
    (2014_01_19 naanhy01001 00:01:00.000-00:01:09.000 natural text)

The prefixation of *ba-* onto the numerals *sakhal* 'one' and *ru* 'two' in (5.113) transforms the noun phrase modifiers into verbal elements, giving a hypothetical stative meaning. The adoption of verbal morphology by numerals has also been attested in the Western Oceanic language of Gapapaiwa spoken in Milne Bay, Papua New Guinea (McGuckin, 2011, p. 301).

5.6 Serial verb constructions

Sequences of juxtaposed verbs are common in Nese. Foley and Olson (1985, p. 18) define serial verb constructions (SVCs) as 'constructions in which verbs sharing a common actor or object are merely juxtaposed, with no intervening conjunctions'. SVCs are a well-known phenomenon in Oceanic languages (Crowley, 2007). Nese makes a distinction between nuclear layer SVCs and core layer SVCs and these two layers are defined in line with Foley and Van Valin's (1984) description; that is, the nucleus contains the predicate and the core layer contains the nucleus and its arguments. The current data provides good evidence for the existence of nuclear layer and core layer SVCs.

5.6.1 Nuclear layer SVCs

Nuclear layer SVCs in Nese are constructions in which two or more verbs are juxtaposed, and they are distinguished in Nese from core layer constructions by the behaviour of negation in relation to the serial verbs and by the argument and TAM sharing properties. Firstly, verbs in sequence are independent roots, which if negated are contained within both negative discontinuous markers. Also there is a sharing of both a single set of arguments, both subject and objects, as well as a sharing of same TAM marking. Nese exhibits causative serialisation (§5.6.1.1) and asymmetrical serialisation (§5.6.1.2).

5.6.1.1 Causative serialisation

Causative SVCs are those in which V2 expresses a process or result experienced by the object, while V1 describes the action leading up to or causing the result. An example is given in (5.114) where V1 is a transitive verb while an intransitive stative verb occupies V2 position.

5.114 *Je-**bet*** ***khojkhoj*** *natan.*
1SG:IRR-make be.proper ground
'I will make the ground better.'
(Fieldnotes, elicitation)

In (5.114), the subject of V1 is the 1SG cross-index and the object of transitive V1 occurs after the intransitive stative V2. In other causative SVC constructions involving an active intransitive V2, the lexical noun phrase object also occupies the slot after V2.

5.115 John   Ø-ti-**rub**   **nas**   *namat*.
      John   3SG:REAL-ASP-beat   die   snake
      'John beat the snake to death.'
      (Fieldnotes, elicitation)

In (5.115), a sequential reading cannot be deduced, although this is possible in the serial construction in (5.116) where the verb *nas* occurs after the object.

5.116 John   khai   Ø-**rub**   *namat*   **nas**.
      John   3SG   3SG:REAL-beat   snake   die
      'John beat the snake, (and) it died.'
      (Fieldnotes, elicitation)

5.6.1.2 Asymmetrical nuclear layer serialisation

Asymmetrical nuclear layer serialisation is made up of two verbs in serial formation, the first of which emanates from a large open class while the verbs occurring in V2 are restricted. More specifically, following Aikhenvald (1999, p. 472), the verb from the large class describes the 'single event while the verb from the small closed class provides additional directional or aspectual specification'. In (5.117), V1 is the main verb and V2 may be analysed as providing additional directional information regarding the main verb and not necessarily contributing to a complex event. The 3SG object pro-index is indexing a lexical noun phrase expressed in a previous clause.

5.117 *Rri-si-**takh**-e*   ***v'an***.
      1PLINCL-IRR-take-3SGOBJ   go
      'We will take it there.'
      (2014_01_19 naanhy01001 00:32:01.000-00:32:02.000 natural text)

5.118 *Ne-ve*   *kho-**takh**-e*   ***ma***.
      1SG:REAL-say   2SG:REAL-take-3SGOBJ   come
      'I said take (bring) it here.'
      (2014_01_19 naanhy01001 00:08:36.000 natural text)

The verbs *ma* 'come' and *v'an* 'go', which occupy V2 in constructions (5.117) and (5.118), can also occur as independent main verbs in verb clauses, as shown in (5.119) and (5.120).

5.119 *Rri-**v'an**   lanus.*
1SG:REAL-go   bush:LOC
'We are going to the bush.'
(2012_05_16 obanhy01003 00:00:08.000 natural text)

5.120 *Lana   ri-si-**ma**   khe.*
Lana   3PLINCL-IRR-come   DEM
'Lana them will be coming.'
(2014_01_19 naanhy01001 00:05:56.000-00:05:57.000 natural text)

Nese employs the verb *v'an* in serial formation with other verbs to encode the aspectual durative meaning translated as 'keep on doing' for an unspecified amount of time. The verb that precedes it may be an active intransitive (5.121), a stative intransitive verb (5.122) or a transitive verb (5.123), in which case the 3SG object pro-index is co-referential with a lexical noun phrase in an antecedent clause.

5.121 *Khai   Ø-use   **v'an**   **v'an**   bung.*
3SG   3SG:REAL-rain   go   go   night
'It rained until dark.'
(2014_01_19 naanhy01001 00:00:15.000-00:00:16.000 natural text)

5.122 *Khai   Ø-nakis   **v'an**   **v'an**   **v'an**   Ø-sat.*
3SG   3SG:REAL-good   go   go   go   3SG:REAL-bad
'It was good for some time then it went bad.'
(2014_01_19 naanhy01001 00:22:09.000-00:22:12.000 natural text)

5.123 *Re-jnejne   **v'an**   **v'an**...*
1SG:REAL-make-3SGOBJ   go   go
'They fished for some time...'
(2014_01_19 naanhy01001 00:20:02.000-00:20:04.000 natural text)

When the verb with a durative function follows a transitive verb, it occurs after the object of the verb complex, which may be realised by way of the object pro-index (5.124) or a lexical noun phrase (5.125).

5.124 *Je-var-i* ***v'an*** ***v'an*** *je-rov.*
1SG:IRR-say-3SGOBJ go go 1SG:IRR-finish
'I will say it until I will finish.'
(2014_01_19 naanhy01001 00:28:35.000-00:28:36.000 natural text)

5.125 *Ø-bet* *tangatarr* ***v'an*** ***v'an***
3SG:REAL-make thing go go
'He did the things (to an unspecified point in time)

Ø-s-be-bet-khojkhoj-te *mu.*
3SG-IRR-NEG1-make-be.proper-NEG2 any more
and he no longer did it well.'
(2014_01_19 naanhy01001 00:46:09.000-00:46:13.000 natural text)

At this stage, there is no example in the current data to account for the existence of negated asymmetrical SVCs involving the aspectual durative *v'an,* the continuative *wor* or the completive marker *rov*.

5.6.1.3 Tightly bound nuclear layer serialisation

Nese also has serial verb constructions in which a functional restriction holds regarding forms that may occupy V2 position, where there is no evidence for these forms existing as independent verbs. Four examples of these types of V2 are presented in Table 5.5.

Table 5.5: V2 verbs that cannot be independent verbs

V1	V2	
ver 'say'	*khorr* 'block'	'verbally block'
vitei 'put'	*khorr* 'block'	'physically block' 'engage'
tekh 'take'	*lue* 'out'	'take out'
kol 'carry'	*lue* 'out'	'carry out'
khil 'dig'	*lue* 'out'	'dig out'
rub 'beat'	*vej* 'break'	'smash' 'strike'
rong 'hear'	*vuson* 'ability'	'can hear'
les 'see'	*vuson* 'ability'	'can see'
woj 'eat'	*vuson* 'ability'	'can eat'

When the object is a lexical noun phrase, it occurs after V2, as shown in (5.126) and (5.127).

5.126 Ne-**tekh**   **lue**   sospen   rengen   nakhad.
       1SG:REAL-take   out   saucepan   LOC   fire
       'I removed the saucepan from the fire.'
       (Fieldnotes, elicited)

5.127 Nalangrub   **rub**   **vej**   naine   Ø-ti-jov.
       Hurricane   beat   break   house   3SG:REAL-ASP-fall
       'The hurricane smashed the house and it fell.'
       (2012_08_22 anhy01007 0:04:32.000-00:04:36.000 elicitation)

5.6.2 Core layer serialisation

In Takau (2016), I proposed that while nuclear layer serialisation is easier to identify, the category of core layer SVCs is much more difficult to establish in Nese and, at this stage, there is no convincing evidence to account for its existence. These constructions may be defined on the basis of their ability to have cross-indexes attached to all the verbs in serial formation, as shown in (5.128). However, this is problematic because in Nese subject cross-indexes are always obligatory and where two verbs with similar cross-indexes are juxtaposed side by side, they may be analysed as sequences of independent clauses.

5.128 No-kol-o,   navij,   **ne-tei**
       1SG:REAL-carry-OBJ   banana   1SG:REAL-CUT:3SGOBJ
       'I took it, the banana, I cut it

       ne-vitai   rengen   bak.
       1SG:REAL-put:3SGOBJ   LOC   bag
       I put it inside the bag.'
       (2012_05_16 obanhy01003 00:02:06.000-00:02:10.000 natural text)

In (5.128), the two verbs *tei* 'cut' and the extended transitive verb *vitai* 'put' share the same object and subject, and the subject pro-indexes must be expressed otherwise the construction will be ungrammatical, as shown in (5.129) and (5.130). The translations given for the ungrammatical examples (5.129) and (5.130) are the intended meanings had the constructions been grammatical.

5. THE VERB COMPLEX

5.129 *No-kol-o,   navij,   **-tei**   **ne-vitai**.
       1sg-carry-3sgObj   banana   cut   1sg:real-put
       'I carried it, the banana, cut and I put it.'
       (Fieldnotes, elicitation)

5.130 *No-kol-o,   navij,   **ne-tei**   **-vitai**.
       1sg-carry-3sgObj   banana   1sg:real-cut   1sg:real-put
       'I carried it, the banana, I cut it and put it.'
       (Fieldnotes, elicitation)

However, constructions that were formerly analysed as nuclear-level manner serialisation are now reanalysed as core layer serial constructions given that there is no tight binding of the verbs in serial formation, even though there is sharing of arguments.

Nese manner serial verbs are those in which V2 gives information regarding the manner in which the action is carried out. V2 in this case is usually a stative intransitive verb and V1 can only be an active transitive verb or an active intransitive verb. The arguments are shared and the negative discontinuous marker -*s-be*-Verb-*te* encloses both verbs and any arguments. Construction (5.131) is composed of an active intransitive verb occupying V1 position and a stative intransitive verb occupying V2 position and they both share the subject argument. In (5.132), both verbs are enclosed by the negative discontinuous marker -*s-be*-Verb-*te*.

5.131 *Khunokh*   *kho-**rej***   ***ralral**.*
       2sg   2sg:real-asp-talk   be.crazy
       'You're speaking crazily.'
       (2012_06_19 obfaha01004 00:01:20.000-00:01:24.000 natural text)

5.132 *Khina*   ***j-be-rej ralral-te***
       3sg   irr-neg1-talk be.crazy-neg2
       'I am not talking crazily.'
       (2012_06_19 obfaha01004 00:01:27.000-00:01:28.000 natural text)

The placement of the lexical object noun phrase poses problems given that in affirmative sentences the lexical noun phrase object occurs immediately after V1, as shown in (5.133); however, in negative sentences it can be enclosed by the negative discontinuous markers or after the negative discontinuous marker, as shown in (5.134) and (5.135) respectively. Example (5.134) suggests tight bonding bonding between the two verbs since both verbs along with lexical noun phrase object may be enclosed by the negative discontinous marker; however, example (5.135) explicitly shows the absence of a tightly bound relationship given the placement of the negative discontinuous marker and the placement of the lexical noun phrase object.

5.133 *Khar* ***ri-khil*** *nual mavos.*
 3PL 3PL:REAL-dig hole be.correct
 'They dug the hole correctly.'
 (Fieldnotes, elicitation)

5.134 *Khar* ***ri-s-be-khil*** *nual khe mavos-te.*
 3PL 3PL-IRR:NEG1-dig hole DEM correct-NEG2
 'They did not dig the hole correctly.'
 (Fieldnotes, elicitation)

5.135 *Mak* *kha* ***s-be-bet-te*** *naine* ***Ø-ti-mavos.***
 Mark 3SG IRR-NEG1-make house 3SG:REAL-ASP-correct
 'Mark did not build the house correctly.'
 (2012_08_08 elanhy01002 00:00:42.000-00:00:45.000 elicitation)

When the object is an object pro-index, it is expressed in V1, as shown in (5.136).

5.136 *Nalang* *khai* ***Ø-ti-sirsir-ia*** *terrterr.*
 Wind 3SG 3SG:ASP-blow-1SGOBJ be.strong
 'The wind blew at me strongly.'
 (2012_08_22 anhy012 00:17:28.000-0017:31.000 elicitation)

Table 5.6 contains some examples of possible V1 and V2 combinations of manner core layer serial verb constructions.

5. THE VERB COMPLEX

Table 5.6: V1 and V2 verbs in manner nuclear layer SVCs

Verb in V1 position	Verb in V2 position
rej 'talk' (intrans)	*ralral* 'crazily, crazy' (intrans stative)
rej 'talk' (intrans)	*khojkhoj* 'be proper' (intrans stative)
bat-e 'make it' (trans)	*mavos* 'correct' (intrans stative)
bat-e 'make it' (trans)	*derr* 'crooked' (intrans stative)
bat-e 'make it' (trans)	*sirsir* 'quickly' (intrans stative)
vala 'run' (intrans active)	*nalub* 'slow' (intrans stative)
sakhsakh 'work' (intrans active)	*khokhorr* 'difficult' (intrans stative)

5.7 Valency

Nese makes little use of verbal derivational morphology and the only derivational process occurring in Nese involves valency reduction. There are no morphological means on the verb through which valency is increased. However, valency is reduced via the reduplication and nominalisation processes. As mentioned in §2.5.4, both transitive and intransitive verbs are susceptible to reduplication. The process does not have a marked effect on the argument structure of intransitive verbs, given that there is no decrease in the number of arguments when intransitive verbs are reduplicated. However, reduplication of transitive verbs entails the elimination of either the object pro-index or the object noun phrase in the clause, consequently changing a transitive verb into an intransitive one. This is illustrated in examples (5.137) and (5.138).

5.137 *Je-**sob***   *nokhobu?*
      1SG:IRR-talk about   bamboo
      'Will I talk about bamboos?'
      (2012_08_27 obnesp01001 00:02:39.000-00:03:05.000 natural text)

5.138 *Ne-**sob-sob***   *Ø-ti-rov*   *khe.*
      1SG:REAL-REDUP-talk about   3SG:REAL-ASP-finish   DEM
      'I've been talking it's over now.'
      (2012_08_22 elanhy01001 00:06:02.000-00:06:04.000 natural text)

In (5.138), the deleted object is implied but specific expression of the object of reduplicated verb forms can be made to in the clause by means of prepositional phrases. This is illustrated in (5.139), where the object argument is introduced by the verbal preposition *khin*.

5.139　*Ri-s-be-**sob-sob**-te*　　　　　　　　　　*khin*　　*tenge*　*sakhal.*
　　　　1PLINCL-IRR-NEG1-REDUP-talk about-NEG2　　PREP1　　thing　one
　　　　'We aren't talking about anything.'
　　　　(2014_01_19 naanhy01001 00:57:14.000-00:57:17.000 natural text)

Verbal reduplication in Nese has an iterative function; therefore, in (5.138) the speaker states that she will commence speaking and speaks for a lengthy period of time. This iterative function also applies to example (5.139), where a discussion that had been going on for some time is considered as trivial.

Intransitive verbs that undergo reduplication exhibit a change in the ordering of arguments compared to that exhibited in their un-reduplicated form. For example, the intransitive verb *rej* 'talk' takes an argument with recipient role, introduced by the verbal prepositions *khin* or *min*. This is illustrated in (5.140), where the patient is represented by the 3PL object pro-index on the verbal preposition *min*.

5.140　*Khina*　*ne-**rej***　　　*min-**er***　　　*v'an*　*v'an*　*ne-kurkurakh*
　　　　1SG　　1SG:REAL-talk　　PREP2-3PLOBJ　　go　　go　　1SG:REAL-tired

　　　　buro.
　　　　GENMOD
　　　　'I have been talking to them and I am just sick of them.'
　　　　(2014_01_19 naanhy01001 00:50:29.000-00:50:32.000 natural text)

When the verb is reduplicated the direct object argument represents the instrumental role rather than the patient role expressed by the possessive lexical noun phrase *nale jinkrre*, as shown in (5.141).

5.141　*Kirr-**rej-rej***　　　　　　*min*　　　*nale*　　　　*jin-krre.*
　　　　2PL:REAL-REDUP-talk　　　PREP2　　language　　POSS-1PLINCL
　　　　'You guys talk in our language.'
　　　　(2012_08_27 nsesp01002 00:00:54.000-00:00:46.000 natural text)

5. THE VERB COMPLEX

While reduplication removes the object pro-index or the lexical noun phrase object from a transitive verb, nominalisation reduces valency to zero so that neither subject nor object arguments are referred to in the expression of a nominalised verb. When an intransitive active verb undergoes nominalisation the subject argument is eliminated, as shown in (5.142) and (5.143) for the verb *roj* 'be sick'.

5.142   *Khai*   *Ø-**roj**?*
       3SG   3SG:REAL-be.sick
       'Is he sick?'
       (2014_01_19 naanhy01001 00:46:32.000 natural text)

5.143   *Tua*   ***norojian***   *sikh-sikha.*
       before   sickness   REDUP-NEG
       'In the past, there were no sicknesses.'
       (Fieldnotes, elicitation)

In (5.144), the unreduplicated instance of the transitive verb *vis* 'squeeze out coconut milk' takes subject and object marking. In (5.145), the verb root *vis* is reduplicated and nominalised and the subject and object arguments are not expressed in the clause.

5.144   *Ne-**vis-vis***   *lalon*   *ale*   *ne-tekh*   *tenge*
       1SG:REAL-REDUP-squeeze out milk inside CONJ 1SG:REAL-take thing
       'I squeezed out the milk on the inside part then I took

       os   *ale*   *ne-vitai*   *nalok*   *v'an*   *rangan,*
       different CONJ 1SG:REAL-put laplap DIR LOC
       a different thing and I put the laplap (pudding) into it

       ale   ***ne-vis-i.***
       CONJ   1SG:REAL- squeeze out milk-3SGOBJ
       then I squeezed it.'

5.145   *Letang* ***no-vis-vis-ian***   *khai* *Ø-ti-rov.*
       sister   NOM-REDUP-squeeze out milk-NOM 3SG 3SG:REAL-ASP-be finish
       'Sister! The squeezing of the milk is over.'
       (2012_07_12 obaksi01001 00:10:36.000-00:10:38.000 natural text)

6

Simple sentences

6.1 Introduction

In this chapter, I describe the constituents of a simple sentence. The chapter consists of a discussion of verbal clauses (§6.2), non-verbal clauses (§6.3), existential clauses (§6.4), topicalisation and left dislocation (§6.5), adjuncts (§6.6), interrogative clauses (§6.7), imperative clauses (§6.8), comparative clauses (§6.9) and passive clauses (§6.10).

6.2 Verbal clauses

In Nese the basic constituent order of underived clauses consisting of only the core constituents is (S)V(O). The minimal elements (cf. §4.4) of a verb clause are the verb root and the subject cross-index, if intransitive (6.1), as well as the object pro-index, in transitive (6.2).

6.1   *Ne-v'an.*
      1SG:REAL-go
      'I went.'
      (2014_01_19 naanhy01001 00:04:37.000-00:04:39.000 natural text)

6.2   *Ne-les-i*
      1SG:REAL-see-3SGOBJ
      'I saw him/her.'
      (2014_01_19 naanhy01001 00:38:18.000 natural text)

A maximal clause consists of the verb root and all the associated core and non-core arguments.

6.2.1 Verbal equational clauses

Nese employs the copula verb *ve* 'be', which is placed between two noun phrases of equal status. The status of *ve* 'be' as a verb can be seen in its ability to take subject cross-indexes, as shown in (6.3).

6.3	*Kanan*	*bir-**ve***	*nemere*	*b'khab'khe.*
	1PLEXCL	1PLEXCL:REAL-be	people	short

'We are short people.'
(Fieldnotes, elicitation)

In (6.4), the copula *ve* is used to express an equal relationship between a noun phrase headed by a common noun and one that has a proper noun functioning as the head noun.

6.4	*Morron*	*khai*	*Ø-**ve***	*Fraere.*
	Today	3SG	3SG:REAL-be	Friday

'Today is Friday.'
(2012_07_12 obaksi01001 00:00:16.000-00:00:22.000 natural text)

The complement of *ve* 'be' may be a noun that is modified by an adjective, as shown in (6.5) where the adjectives *khorkhor* 'hard' and *sakhal* 'one' are modifiers of the noun phrase *tenge* 'thing'.

6.5	*Khai*	*Ø-**ve***	*tenge*	*khorkhor*	*sakhal*	*khe.*
	3SG	3SG:REAL-be	thing	hard	one	EMP

'That is really one hard thing.'
(2014_01_19 naanhy01001 00:07:10.000-00:07:14:000 natural text)

Furthermore, the copula *ve* may establish an equal relationship between two noun phrases headed by proper nouns, as illustrated in (6.6).

6.6 | *Tontar* | *asuv* | *Katolik,* | *Tontar* | *asakh* | *SDA* | *ale* | *Senbokhas*
Tontar | left | Catholic | Tontar | right | SDA | CONJ | Senbokhas

*Ø-**ve*** *Presbyterian.*
3SG:REAL-be   Presbyterian

'The left side of the Tontar area is Catholic, the right side of Tontar is SDA and Senbokhas is Presbyterian.'
(2012_08_22 anhy01005 00:03:05.000-00:03:14.000 natural text)

Although the final clause in (6.6) is an equational clause (cf. §6.2.1) in which *ve* is employed to express equal status between two noun phrases headed by the proper nouns *Senbokhas* and *Presbyterian* respectively, previous clauses in this example also exhibit an equal relationship between noun phrases without the copula *ve*. In these cases, a pause occurs between the two noun phrases.

As with negation of other verbal clauses, negation of the copula *ve* 'be' is achieved through the negative discontinuous marker *-be*-Verb-*te* (§5.5.1.1). An example is given in (6.7).

6.7 | *Lokhsa* | *khai* | *Ø-s-be-ve-te* | *Malo,* | *Santo* | *khe.*
DIR | 3SG | 3SG-IRR-NEG1-be-NEG2 | Malo | Santo | DEM

'Over there is not Malo, that's Santo.'
(2014_01_19 naanhy01001 00:04:30.000-01:04:33.000 natural text)

Examples (6.4) and (6.7) display topicalisation of the time adverbial *morron* 'today' and the directional *lokhsa* 'there' respectively. When not topicalised, the time adverbial and directional typically occupy the position after the noun phrases (*Fraere* 'Friday' and *Malo* 'Malo') in the predicate.

6.3 Non-verbal clauses

Non-verbal clauses are not as frequently attested in the data as verbal clauses, but there are a number of different non-verbal clause types that occur.

6.3.1 Non-verbal equational clauses

As stated in §6.2.1, equational clauses are expressed in Nese not only by means of the copula *ve* but also by simple juxtaposition of two noun phrases, as illustrated by the two initial clauses in example (6.6) with no intervening copula. Non-verbal equational clauses in Nese are based on the structure subject + predicate, the latter consisting of another noun phrase adding further information regarding the subject. The subject position may be occupied by independent pronouns, common nouns and proper nouns. Generally, Nese non-verbal clauses may be used to assert the identity of the subject noun phrase and to assert the numerical value of the referents represented by the subject noun phrase.

In (6.8), the subject noun phrase is represented by the 1SG independent pronoun, with the predicate noun phrase represented by a proper noun functioning as the head.

6.8 [Khina]   [pasta   Louis Ross.]
     1SG   pastor   Louis Ross
     'I am pastor Louis Ross.'
     (2012_01_18 obrolo01001 00:00:02.000-00:00:07.000 natural text)

In (6.8), the predicate noun phrase establishes the identity of the subject noun phrase. This contrasts with example (6.9) in which the predicate noun phrase, consisting of a common noun is modified by a stative intransitive verb, giving further information about the type of person represented by the 1SG independent pronoun.

6.9 [Khina]   nemerre   [Ø-sat.]
     1SG   man   3SG-REAL-bad
     'I am a bad man.'
     (2012_04_26 obmach01001 00:00:50.000-00:00:55.000 song)

Subjects of non-verbal clauses may be occupied by an independent pronoun modified by a demonstrative, as shown in (6.10), where a demonstrative also modifies a possessed noun phrase forming the head of the predicate.

6.10 [Khai   khe]   [tete   s-ak   khe.]
     3SG   DEM   father   CLGEN-1SG:POSS   DEM
     'He is my father.' (literally 'that one is my father'.)
     (2014_01_19 naanhy01001 00:12:42.000-00:12:44.000 natural text)

In (6.11), the pronoun as head of the subject noun phrase is modified by the numeral *til* 'three' and the predicate is made up of the single noun phrase *tav'at* 'woman'.

6.11 [Kanan   til]   [tav'at.]
     1PL   three   woman
     'The three of us are women (females).'
     (2012_05_22 obcero01001 00:00:26.000-00:00:29.000 natural text)

A comparison of non-verbal equational clauses and verbal equational clauses employing the copula *ve* show that if the head of the predicate noun phrase is a common noun, then either the non-verbal or verbal construction can be employed. Compare example (6.12) with examples (6.10) and (6.11).

6.12 *John*   *khai*   *Ø-ve*   *tija*   *sakhal.*
     John   3SG   3SG:REAL-be   teacher   one
     'John is a teacher.'
     (Fieldnotes, elicitation)

However, if the head of the noun phrase in the predicate of an equational clause is a proper noun, a similar identificational clause cannot be constructed via the copula *ve* in which an independent pronoun occupies subject position and a proper noun occupies the predicate slot, as indicated by ungrammatical (6.13).

6.13 **Khina*   *ne-ve*   *Louis*   *Ross.*
     1SG   1SG:REAL- be   Louis   Ross
     'I am Louis Ross.'
     (Fieldnotes, elicitation)

A predicate noun phrase with a proper noun as its head can have a proper noun as its subject, as illustrated in example (6.6), repeated here as (6.14), where it is clear that Nese allows a structure containing the copula *ve* and one without a copula *ve* to express an equal status in clauses containing proper nouns functioning as both the subjects of the clause and the head of the noun phrases in the predicate of the clause.

6.14 [Tontar asuv] [Katolik,] [Tontar asakh] [SDA]   ale   Senbokhas
     Tontar   left   Catholic   Tontar   right   SDA   CONJ   Senbokhas
     Ø-ve   *Presbyterian.*
     3SG:REAL-be   Presbyterian
     'The left side of the Tontar area is Catholic, the right side of Tontar is SDA and Senbokhas is Presbyterian.'
     (2012_08_22 anhy01005 00:03:05.000 00:03:17.000 natural text)

Similarly, a predicate noun phrase can also have a common noun phrase as its subject, as illustrated in non-verbal (6.15), in which the subject is a possessive noun phrase, incorporating a fronted possessor expressed by the adverbial demonstrative *iekhetan*. As shown in §4.5.8.2.2, possessors typically occupy the position immediately after the possessive classifier *sen* and not necessarily after the predicate.

6.15 [*Iekhetan   neng s-an*]   [*Natanv'at.*]
     DEM   name-CLGEN-3SG:POSS   Matanvat
     'Down here is called Matanvat.'
     (Fieldnotes, elicitation)

As stated in §5.1, a noun phrase in the predicate of a clause may be used to assert the numerical value of the subject noun phrase. This is illustrated in (6.14), where the numeral *line* 'five' constitutes the head of the noun phrase in the predicate with no further modification. In such cases, the head of the subject noun phrase is usually an independent pronoun.

6.16 [*Kanan*]   *line*
     1PLEXCL   five
     'There's five of us.'
     (2012_05_22 obcero01001 00:00:03.000-00:00:04.000 natural text)

Moreover, a non-verbal existential clause may simply consist of an independent pronoun and an adverb as illustrated in the second clause in (6.15).

6.17 *Nemerrte   sikh-sikha,   [kanan]   [buro.]*
     Man:PL   REDUP-NEG   1PLEXCL   GENMOD
     'There was no one, it was just us.'
     (2014_01_19 naanhy01001 00:10:48.000-00:10:52.000 natural text)

Nominalised verbs may also occupy subject position in non-verbal existential clauses, as illustrated in (6.18), where the predicate part of the clause has the independent pronoun functioning as the head of the noun phrase, modified by the demonstrative *khe* and the adverb *buro*.

6.18 [*Norojian*]   [*khai*   *khe*   *buro.*]
     disease   3SG   DEM   GENMOD
     'That is all the diseases which exist.'
     (Fieldnotes, natural text)

6.3.2 Non-verbal locational clauses

A non-verbal locational clause is used to predicate the location of the subject referent. Local adverbial demonstratives, which can also occur as clause-level adjuncts, form the predicate of this clause type. This is illustrated with the local adverbial demonstratives *iekhe* 'here' in (6.19) and (6.20) and with *iekhetan* 'down here' in (6.21).

6.19 *[Khai]*   *[iekhe.]*
      3SG   DEM:LOC
      'She is here.'
      (Fieldnotes, elicitation)

In (6.19), the local adverbial demonstrative *iekhe* forms the predicate of the clause indicating the location of the subject noun phrase expressed by the 3SG independent pronoun.

6.20 *[Nav'at s-am]*   *[iekhe.]*
      stone   CLGEN-2SG:POSS   DEM:LOC
      'Here is your money.'
      (2014_01_19 naanhy01001 00:04:22.000-00:04:23.000 natural text)

In (6.20), the head of the subject noun phrase is the possessed common noun *nav'at* 'money' and the predicate is composed of the demonstrative *iekhe*, which indicates the location of the subject noun phrase.

6.21 *[Khai]*   *[iekhetan.]*
      3SG   DEM
      'She's down here.'
      (Fieldnotes, elicitation)

Lastly, in (6.21), the local adverbial demonstrative *iekhetan* occupies the predicate slot in the clause with the 3SG independent pronoun functioning as the subject of the clause.

Non-verbal clauses are structurally akin to verbal equational clauses in certain points relating to the type of nouns functioning as subjects and those that occur in the predicate. Both clause types allow independent pronouns and proper nouns to function as subjects, when either a common noun or proper noun are functioning as the predicate. Similarly, both clause types may have independent pronouns functioning as subjects with a noun phrase composed of a head noun modified by a stative intransitive verb functioning as the predicate. A point of divergence lies in the fact that verbal clauses permit independent pronouns to function as subjects with numerals and adverbs functioning as the predicates. Also, nominalised verbs may function as subjects in non-verbal clauses with independent pronouns as predicates; however, the absence of this pattern in verbal clauses may be due to insufficient data rather than a property inherently lacking.

6.4 Existential clauses

Nese employs the existential verb *tokh* 'to exist' to assert the existence of an entity as shown in example (6.22).

6.22 | *Sande* | *skul* | *khai* | *Ø-**tokh*** | *be* | *nemerrte* | *sikh-sikha*
 | Sunday | school | 3SG | 3SG:REAL-exist | CONJ | man:PL | REDUP-NEG

| *te* | *ba-sesre-rr.* |
| SUB | POT-to teach-3PLOBJ |

'There is a Sunday school but there is no one to teach them.'
(2014_01_19 naanhy01001 00:12:34.000-00:12:37.000 natural text)

There is no evidence in the data to prove that a negated existential clause is composed of the negated verb *tokh* 'to exist'. On the other hand, negative existential clauses are formed by the negative predicate verb *sikha*, as discussed in the following subsection.

6.4.1 Negative existential clauses

As stated in §5.5.1.2, Nese has a negative predicate verb *sikha*, which is employed in negative existential clauses to assert that the subject of the clause does not exist. Clauses are negated with the verbal *sikha* occurring after the noun over which negation has scope to render the meaning *There is no…*. Although it may take the ASP marker *-ti-*, *sikha* does not take any of the subject cross-indexes. The negative predicate verb may also be used as an interjection, which means 'no'.

To begin with, *sikha* negates the existence of an entity represented by a lexical noun phrase, as illustrated in (6.23).

6.23 **Nemerrte**   sikh-sikha.
      men:PL   REDUP-NEG
      'There is no one.'
      (2014_01_19 naanhy01001 00:10:49.000 natural text)

Similarly, it may negate the existence of an entity realised by an independent pronoun, as illustrated in (6.24).

6.24 **Khai**   khe   sikh-sikha.
      3SG   DEM   REDUP-NEG
      'That one is not present.'
      (2014_01_19 naanhy01001 00:29:20.000-00:29:23.000 natural text)

Given that *sikha* does not take any subject cross-index, when the identity of a noun phrase has already been established in an antecedent clause, a negative presentative clause does not require the overt expression of the subject noun phrase and may simply consist of the predicate *sikha* and an adverbial adjunct, as illustrated in (6.25).

6.25 **Tua**   sikh-sikha.
      Before   REDUP:NEG
      'In the past there was none.'
      (2012_08_27 obnesp01001 00:11:58.000-00:12:05.000 natural text)

6.5 Topicalisation and left dislocation

In discussing topicalisation and left dislocation, I follow Ross's (1973, p. 137) definition, which describes topicalisation as a structure in which an NP (either core or adjunct) has been moved to a clause external position with no trace left behind within the clause, contrasting with left dislocation, which sees the sentence internal NP being dislocated to the left but leaving behind a trace in the position it once occupied. Nese allocates the left-most periphery of the clause to topicalised, emphasised or focused elements whose arrival at this destination could be either via the topicalisation or left dislocation processes. Core or adjunct noun phrases in Nese undergo topicalisation in two distinct ways: firstly, by movement with no trace in the clause and, secondly, with no movement because the landing sites are synonymous with their original position.

The first scenario applies specifically to noun phrases functioning as complements of the true preposition *rengen* (cf. §6.6.2). Complements of the true preposition *rengen* 'in, at' typically occur after the preposition; however, when the noun phrase complement is focused, for example *plen* 'plane' in (6.26), there is no trace left behind in the site of extraction.

6.26 **Plen**   tenge   rov   jelekh   ri-nas   **rangan**.
     plane   thing   MOD   MOD   3PL:REAL-to.die   LOC
     'As for planes, every single thing dies in it.'
     (2014_01_19 naanhy01001 00:07:15.000-00:07:18.000 natural text)

The second scenario applies to subject cross-indexes occurring in conjunction with either lexical noun phrase subjects or noun phrase adjuncts, all of which have the same referent. As mentioned in §4.6, repeated here as example (6.27), the noun phrase *teverik khe* establishes the participant as a topic with the 3PL independent pronoun being the subject, and these two elements cannot be argued to have been moved from another position to this position.

6.27 Ale   **teverik khe khar re**-*v'an*   re-ve   rusu-num
     CONJ   men   DEM 3PL 3PL:REAL-go   3PL:REAL-say   3PL:IRR-drink

     nanalokh.
     kava
     'Then these men they went and they said 'we will drink kava.'
     (2014_01_19 naanhy01001 00:01:35.000-00:01:38.000 natural text)

It may be tempting to consider the presence of the 3PL realis subject cross-index in conjunction with either, the 3PL independent pronoun and the lexical noun phrase as being a case of left dislocation in which the subject cross-index is the trace in the clause. This, however, is not plausible given that the extraction site and landing sites are the same and the 3PL realis subject cross-index cannot be considered as a trace.

Left dislocation is clearly expressed by object arguments, where a trace, by way of the object pro-index, is left behind in the clause. Object arguments of transitive verbs and complements of verbal prepositions may be dislocated to the left-most clause external position. To begin with, object noun phrases may be dislocated to the left, leaving behind a trace in the clause by means of an object pro-index, as shown in (6.28).

6.28 Sikha, **nokhnaine khe**, khar rri-lijkhor-**o** khe.
     NEG   door   DEM   3PL   3PL:REAL- to close-3SGOBJ   EMP
     'No, this door, they do close it.'
     (2014_02_18 naaksi01001 00:00:33.000-00:00:37.000 natural text)

In example (6.28), the object noun phrase *nokhnaine* 'door' has been dislocated to the left and there is a trace realised by the object pro-index *-o* in the clause. If the core noun phrase had not been dislocated to the left, the construction would be as in (6.29), where the object noun phrase occupies a post-verbal position, with no pro-index on the verb.

6.29 khai   Ø-v'an   Ø-lijkhor   na   **sospen**.
     NEG   3SG:REAL-go   3SG:REAL-to close umm   saucepan
     'S/he went and closed umm the saucepan.'
     (2012_08_22 anhy012 00:35:47.000-00:37:50.000 elicitation)

In addition to object noun phrases that may be dislocated to the left, a complement of the verbal preposition *min* (cf. Chapter 3), with a conjunctive function, may also be dislocated to the left of the noun phrase containing the verbal preposition. This is illustrated in (6.30).

6.30 **Nemerjian khe**, kanan   min-**i**   bir-sukul.
     Old person DEM   1PLEXCL   CONJ-3SGOBJ   1PLEXCL:REAL-school
     'That old person, us with him we go to school.'
     (2014_01_19 naanhy01001 00:12:14.000-00:12:17.000 natural text)

In (6.30), the object of the prepositional verb *min*, which forms part of the subject noun phrase of the clause, has been dislocated to the left, bringing it into a more discourse-prominent position.

Similarly, clause-level adjuncts of various types may also be dislocated to a clause external position, as illustrated by the topicalised object noun phrase *nuaknatan* in (6.31).

6.31 **Nuaknatan,**   Ø-vala   **khin-i,**   Ø-v'an.
     truck   3SG:REAL- run   PREPI-3SGOBJ   3SG:REAL-go
     'The truck, she ran by it and went.'
     (2012_08_22 anhy01005 00:02:21.000-00:02:24.000 natural text)

Example (6.31) contains two clauses with the intransitive verbs *vala* 'run' and *v'an* 'go', the former constituting the initial clause. The initial clause contains a prepositional phrase headed by the verbal preposition *khin*, which introduces an adjunct of the intransitive clause. The complement of this verbal preposition is co-referential with the noun phrase *nuaknatan* 'truck'. It is, therefore, clear that the noun phrase *nuaknatan* is a left dislocated argument of the intransitive transitive verb *vala* 'run'.

It is easy to ascribe left dislocation to cases like (6.31), where an adjunct argument introduced by a verbal preposition is co-referential with a preverbal lexical noun phrase object. Other adjunct arguments such as nouns functioning as temporal adjuncts, local demonstratives, temporal nouns may also occupy clause external positions (clause initially and clause finally) and, in such cases, they are not instances of either topicalisation or left dislocation, as defined by Ross (1973) (cf. §6.6.3, §6.6.4 and §6.6.6 respectively).

6.6 Adjuncts

Adjuncts in Nese are non-obligatory constituents that modify the core of the clause, providing further information about the action encoded in the verb. Functionally, this includes spatial and temporal information, manner and other circumstantial information relating to the event. Following Dixon (2010, p. 429), adjuncts are non-core arguments expressing notions such as instrument, accompaniment, recipient, beneficiary, time, place and manner. Thus, semantic roles rather than syntactic criteria are employed to identify whether a given participant is formally an adjunct or an obligatory argument. In Nese, adjuncts occur in the non-core area and may either occur clause initially, before the subject, or they may occur clause finally. In intransitive clauses, adjuncts occur before the subject noun phrase or the subject cross-index or after the verb. In transitive clauses, a clause initial position is one that is located before the subject noun phrase or the subject cross-index and a clause final position occurs after the object noun phrase, object pro-index or any other core arguments in transitive clauses.

Syntactically, Nese has a number of different types of adjuncts and these may be expressed through true prepositions, verbal prepositional phrases, adverbs, demonstratives, locational nouns and temporal nouns. The category of nouns functioning as temporal adjuncts, locational demonstratives and temporal nouns may occur in both clause final and clause initial non-core positions. However, adjunct arguments expressed by means of verbal prepositions and the true preposition *rengen* can only occupy clause final position. This also applies to locational nouns. In the following subsections, I discuss the status of complements of verbal and true prepositions, adverbs, demonstratives, locational nouns and temporal nouns functioning as adjuncts.

6.6.1 Verbal prepositions

A prepositional phrase in Nese consists of the head preposition and either an object suffix or a noun phrase as the complement. The type of preposition determines what form the complement can take, either a noun phrase or an object suffix. These object suffixes are presented in Table 3.14 in Chapter 3. A verbal preposition never takes as its complement a noun phrase with a locative noun as head. The order of elements in a prepositional phrase is presented in Table 6.1.

Table 6.1: Order of elements in a prepositional phrase

Verbal prepositions	NP	Object suffix	Demonstrative
khin	✓	✓	✗
min	✓	✓	✗
ngin	✓	✓	✗
sur		✓	✗
belek	✓	✗	✓

The category of verbal prepositions is composed of *min* 'to, with, towards', *khin* 'with, for, to', *ngin* 'for', *sur* 'for' and *belek* 'like', and there is considerable overlap between the functions of these prepositions. This category is further divided into two subcategories, one of which is characterised by the ability to take verbal object marking and the other by its ability to take aspect/polarity marking. Distinguishing between core arguments and adjuncts is dependent on whether a verb is a transitive or intransitive verb, and in the case of transitive verbs, whether they are extended transitive verbs. For underived intransitive verbs, the issue is perhaps less complex since any argument added by means of a verbal preposition is not a core argument and is, therefore, an adjunct. It ought to be noted at the outset, however, that a single verbal preposition can only be used once to introduce an argument. It cannot be used in consecutive sequence to express different arguments in a single clause.

The functions of the verbal prepositions are outlined in Table 6.2.

Table 6.2: Functions of verbal prepositions

min	dative 'to' (used interchangeably with *khin*)
	comitative 'with'
	allative 'towards'
	general locative 'on'
khin	instrumental 'with'
	purposive 'for'
	dative 'to' (used interchangeably with *min*)
	stimulus 'about'
sur	purposive 'for'
ngin	purposive 'for'
belek	*similitive* 'like'

The phonological shapes of *min*, *khin* and *ngin* closely resemble that of the Proto Oceanic remote or long transitive suffix *aki(ni), which, when attached to the verb root, transforms a peripheral noun phrase with an instrumental, beneficiary or any other function, into one that functions as an object argument of the verb clause (Lynch et al., 2011, p. 82). Although Lynch et al. state that the history of the Proto Oceanic remote or long transitive suffix is still a controversial issue, they acknowledge that, in general, Oceanic languages employ a reflex of the Proto Oceanic remote or long transitive suffix *aki(ni) to derive transitive verbs from intransitive verbs by increasing the valency of the verb (2011, p. 82). Evans (2003, p. 236) states that prepositional reflexes of *aki(ni) in Oceanic languages come in the form of verbal prepositions that use object markers to index the person and number of their object. There are some Oceanic languages that have prepositions that are reflexes of *aki(ni) such as Woleian (Evans, 2003, p. 148).

It is evident from Table 6.2 that the verbal prepositions in Nese have overlapping functions; for example, *khin*, *min* and *ngin* all have dative function and it is difficult to account for when one is used instead of the other. This may be partly explained by the fact that *aki(ni) occurs in many Oceanic languages with a thematic consonant, which has been understood to originate from original final consonants of the verb it attaches to, which were later reanalysed as part of the suffix instead of the verb (Evans, 2003). Thus *khin*, *min* and *ngin* have different initial consonants but overlapping functions.

While the above explanation may offer a plausible analysis for the possible origin of these verbal prepositions in Nese, the reconstructions given for Proto Oceanic verbal prepositions suggest a counter analysis. According to Lynch et al. (2011, p. 87), Proto Oceanic had two types of prepositions, local and temporal prepositions and verbal prepositions, the latter of which had benefactive, ablative, instrumental, allative and comitative functions. The reconstructed forms of these verbal prepositions are *pani benefactive, *tani ablative, *kini instrumental, *suri allative and *mai comitative. These functions are all reflected in those outlined in Table 6.2 for verbal prepositions in Nese apart from ablative *tani. Given that Nese *khin, min* and *ngin* have overlapping dative/benefactive functions, it is not clear whether they are all reflexes of Proto Oceanic dative *pani or whether *khin* and *min* are reflexes of Proto Oceanic instrumental *kini, given that they both also have the instrumental function in contrast to *min*, which does not have that function.

6.6.1.1 *Khin*

The verbal preposition *khin* has dative, instrumental, purposive and stimulus functions. The dative function is restricted to the extended transitive verbs *vervis* 'to reveal' and *var* 'to tell'. When the verbal preposition has a dative function, the indirect object is the person who is the recipient of an action, as shown in (6.32), where the direct object of the prepositional verb is the elided 3sg object pro-index. This dative function is also shown in (6.33), where the object of the verbal preposition is the 3sg object suffix.

6.32 *J-be-vervis-te* **khin** *nelekhterr khe.*
1sg:IRR-NEG1-reveal-NEG2 PREP1 woman DEM
'I did not reveal it to the woman.'
(2012_08_22 anhy01005 00:02:21.000-00:02:24.000 natural text)

6.33 *Na-var-i* **khin**-*er belek khe.*
1sg:REAL-tell-3sgObj PREP1-3plObj like dem
'I told it to them like this.'
(2014_01_19 naanhy01001 00:10:07.000-00:10:09.000 natural text)

In (6.34), however, the complement of *khin* has an instrumental function representing the means through which an action is performed, and cannot be classified as a core argument because it is not obligatory.

6.34 Kho-se-var-i **khin** nale jin-krre.
      2SG-IRR-to tell-3SGOBJ PREP1 language CLGEN-1PLEXCL:POSS
      'You'll tell it in our language.'
      (2014_01_19 naanhy01001 00:41:57.000-00:42:00:00 natural text)

Nese permanently restricts direct objects of the verb *var* to those that assume the theme role. As shown in (6.35), the direct object slot is occupied by a lexical noun phrase functioning as the direct object representing the theme. On the other hand, there is flexibility regarding the complements of the preposition *khin* in that they can encode either the beneficiary or the instrumental roles.

6.35 Khai Ø-ver   nel-en   nasub maro **khin**
      3SG   3SG:REAL-to tell message-3SG:POSS chief DIR PREP1
      'She told the message of the chief up there (God)

      kanan   jelekh.
      1PLEXCL   all
      to us.'
      (2014_01_19 naanhy01001 00:09:25.000-00:09:40.000 natural text)

In (6.33) and (6.35), the complements of *khin* assume the beneficiary role, contrasting with the instrumental role in (6.34). This is thus in keeping with Dixon's (2010) definition of adjuncts in that, although an argument of the verb *var* introduced by *khin* expressing the instrumental function can easily be classed as an adjunct in Nese, an indirect object bearing the beneficiary role cannot be considered as an adjunct.

Although the direct objects of the extended transitive verbs *vervis* and *var* are expressed via direct affixation to the verb root, the direct object of the transitive verb *volvol* 'sell' expresses its direct object as a complement of the verbal preposition *khin*, as shown in (6.36).

6.36 Khai khe nat-ne,   ro-volvol   **khin** melon.
      3SG   DEM child-3SG:POSS 3PL:REAL-sell PREP1   melon
      'That's her child, they sell melons.'
      (2014_01_19 naanhy01001 00:11:53.000-00:11:56.000 natural text)

6. SIMPLE SENTENCES

Ditransitive verbs that require two core arguments may have a third non-core argument expressed as a complement of the verbal preposition *khin*, encoding the instrumental, accompaniment and locational concepts, as shown in (6.37), (6.38) and (6.39) respectively.

6.37 *Khar   ri-s-be-viteikhor-te   tav'at   **khin**   tenge*
     3PL   3PL-IRR-NEG1-put.block-NEG2   woman   PREP1   thing
     'As for them, they do not block women with any

   sakhal   be   nejal   buro.
   one   CONJ   mat   GENMOD
   thing but just mats.'
   (2014_01_19 naanhy01001 00:31:53.000-00:31:58.000 natural text)

6.38 *No,   tenge   ververik   buro,   belek   te   vosvos   nalok,*
     No   thing   small   GENMOD   like   SUB   right   laplap
     'No they are simply those small ones, like the ones which are right for laplap

   *rri-ba-bat-e   **khin**   nalok.*
   3PL:REAL-POT- make-3SGOBJ   PREP1   laplap
   we will make it with laplap.'
   (2014_01_19 naanhy01001 00:25:19.000-00:25:25.000 natural text)

6.39 *Khai   Ø-rong-o   ba-rongvuson-i   neten*
     3SG   3SG:REAL-to hear-3SGOBJ   POT-to understand-3SGOBJ   PURP2
     'She heard it and she will understand it because

   te   khar   re-ve   Ø-se-sesre   tejiblakh
   SUB   3PL   3PL:REAL-to say   3SG-IRR-to teach   children
   they said that she will teach the children

   ***khin**   naul.*
   PREP1   school
   in school.'
   (2014_01_19 naanhy01001 00:08:24.000-00:08:32.000 natural text)

253

Intransitive verbs, on the other hand, inherently have only one core argument; therefore, the verbal preposition *khin* extends the coding of participant roles, specifically by introducing participants bearing the instrumental, purposive and stimulus functions. As illustrated in (6.38), the verbal prepositional *khin* introduces an instrumental participant represented by the 3SG object suffix, which is co-referential with the left dislocated noun phrase *nuak natan* 'truck'.

6.40 *Nuak natan,* Ø-*vala* **khin-i,** Ø-*v'an.*
 truck 3SG:REAL-run PREPI-3SGOBJ 3SG:REAL-go
 'The truck, she went by it and went.'
 (2012_08_22 anhy01005 00:02:21.000-00:02:24.000 natural text)

In (6.41), the complement of *khin* states the purpose of the action encoded in the intransitive active verb *ma* 'come'.

6.41 *Khai* Ø-*se-ma* **khin** *noroblat s-an te*
 3SG 3SG:IRR-ma PREPI paper CLGEN-3SG:POSS SUB
 'She will come for her paper which

 Ø-*ti-vitai iekhe.*
 3SG:REAL-ASP-put DEM:LOC
 she had left here.'
 (2014_0_19 naanhy01001 00:16:22.000-00:16:26.000 natural text)

With the intransitive active verb *sobsob* 'to relate a story', which is derived via reduplication of the transitive *sob,* the complement of the verbal preposition does not encode the dative function. However, it refers to the theme being discussed. As stated in §5.7, reduplication transforms a transitive verb into an intransitive verb by eliminating its object argument, which may be expressed by either a lexical noun phrase or by the object pro-index. In its transitive form, the object argument of the verb *sob* expresses what is being discussed, as shown in example (6.42).

6.42 *ne-sob na* **tejiblakh.**
 1SG:REAL-talk about umm house
 'I am talking about children.'
 (2012_05_16 obanhy01005 00:00:04.000-00:00:07.000 natural text)

Example (6.41) presents *sob* in its intransitive reduplicated form with the prepositional verb introducing what would normally be the object argument.

6.43 *Rri-s-be-**sob-sob**-te*   ***khin***   *tenge*   *sakhal.*
      1PLINCL-IRR-NEG1-REDUP-talk about-NEG2   PREP1   thing   one
      'We aren't talking about anything.'
      (2014_01_19 naanhy01001 00:57:14.000-00:57:17.000 natural text)

In fact, when *sob* is intransitive it may also employ the preposition *rengen* to introduce an argument with a similar function (cf. §6.6.2).

Lastly, the stimulus function is embedded in the complement of verbal preposition co-occurring with the intransitive stative verbs *ralral* 'crazily, crazy' and *wun* 'be full', as shown in (6.44) and (6.45) respectively. In both examples, the intransitive stative verbs acquire another argument, apart from the subject argument with the former associated with stimulus functions.

6.44 *Kirr-ralral*   ***khin***   *nanalokh?*
      2PL:REAL-be.crazy   PREP1   kava
      'You guys are crazy about kava?'
      (2014_01_19 nanhy01001 00:50:19.000-00:50:21.000 natural text)

This analysis conforms with that presented in §5.7, where it was shown that intransitive verbs derived from transitive verbs via reduplication acquire another argument by means of verbal prepositions (cf. example 5.139).

6.45 *Belek*   *nakhariv*   *natas*   *neren*   *te*   *nesim'-en*   *Ø-wun*
      like   crab   sea   when   SUB   belly-3SG:POSS   3SG:REAL-be.full
      'Like the sea crab when its belly is full

      khin   *natas.*
      PREP1   sea
      of saltwater.'
      (2014_01_19 naanhy01001 00:53:13.000-00:53:19.000 natural text)

6.6.1.2 *Min*

The verbal preposition *min* specifies the broadest range of semantic roles of the participant, marking the dative, ablative, allative, temporal, instrumental and comitative functions. The comitative function has been dealt with in §3.2.1, and given that the comitative function is not a prepositional one, it will not be dealt with here. The justification for treating *min* as a verbal preposition is that it can take both nominal arguments, as shown in (6.46), and arguments realised by object pro-indexes, as shown in (6.47).

6.46 *khai   khe,   rro-so-kron-i   min   tav'at.*
     3SG   DEM   1PL-IRR-give-3SGOBJ   PREP2   woman
     'That one we'll give it to the woman.'
     (2014_01_19 naanhy01001 00:31:40.000-00:31:44.000 natural text)

6.47 *Namalvar   Ø-rej   min-a.*
     High person   3SG:talk   PREP2-1SGOBJ
     'The high person talks to me.'
     (2012_04_17 obloro01002 00:00:06.000-00:00:10.000 song)

The preposition *min* resembles *khin* in that the arguments introduced by the former may constitute core as well as adjunct arguments, depending on the valency of the verb. Thus, with extended transitive verbs such as *kron* 'give', *rej* 'to speak', *us* 'to ask', *var* 'to tell', and *vitai* 'to put', *min* expresses a third core argument. Adjunct arguments, however, are those that serve instrumental, accompaniment and purposive semantic roles.

Examples (6.46), (6.47), (6.48) and (6.49) contain complements of *min* functioning as a third core argument of the extended transitive verbs *kroon* 'to give', *rej* 'to speak', *var* 'to tell' and *vitai* 'to put' respectively, with the complements bearing the dative or beneficiary semantic roles.

6.48 *Ale   ne-var-i   min   lekhtarr.*
     CONJ   1SG:REAL-tell-3SGOBJ   PREP2   woman
     'Then I mentioned it to the woman (wife).'
     (2012_06_11 obro01005 00:01:31.000-00:01:34.000 natural text)

6.49 *Nakhad   khai   Ø-ti-v'an   atan,   ne-lev   nadatav*
      Fire   3SG   3SG:REAL-ASP-go   down   1SG:REAL-take   breadfruit
      'The fire has gone down, I am taking the breadfruit

   *ne-vita-i   **min**   nakhad.*
   1SG:REAL-put-3SGOBJ   PREP2   fire.
   and am putting it on the fire.'
   (2012_06_12 obaksi01001 00:01:21.000-00:01:22.000 natural text)

Contrasting example (6.34) and (6.48) shows that the dative *min* is restricted to being used interchangeably with dative *khin* when the preceding lexical verb is *var* 'tell' to mark an extended core argument.

Adjunct arguments are encoded in the allative, instrumental, purposive and temporal semantic roles. Expression of the allative function is attested only in conjunction with the verb *v'an* 'go' when *v'an* occurs as the last verb in a serial verb construction. This is shown in (6.50), where the speaker is agreeing for her voice (recording) to be placed in an archive.

6.50 *Ne-najnge   te   kho-se-lev   ral-ok   v'an*
      1SG:REAL-agree   SUB   2SG:IRR-take   voice-1SG:POSS   go
      'I agree that you will take my voice (record) to

   ***min**   akaev.*
   PREP2   archive
   the archive.'
   (2012_06_12 obaksi01001 00:00:37.000-00:00:46.000 natural text)

The instrumental semantic role embedded in the noun phrase functioning as the complement of *min* in (6.51) indicates the means through which the action encoded by the transitive verb is carried out.

6.51 *Khar   ri-bat-e   **min**   nokhobu   buro.*
      3PL   3PL:REAL-do-3SGOBJ   PREP2   bamboo   GENMOD
      'They did it with just bamboos.'
      (2012_08_27 obnesp01001 00:14:15.000-00:14:25.000 natural text)

An argument serving the accompaniment semantic role is expressed as the complement of *min* in (6.52), where *min* adds a non-core argument to the intransitive active verb *khro*.

6.52 | *Neduru* | *khe* | *wor,* | *rro-khro* | **min**-*er,* | *nabat-rre*
those two | DEM | ADV | 3PL:REAL-stay | PREP2-3PLOBJ | head-3PLOBJ

'Just those two, if you stay with them, their heads

Ø-ti-terter   *Ø-terter*   *Ø-terter.*
3SG:REAL-ASP-be.strong   3SG:REAL-be.strong   3SG:REAL-be.strong

are so strong (they are really stubborn).'
(2014_01_19 naanhy01001 00:35:00.000-00:35.00.000 natural text)

A purposive role is borne by the argument functioning as the complement of the verb *takh* 'to take', as illustrated in (6.53).

6.53 | *Khina* | *ne-rong* | *te* | *de-waj-i* | *buro,*
1SG | 1SG:REAL-want | SUB | 1SG:IRR-to.eat-3SGOBJ | GENMOD

'As for me, I simply want to eat it,

khise | *khai* | *ba-takh-e* | **min**-*a.*
who | 3SG | POT-to.take-3SGOBJ | PREP2-1SGOBJ

but who will take it for me.'
(2014_01_19 naanhy01001 00:22:17.000-00:22:20.000 natural text)

In cases where the verbal preposition has a temporal function, its object indicates the time at which an event takes place. This is shown in example (6.54), where the complement is a proper noun.

6.54 | *Khai* | *iekhe* | *neten* | *rri-sid-e* | **min**
3SG | DEM:LOC | PURP2 | 1PLINCL:REAL-cut-3SGOBJ | PREP2

'This one, because we had already cut it on

sande | *di* | *bet* | *balak* | *khai* | *Ø-ti-nanas* | *khe*
sunday | already | make | like | 3SG | 3SG:REAL-ASP-be.dry | DEM

Sunday, it has already dried.'
(2012_07_12 obaksi01001 00:17:03.000-00:17:06.000 natural text)

Finally, in (6.55), the un-reduplicated form of the head verb in the clause is the extended transitive verb *rej*. Reduplication, as stated in §2.5.4, transforms a transitive verb into an intransitive verb. In (6.55), reduplication has eliminated both the object and extended arguments, consequently transforming the extended transitive verb into an intransitive one. The verbal preposition *min* adds a non-core argument, with an instrumental function, to the intransitive verb *rejrej*.

6.55 *Kirr-rej-rej* **min** *nale* *jin-krre.*
2PL:REAL-REDUP-talk PREP2 language CLGEN-1PLINCL:POSS
'You (PL) talk in our language.'
(2012_08_27 nsesp01002 00:00:45.000-00:00:54.000 natural text)

6.6.1.3 Ngin

Unlike *min* and *khin, ngin* being the least commonly used verbal preposition merely has the purposive and thematic functions. Complements are marked either by way of an object pro-index, as shown in (6.56), or by a lexical noun phrase, as shown in (6.57), where they encode the purposive function in association with intransitive active verbs.

6.56 *Ne-najnge* **ngin**-*i.*
1SG:REAL-agree PURP1-3SGOBJ
'I agree for it.'
(2012_05_16 obanhy01001 00:00:08.000-00:00:09.500 natural text)

6.57 *Khai* *Ø-ba-ma* **ngin** *nanalokh.*
3SG 3SG:REAL-POT-to.come PURP1 kava
'He will come for kava.'
(2014_01_19 naanhy01001 00:13:00.000-00:13:03.000 natural text)

Conversely, the verbal preposition is also used to indicate a core argument of the verb clause, as illustrated in (6.58), where the speaker uses *ngin* to introduce the theme of the action expressed by the transitive head verb.

6.58 *Rri-serrteng* **ngin** *voli-n* *netenge* *mandarin* *khe*
1PLINCL:REAL-count PURP1 cost-3SG:POSS thingummy mandarins DEM
'We count the cost of the thingummy, the mandarins.'
(2014_02_18 naaksi01001 00:13:55.000-00:13:58.000 natural text)

6.6.2 True prepositions

True prepositions are those whose complements are restricted to noun phrases. Nese only has three true prepositions: *rengen* 'to, into, on', *neten* 'for, for the purpose of' and *belek* 'like'. The preposition *rengen* is a general locative preposition, encoding the meanings 'to', 'into', 'on' and indicating the place or thing to which an action is directed or at which an action is taking place. Although there is evidence to suggest that it also introduces a participant marked for the semantic role of stimulus, due to the fact that in the majority of cases this preposition introduces a participant that has a locative role, the preposition is labelled as LOC.

The use of *rengen* in expressing a core argument is restricted to verbs that obligatorily require not necessarily a physical location as a third argument, but a locus affected by the action encoded in the verb(s) such as 'calico' in (6.59) and 'saucepan' in (6.60).

6.59 *Re-takh-e   ri-vita-i   **rengen**   norrurr*
     3PL:REAL-take3SGOBJ 3PL:REAL-put-3SGOBJ LOC   calico
     'They take it, they put it in

   sakhal buro.
   one   GENMOD
   just a calico.'
   (2014_01_19 naanhy01001 00:29:04.000-00:29:10.000 natural text)

In (6.60), the locative preposition specifically has the meaning of 'into' as the preceding serial verbs *vreng-* 'throw' and *ling-* 'leave' and the directional verb *v'an* indicate motion into something.

6.60 *Ale   vreng-i   ling-i   v'an   **rengen**   sospen.*
     CONJ   throw-3SGOBJ   leave-3SGOBJ   go   LOC   saucepan
     'And she threw it into the saucepan.'
     (2014_01_19 naanhy01001 00:05:32.000-00:05:35.000 natural text)

Expression of a locational semantic role is not a property limited to core arguments, as arguments that function as adjuncts also encode locational as well as instrumental and temporal semantic roles. A locational function encodes the meaning 'to' or 'into', as shown in (6.61), where *rengen* bears the meaning 'to', indicating the location or intended destination of the action expressed by the intransitive active verb *v'an* 'go'.

6. SIMPLE SENTENCES

6.61 | *Gregory* | *khai* | *Ø-s-be-v'an-te* | ***rengen*** | *sukul.*
| Gregory | 3SG | 3SG-IRR-NEG1-go -NEG2 | LOC | school

'Gregory, he did not go to church.'[1]

(2014_01_19 naanhy01001 00:16:59.000-00:17:03.000 natural text)

When *rengen* has an instrumental function, the preposition expresses the means by which an action is carried out, as shown in examples (6.62) and (6.63), where the prepositional phrases are adjuncts of the verbal clause.

6.62 | *Edwin* | *khe* | *Ø-ti-vala* | ***rengen*** | *baskel.*
| Edwin | DEM | 3SG:REAL-ASP-run | LOC | bicycle

'That's Edwin, running (riding) on the bike.'

(2014_01_19 naanhy01001 00:38:10.000-00:38:13.000 natural text)

6.63 | *Benetil* | *khai* | *Ø-v'an* | ***rengen*** | *nuaknakis.*
| Three days ago | 3SG | 3SG:REAL-go | LOC | canoe

'Three days ago he went by canoe.'

(2014_01_19 naanhy01001 00:24:54.000-00:24:57.000 natural text)

A temporal meaning is equivalent to 'on', indicating the date at which an event or action takes place, as illustrated in (6.64) and (6.65).

6.64 | *Khina* | *ne-v'an* | *khe,* | *rri-v'an* | | ***rengen***
| 1SG | 1SG:REAL-go | DEM | 1PLINCL:REAL-go | | LOC

'I went, we went on

mande | *khe,* | *no-khro* | *v'an* | *v'an* | *ne-les* | *te*
Monday | DEM | 1SG:REAL-stay | go | go | 1SG:REAL-see | SUB

Monday, I stayed until I saw them

ri-ma.
3PL:REAL-come

coming.'

(2014_01_2019 naanhy01001 00:32:06.000-00:32:12.000 natural text)

---

1   The speaker is using 'school' in this instance to refer to 'church' rather than 'school'. In general, older Ni-Vanuatu tend to use 'school' to refer to either 'a school' or 'a church' while the younger generation restrict its meaning to the commonly understood meaning of 'school'.

6.65 | *Ale* | *re-v'an* | *re-takh-e* | **rengen** | *namba* | *wan.*
CONJ | 3PL:REAL-go | 3PL:REAL-take-3SGOBJ | LOC | number | one

'Then they went and took it on the first (of January).'
(2014_01_19 naanhy01001 00:52:07.000-00:52:10.000 natural text)

All the examples involving *rengen* in this subsection show the complements occurring in their typical position – that is, after the preposition. As shown in §6.6.1.1, adjunct arguments introduced by the verbal preposition *khin* may be left dislocated with a trace left behind in the site of extraction in the form of an object pro-index. The preposition *rengen* does not take object marking via a pro-index, so when a lexical noun phrase functioning as the complement of *rengen* is topicalised, there is lowering of the /e/ vowels resulting in *rangan* (cf. §2.5.2.5), as illustrated in (6.66), where an adjunct noun phrase, bearing the locational meaning 'on', has been topicalised.

6.66 | **Nejal** | **iekhe** | *rri-yat* | **rangan.**
mat | DEM:LOC | 1PL:REAL-sit | LOC

'This one here is a mat, we are sitting on.'
(2014_01_19 naanhy01001 00:29:41.000-00:29:42.000 natural text)

The topicalised complement of *rengen* may also encode the adjunct related locational meaning equivalent to 'in', as shown in (6.65).

6.67 | *Plen,* | *tenge* | *rov* | *jelekh* | *ri-nas* | **rangan.**
plane | thing | COMPL | all | 3PL:REAL-die | LOC

'As for planes, everything dies in it.'
(2014_01_19 naanhy01001 01:07:15.000-00:07:18.000 natural text)

While *rangan* may be co-referential with dislocated noun phrase arguments, example (6.68) shows that it may also be co-referential with the object noun phrase argument of a main clause. In (6.68), *rangan* occurs in a subordinate clause while its co-referential noun phrase is a core object argument *nalok* 'laplap' in the main clause.

6.68 | *Bor-woj* | **nalok** | **lokbusbuak,** | *te* | *ne-bet*
1PLEXCL:REAL-eat | laplap | laplap.taro | SUB | 1SG:REAL-make

nolulngun | **rangan.**
laplap.type | LOC

'We ate laplap taro which I used to make laplap wrapped with cabbage.'
(2012_05_16 obanhy01001 00:01:26.000-00:01:32.000 natural text)

Furthermore, *rangan* may occur in a main clause with its co-referential noun phrase occurring in an antecedent main clause, as shown in (6.69).

6.69 *Khai khe na,* **sukul** *v'at* *khe,* *re-ma* *re-vita-i*
      3SG DEM EMP   school four DEM 3PL:REAL- 3PL:REAL-put-3SGOBJ
                                                     come

  'That's the one, those four churches, they came and established them

  iekhetan *iekhe,* *nemere* *sikh-sikha* *mu* **rangan**.
  DEM   DEM:LOC people   REDUP-NEG   ADV   LOC
  down here, there is no longer anyone in them.'
  (2012_08_22 anhy01005 00:03:17.000-00:03:22.000 natural text)

In (6.69), *rangan* is co-referential with the lexical noun phrase *sukul v'at* functioning as a left dislocated object argument of the antecedent main clause with the verbal head *rre-vita-i*, as well as a topicalised noun phrase argument of the true preposition *rengen*.

The preposition *neten* means 'for' or 'for the purpose of'. It provides the purpose for an action expressed by the verb, by way of a lexical noun phrase object. Like *belek,* prepositional *neten* may combine with the subordinator *te* to introduce adverbial clauses of purpose (cf. §7.5.3.3). The only type of objects that *neten* may take is common nouns. This is illustrated in (6.70) and (6.71).

6.70 *...Ne-v'an* **neten** *navij* *sakhal.*
      1SG:REAL-go PURP2   banana one
  'I went for a banana.'
  (2012_05_16 obanhy01003 00:01:44.000-01:46.000 natural text)

6.71 *Kirr-bat* *kavrra* **neten** *nav'at.*
      2PL:REAL-make copra PURP2   money
  'You (PL) make copra for money.'
  (Fieldnotes, elictitation)

Neten resembles *ngin* 'for' in that both can only take common nouns as objects; however, *ngin* does not combine with the subordinator *te* to introduce adverbial clauses.

The form *belek* has a prepositional similitive function meaning 'like'. It is used to describe similarities between states and actions indicating that something or an action is like something else or like another action. Apart from functioning as a preposition, *belek* also has properties that are verbal, evidence of which is given in examples (6.72), where it takes the aspectual prefix *ti*, and in (6.73), where it is negated with the negative discontinuous markers.

6.72 *Navar-am   Ø-khus-khus   je   neten   te   Ø-ti-yat*
     Hand-2SG:POSS 3SG:REAL-REDUP-   ADV   PURP2   SUB   3SG:REAL-ASP-sit
                    shake

'Your hand is shaking a lot because he was sitting and

*Ø-ti-les   te   **Ø-ti-belek**   khe.*
3SG:REAL-ASP-see   SUB   3SG:REAL-ASP-like   DEM

saw that it's like this.'

(2014_01_2019 naanhy01001 00:39:02.000-00:39:06.000 natural text)

6.73 *Neten   te   tua   **Ø-s-be-belek-te**   nekrre   sana.*
     PURP2   SUB   before   3SG-IRR-NEG1-like-NEG2   1PLEXCL   today

'Because before (the past) was not like us today.' ('Because things were different in the past compared to our situation today.')

(Fieldnotes, natural text)

However, since *belek* cannot take subject prefixes, a criterion used to distinguish verbs from other word classes, I therefore classify it as a preposition. *Belek* may combine with the subordinator *te* to introduce an adverbial clause of manner (cf. §7.5.3.2). Prepositional *belek* 'like' may take a noun phrase or a nominal demonstrative as its object. It may also function as the predicate of a non-verbal clause.

A noun phrase with a proper noun as the head may function as the object of *belek*, as shown in (6.74), and in such cases the 3SG object pro-index suffixed to the transitive verb *les* 'see' has been elided. This elided argument is co-referential with the object of *belek*; however, the prepositional phrase is a non-core argument.

6.74 *Ne-les*   ***belek***   Edwin.
      1SG:REAL-see   like   Edwin
      'It looks like Edwin/I see as if that's Edwin.'
      (2014_01_19 naanhy01001 00:38:07.000-00:38:09.000 natural text)

In example (6.74), the speaker is sitting down and saw a person far off in the distance and suggests that it might be Edwin. Example (6.75) shows *belek* functioning as the head of a prepositional phrase that forms the predicate component of the clause with the 3SG independent pronoun filling the subject slot. In this example, *belek* is used for comparative purposes, identifying the 3SG subject argument as being identical to the argument represented by the common noun phrase *takharr khe*.

6.75 *Khai*   ***belek***   ***takharr***   *khe.*
      3SG   like   whiteman   DEM
      'He is like that whiteman.'
      (2014_01_19 naanhy01001 00:45:47.000-00:45:48.000 natural text)

A common noun may be the head of an NP functioning as the object of a prepositional phrase with *belek* as the head, as shown in (6.76), where the prepositional phrase is an adjunct argument of the intransitive active verb *vala* 'run'.

6.76 *Nuak*   *sakhal*   *khe*   *khai*   *Ø-vala*   ***belek***   ***plen.***
      Boat   one   DEM   3SG   3SG:REAL-run   like   plane
      'That boat, it runs like a plane.'
      (2014_01_19 naanhy01001 01:06:27.000-01:06:30.000 natural text)

When the preposition has the demonstrative *khe* as its object it may indicate an action that is accompanied by a gesture, as shown in (6.77). There are cases, however, where the object *khe* does not need an accompanying gesture because it refers rather to an antecedent statement rather than to a motion or action. This is shown in (6.77) and (6.78), where the prepositional phrases are adjunct arguments.

6.77 *Navar-ak*   *iekhe*   *khai*   *Ø-khus-khus*   ***belek***   ***khe.***
      Hand-1SG:POSS   DEM   3SG   3SG:REAL-REDUP-shake   like   DEM
      'My hand here, it's shaking like this.'
      (2019_01_19 naanhy01001 00:39:09.000-00:39:11.000 natural text)

6.78   *Ne-ve*   *"no*   *khina*   *na-v'an*   *te*   *nemerrte..."*
1SG:REAL-say   'no   1SG   1SG:REAL-go   SUB   man...

na-var-i   **belek**   **khe**.
1SG:REAL-say-3SGOBJ   like   DEM
'I said, "no I went so that the men...". I said it like that.'
(2014_01_19 naanhy01001 00:09:54.000-00:10:09.000 natural text)

In (6.78), the object of the preposition *khe* refers to the antecedent statement in quotation marks.

Another use of the prepositional construction *belek khe* is that it may mean 'for example'. This is shown in (6.79).

6.79   *Neren*   *sakhal*   *ru,*   **belek**   **khe,**   *je-v'an*   *kele*   *te*
Time   one   two   like   DEM   1SG:IRR-go   again   SUB
'Once or twice, for example, I will go again to

je-jer   *naute.*
1SG:IRR-clean   garden
clean the garden.'
(2012_08_27 obnesp01003 00:08:14.000-00:08:25.000 natural text)

So in (6.79), the speaker is talking about clearing the bush for gardening and uses *belek khe* to give an example of how many times the clearing of the bush may be done.

6.6.3 Adverbs

Adverbs occur outside of the clausal core and are, therefore, non-core constituents that modify the whole clause (cf. §3.6). Clause-level adverbs include nouns functioning as temporal adjuncts, such as *amu* 'before', *benetil* 'three days ago', indicating the temporal setting of the clause, and *naleng* 'maybe', which denotes uncertainty about the proposition expressed by the verb.

6.80   *Kanan*   *wor*   *bir-v'an*   ***amu***.
1PLEXCL   MOD   1PLEXCL:REAL- go   before
'It was us who went first.'
(2012_05_16 obanhy01005 00:03:59.000-00:04:01.000 natural text)

In (6.80), *amu* occupies a clause final position in contrast with *benetil*, which occupies a clause initial position, as shown in (6.81).

6.81 **Benetil**   khai   Ø-v'an   rengen   nuaknakis
      Three days ago   3SG   3SG:REAL-go   LOC   canoe
      'Three days ago she went on the canoe.'
      (2014_01_19 naanhy01001 00:24:54.000-00:24:57.000 natural text)

As illustrated in (6.80) and (6.81), adjunct clausal adverbs with temporal denotations normally may occupy both clause initial and clause final positions.

Unlike temporal adverbs that may occupy clause initial and clause final positions, the occurrence of the adverb *naleng* is restricted to clause initial position, as illustrated in (6.82).

6.82 Khina   **naleng**   je-kilaik   nani   s-ak
      1SG   maybe   1SG:IRR-check on   coconut   CLGEN-1SG:POSS
      'Maybe I will go and check on my coconuts

      ev'an   vila.
      DIR   seawards
      down there towards the sea.'
      (2014_01_19 nanhy01001 00:58:12.000-00:58:16.000 natural text)

In (6.82), *naleng* occupies the slot between the subject pronoun and the subject cross-index marking. This contrasts with *benetil* in (6.81), which occupies the slot before the subject pronoun.

6.6.4 Demonstratives

As stated in §3.11, the demonstratives *khe, iekhe* and *iekhatan* have spatial denotations. The latter two are classed as local adverbial demonstratives while *khe* is predominantly a nominal demonstrative in spite of the fact that it encodes spatial meanings in some respects. When these demonstratives express a spatial meaning, they function as locational adjuncts.

When *khe* functions as a locational adjunct, it encodes the meaning 'here' or 'there' or any location that may be indicated by the speaker via gestural means.

6.83 | Khai | Ø-khro | buro | **khe** | ale | Ø-ma
| 3SG | 3SG:REAL-stay | GENMOD | DEM | CONJ | 3SG:REAL-come

'She was just here and she came

Ø-ma **khe**
3SG:REAL-come DEM
she came here.'
(2014_01_19 naanhy01001 00:15:46.000-00:15:49.000 natural text)

In (6.83), the location to which the initial instance of *khe* refers is different to that referred to by *khe* in the last clause. The expression of both instances of *khe* in this utterance is accompanied by eye gesture indicating the contrast between the two occurrences of *khe*. In some cases, *khe* is further modified by other directional particles like *vila* 'seawards' to further indicate the location of an event or action expressed by the verb.

Iekhe 'here' indicates a position that is proximal to the speaker or the location in which the speaker is located in, as illustrated in (6.84).

6.84 | Ne-var-i | khin | vinelekh | ne-ve | ma
| 1SG-tell-3SGOBJ | PREP | daughter in law | 1SG:REAL- say | come

'I told the daughter-in-law, I said, "come

yat **iekhe**!
sit DEM:LOC
sit here".'
(2014_01_19 naanhy01001 00:01:18.000-00:01:22.000 natural text)

In (6.84), *iekhe* occupies a clause final non-core position. Contrasting with *khe*, which can never occupy a clause initial non-core position, Nese allows *iekhe* to fill a clause initial non-core position slot, as illustrated in (6.85).

6.85 | **Iekhe,** | khunokh | khe | kho-se-lol | v'an | v'an.
| DEM | 2SG | DEM | 2SG-IRR- to live | go | go

'Here you will live on and on.'
(2014_02_18 naaksi01001 00:21:09.000-00:21:11.000 natural text)

Iekhe may also occupy a clause initial non-core position within a subordinate clause, as illustrated in (6.86).

6.86	*Ne-var-i*	*khin-er*	*ne-ve*	*khai*
	1SG:REAL-tell-3SGOBJ	PREP-3PLOBJ	1SG:REAL-say	3SG
	'I told them, I said, "She			

	Ø-se-evlakh	*neten*	*te*	*sana*	***iekhe***	*te-jiblakh*
	3SG-IRR- be happy	PURP2	SUB	ADV	DEM:LOC	PL-child
	will be happy because today, here					

sikh-sikha.

3SG:REAL-REDUP-NEG

there are no kids".'

(2014_01_2019 naanhy01001 00:35:34.000-00:35:41.000 natural text)

The locational demonstrative *iekhetan*, as used in construction (6.87), indicates a downward location in close proximity to the speaker.

6.87	*Tav'at*	*yat!*	*Yat*	***iekhetan***	*khe.*
	woman	sit	sit	DEM	EMP
	'Woman sit! Sit down here.'				

(2012_06_12 obaksi01001 00:11:07.000-00:1:10.000 natural text)

6.6.5 Locational nouns

Locational nouns, occurring in clause final position, may function as adjuncts of intransitive clauses, indicating the location at which an action takes place. An example is given at (6.87).

6.88	***Tawu***	***Ø-ti-natur***	***latas.***
	cone shell	3SG:REAL-ASP-sleep	sea:LOC
	'The coneshell slept in the sea.'		

(2012_05_16 obanhy01004 00:00:07.000-00:00:09.000 natural text)

In (6.88), the locational noun *latas* indicates the location in which the action expressed by the intransitive active verb *natur* 'sleep' takes place. Although locational nouns normally occupy a clause final position, as shown in (6.88), they may also occupy a focused clause initial position, as illustrated by example (6.89).

6.89 Khina **leut-ak** nobukhas khai Ø-ti-v'an woj maniok
1SG garden:LOC pig 3SG 3SG:REAL-ASP-go eat manioc
'As for me, in my garden, the pig went and ate

s-anan, woj maniok s-ak.
CLGEN-1PLEXCL:POSS eat manioc CLGEN-1SG:POSS
our manioc, my manioc.'
(2012_05_16 obanhy01003 00:05:56.000-00:06:02.000 natural text)

6.6.6 Temporal nouns

Nouns functioning as temporal adjuncts may occupy either a clause initial or clause final position, indicating the temporal setting of the event described by the verb. In example (6.90), the noun functioning as a temporal adjunct is in clause initial position.

6.90 **Benanev** no-khro buro laine.
yesterday 1SG:REAL-stay GENMOD home:LOC
'Yesterday I just stayed at home.'
(2014_01_19 naanhy01001 00:00:02.000-00:00:05.000 natural text)

When it occurs in a clause final position, a noun functioning as a temporal adjunct occupies clause final slot, as illustrated in (6.91), where it occurs clause finally after the intransitive verb *sakhsakh* 'to work'.

6.91 Khina no-rong-o sikha, no-rong te
1SG 1SG:REAL-feel-3SGOBJ NEG 1SG:REAL-feel SUB
'I don't want to, I feel that

rri-**sakhsakh** **benanev** v'an v'an...
1PL:REAL-work yesterday go go
we worked so much yesterday, I'm tired.'
(2012_05_16 obanhy01003 00:00:37.000-00:00:41.000 natural text)

6.7 Interrogative clauses

Polar questions are distinguished from declarative clauses by a question intonation. Content questions are formed by using the following proforms that tend to seek information otherwise provided by noun phrases. In general, these proforms, listed in Table 6.3, occupy the same structural slot occupied by the item being questioned. Apart from using proforms, Nese also employs a question tag formed with the conjunction *deve* 'or' with the negative verb *sikha*.

Table 6.3: Interrogative proforms

Proform	
khise	'who'
vise	'how many'
verse	'how'
nese	'what'
sev'elnge	'when'

6.7.1 *Khise*

An interrogative clause containing *khise* 'who' seeks information about the identity of a participant in a clause – information that is absent in the clause but is typically expressed via noun phrases or independent pronouns. As stated in §4.3, noun phrases may function as a subject argument of a verbal clause, a subject argument of a non-verbal clause, an object argument of a verbal clause or an object argument of a true preposition. Thus, it is expected that in an interrogative clause where the identity of the noun phrase occupying those structural slots is questioned via the interrogative preform *khise*, the latter will occur in the position preceding the structural positions occupied by those noun phrases in the clause.

Given that subjects occupy a clause initial position, the form *khise* occupies the preceding structural slot, as illustrated in (6.92), where the interrogative *khise* occupies the slot preceding the subject position in the verbal clause with an intransitive verb head.

6.92 Tua   norojian   sikh-sikha,   nemerrte Ø-s-be-roj-te,
      ADV   sickness   REDUP-NEG   people   3SG-IRR-NEG1-be sick-NEG2
      'In the past there was no sickness, no one was sick,

   khise khai   Ø-roj?
   INT   3SG   3SG:REAL-be sick
   who was sick?'

Noun phrases may also function as subjects of non-verbal clauses, which means that an interrogative clause may be composed of a non-verbal clause seeking information about the identity of a participant by means of *khise* occupying the slot preceding subject position. This is illustrated in (6.93).

6.93 Rri-bet   norrian   lemje   je,   **khise** nemerrte nen?
      3PL:REAL-make   food   a.lot   ADV   INT   man   POSS
      'We made so much food, who is its man? (who is the person who is supposed to eat this)'
      (2014_01_19 naanhy01001 00:15:00.000-00:15:03.000 natural text)

The last clause in (6.93) represents a non-verbal clause in which *khise* occupies the slot preceding subject position and the possessive noun phrase *nemerrte nen* forms the predicate. The position occupied by interrogative *khise* in non-verbal clauses is not restricted to clause initial position since it may also occupy a clause final position, as shown in (6.94).

6.94 Nat-ne   **velvele**   khe   nengs-an   **khise**?
      Child-3SG:POSS   small   DEM   name-3SG:POSS   INT
      'That small child of hers what's his name?'
      (2014_01_19 naanhy01001 00:34:48.000-00:34:50.000 natural text)

Example (6.94) shows an interrogative clause in which the subject is a directly possessed noun phrase. Nese also allows indirectly possessed nouns to occupy the subject slot in non-verbal clauses and, in such cases, since a lexical noun phrase may constitute the possessor in an indirect possessive relationship, interrogative *khise* may occupy the possessor slot, as shown in (6.95).

6.95 Nale   jin   **khise**   khe?
      language   POSS   INT   DEM
      'Whose language is this?'
      (Fieldnotes, natural text)

Nese allows the option of the interrogative *khise* either occupying the slot preceding the subject, as illustrated in (6.96), or the predicate slot in non-verbal clauses, as illustrated by example (6.94). There is a restriction on the type of non-verbal clause in which this option is permissible. Non-verbal clauses in which the predicate slot is occupied by a demonstrative do not allow *khise* to occupy the two alternative slots. As shown in (6.96), in non-verbal clauses containing a demonstrative functioning as an argument, the demonstrative can only occupy the predicate slot.

6.96 **Khise**   khe?
     INT   DEM
     'Who is this?'
     (2014_01_19 naanhy01001 00:22:43.000 natural text)

Furthermore, an interrogative clause may be a subordinate clause, as illustrated in (6.97), where interrogative *khise* precedes the subject of the subordinate clause.

6.97 Kho-rong   te   **khise** khai   rongvuson-i?
     2SG:REAL-want   SUB   INT   3SG   understand-3SGOBJ
     'Who do you want who will understand it?'
     (2014_01_19 naanhy01001 00:40:08.000-00:40:10.000 natural text)

The subject position of an interrogative clause may be occupied by a lexical noun phrase composed of a noun phrase conjoined by the comitative *min* with the interrogative form *khise*. As stated in §3.2.1, the initial noun phrase occurring before the conjunction always contains a superset free pronoun, namely the 1PL EXCL and 3PL independent pronouns, and the noun phrase occurring after the conjunction is an included subset noun phrase. Since the initial position is restricted to the 1PL EXCL and 3PL independent pronouns, it is the second noun phrase slot that may be occupied by interrogative *khise*, as shown in (6.98).

6.98 Khar   min   **khise** khe?   no   khar   min   jokh-ok
     3PL   CONJ   INT   DEM   NEG   3PL   CONJ   uncle-1SG:POSS

     Priscilla   khe.
     Priscilla   DEM
     'Who is that with them? No that's my uncle Priscilla with them.'
     (2014_01_19 naanhy01001 00:16:39.000-00:16:43.000 natural text)

There are no examples in the data of an interrogative clause formed by *khise* occupying the object position and co-occurring with a transitive verb head or a verbal preposition introducing an argument of an extended transitive verb such as *var* 'to tell'.

6.7.2 Vise

An interrogative clause may be formed when the quantity of a noun phrase is not mentioned and numerical information is, therefore, sought after. This is achieved by way of the interrogative proform *vise* 'how many'. As stated in §4.5.5 and §4.5.6, quantifiers and numerals may modify heads of noun phrases indicating their numerical value. It would, therefore, follow that the interrogative proform *vise* would occupy the structural slots occupied by these modifiers in an interrogative clause. Numerical modifiers occur post-nominally, thus, as shown in (6.99), *vise* also occupies a post-nominal position.

6.99   *Ne-ve*   *Jokh-ok*   *nenet-en*   *nial*   ***vise?***
       1SG:REAL-say   uncle-1SG:POSS   eye-3SG:POSS   sun   how many
       'I said, "uncle how many eyes does the sun have?" (what is the time?)'
       (2014_01_19 naanhy01001 00:33:04.000-00:33:08.000 natural text)

However, an interrogative clause may also be formed when the proform *vise* is topicalised, occupying a pre-nominal position, as illustrated in (6.100).

6.100   *Be*   ***vise***   *nemere*   *khar*   *ru-sul*   *kavra.*
        CONJ   how many   man   3PL   3PL:REAL-burn   copra
        'But how many men burnt the copra?'
        (Fieldnotes, elicitation)

In (6.100), *vise* occupies the slot before noun phrase functioning as the subject of the intransitive clause

6.7.3 Verse

Interrogative clauses that inquire about the means through which or the manner in which an action is carried out use the proform *verse* 'how' in addition to its usage as a subordinator to introduce an adverbial clause (cf. §7.5.3). It was highlighted in §3.6 that a subclass of adverbs modifies heads of verb complexes providing aspectual, manner and intensification information regarding the head of the verb. These occupy a post-verbal position; therefore, *verse* also occupies a post-verbal position.

In (6.101), the interrogative *verse* occupies a post-verbal slot, functioning as an adverbial adjunct.

6.101 *Khar   ro-vol-i   **verse?***
      3PL   3PL:REAL-buy-3SGOBJ   how
      'How did they buy it?'
      (2014_01_19 naanhy01001 00:28:50.000-00:28:52.000 natural text)

Verse may also occupy a preverbal position, as illustrated in (6.102), in which the interrogative proform occupies the slot prior to the 3PL independent pronoun functioning as the subject of the transitive clause.

6.102 ***Verse***   *nemere*   *re-bet*   *nalok?*
      how   3PL   3PL:REAL-make   laplap
      'How do people make laplap?'
      (2012_07_29 elloro01001a 00:02:47.000-00:02:49.000 elicitation)

When *verse* occurs in post-verbal position in transitive clauses, it occupies the slot after the object noun phrase, as shown in (6.103).

6.103 *Bir-tu-tun*   *navij*   ***verse?***
      1PLEXCL:REAL-REDUP-roast   banana   how
      'How do we roast bananas?'
      (Fieldnotes, elicitation)

The interrogative proform *verse* may also function as the predicate of a non-verbal clause, as shown in (6.104).

6.104 *Dev'e*   *khunokh*   ***verse?***
      mother   2SG   how
      'Mother, how about you?'
      (Fieldnotes, natural text)

6.7.4 Khade

The form *khade* means 'where' and indicates the location of something. The proform usually occurs either after a verb complex where it has a locative adverbial function, as shown in (6.105), or as the predicate of a non-verbal clause, as shown in (6.106).

6.105 Khar   re-ve   khai   Ø-se-ma   Ø-se-v'an   **khade?**
      3PL   3PL:REAL-say   3SG   3SG-REAL-come   3SG-IRR-go   where
      'They said, "he will come and go where?"'
      (Fieldnotes, natural text)

6.106 *Nev'enu-n*   *tama-m*   **khade?**
      place-3SG:POSS   father-2SG:POSS   where
      'Where is your father's place?/Where is your father from?'
      (2014_01_19 naanhy01001 00:19:49.000-00:19:52.000 natural text)

Nese makes no lexical distinction between the interrogative form for where an action performed by a subject takes place, as shown in (6.105), and the location of something as shown, as illustrated by the use of *khade* in (6.106) and (6.107).

6.107 *Nesde*   *s-ak,*   *khai*   **khade?**
      Knife   CLGEN-1SG:POSS   3SG   where
      'My knife, where is it?'
      (2012_07_12 obaksi01001 00:22:09.000 natural text)

Like the other interrogative forms previously discussed, *khade* may also occupy a clause initial position, as shown in (6.108).

6.108 **Khade**   *nobukhas*   *Ø-tab*   *belek*   *khe.*
      where   pig   3SG:REAL-lost   like   DEM
      'Where did the pig get lost like this?'
      (2012_05_16 oanhy01010 00:06:56.000-00:06:59.000 natural text)

6.7.5 Nese

The interrogative form *nese*, which is equivalent to 'what' in English, is used to question the identity of noun phrases that occupy the structural slot in which *nese* occupies. To begin with, *nese* may occupy the position of verbal complement, as shown in (6.109).

6.109 *Rri-si-terev*   **nese?**
       1PLINCL-IRR-wait   what
       'What will we wait for?'
       (2014_01_19 00:01:33.000-00:01:34.000 natural text)

It may also function as the complement of a verbal preposition functioning as an argument of the clause, as shown in (6.110).

6.110 *Re-ve*   *Khunokh*   *kho-se-visvisen-i*   *min*   **nese?**
       3PL:REAL-say   2SG   2SG-IRR-show-3SGOBJ   PREP   what
       'They said, "What will you show her?"'
       (2014_01_19 00:01:33.000-00:01:34.000 natural text)

The interrogative proform may also occur after the subordinator *neten* to seek specific reasons, as shown in (6.111).

6.111 *Khai*   *Ø-nas*   *neten*   **nese?**
       3SG   3SG:REAL-die   PURP2   what
       'Why did he die?'
       (2014_01_19 naanhy01001 00:45:21.000-00:45:22.000 natural text)

6.7.6 Sev'elnge

Lastly, Nese employs the clause final form *sev'elnge* to question the date and time of a particular proposition, as shown in (6.112). Nouns functioning as temporal adjuncts also indicate the date and time of an action expressed by a head verb may occupy both clause initial and clause final positions. The proform *sev'elnge*, however, can only occupy a clause final position.

6.112 *Rri-si-v'an*   **sev'elnge?**
       1PLINCL-IRR-go   when
       'When will we go?'
       (2012_07_29 elloro01001a 00:01:40.000-00:01:41.000 elicitation)

6.8 Imperative clauses

Nese exhibits two types of imperative clauses: affirmative imperative clauses and negative imperative clauses. They may be articulated either as direct speech or as reported speech and are distinguished by the lack of subject cross-indexing on the verb. This is illustrated in (6.113) where there are no subject cross-indexes present on the verbs in the imperative clause.

6.113 *Letang   lev   sospen   ma   iekhetan!*
      Sister   bring   saucepan   DIR   DEM
      'Sister bring the saucepan here!'
      (2012_06_12 obaksi01001 00:03:52.000-00:03:56.000 natural text)

In (6.113), the noun phrase *letang* has a vocative function. Noun phrases with vocative functions may also be optional in imperative clauses, as illustrated in (6.114), where there is no vocative noun phrase.

6.114 *V'an   tekh   norobne!*
      go   take   umbrella
      'Go and take the umbrella!'
      (2012_05_16 obanhy01003 00:01:37.000-00:01:38.000 natural text)

The two examples above constitute commands given in direct speech. Commands may also be given as reported speech and, in such cases, the subject noun phrase is not emphasised, as illustrated in (6.115).

6.115 *Re-ve   'No   v'an   jalin   les   kher   jalin!'.*
      3PL:REAL- say   No   go   outside   see   3PL   outside
      'They said, "No, go outside and see them outside!"'
      (2014_01_19 naanhy01001 00:16:02.000-00:16:05.000 natural text)

A command may be given as a warning, in which case the dehortative *khota* is used, as illustrated in (6.116).

6.116 *Ey   **khota**   kho-bet   nebet   terrterr   belek   khe!*
      hey   DEHORT   2SG:REAL-make   head   strong   like   DEM
      'Hey stop being stubborn like this!'
      (2012_05_16 obanhy010 00:04:03.000-00:04:05.000 natural text)

When a command employs the dehortative marker, the subject cross-indexes must be expressed on the verb, as shown in (6.116), contrasting with imperative clauses that are not expressed as warnings, as shown in (6.115). This contrast is made clearer in (6.117), where the second clause is a command containing the dehortative mood marker. In this clause, the addressee is sleeping and a command is given as a warning not to sleep, or to discontinue the activity. The last two clauses are affirmative imperative clauses that do not convey any warning, therefore, displaying a lack of mood expression on the verb.

6.117 *Re-ve* '*mama mama* **khota** **kho**-*natur!* *Lana*
3PL:REAL-say mum mum DEHORT 2PL:REAL-sleep Lana
'They said, "Mum, Mum don't sleep! Lana

Ø-ti-ma *v'an* *jalin!* *Rakhtakh* *v'an* *jalin!*'
3SG:REAL-ASP-come go outside get up go outside
has come go outside! Get up and go outside!"'
(2014_01_19 naanhy01001 00:15:50.000-00:15:56.000 natural text)

An imperative clause may also be composed of a warning expressed via a negated verb marked for the dehortative mood. This is illustrated in (6.118), where the speaker is expressing a warning-like command to herself not to divulge information.

6.118 *Ne-ve* **khota** *j-be*-*vervis-i-te!*
1SG:REAL-say DEHORT 1SG:IRR-NEG1-reveal-3SGOBJ-NEG2
'I said, "I must not reveal it!"'
(2014_01_19 naanhy01001 00:33:00.000-00:33:02.000 natural text)

All the examples in the data show that when *khota* co-occurs with a verb marked for negation, the latter is fused with the irrealis mood rather than the realis mood, thereby expressing a proposition whose realisation has not yet occurred at the time of utterance, or one expressing a hypothetical situation. It is, therefore, clear that when an imperative clause contains *khota* occurring in conjunction with a verb head marked for realis mood, it signals an order to cease an action that is in progress. On the other hand, when an imperative clause is composed of preverbal *khota* followed by a negated verb marked for the irrealis mood, the action expressed by the verb signals a command to prohibit the realisation of an action.

6.9 Comparative clauses

Comparative and superlative relationships are not expressed in Nese via derivational processes affecting the lexical root, unlike in English. In fact, there is no distinction in the expression of comparative or superlative relationships since one single stative intransitive verb can encode a comparative or superlative denotation, as illustrated in (6.119).

6.119 *Khai*   *Ø-skhaskho*   ***nakis***.
      3SG   3SG:REAL-sing   good
      'She sings well.'/'She sings better.'/'She sings the best.'
      (Fieldnotes, elicitation)

The expression of a comparative relationship existing between two participants is achieved via the verb *jov* 'to win'. This is shown in (6.120).

6.120 *Khai*   *Ø-skhaskho*   ***nakis***   *Ø-jov*   *John.*
      3SG   3SG:REAL-sing   good   3SG:REAL-win   John
      'She sings better than John.'
      (Fieldnotes, elicitation)

6.10 Passive clauses

Nese does not possess passive constructions; however, agentless constructions in Nese are expressed by means of the 3PL independent pronoun *khar* or simply by the 3PL subject pro-index with no co-referential independent pronoun or lexical noun phrase subject. The use of *khar* or the 3PL subject pro-index, without any preceding subject noun phrase, indicates that the action described by the verb has no specific agent referred to within the clause or in any preceding clauses. This is illustrated in (6.121), where *khar* is used with no preceding subject noun phrase. The elicitation prompt used was the agentless construction in Bislama *Oli tekem i kam* 'they brought it hither' or 'it was brought hither', a construction resembling those identified as subjectless predicate constructions by Crowley (2004, p. 121), which are functionally equivalent to passive constructions in English.

6.121 **Khar** re-takh-e ma.
3PL 3PL:REAL-take-3SGOBJ come
'They brought it hither.'/'It was brought hither.'
(2012_08_22 anhy012 00:48:38.000-00:48:40.000 natural text)

The use of the 3PL independent pronoun in agentless constructions does not necessarily mean that the unspecified subject is a plural entity. It could also be used to refer to a singular entity, as illustrated in (6.122).

6.122 **Khar** ri-us-i kele, kirr-var-i.
3PL 3PL:REAL-ask-3SGOBJ again 2PL:REAL-say-3SGOBJ
'They are asking it again, you guys talk about it.'
(Fieldnotes, natural text)

In (6.122), a question was being asked by a single person and reference to that single person is made by the speaker through the 3PL independent pronoun.

7
Complex sentences

7.1 Introduction

In this chapter, I describe the means by which independent clauses are conjoined and how subordinate clauses are linked to their main clauses. Independent clauses can stand on their own, expressing a complete proposition, while subordinate clauses are those that cannot stand on their own and are linked to a main clause by way of subordinators. In §7.2 and §7.3, I describe coordinate clauses, including a discussion on juxtaposition and three coordinators. Apart from these, adversative and disjunctive coordination are discussed in §7.3.5 and §7.4 respectively. Subordination is dealt with in §7.5 with a focus on complement clauses (§7.5.1), relative clauses (§7.5.2), adverbial clauses (§7.5.3), conditional clauses (§7.5.4), negative conditionals (§7.5.5) and concessive clauses (§7.5.6).

7.2 Coordinate clauses

Nese employs three types of coordination strategies to link clauses and phrases: conjunctive, adversative and disjunctive coordination; these are presented in Table 7.1. Expression of conjunctive coordination comes in six different forms, compared to the adversative and disjunctive coordination patterns each of which only takes one form. Noun phrases may be linked via juxtaposition along with the conjunctions *rrun* and *min* and via disjunctive *deve*. Prepositional phrases, however, can only be linked via the conjunction *din* while clauses allow more conjunction patterns compared to noun phrases and prepositional phrases, as shown in Table 7.1.

Table 7.1: Coordination strategies

Type of coordination	Coordination strategy	NP	PP	Clauses
Conjunctive	Juxtaposition	✓	✗	✓
	rov	✗	✗	✓
	din	✗	✓	✓
	ale	✗	✗	✓
	rrun	✓	✗	✗
	min	✓	✗	✗
Adversative	*be*	✗	✗	✓
Disjunctive	*deve*	✓	✗	✓

7.3 Conjunctive coordination

7.3.1 Juxtaposition

Nese clauses and noun phrases may be joined paratactically, with no overt coordinator. Lynch et al. (2011, p. 89) state that in Proto Oceanic, clauses were linked paratactically as well as through the medium of coordinating conjunctions, and in many Oceanic languages today clauses can be coordinated with no coordinator, thus it is not surprising that this is also the case in Nese. Clauses joined paratactically in Nese can be identified by intonation patterns, whereby the end of a clause is characterised by a falling intonation and a short pause and the beginning of a new clause by a rising intonation. Construction (7.1) is an example of three clauses in Nese that are linked paratactically with no overt coordinator.

7.1 *Ale   bur-lol,   bir-v'an,   bur-suwo.*
    CONJ   1PLEXCL:REAL-stay 1PLEXCL:REAL-go   1PLEXCL:REAL-swim
    'Then we stayed and we went and swam.'
    (2011_12_21 obrojo01003 00:00:26.000-00:00:30.000 natural text)

In (7.1), a sequential reading of the events described by each clause may be deduced: each clause has the same subject and the speaker is relating these events in the order in which they occurred.

Nese also allows the conjoining of clauses containing different subjects to be joined with no overt means of coordination. When two clauses with different subjects are joined paratactically, a contrast is being made of the activities the two subjects will be involved in simultaneously. For example, in (7.2), while the subject of the first clause will be at church, the subject of the second clause will be at home, cooking.

7.2 *Kani   kirr-v'an   rengen   sukul,   khina   jo-khro*
     2PL   2PL:REAL-go   LOC   school   1SG   1SG:IRR-stay
     'You guys go to church, I will stay

jo-kuk-u.
1SG:IRR-cook-3SGOBJ
I'll cook.'
(2012_01_19 naanhy01001 00:03:36.000-00:03:38.000 natural text)

Noun phrases may also be juxtaposed, as illustrated in (7.3), where they are given as a list of items.

7.3 *Rrisi-vita-i   nese?   naram   sikh-sikha,   **navij**   buro*
     1PL:IRR-put-3SGOBJ   what   yam   REDUP-NEG   banana   GENMOD
     'What are we going to put? There is no yam, only bananas,

novusbuak,   **maniok**,   **kumala**.
taro   manioc   kumara
taros, maniocs and kumara.'
(2012_05_16 obanhy01003 00:08:14.000-00:08:23.000 natural text)

In clauses where noun phrases are joined paratactically, there is a pause after each noun phrase to indicate the phrasal boundary. The intransitive verb *rov* 'finish' is also used in Nese as a completive marker, and when it occurs at the end of a clause that is joined paratactically with another clause, it indicates that the event described in the first clause has ended, therefore inferring a sequential order of events. It does not have this function in relation to noun phrases or prepositional phrases. So in (7.4) the cleaning takes place after the registration. The two clauses, which are joined paratactically with *rov*, indicating that the event in the first clause has ended, do not necessarily have to have the same mood and subjects. This is shown in example (7.4), where the mood of the borrowed Bislama verb *rejista* 'register' is realis and the subject is 2PL while the mood of the clause after the coordinator *rov* is irrealis and the subject is 3PL.

7.4 | *Rri-si-ma,* | *birr-rejista* | *v'an* | ***rov,*** | *rri-si-vekhsein*
| 3PL-IRR-come | 2PL:REAL-register | go | COMPL | 3PL-IRR-clean

'They will come, we will get registered and when this is over, they will clean

| *naine* | *te* | *rri-si-natur* | *min-i…*
| house | SUB | 3PL-IRR-sleep | PREP-3SGOBJ

the house in which they will sleep.'

(2014_02_18 naaksi01001 00:07.000-00:07:05.000 natural text)

Apart from being used as an indicator of sequential events expressed by clauses joined paratactically, *rov* is also used in conjunction with the coordinator *ale*. This is illustrated in (7.5).

7.5 | *Rri-si-vita-i* | *khojkhoj* | *v'an* | ***rov*** | ***ale*** | *rri-si-bin-i…*
| 1PLINCL-IRR-PUT-3SGOBJ | be.proper | go | COMPL | CONJ | 1PLINCL-IRR-pin-3SGOBJ

'We put it and once that is over then we have it pinned…'

(2012_07_12 obaksi01001 00:16:11.000-00:16:14.000 natural text)

7.3.2 *Din* 'and'

Din 'and' is a coordinator that is used to conjoin independent clauses; however, it is no longer used productively in current speech. Its only attestation in the current data is during a recording session in which seven Nese speakers were involved in a conversation and prior to the commencement of the recording they had been discussing the status of *din* and resolved that *din* should be the coordinator they ought to be using rather than Bislama *ale*, which is an introduced form. They thus indicated their awareness that *din* was originally a productively occurring coordinator in Nese, and that it has been replaced by *ale*. The use of *din* in this context is shown in (7.6), where the referent of the subjects in the coordinated clauses are the same.

7.6 | *Ø-derr* | *natan* | ***din*** | *ale* | *Ø-v'an* | *maro.*
| 3SG:REAL-dig | ground | CONJ | CONJ | 3SG:REAL-go | up

'He digs the ground and then, then he goes up.'

(2012_08_27 obnesp01001 00:13:56.000-00:14:05.000 natural text)

In (7.6), the second speaker (Louis Ross) uses both *din* and *ale*, which shows that he is probably more familiar with using *ale* rather than *din* and has, therefore, used both in this sentence because the use of this coordinator during this conversation was something that the speakers made great effort to remember.

7.3.3 Ale 'so', 'then'

Ale, a borrowing from French *allez* 'you (PL) go' via Bislama *ale* 'so, then, ok', functions as a clausal coordinator as well as the interjection 'okay'. It is the only commonly used coordinator in the current speech of all Nese speakers. The use of *ale* as a conjunction excludes phrases and is restricted to clauses, linking sequential actions as well as signalling the result of an action as illustrated in (7.7).

7.7 *Bir-v'an   bir-kij   nani   jin   Mosli,*
1PL:REAL-go   1PL:REAL-remove flesh of coconut   coconut   POSS   Mosli
'We went and removed the coconut flesh of Mosli's coconuts

*bir-kij-i   ko   **ale**   bir-bat-e,*
1PL:REAL-remove flesh of coconut   go   CONJ   1PL:REAL:make-3SGOBJ
we removed the coconut flesh to a certain point where we made it

Bag   khesve.
Bag   seven
seven bags.'
(2011_12_21 obrojo01003 00:00:05.000-00:00:01.000 natural text)

In (7.7), a resultative reading can be deduced from the use of the conjunction *ale* where the speaker is saying that they had been making copra and as a result they made seven bags. In (7.8), the first instance of *ale* is a lexical interjection and it is the second instance of *ale* that is functioning as a coordinator, coordinating two clauses with similar subject noun phrases. In this instance, the coordinator implies a relationship of temporal sequence where the praying will take place before the eating starts.

7.8	*Tav'at*	*yat!*	*Yat*	*iekhetan*	*khe*	*na!*	**ale**
	woman	sit	sit	DEM	DEM	now	CONJ

'Woman sit, sit down here now! Okay

	rri-si-varvar	*min*	*norian*	*s-ar*	**ale**
	1PL-IRR-pray	PREP2	food	CLED-1PLINCL:POSS	CONJ

we will pray for our food then

	rri-si-woj	*norian*	**ale**	*khorkhorbul!*
	1PL-IRR-eat	food	CONJ	close.eyes

we'll eat the food, okay close your eyes.'
(2012_06_12 obaksi01001 00:11:07.000-00:11:17.000 natural text)

7.3.4 *Rrun* 'and'

Rrun is a coordinator that links noun phrases. Noun phrases coordinated by *rrun* may occupy subject position, as shown in (7.9), or object position, as illustrated in example (7.10).

7.9	*Khai*	***rrun***	*nat-ne*	*ri-vial*	*ri-ma*	*khe.*
	3SG	CONJ	child-3SG:POSS	3PL:REAL-walk	3PL:REAL-come	DEM

'She and her daughter they walked to here.'
(2014_02_18 naaksi01001 00:00:20.000-00:00:22.000 natural text)

As shown in (7.9), a subject noun phrase composed of two coordinated noun phrases may consist of an independent pronoun and a lexical noun phrase. Full noun phrase objects may also be coordinated by *rrun* as shown in (7.10).

7.10	*No-vol*	*tin*	*nanaj*	*sakhal*	***rrun***	*makrroni*	*khe*	*rru.*
	1SG:REAL-buy	tin	fish	one	CONJ	noodles	DEM	two

'I bought one canned fish and two noodles.'
(2014_01_19 naanhy01001 00:04:37.000-00:04:44.000 natural text)

There are cases showing *rrun* linking a verb complex containing an object pro-index and a full noun phrase, as illustrated in (7.11). In these cases, however, *rrun* may be better analysed as a preposition meaning 'with'. This prepositional meaning is perhaps more evident in example (7.12), where *rrun* acts as a link between the subject of the intransitive active verb *khro* with a possessive noun phrase.

7.11 | *Bur-kuk-u* | | *ale* | *bir-waj-i* | | ***rrun***
1PLEXCL:REAL-cook-3SGOBJ | CONJ | 1PLEXCL:REAL-eat-3SGOBJ | | CONJ

'We cooked it and we ate it with

norrulnasasakh.
rice
rice.'
(2012_06_11 obrojo01005 00:02:45.000-00:02:49.000 natural text)

7.12 | *Ro-khro* | ***rrun*** | *nenetin* | *Tomatin.*
3PL:REAL-stay | CONJ | child-3SG:POSS | Tomatin

'They stayed with Tomatin's child.'
(2014_01_19 naanhy01001 00:37:17.000-00:37:20.000 natural text)

7.3.5 Adversative *be* 'but'

Adversative *be* 'but', a borrowing from Bislama *be* 'but', is used to contrast propositions. Nese only allows clauses to be coordinated by adversative *be*. In (7.13), two clauses are conjoined using *be* where the subject of the first clause is the same as the subject of the second clause.

7.13 | *Nemere* | *khar* | *ro-khro* | ***be*** | *khar*
people | 3PL | 3PL:REAL-stay | CONJ | 3PL

'The people were there but they

ro-rong-o | *sikha* | *te* | *re-bet* | *sukul.*
3PL:REAL-want-3SGOBJ | NEG | SUB | 3PL:REAL-make | school

didn't want to go to church.'
(2014_01_19 naanhy01001 00:11:19.000-00:11:23.000 natural text)

In (7.14), the subjects of the two coordinated clauses are different and, in this case, the clause is elliptical since the verb is omitted because it is understood as being similar to the one in the first clause. The verb *ma* in the main clause is functioning as a directional particle that is not necessarily indicating physical direction toward the speaker but expresses a direction in temporal terms toward a specific point of reference, which is the point at which the speaker is speaking.

7.14 Khai   Ø-s-be-num-num-te   rrenrran   ma   **be**
      3SG   3SG-IRR-NEG1-REDUP-drink-NEG2   always   come   CONJ
      'He does not always drink it,

   Gregory,   bentaru   benanev.
   Gregory   two days ago   yesterday
   but Gregory, two days ago, yesterday. (He drank it two days in a row.)'
   (2014_01_19 naanhy01001 00:48:51.000-0049:00.000 natural text)

7.4 Disjunctive *deve* 'or'

The conjunction *deve* 'or' is employed to express alternative or contrastive choices. It is used to conjoin noun phrases (7.15) and clauses (7.16). In (7.15), the two noun phrases have temporal meanings and function as adjuncts in the main clause. In example (7.16), two clauses are being conjoined with *deve* in which the referent of the subject of the second clause is the same as that of the object of the first clause.

7.15 Bur-khos   laine   bung,   naleng   haf
      1PLEXCL:REAL-reach   house:LOC   night   maybe   half
      'We reached the house at night, at maybe half

   pas   fo   **deve**   haf   pas   faef.
   past   four   CONJ   half   past   five
   past four or half past five.'
   (2011_12_21 obrojo01003 00:00:20.000-00:00:26.000 natural text)

7.16 Je-kol-o   lue   nua   **deve**   Ø-se-tokh   buro?
      1SG:IRR-carry-3SGOBJ out   water   CONJ   3SG-IRR-stay   GENMOD
      'Should I take out the water or should it just stay?'
      (Fieldnotes, natural text)

When *deve* is followed by a clause consisting only of negative *sikha*, it expresses an alternative that is the negated proposition in the first clause (7.17).

7.17 *Khina j-be-rongvuson-te   sakhal Ø-se-ma   **deve** sikha.*
      1SG   1SG:IRR-NEG1-know-NEG2   one   3SG-IRR-come   CONJ   NEG
      'I don't know whether one will come or not.'
      (2014_02_18 naaksi01001 00:04:01.000-00:04:05.000 natural text)

7.5 Subordinate clauses

The types of subordinate clauses that exist in Nese are complement clauses (§7.5.1), relative clauses (§7.5.2) and adverbial clauses (§7.5.3). Nese does not have a complicated system of overtly marking subordination; instead, there is a general subordinator *te*, which is used to introduce both complement clauses and relative clauses. This general subordinator combines with other forms to introduce adverbial clauses. The subordinators are laid out in Table 7.2.

Table 7.2: Subordinators and functions

te	introduces a complement clause
te	introduces a relative clause
neten te	introduces a temporal adverbial clause of reason 'because'
neren te	introduces a temporal adverbial clause 'when'
neren	'during', 'at'
belek te	introduces a similitive adverbial clause

Table 7.2 shows that all forms of the subordinator include *te* except for *neren*, which may or may not co-occur with *te*, the two forms being semantically distinct from each other.

7.5.1 Complement clauses

Complementation is defined by Noonan as 'the syntactic situation which arises when a notional sentence or predication is an argument of a predicate' (1985, p. 44). The two types of clauses in Nese are transitive and intransitive clauses, the former having two core arguments and the latter possessing a single core argument that is the subject. Nese allows clauses to occupy subject and object position. There are only two examples showing clauses occupying subject position, although a greater number of transitive verbs can take sentential complements as objects. These verbs fall into different semantic categories, which Dixon (2006, p. 9) describes as primary and secondary types. Verbs in the primary type are those that can take both arguments as NPs, with a distinction made between Primary A type and Primary B type based on the former obligatorily taking both arguments as NPs while the latter being permitted to take one argument as a clause instead. However, verbs in the secondary type are those in which one argument must be a clause with the distinction between Secondary B and Secondary C based on the latter having the tendency to contain different subjects in the main and complement clauses (Dixon, 2006, pp. 9–13). The current data shows that Nese has verbs that come under the Primary B type and Secondary C types. Complementation in Nese is expressed in two distinct ways. Firstly, via the subordinate marker which signals the commencement of the complement clause. Secondly, in the absence of *te*, Nese requires the verb in the complement clause to be marked with the aspectual marker *-ti-*.

7.5.1.1 Verbs that take one clausal argument

As stated above, some Nese verbs fall into the category of Primary B verbs as defined by Dixon (2006, p. 10), a category that is composed of verbs falling into four semantic types: verbs of attention, thinking, liking and speaking. Each of these semantic types is explored in this subsection. Verbs of attention include *les* 'see' and *rong* 'hear'. The transitive verb *les* 'see' can take either a complement clause (7.18), where the complement clause is introduced by the subordinator *te*, or an NP as the object argument (7.19).

7.18 *Kho-**les**   [**te**   tenge   Ø-s-be-khirkhir-vusokh-te.]*
2SG:REAL-see   SUB   thing   3SG-IRR-NEG-move-proper-NEG2
'You see that (how) the thing does not move the properly.'
(2014_01_19 naanhy01001 00:39:12.000-00:39:16.000 natural text)

In (7.18), the complement clause consists of a negated clause.

7.19 *Mary   khai   Ø-les   **saen**   **sakhal**.*
Jayven   3SG   3SG:REAL-come   sign   one
'Mary she saw a sign.'
(2012_08_22 elanhy01011 00:19:30.000-00:19:33.000 elicitation)

In the absence of the subordinator *te*, complement relationships are expressed via the presence of the aspectual marker *ti* in the complement clause, as shown in (7.20), where the subject of the main clause is not expressed but is different to that of the complement clause.

7.20 *Wolei!* **les** **nemerjian** *khe* *Ø-ti-mul* *nge.*
Oh! see old man DEM 3SG-ASP-return DEM
'Oh! see that old man returning.'
(2014_01_19 naanhy01001 00:11:28.000-00:11:30.000 natural text)

In cases such as (7.20) where the subject of the complement clause is a 3SG noun phrase, it is mandatory for the verb in the complement clause to carry the aspectual marker *ti* when the associated action is set in a non-future temporal setting and when the subordinator *te* is absent. However, the mandatory presence of the aspect marker is not relevant when the subordinator *te* is present, as illustrated in (7.21), which is also a case of the verb *les* taking a complement clause as its object with the meaning of understanding or knowing rather than actual seeing. In this example where the subject of the main clause is different to that of the complement clause, *les* is functioning as a perception verb rather than one that is related to the sense of seeing.

7.21 *Kho-**les*** [*te* *Aklyn,* *khai* *Ø-rong-o* *Ø-se-ma.*]
2SG:REAL-see SUB Aklyn 3SG 3SG-want-3SGOBJ 3SG-IRR-come
'You see that Aklyn, she wants to come.'
(2014_01_19 naanhy01001 00:08:16.000-00:08:18.000 natural text)

The verb *les*, with a sensory denotation, undergoes haplology when negation is involved and the object is a complement clause introduced by the subordinator *te*. Haplology involves the deletion of one of two identical syllables and with sensory *les* haplology affects NEG2. This is shown in (7.22), where the subordinator *te* is not present, although in a non-negated construction the subordinator *te* is used, as shown in (7.23).

7.22 *J-be-les-**te*** *nause* *Ø-se-ma.*
1SG:REAL-NEG1-see-NEG2 rain 3SG-IRR-come
'I don't see that it's going to rain.'
(Fieldnotes, elicitation)

7.23   Ne-**les**   [te   nause   Ø-se-ma.]
       1SG:REAL-see   SUB   rain   3SG-IRR-come
       'I see that the rain will come.'
       (Fieldnotes elicitation)

Three Nese verbs encountered that come under the same sub-classification of verbs such as *les* are derived from the root *rong*. These are presented in Table 7.3.

Table 7.3: Nese verbs derived from the root *rong*

rong 'hear', 'listen', 'want', 'like' and 'feel'
rongvuson 'know'
rongneleng 'forget'

When a nominal object argument of *rong* 'hear' 'listen' is present, the subordinator *te* is absent, as shown in (7.24), contrasting with instances where the complement of the verb *rong* 'hear' is obligatorily introduced by the subordinator *te*, as illustrated in (7.25).

7.24   Iven   Ø-ti-rong   **natas**   **khe.**
       Iven   3SG:REAL-ASP-hear   sea   DEM
       'Iven heard the sea.'
       (2014_01_19 naanhy01001 00:28:01.000-00:28:02.000 natural text)

7.25   John   khai   **Ø-rong-o**   [te   khar
       John   3SG   3SG:REAL-hear-3SGOBJ   SUB   3PL
       'John heard that they

       ri-ve   Pita   Ø-se-lakh.]
       3PL:REAL-say   Peter   3SG-IRR-marry
       said that Peter will get married.'
       (Fieldnotes, elicitation)

I have indicated (§4.4) that an object argument is realised either by a noun phrase or by an object suffix, the simultaneous co-occurrence of both being impermissible. However, although most complement-taking verbs abide by this, there are sporadic instances only in relation to the verb *rong* where the object pro-index co-occurs referring to the complement clause. Compare examples (7.25) and (7.26), the latter example being the most predominant where the object pro-index is not present.

7.26 Ne-turo   v'an   v'an   **ne-rong**   *te*
      1SG:REAL-stand   go   go   1SG:REAL-feel   SUB
      'I stand until I feel that

      Ø-se-rurrngo   ale   je-yat.
      3SG:IRR-sore   CONJ   1SG:IRR-sit
      it's going to be painful then I'll sit.'
      (2014_01_19 naanhy01001 00:58:33.000-00:58:37.000 natural text)

As seen also with the examples containing *les* 'see' in (7.23), the object suffix does not co-occur with a complement clause object. On the other hand, example (7.27) suggests that the presence of the subordinator *te* is not necessary, and the complement clause may be simply juxtaposed to the main clause.

7.27 **Ne-rong-o**   kho-skhaskho   rengen   nebe   sakhal.
      1SG:REAL-hear-3SGOBJ   2SG:REAL-sing   LOC   song   one
      'I heard that you sang a song.'
      (Fieldnotes, elicitation)

Verbs that fall into the semantic category labelled as 'thinking' are *rromrrom* 'think, believe', *rongvuson* 'know' and *rongneleng* 'forget'. While the verb *rromrrom* may take a noun phrase as an argument, as illustrated in (7.28), it may also take a complement clause that is introduced by *te* (7.29), or the main clause containing *rromrrom* may be simply juxtaposed beside its complement clause, as shown in (7.30).

7.28 Khai   **Ø-rromrrom**   nau-ne
      3SG   3SG:REAL-think   spouse-3SG:POSS
      'He is thinking about his spouse.'
      (Fieldnotes, elicitation)

7.29 Khina   **no-rromrrom**   [te   khai   Ø-s-be-rrorrovokh-te]
      1SG   1SG:REAL-think   SUB   3SG   3SG:IRR-NEG1-play-NEG2
      'I think that she won't play.'
      (Fieldnotes, elicitation)

7.30   **No-rromrrom**   terrterr   je-rov   naul   s-ak.
       1SG:REAL-think   strong   1SG:IRR-finish   school   CLGEN-1SG:POSS
       'I am thinking strongly that I will finish my studies.'
       (Fieldnotes, elicitation)

The verb *rongvuson* 'know' takes either a nominal argument, as shown in (7.31), or a complement that is obligatorily introduced by the subordinator *te*, as shown in (7.32).

7.31   Khai   **Ø-rongvuson**   nanalokh   buro.
       3SG   3SG:REAL-know   kava   GENMOD
       'He knows kava only.' (i.e. kava is all he knows)
       (2014_01_19 naanhy01001 00:24:46.000-00:24:48.000 natural text)

7.32   Nev'enu   khai   Ø-ti-nanas   **ne-rongvuson-i**
       place   3SG   3SG:REAL-ASP-be.dry 1SG:REAL-know-3SGOBJ
       'The place is dry, I know

       [te   nevle   nokhobonian.]
       SUB   month   garden
       that it is the gardening month.'
       (2012_08_27 obnesp01003 00:03:36.000-00:03:42.000 natural text)

Although the constituent occurring after *te* resembles a noun phrase, it is analysed here as a complement clause because it does not mean that 'I know the gardening month', but rather it means that 'I know that it is the gardening month', which means that it predicates the existence of the month rather than simply referring to it.

The verb *rongneleng* 'forget' may take a nominal object argument, as shown in (7.33), and a complement clause as the object, illustrated in (7.34). Sentence (7.34) with the complement-taking verb *rongneleng* 'forget' illustrates an example where the 3SG subject of the complement clause is co-referential with the subject of the main clause and the verb taking the potential mood. When the verb in the subordinate clause is marked for the potential mood, the 3SG subject is not marked on the verb in the complement clause. This can be seen in (7.34) in which the verb is only marked with the potential *-bo-*. The data does not contain any examples

7. COMPLEX SENTENCES

where the subject in the complement clause is not co-referential with that of the main clause and where the verb in the subordinate clause is marked for the potential mood.

7.33 **No-rongneleng**   neng   s-en   nuak   khe.
      1SG:REAL-forget   name   CLGEN-3SG:POSS   boat   DEM
      'I forgot the name of that boat.'
      (Fieldnotes, elicitation)

7.34 Sera   khai   **Ø-rongneleng**   [te   **ba-kuk.**]
      Sera   3SG   3SG:REAL-forget   SUB   POT-cook
      'Sera she forgot to cook.'
      (2012_08_22 elanhy01011 00:11:16.000-00:11:20.000 elicitation)

Verbs that come under the semantic category of 'liking' always take the subordinator *te* to introduce their complement clauses and these are *rongo sat* 'be sorry', *rronrronivele* 'regret' and *rong* 'want'. The former two verbs do not take nominal object arguments. When the verb *rongo sat* 'be sorry' takes a complement clause as its object, the subject of the subordinate clause is not required to be co-referential with the subject of the main clause, as illustrated in (7.35). In this example, the main clause has the head verb *rongo sat*, with the subject position being filled by the 1SG subject cross-index, while the subject of the complement clause is represented by the 3SG pronoun.

7.35 **No-rong-o**   sat   [te   khai   Ø-nas.]
      1SG:REAL-feel-3SGOBJ   bad   SUB   3SG   3SG:REAL-bad
      'I am sorry that he died.'
      (Fieldnotes, elicitation)

Unlike the two verbs described previously under the semantic category of 'liking', the verb *rong* may take both a nominal object argument, as illustrated in (7.36), and a complement clause as an object argument.

7.36 Khai   **Ø-rong**   tenge   nial.
      3SG   3SG:REAL-want   thing   red
      'He wants the red thing.'
      (2012_08_22 elanhy01011 00:15:59.000-00:16:02.000 elicitation)

Example (7.37) illustrates the verb *rong* 'want' with a complement clause as object, where the subject of the complement clause being the 3SG pronoun is co-referential with the subject of the main clause. In both cases, the subject is not marked on the verb in the complement clause, and the verb is marked for potential mood. In a desiderative complement with the verb *rong* 'want', the verb cannot take realis marking as the event of the complement is a potential rather than a real event. The subordinator *te* cannot be omitted with a desiderative complement. When the subject of the complement clause is not co-referential with that of the main clause, the subject pro-index must be affixed to the verb in the complement clause, as shown in (7.38).

7.37 Khai **Ø-rong** [te Ø-ba-num nanalokh buro.]
3SG 3SG:REAL-want SUB 3SG:REAL-POT-drink kava GENMOD
'He only wants to drink kava.'
(2014_01_19 naanhy01001 00:13:03.000-00:13:06.000 natural text)

7.38 **Ø-Se-rong** [te rri-si-rej-rej min-i.]
3SG-IRR-want SUB 1PLINCL-IRR-REDUP-speak PREP2-3SGOBJ
'She wants for us to speak it.'
(2014_01_19 naanhy01001 00:08:18.000-00:08:21.000 natural text)

The current data indicates a preference for the use of the potential mood marker *ba* to be indexed on the head verb in the complement clause, when the subjects of the main and complement clause are co-referential and the main clause contains the verb *rong* marked for the realis mood, although the action or event expressed by the verb in the complement clause is irreal. Another example is given in (7.39) where the subject of the main clause is expressed via the 2PL realis cross-index and the verb in the complement clause is also indexed by the 2PL realis pro-index in conjunction with the potential marker *ba*.

7.39 Seve **kirr-rong** [te **kirr-be-les-ia**,
COND 2PL:REAL-want SUB 2PL:REAL-POT-see-1SGOBJ
'If you guys want to come and see me,

kirr-ma.]
2PL:REAL-come
you guys come.'
(2014_01_19 naanhy01001 00:05:59.000-01:06:03.000 natural text)

The only deviation from this pattern involving the usage of potential *ba* in conjunction with co-referential subjects is when the subject of both the main and complement clauses is expressed by the 1SG, as shown in (7.40), where the 1SG subject cross-index in the complement clause is expressed by the 1SG irrealis form *de-*.

7.40   **Ne-rong**   [te   ***de-natur.***]
       1SG:REAL-want   SUB   1SG:IRR-sleep
       'I want to sleep.'
       (2014_01_19 naanhy01001 00:06:41.000-00:06:43.000 natural text)

There is no evidence to suggest that the head verb in the complement clause is marked with the irrealis subject cross-index when the subjects of both clauses are co-referential and the head verb in the main clause is marked for realis mood. Negation of the verb *rong* 'want' is achieved via the negative *sikha* occupying the slot preceding the subordinator *te*, as shown in (7.41).

7.41   Khai   **Ø-rong-o**   ***sikha***   [te   *bo-sukul.*]
       3SG   3SG:REAL-want-3SGOBJ   NEG   SUB   POT-school
       'He does not want to go to school.'
       (2014_01_19 naanhy01001 00:13:06.000-00:13:19.000 natural text)

When the verb *rong-* 'want' is negated, the 3SG object pro-index is always present. Lastly, the intransitive verb *rronrronivele* 'regret' does not take any nominal object argument, although it takes a complement clause as an argument.

7.42   **No-rronrronivele**   [te   *je-be-v'an-te.*]
       1SG:REAL-regret   SUB   1SG:IRR:NEG1-go-NEG2
       'I regret that I did not go.'
       (Fieldnotes, elicitation)

In (7.42), the intransitive verb *rronrronivele* takes an extended argument in the form of the complement clause whose subject is co-referential with the subject of the main clause.

The last semantic category into which Nese verbs taking complement clauses fall is associated with the notion of speaking. Generally, the argument occupying the position of subject in a verbal clause containing a verb of locution as the head verb conveys information to an addressee.

On the other hand, the information in the complement of the predicate refers to whether or not the reported speech is quoted directly (i.e. repeated word for word) as it was originally uttered. The verbs of locution in Nese are *ver* 'tell', *ve* 'say', *vervis* 'reveal' and *us* 'ask'. The predicates *ver* 'tell', *ve* 'say' and *vervis* 'reveal/disclose' do not take subordinators or complementisers to introduce their complement clauses. In these cases, the complement clauses are simply juxtaposed paratactically and a pause is made to signal the clausal boundary.

The predicate *ve* takes a noun phrase (7.43) and an indirect or direct reported speech as its complement (7.44).

7.43 *Khina* **ne-ve** **nokhod-me** **khe**.
 1SG 1SG:REAL-say grandchild-1SG:POSS DEM
 'I say this is my grandchild.'/I call her grandchild.'
 (2012_05_16 obanhy01003 00:09:11.000-00:09:13.000 natural text)

7.44 **Ne-ve** *sikha* *khai* *Ø-ve* *Ø-se-ma* *khe*.
 1SG:REAL-say NEG 3SG 3SG:REAL-say 3SG-IRR-come DEM
 'I said, "no she said that she will come, she will really come".'
 (2014_01_19 naanhy01001 00:16:14.000-00:06:18.000 natural text)

In (7.44), the subject of the main clause expressed via the 1SG independent pronoun is not co-referential with the subject of the complement of the predicate. The complement of the predicate also contains the same verb *ve* and in this instance the speaker is reporting what she had mentioned about someone else planning to visit her.

Nese does not make tense distinctions; therefore, the only way in which direct speech may be distinguished from indirect speech is through the use of the independent pronouns and the subject cross-indexes. When the subject of the complement clause is expressed by the 1SG irrealis cross-index, it is the choice between *de* and *je* (§5.4.1.2) that could determine whether the complement clause is direct speech or indirect speech. The form *de* is never used in main clauses and is only used in clauses that are functioning as complements of the verb *rong* when it means 'want' and of the verb *ve* 'say'. In contrast, *je* cannot be used in complement clauses and can only be used in matrix clauses.

7.45	*Khina*	**ne-ve**	**de-vile**	*bin*	*khe…*
	1SG	1SG:REAL-say	1SG:IRR-clean	bean	DEM

'I said that I will clean these beans…'

(2014_01_19 naanhy01001 00:04:11.000-00:04:13.000 natural text)

Since *de* cannot be used in main clauses, the complement clause in (7.45) can be understood as being a case of reported speech rather than direct speech. Example (7.46) is not a grammatical construction if it is occurring as a main clause, although (7.47) is grammatical.

7.46	***De-vile***	*bin.*
	1SG:IRR-clean	bean

(Fieldnotes, elicitation)

7.47	***Je-vile***	*bin.*
	1SG:IRR-clean	bean

'I will clean the bean.'

(Fieldnotes, elicitation)

Another example involving the 3SG pronoun is given in (7.48), where the subject of the main clause is co-referential with the subject of the complement clause.

7.48	***Khai***	*Ø-ve*	*Ø-se-ma.*
	3SG	3SG:REAL-say	3SG-IRR-come

'She said she will come.'

(2014_01_19 naanhy01001 00:16:14.000-00:06:18.000 natural text)

The use of the 3SG cross-index in the complement clause indicates that it is indirect speech since if it was a case of direct speech the 1SG cross-index *je* would have been used, as that would have been the words that the speaker who is here referred to by the 3SG pronoun would have said. This is illustrated in (7.49).

7.49	*Khai*	*Ø-ve*	***'je-ma.'***
	3SG	3SG:REAL-say	1SG:IRR-come

'She said, "I will come".'

(Fieldnotes, elicitation)

A similar analysis applies to (7.50) where the use of the subject 1PL EXCL pronoun in the complement clause suggests that it is a case of direct speech because if the speaker had reported what was spoken by the people represented by the 3PL subject noun phrase of the verb *ve*, the construction would be as shown in (7.51) where the 3PL pronoun is used as the subject of the first clause in the complement clause.

7.50 *Re-ve*   [*no* **kanan**   *bir-si-khro*   *v'an*   *v'an...*]
      3PL:REAL-say   no   1PLEXCL   1PLEXCL-IRR-stay   go   go
      'They said, "no as for us, we will stay here for some time".'
      (2014_01_19 naanhy01001 00:18:46.000-00:18:50.000 natural text)

7.51 *Re-ve*   [*no* **khar**   *ri-si-khro*   *v'an*   *v'an...*]
      3PL:REAL-say   no   3PLEXCL   3PLEXCL-IRR-stay   go   go
      'They said, "no as for them, they will stay here for some time".'
      (Fieldnotes, elicitation)

It is more problematic to differentiate between direct speech and indirect speech when the subjects of the matrix clause and the complement clause are not co-referential and when the subject in the complement clause is a proper noun phrase, as shown in (7.52).

7.52 *Re-ve*   [*mm* *Lana*   *khota*   *Ø-s-be-me-te*   *khe.*]
      3PL:REAL-say   um   Lana   DEHORT   3SG-IRR-NEG1-come-NEG2   DEM
      'They said, "umm Lana will not come here".'
      (2014_01_19 naanhy01001 00:06:11.000-00:06:14.000 natural text)

Nese does not use any morphological means to distinguish whether participants represented by pronouns or cross-indexes functioning as subjects of the matrix clause and the complement clause are co-referential, and speakers rely solely on contextual information to distinguish the referents of the subjects represented by pronouns functioning as subjects of clauses. For example, in construction (7.53), the referent of the subject of the complement clause could be the subject of the matrix clause or it could be another person.

7.53 *Khai*   *Ø-ve*   *Ø-se-ma...*
      3SG   3SG:REAL-say   3SG-IRR-come
      'She said she will come.'
      (2014_01_19 naanhy01001 00:06:16.000-00:06:17.000 natural text)

When pronouns and cross-indexes are used as subjects of the matrix and complement clauses, there is ambiguity in distinguishing between the referents; however, when proper nouns occur in subject position in both matrix and complement clauses, there is no ambiguity in the distinction regarding the co-referentiality of the subject arguments.

Ver 'to tell, say' is an extended transitive verb that can take four arguments: the subject noun phrase that may be represented by a pronoun; a lexical noun phrase or a cross-index; the direct object, which may be represented by a lexical noun phrase or a pro-index; and an optional prepositional phrase indicating the addressee. *Ver* contrasts with *ve* in that the latter is used primarily to report direct speech or indirect speech and does not take noun phrase arguments. When *ver* takes a direct object in the form of an object pro-index, the medial vowel in the verb is lowered to /a/, resulting in the form *var-i*. In (7.54), the complement is a possessive noun phrase and, in (7.55), the direct object is realised by the object cross-index, the dative prepositional phrase expresses the addressee and the complement clause has *ve* as its head verb. The complement of the verb *ver* can be either a complement clause where the head of the complement clause is the verb *ve* (7.55) or the verbal preposition *belek* 'like' (7.56).

7.54 **Kirr-ver**   neng   s-an   O!
      2PL:REAL-say   name   CLGEN:3SG:POSS   O
      'Oh you guys say its name!'
      (2012_08_27 obnesp01003 00:05:56.000-00:05:58.000 natural text)

7.55 **Ne-var-i**   khin   vinelekh   ne-**ve**
      1SG:REAL-tell-3SGOBJ   PREP1   daughter in law   1SG:REAL-say
      'I told my daughter-in-law, I said,

      ma   yat   iekhe   ale   v'an   te   kuk   na   netenge
      come   sit   DEM:LOC   CONJ   go   SUB   cook   HESIT   thingummy
      "come sit here and go and cook um, the thingummy,

      tubunbun   nen   norrulnasasakh.
      meat   ASSOC   rice
      the meat for the rice".'
      (2014_01_19 naanhy01001 00:01:19.000-00:01:28.000 natural text)

In example (7.55), the complement clause with *ve* as the head verb is composed of a clause in imperative form. As illustrated in (7.56), *belek* is always inflected for third person singular when it occurs as an adjunct argument of the matrix verb *ver* and the content of the noun phrase functioning as the object of *belek* has already been established earlier in discourse.

7.56   'Nua   Ø-kol'   **Ø-var-i**   belek   khe   buro
       water   3SG:REAL-flow   1SG:REAL-say-3SGOBJ   like   DEM   GENMOD
       '"The water is running," she said it just like that.'
       (2012_01_18 obrolo01001 00:02:07.000-00:02:10.000 natural text)

In (7.57), the verb *vervis* 'reveal, disclose' takes an NP complement representing the addressee and a complement clause representing the content of the speech.

7.57   Ne-var-i   khin-err   belek   khe.   be
       1SG:REAL-say-3SGOBJ   PREP1-3PLOBJ   like   DEM   CONJ
       I told them like this but (That's what I told them but)

       j-be-vervis-te   khunokh   te   khai   Ø-se-ma.
       1SG:IRR:NEG1-reveal-NEG2   2SG   SUB   3SG   3SG-IRR-come
       I did not tell you that she will come.'
       (2014_01_19 naanhy01001 00:10:07.000-00:10:13.000 natural text)

The complement of the verb *us* 'ask' expresses reported speech as shown in (7.58). When the object expressed via a complement clause is present, the 3SG object pro-index is not present. This supports the fact that the complement clause is filling the object function. In this example, *naleng* is part of the second matrix clause with the head verbs marked for realis mood.

7.58   Khina   j-be-rongvuson-i   naleng   khunokh   kho-v'an
       1SG   1SG:IRR:NEG1-know-3SGOBJ   maybe   2SG   2SG:REAL-go
       'I don't know how about you go

       kho-us   te   khai   Ø-se-ma.
       2SG:REAL-ask   SUB   3SG   3SG-IRR-come
       and ask for him to come.'
       (2014_02_18 naaksi01001 00:00:57.000-00:01:02.000 natural text)

The verb *us* 'ask' may also take a nominal argument in object position, as shown in (7.59), where the noun phrase *tenge kher khe* 'these things' forms the object argument.

7.59 Khai   Ø-us   **tenge**   **kher**   **khe.**
      3SG   3SG:REAL-ask   thing   PL   DEM
      'She is asking all these things.'
      (Fieldnotes, elicitation)

7.5.1.2 Verbs with an obligatory clausal argument

Dixon's subclass of Secondary C verbs comprises verbs of causation. Nese verbs that fall under this category are *bat-e* 'make/cause' (7.60), *ver terrterr* 'force verbally' (7.61) and *najnge* 'agree, allow, let' (7.62).

7.60 **Ne-bat-e**   te   Ø-se-naskhe   sirrsirr.
      1SG:REAL-make-3SGOBJ   SUB   3SG-IRR-cooked   be.quick
      'I made/did it in such a manner that it will be cooked quickly.'
      (Fieldnotes, elicitation)

In (7.60), the referent of the object of the matrix clause is the same as that of the subject of the complement clause. This does not apply to similar referents in (7.61) and (7.62), where the referents of the subjects of the matrix clause and that of the complement clauses are not co-referential.

7.61 **Ne-ver**   terrterr   te   khai   Ø-se-vervis-i.
      1SG:REAL-say   be.strong   SUB   3SG   3SG-IRR-reveal -3SGOBJ
      'I forced (verbally) him to reveal it.'
      (Fieldnotes, elicitation)

7.62 Khina   **ne-najnge**   te   Ø-se-tekh   ral-ok   rengen
      1SG   1SG:REAL-agree   SUB   3SG-IRR-take   voice-1SG:POSS   LOC
      'I agree for her to record my voice using

      tangatarr   s-an   khe.
      thing   CLGEN-3SG:POSS   DEM
      those things of hers.'
      (2012_05_16 obanhy01001 00:00:26.000-00:00:33.500 natural text)

7.5.1.2.1 Clauses in subject position

The only two examples in the data in which clauses occupy subject position is when the subject is composed of a verbal equational clauses (cf. §6.2.1), as illustrated in (7.63). In (7.63), the verbal clause in subject position is comprised of the copula verb *ve* functioning as the head verb occupying the slot between two noun phrases of equal status. The complement clause is introduced by the subordinator *te*.

7.63 *Khai   Ø-ve   tenge   lukho   te   kho-ma   les*
     3SG   3SG:REAL-be   thing   fearful   SUB   2SG:REAL-come   see
     'It's a very fearful thing that you came to see

   kanan.
   1PLEXCL
   us.' ('It's an honour that you came to see us.')
   (Fieldnotes, elicitation)

The other example in the data contains a non-verbal clause in subject position of the matrix clause. This is shown in (7.64).

7.64 *Norromian   s-ak   khai   Ø-ti-terrterr   te*
     thinking   CLGEN-1SG:POSS   3SG   3SG:REAL-ASP-be.strong   SUB
     'As for my thoughts, it is strong that

   Ø-se-mavos.
   3SG-IRR-be.correct
   it will be good.' ('I strongly believe that it will be good.')
   (Fieldnotes, elicitation)

In (7.64), the subject of the matrix clause and that of the subordinate clause that is represented by the 3SG irrealis subject cross-index are not co-referential. The matrix clause contains the topicalised noun phrase *norromian sak*.

7.5.2 Relative clauses

A relative clause is one that modifies the head noun in an NP and is embedded within that NP. The argument being modified must be co-referential with one of the arguments of the relative clause. Nese uses either the subordinator *te* to introduce relative clauses or, in cases where

7. COMPLEX SENTENCES

te is not used, there is a lack of pausing and change of intonation between the NP head and the relative clause that marks a relative clause boundary. The discussion of relative clauses in this section will be mainly focused on their internal syntactic properties.

In (7.65), the head noun of the main clause is followed by a relative clause that gives additional information about that head noun. The head noun and the co-referential prepositional object pro-index make up the common argument, and they are underlined in (7.65). The common noun *naine* in this example is an extra clausal object of the clause and it is being modified by the relative clause.

7.65 …*rri-si-vekhsein-i,*   **<u>naine</u>**   *te*
       3PL-IRR-clean-3SGOBJ   house   SUB
       '…they will clean it, the house which

       rri-si-naturr   *min-**i**,*   *domitri.*
       3PL:IRR-sleep   PREP2-3SGOBJ   dormitory
       they will sleep in it, the dormitory.'
       (2014_02_18 naaksi01001 00:07:02.000-00:07:05.000 natural text)

In the examples that follow, the common arguments will be distinguished from other elements by the use of bold font with underlining. Keenan (1985, p. 143) distinguishes two types of relative clauses, based on whether the common argument occurs outside or inside of the relative clause. These are called external or internal relative clauses respectively. The former is the prevalent pattern in SVO languages and is also applicable to Nese, as can be seen in (7.65), where the common noun is outside of the relative clause. Contrastively, internally headed relative clauses are those where the head noun is inside the relative clause. However, this is not applicable to Nese. The class of external relative clauses is further divided into two subclasses called post-nominal and prenominal external clauses. In the former, the relative clause occurs to the right of the domain noun and, in the latter, the relative clause occurs to the left of the common argument. Nese exhibits post-nominal external clauses only. Modifiers have a tendency to occur after the head noun in an NP; therefore, relative clauses, which also have a modifying function, occur post-nominally, although they are embedded in the NP.

7.5.2.1 Marking of the relative clause

Nese employs the subordinator *te* to mark relative clauses, as shown in (7.66), and when *te* is not present the relative clause is simply juxtaposed beside the common argument and there is no pause or change in intonation between the head of the NP and the following clause, as exemplified in (7.67).

7.66 *Kho-so-khuban   rengen   **navle**   te   rri-les   nalang*
2SG-IRR-garden   LOC   month   SUB   1PLINCL:REAL-see   wind
'You will do your gardening in the month in which we see the wind

Ø-sirsir.
3SG:REAL-blow
blowing.'
(2012_08_27 obnesp01003 00:07:38.000-00:07:48.000 natural text)

7.67 *Vave!   khunokh,   netenge,   **nalok   s-am**   **khe***
Aunty   2SG   thingummy   laplap   CLGEN-2SG:POSS   DEM
'Aunty, that thingummy, your laplap

kho-var-i   kho-bat-e   khe,   sobonon   khai
2SG:REAL-say-3SGOBJ   2SG:REAL-make-3SGOBJ   DEM   some   3SG
that you said you made, are there still some

Ø-ti-tokh?
3SG:REAL-ASP-stay
left?'
(2012_05_16 obanhy01003 00:07:24.000-00:07:29.000 natural text)

In (7.66), the noun phrase, the object of the prepositional phrase, which is functioning as a non-core argument of the main clause, is being modified by the relative clause giving more information about the co-referential participant so that it is more easily identifiable. Example (7.67) shows the relative clause occurring beside the co-referential participant *nalok* 'laplap' with no intervening subordinator. In these cases, there is no pause after the noun phrase *nalok* 'laplap' and the beginning of the relative clause.

7.5.2.2 Marking of the common argument

A noun phrase, independent pronoun, pro-index or cross-index that is the common argument, regardless of its function in the matrix clause, must always be co-referenced with an argument in the relative clause either by means of an independent pronoun or an object cross-index. A co-referential constituent in the relative clause is never expressed as an NP. In cases where there is more than one argument in the main clause, the cross-indexes or pro-indexes on the verb in the relative clause can assist in identifying which argument in the main clause is being co-referenced.

In (7.68), the common argument in the main clause is the 3SG object pro-index and the object pro-index in the relative clause is marked for singular, indicating co-referentiality between the 3SG object pro-index in the matrix clause and the object pro-index in the relative clause.

7.68 Tentan-***i***   *jelekh*   te   kho-rong   kho-se-milj-***i***   sirsir.
pin-3SGOBJ   all   SUB   2SG:REAL-want   2SG-IRR-tie-3SGOBJ   quickly
'Pin all of it which you want to tie quickly.'
(2012_07_12 obaksi01001 00:16:22.000-00:16:25.000 natural text)

Although it is easy to determine a co-referential relationship between the singular noun in the matrix clause and the object pro-index in the relative clause in (7.68), there are cases where a certain degree of ambiguity exists. This is illustrated in (7.69) where the subject of the relative clause, given that it is 3SG, is not overt, therefore triggering ambiguity as to whether the referent of the non-overt pro-index is an argument in the matrix clause or is information that ought to be able to be deduced from context.

7.69 Ne-ve   'wolei   Yvon   khai   Ø-s-bo-kuk-te   ***bin***
1SG:REAL-say   Oh   Yvonne   3SG   3SG-IRR-NEG1-cook -NEG2   bean
'I said, "Oh Yvonne she did not cook some of the beans

sobonon   ***khe***   te   Ø-ti-takh-e.'
some   DEM   SUB   3SG:REAL-ASP-take-3SGOBJ
which she took".'
(2014_01_19 naanhy01001 00:03:59.000-00:04:04.000 natural text)

In fact, the object pro-index on the verb in the relative clause is co-referential with the object of the main clause realised by the noun phrase *bin* 'bean'. Nese does not make any morphological distinction between singular and plural categories in inanimate common nouns (cf. §4.5.4), and the object is invariably 3SG even though its co-referential noun phrase in the main clause may be modified by a numeral or quantifier specifying plurality. Plural animate nouns functioning as either subjects or objects in a main clause must have their corresponding co-referential entities in the relative clause marked for number. Although possessive suffixes are marked for number, they bear no import in distinguishing co-referentiality between a lexical noun phrase in the matrix clause and an object pro-index in the relative clause. Given that Nese does not permit a lexical noun phrase inside a relative clause to be co-referential with a lexical noun phrase in the matrix clause and possessive suffixes can only modify full lexical noun phrases, possessed full noun phrases co-referential with an argument in the matrix clause are non-existent.

On the other hand, there is evidence of a lexical noun phrase in the matrix clause being modified by a possessive classifier, as shown in (7.70). In such cases, the numerical value indicated on the possessive classifier does not have any relevance in terms of distinguishing whether an object pro-index in the relative clause is co-referential with the noun phrase it is modifying.

7.70 **_Nemer-re_**   **_s-an_**   te   **_rri-ti-ma_**.
Man-PL   CLGEN-3SG:POSS   SUB   3PL:REAL-ASP-come
'His people who came.'
(2012_06_24 obgisa01001 00:00:43.000-00:00:47.000 natural text)

In (7.70), the head noun in the possessive noun phrase is plural, even though the general possessive classifier is marked for 3SG and the plural head noun *nemerre* is co-referential with the 3PL subject cross-index in the relative clause. In cases where number is not encoded in the lexical noun phrase functioning as an argument in the matrix clause, which is co-referential with an object pro-index in the relative clause, the presence of a possessive classifier does not bear any significance in determining whether an object pro-index is co-referential with the lexical noun phrase. This is illustrated in (7.71), where there is no number encoded in the head noun *nokhobu* in the matrix clause and the co-referential object pro-index in the relative clause is specified for the 3SG person and number. Although the object pro-index is singular, a plural reading is also possible. In such cases, the presence of the possessive classifier does not assist in adding any numerical information to the object pro-index, a factor that is pivotal in establishing a co-referential relationship.

7.71   ***Nokhobu***   *s-am*   *te*   *rri-si-nib-e*.
       bamboo   CLGEN-2SG:POSS   SUB   1PL-IRR-cover-3SGOBJ
       'Your bamboo(s) which we will cover.'
       (2012_07_21 obaksi01001 00:25:03.000-00:25:10.000 natural text)

7.5.2.3 Restrictions on relativisation

There are no restrictions on what kinds of arguments in the main clause may be relativised since Nese permits subjects, objects and non-core arguments to undergo relativisation. However, there is a restriction on the type of nominal element in the matrix clause that may be relativised. In this regard, Nese does not allow independent pronouns bearing any syntactic function such as subject or object arguments in the matrix clause to undergo relativisation. Arguments in the form of lexical noun phrases are the only ones that may be relativised, consequently entering into a co-referential relationship with another argument in the subordinate clause. Furthermore, Nese does not place emphasis in using resumptive independent pronouns in relative clauses as co-referential arguments, contrasting with the predominant use of co-referential subject cross-indexes and object pro-indexes in relative clauses. Evidence from the data points to four different argument types in main clauses that may enter into co-referential relationships with their co-referencing arguments in relative clauses. These are presented in Table 7.4.

Table 7.4: Co-referential arguments in matrix and relative clauses

Co-referential arguments in relative clause	Arguments in matrix clause			
	Subject	Object of transitive verb	Object of PP	Predicate of non-verbal matrix clause
subject	✓ (7.29)		✓ (7.75) (7.81)	✓ (7.78)
object		✓ (7.74)	✓ (7.72)	
rangan		✓ (7.77)	✓ (7.77)	
subject of verbal preposition *belek*			✓ (7.81)	

As shown in Table 7.4, there is a symmetrical relationship between the co-referential properties of subject and object arguments in matrix clauses. Objects of transitive verbs in matrix clauses can only be co-referential with an object argument in the relative clause or the preposition *rangan*. In a similar manner, subjects in matrix clauses are restricted to enter into co-referential relationships only with subject arguments in relative clauses.

Objects of prepositional phrases functioning as non-core arguments in matrix clauses display more flexibility, in that they may be co-referential with either a subject, object, non-core *rangan* 'in, into, at' and subject of the verbal preposition *belek* 'like' of relative clauses. While a co-referential relationship may exist between objects of prepositional phrases in matrix clauses with either a subject, object or non-core argument in the relative clause, there are also cases where Nese does not require any argument in the relative clause to enter into a co-referential relationship with the object of a prepositional phrase in the matrix clause.

To begin with, the subject of an intransitive matrix clause may be co-referential with a zero marked 3SG subject of the relative clause, as illustrated in (7.72), where the 3SG irrealis subject pro-index is co-referential with the non-overt subject argument of the verb *vitai* 'put'. The example also shows a co-referential relationship between the possessed lexical NP object argument of the prepositional phrase functioning as a non-core argument of the matrix intransitive clause with the object argument of the verb *vitai* 'put' in the relative clause.

7.72   **Ø-Se-ma**   khin   **noroblat**   **s-an**   te
       3SG-IRR-come   PREP I   paper   CLGEN-3SG:POSS   SUB
       'She will come for her paper which

   Ø-ti-vita-i   iekhe.
   3SG:REAL-ASP-put-3SGOBJ   DEM:LOC
   she had left here.'
   (2014_01_19 naanhy01001 00:16:23.000-00:16:26.000 natural text)

Furthermore, a subject pro-index in the main clause may be co-referential with another subject pro-index in the relative clause, as illustrated in (7.73). In (7.73), the 2SG irrealis subject pro-index in the matrix clause is co-referential with the 2SG subject pro-index marked for realis mood in the relative clause.

7.73   **Kho-se-kil-kil**   norrian   te   **kho-rong-o.**
       2SG-IRR-REDUP-look for   food   SUB   2SG:REAL-want-3SGOBJ
       'You will look for food that you want.'
       (2014_02_18 naaksi01001 00:16:54.000-00:16:59.000 natural text)

In (7.74), the noun phrase occupying the object position in the transitive matrix clause is co-referential with the object argument in the relative clause. On the contrary, the subject argument in the matrix clause is not co-referential with the subject argument in the relative clause, contrasting with example (7.72) in which the subjects of both the matrix and relative clauses are co-referential.

7.74 *Rri-tekh*   **_norrurr_**   *te*   *Amerika*   *Ø-ti-vreng-**i***   *khe.*
      1PLINCL:REAL-take   clothes   SUB   America   3SG:REAL-ASP-   DEM
                                                                throw-3SGOBJ

'We took the clothes which the Americans threw.'
(2012_06_19 obfaha01003 00:00:07.000-00:00:11.000 natural text)

A common argument in object position in the matrix clause need not necessarily be an object argument of a transitive verb as Nese also permits the object argument of prepositional phrases functioning as non-core arguments in matrix clauses to be co-referential with another argument in the relative clause. This is shown in (7.75), where the common argument in the matrix clause is the object of the prepositional phrase headed by the verbal preposition *min,* which is co-referenced by the resumptive 3SG independent pronoun *khai*, functioning as the subject of the intransitive verb *tokh*.

7.75 *So*   *tete*   *min*   **_norrian_**   *te*   **_khai_**   *Ø-ti-tokh.*
      Thanks   father   PREP2   food   SUB   3SG   3SG:REAL-ASP-stay

'Thank you father for the food which is here.'
(2012_06_12 obaksi01001 00:11:19.000-00:11:22.000 natural text)

Example (7.75) contrasts with example (7.72) in that there is a co-referential independent 3SG resumptive pronoun in the relative clause in (7.75), which is lacking in the relative clause in example (7.72). Nese restricts the use of co-referential independent pronouns in relative clauses to those occupying subject position in relative clauses. When an independent pronoun is present in such contexts, such as in (7.75), it is used as a marker of emphasis, bringing into focus the argument with which it is co-referential. There is no evidence to suggest that an independent pronoun in object position in a relative clause can be co-referential with a lexical noun phrase argument in the matrix clause.

Although, in conjoined independent clauses, it is obligatory for the *rangan* argument to be co-referential with an argument functioning as the object of a prepositional phrase in an antecedent clause, evidence suggests that clauses exhibiting a subordinate relationship do not require the presence of a prepositional phrase with the locative *rengen* as its head in the matrix clause. This is illustrated in (7.76), where the relative clause contains *rangan* bearing no co-referentiality with an argument functioning as the object of the locative preposition *rengen* in the matrix clause. *Rangan* is co-referential, however, with the noun phrase *tenge* 'thing'.

7.76 *Tav'at   khai   Ø-sa-ma   Ø-se-var-i*
     woman   3SG   3SG-IRR-come   3SG-IRR-say-3SGOBJ
     'The woman will come and block

   *Ø-se-verkhorr-o,   tenge   te   Ø-ti-norvo   **rangan**.*
   3SG-IRR-block-3SGOBJ   thing   SUB   3SG:REAL-ASP-depend   LOC
   him from it, the thing on which he depends.'
   (2014_01_19 naanhy01001 00:49:34.000-00:49:41.000 natural text)

In (7.76), the common argument in the matrix clause is *tenge* 'thing', which is functioning as the object of the verb *verkhorr* 'block (verbally)'. The subject of the verb *norvo* is the non-overt 3SG, which is not represented in the matrix clause but is retrievable from context.

As in (7.76) where the common argument is a lexical noun phrase object in the matrix transitive clause, example (7.77) also has a lexical noun phrase functioning as the object of the transitive matrix clause. Given that the relative clause has an intransitive verb as its head, the co-referential form *rangan* is functioning as an adverbial adjunct in this clause.

7.77 *Khar   ru-tu-sul   naine   nge   [te   nemerrte*
     3PL   3PL:REAL-ASP-burn   house   DEM   SUB   man
     'They burnt the house which the man

   *Ø-ti-natur   **rangan.**]*
   3SG:REAL-ASP-sleep   LOC
   was sleeping inside.'
   (Fieldnotes, elicitation)

A noun phrase forming the predicate of a non-verbal matrix clause may also be subject to relativisation, as illustrated in (7.78).

7.78   Khai   iekhe   khe   **nanus**   te   **Ø**-ti-tokh   khe.
       3SG   DEM LOC   DEM   grass   SUB   3SG:REAL-ASP   DEM
       'This one here is the grass which stays here.'
       (2014_02_18 naaksi01001 00:05:26.000-00:05:30.000 natural text)

In (7.78), there is no overt subject index in the relative clause given that 3SG cross-indexes are not realised on the verb and the 3SG independent pronoun is an optional element. The non-overt 3SG subject cross-index in the relative clause is co-referential with the noun phrase in the non-verbal matrix clause *nanus* 'grass'. Nese exhibits a tendency for co-referential relationships to be established between a lexical noun phrase or a cross-index or a pro-index, rather than an independent pronoun in a matrix clause and another argument in a subordinate clause. Therefore, the relative clause in (7.78) can never occupy the slot immediately after the subject of the non-verbal clause.

A lexical noun phrase functioning as the object of a prepositional phrase with the locative preposition *rengen* as its head is also susceptible to relativisation, assuming a co-referential relationship with an independent pronoun functioning as the subject of the relative clause, as illustrated in (7.79).

7.79   Rri-vekhsein-i,   naine   khe,   naleng   rengen   mande,
       3PL:REAL-clean-3SGOBJ   house   DEM   maybe   LOC   Monday
       They clean it, the house, maybe on Monday,

       tusde,   rengen   **wik**   te   **khai**   Ø-se-ma.
       Tuesday   LOC   week   SUB   3SG   3SG-IRR-come
       Tuesday, in the coming week.'
       (2014_02_18 naaksi01001 00:05:31.000-00:05:42.000 natural text)

In (7.80), the common argument in the main clause is the object of a prepositional phrase functioning as a non-core argument and the common argument in the relative clause is functioning as the subject of the relative clause. Another example where the object NP of a prepositional phrase that functions as a temporal non-core argument is not co-referential with any argument in the relative clause is (7.80).

7.80 | *Kho-so-khuban* | *rengen* | **navle** | *te* | *rri-les* | *nalang*
2SG-IRR-to garden | LOC | month | SUB | 1PL:REAL-see | wind
'You'll make a garden in the month in which we see the wind

Ø-sirsir.
3SG:REAL-blow
blow.'
(2012_08_27 obnesp01003 00:07:38.000-00:07:47.000 natural text)

This differs from (7.77), in which a non-core prepositional common argument is realised in the relative clause by *rangan*. A possible explanation is that Nese does not allow the expression of temporal non-core arguments by means of a resumptive *rangan* in the relative clause; however, non-core arguments realised by prepositional phrases with a locative meaning may be co-referenced with *rangan* in the relative clause.

Lastly, the object of a locative prepositional phrase functioning as a non-core argument in the main clause may be subject to relativisation, bearing a co-referential relationship with the subject cross-index of the verbal preposition *belek* in the subordinate clause. This is illustrated in (7.81).

7.81 | *Tejiblakh* | *ri-yat* | *rengen* | **nuak** | *te*
children | 3PL:REAL-sit | LOC | boat | SUB
'The children they sat on the boat which
Ø-belek | *khe.*
3SG:REAL-like | DEM
is like this.'
(2014_01_19 naanhy01001 01:05:16.000-01:05:20.000 natural text)

The common argument in (7.81) is the lexical noun phrase object of the prepositional phrase functioning as an adjunct of the main clause. This prepositional phrase has a locative function and unlike other examples, such as (7.77), it is not co-referential with a non-core *rangan* in the relative clause. On the contrary, it is co-referential with the subject of the relative clause.

7.5.3 Adverbial clauses

Nese employs the following subordinators, outlined in Table 7.5, to introduce adverbial clauses.

Table 7.5: Subordinators and functions

neten te	introduces an adverbial clause of reason 'because'
neren te	introduces a temporal adverbial clause 'when'
neren	'during', 'at'
belek te	introduces a similitive adverbial clause 'as if'

Adverbial clauses are a type of subordinate clause – that is, a clause that is embedded in a main clause and is grammatically dependent on that main clause. Adverbial clauses differ from complement and relative clauses in that complement clauses are arguments of a predicate and relative clauses are modifiers of a noun phrase that functions as an argument of a predicate. Adverbial clauses, on the other hand, are adjuncts of clauses contrasting with relative clauses that are modifiers of phrases. Following Dixon, adjuncts (which he labels as peripheral arguments) are associated with non-core arguments expressing notions such as instrument, accompaniment, recipient, beneficiary, time, place and manner (2010, p. 429). Nese adverbial clauses articulate concepts of time, manner, purpose and conditions under which an action occurs. Adjuncts that express temporal notions are associated with either simultaneous or sequential time frames. Manner clauses describe the way in which an action encoded in the verb in the matrix clause and that of a subordinate clause is carried out. On the other hand, purpose clauses provide the justification in a subordinate clause for an action expressed by the head verb in the matrix clause. Conditional adjuncts establish the condition under which an action occurs.

7.5.3.1 Temporal clauses

Adverbial time clauses in Nese are introduced by the form *neren te* 'when' or simply *neren* 'during, at'. The use of these markers of temporal clauses indicates a temporal relationship between the main clause and the subordinate clause, which can be either simultaneous, as in (7.82), or sequential, as in (7.83). In (7.83), the extraction of coconut milk takes place after the coconuts are collected and not simultaneously.

7.82 Ø-se-viteikhoro   nekrre   min   nause,   nial
      3SG-IRR-block   1PL   PREP2   rain   sun
      'It will shelter us from the rain, sun

      neren   **te**   rri-si-natur   laine.
      when   SUB   1PLINCL-IRR-sleep   house:LOC
      when we will sleep in the house.'
      (2012_07_12 obaksi01001 00:00:56.000-00:01:01.000 natural text)

7.83 Tija   rro-lol   iekhetan   khe   **neren**   **te**
      teacher   3PL:REAL-stay   DEM:LOC   DEM   when   SUB
      'The teachers stay down here and when

      rri-si-vis-vis   rri-v'an   rri-lavi   nani
      3PL-IRR-REDUP-squeeze   3PL:REAL-go   3PL:REAL-pull   coconut
      coconut milk
      they want to use coconut cream, they will go and take the coconut

      atan   khe.
      down   DEM
      down there.'
      (2014_02_18 naaksi01001 00:08:22.000-00:08:28.000 natural text)

7.5.3.2 Manner clauses

Manner clauses are introduced by *belek te* 'as if', which expresses the manner in which the actions or events described in the main clause are carried out. In (7.84), the speaker is telling the addressee to do something in whatever manner he knows best. In (7.85), the speaker is saying that the way in which they filled the ship was as if they were blind.

7.84 Ale   khunokh   kho-so-kot-o   **belek**   **te**   kho-rongvuson-i.
      CONJ   2SG   2SG-IRR-do-3SGOBJ as.if   SUB   2SG:REAL-know-3SGOBJ
      'Okay you'll do it like you want to.'
      (2014_01_19 naanhy01001 00:04:14.000-00:04:17.000 natural text)

7.85 | *Seve* | *rri-narralon,* | *nenete-ni* | *khe* | *khar* | *ri-si-nas*
COND | 1PL:REAL-drown | child-2PL:POSS | DEM | 3PL | 3PL-IRR-die

'If we drown, all your children will die

latas   *neten*   *te*   *nuak*   *velvele*   *je*   *be*
sea:LOC   PURP2   SUB   boat   small   very   CONJ

in the sea because the boat is too small but

kirr-sungun-i   ***belek*** ***te***   *nam'ata-mi*   *Ø-ti-vonvon.*
2PL:REAL-fill-3SGOBJ   as.if   SUB   eye-2PL:POSS   3SG:REAL-ASP-blind

you fill it up as if you are blind.'
(2014_01_19 naanhy01001 01:04:06.000-01:04:22.000 natural text)

With manner clauses, the main clause always precedes the manner clause.

7.5.3.3 Purpose and reason clauses

Nese employs *neten te* 'because' to express a reason or purpose for the occurrence of the action or event expressed by the verb in the main clause. The form is a juxtaposition of the preposition *neten* (cf. §6.6.2) with the subordinator *te*. Thompson, Longacre and Hwang (2007, p. 250) state that it is common for languages to use similar morphological means to express both purpose and reason clauses. This is because both give reasons why certain actions or events happen. Reason clauses, however, describe a motivating event that may be realised at the time of the main clause event while purpose clauses refer to a motivating event that must be unrealised at the time of the main clause event (Thompson, Longacre & Hwang, 2007, p. 250).

This difference is drawn via distinctions in mood in the subordinate clause whereby subordinate clauses are marked for realis mood when expressing reasoning notions contrary to being marked for irrealis mood when conveying a purposive denotation. Example (7.86) has its subordinate clause marked for realis, which means that the action in the subordinate clause has already happened and has brought about the condition expressed by the main clause.

7.86 Khai   Ø-ve   tenge   khorkhor sakhal khe
      3SG   3SG:REAL-be thing   hard   one   DEM
      'That's one difficult thing

      neten **te** nale   Ø-ti-rov   di.
      PURP2   SUB   language 3SG:REAL-ASP-finish   already
      because the language is already finished (no longer spoken).'
      (2014_01_19 naanhy01001 00:07:12.000-00:07:16.000 natural text)

Since the event in the subordinate clause has already happened, the subordinate clause can be referred to as a reason clause. In (7.87) however, the mood of the main clause is realis and that of the subordinate clause is irrealis. The irrealis mood, being compatible with events which are set in the future tense, means that the event in the subordinate clause has not yet occurred at the time when the event described in the main clause occurred. Therefore, the subordinate clause in (7.87) is a purpose clause because the event described in the subordinate clause is still unrealised at the time when the people were going home.

7.87 Rro-mul   v'an **neten** **te** je-luljokhor   nenet-in
      3PL:REAL-return DIR   PURP2   SUB   1SG:IRR-enclose   child-3SG:POSS
      'We went back so that I could put the chickens

      nato.
      fowl
      chickens in.'
      (2014_01_19 naanhy01001 00:33:29.000-00:33:33.000 natural text)

In situations where both the main and subordinate clauses are marked for irrealis mood, a purposive and reason reading may be deduced as shown in (7.88). In this example, the events in both the main and subordinate clause have not happened yet. The reason reading encodes the reason why the action expressed in the main clause will occur and the purpose for the realisation of the event described in the main clause.

7.88 Khai Ø-se-nakis   **neten** **te** nemerrte rri-si-ma.
      3SG   3SG-IRR-good PURP2   SUB   people   3PL-IRR-come
      'It will be good because the people will come/.''It will be good for the people to come.'
      (Fieldnotes, elicitation)

However, when the subordinate clause is marked for realis, a purposive reading is not possible as shown in (7.89) where the only reading which may be deduced from this example is based on reason.

7.89　*Khai*　*Ø-se-nakis*　**neten**　*te*　*nemerrte*　*rri-ma.*
　　　3SG　3SG-IRR-good　PURP2　SUB　people　3PL:REAL-come
　　　'It will be good because the people came.'
　　　*It will be good in order that the people came.
　　　(Fieldnotes, elicitation)

It is therefore clear that when both clauses are marked for realis mood, the subordinate clause is a reason clause. A combination involving a main clause marked for irrealis mood and a subordinate calse marked for realis mood may also have a reason connotation. On the other hand, a strictly purposive reading may be deduced when a main clause is marked for realis mood and a subordinate clause is marked for irrealis mood. It is only when both clauses are marked for irrealis mood that a reason as well as a purposive reading may be deduced. In these cases, semantic factors as well as contextual information may be relied upon to assist in determining the intended connotation.

7.5.4 Conditional clauses

Following Thompson, Longacre & Hwang (2007, p.257), the different parts of conditional clauses are the 'if' clause and the 'then' clause. The 'if' clause is the clause which names the condition and the 'then' clause refers to the main clause. In Nese the 'if' clause is introduced by the conditional marker *seve* 'if' and it always precedes the main clause as shown in (7.90). Nese employs several strategies to mark the beginning of the 'then' clause. There are cases where the 'then' clause is indicated by a pause or a change in intonation. In other cases, the 'then' clause is introduced by the coordinators *ale* 'and' as shown in (7.91).

7.90　**Seve**　*na-ma,*　*j-be-vervis-te*　*khin-i.*
　　　COND　1SG:REAL-come　1SG:IRR:NEG1-reveal-NEG2　PREP1-3SGOBJ
　　　'If/when I come, I won't tell him.'
　　　(2014_01_19 naanhy01001 00:32:54.000-00:32:57.000 natural text)

7.91 | Lana | **seve** | Ø-se-ma | ale | bir-sakhsakh | kele.
Lana | COND | 3SG-IRR-come | CONJ | 1PL EXCL:REAL-work | again
'Lana, if she comes, then we will work again.'
(2014_01_19 naanhy01001 00:08:57.000-00:09:03.000 natural text)

In (7.91) the conditional *seve* follows the subject of the 'if' clause. The subject of the 'if' clause normally follows the conditional *seve* as illustrated in (7.92) where the subject is realised by the 1SG subject cross-index. However in (7.91) the subject is topicalised.

7.92 | Seve | **khunokh** | kho-rong | te | kho-ba-num-u | ba-lemje
COND | 2SG | 2SG:REAL-want | SUB | 2SG-POT-drink-3SGOBJ | POT-a.lot

'If you want to drink lots of it,

ale | kho-vol-i | vol-i | v'an.
CONJ | 2SG:REAL-buy-3SGOBJ | buy-3SGOBJ | go

then you go buying it.'
(2014_01_19 naanhy01001 00:48:36.000-00:48:40.000 natural text)

Thompson, Longacre & Hwang (2007, p.258) divide conditional constructions into two different categories: reality conditionals and unreality conditionals, with the distinction being based on semantic grounds. Reality conditionals are conditional constructions that refer to real, present, habitual, generic or past situations. Unreality conditionals are further subdivided into two groups: imaginative and predictive conditionals. The subcategory of imaginative conditionals is further subdivided into hypothetical conditionals and counterfactuals. The former refers to situations which might happen while constructions in the latter subcategory refer to situations which did not or could not happen. As in reason and purposive clauses, Nese relies on mood marking on the verb of the main clause to determine whether a construction is a reality or unreality conditional. Constructions in which the mood of the verb in the main clause is realis are reality conditionals, given that they are situations that have happened, are happening or are habitual. A reality conditional construction may be comprised of an 'if' clause marked for realis mood and a subordinate clause marked for irrealis mood as shown in (7.93) or it can be made up of both clauses marked for realis mood, as shown in (7.94).

In (7.93) the realis mood marking in the 'if' clause encodes a habitual meaning. The action expressed by the verb in the 'then' clause, whose realisation is dependent on the occurrence of the activity in the main clause, is marked for irrealis mood. This means that it is expected that when kava is prepared for ceremonial purposes, it will be drunk by that person.

7.93   *Khai   num-u   rengen   seremoni   khin   tenge   sakhal,*
        3SG   drink-3SGOBJ   LOC   ceremony   PREP1   thing   one
        'He drinks it during a ceremony that is done for something

        *ri-si-bat-e   ale   **seve**   re-bet   nanalokh,*
        3PL-IRR-make-3SGOBJ   CONJ   COND   3PL:REAL-make   kava
        that they do and if/when kava is made,

        khai   Ø-se-num-u
        3SG   3SG-IRR-drink-3SGOBJ
        he is going to drink it.'
        (2014_01_19 naanhy01001 00:50:02.000-00:50:11.000 natural text)

This habitual connotation is also evident in the 'if' clause in (7.94) where the head verb is marked for the realis mood. The 'if' clause is made up of a complement clause while the 'then' clause is composed of an equational clause where the head verb is the copula *ve* marked for realis mood.

7.94   *Nekrre   rri-sakhsakh   min   sisen   buro,   **seve**   khina*
        1PL   1PL:REAL-work   PREP2   season   GENMOD   COND   1SG
        'We only work in seasons, if I

        ne-les   te   nalang   khai   Ø-ti-sirrsirr,   nev'enu   khai
        1SG:REAL-see   SUB   wind   3SG   ASP-blow   place   3SG
        see the wind is blowing, the place is

        Ø-ti-narang   ne-rongvuson-i   khai   Ø-ve
        3SG:REAL-ASP-be.dry   1SG:REAL-know-3SGOBJ   3SG   3SG:REAL-be
        is hot, then I know that

        nevle   nokhobonian.
        month   gardening
        it's the gardening month.'
        (2012_08_27 obnesp01003 00:03:27.000-00:03:41.000 natural text)

As shown in (7.95), an 'if' clause may be composed of a complement clause containing a verb in the main clause marked for realis mood while the complement is marked for the potential mood. The 'then' part of the clause is marked for realis mood. A habitual connotation may also be deduced from the realis marking expressed on the main verb in the 'if' clause.

7.95 **Seve** *kirr-rong* *te* *kirr-be-les-ia* *kirr-ma.*
COND 2PL:REAL-want SUB 2PL:REAL-POT-see-1SGOBJ 2PL:REAL-come
'If you people want to see me, then come.'
(2014_01_19 naanhy01001 01:05:59.000-01:06:03.000 natural text)

Unreality conditionals in Nese are indicated by the conditional clause being marked for the irrealis mood as shown in (7.96). In (7.96) both clauses are specified in the irrealis mood and as long as the event described in the main clause eventuates, then the event described in the subordinate clause will occur.

7.96 **Seve** *natas* *Ø-se-tamat* *kani* *kurr-su-mul,*
COND sea 3SG-IRR-peace 2PL 2PL-IRR-return
'If the sea is calm, you (PL) will return

nuak *tu* *khai* *Ø-vala.*
Boat too 3SG 3SG:REAL-run
and the boat will also run.'
(2014_01_19 naanhy01001 01:01:09.000-01:01:16.000 natural text)

Counterfactuals in Nese do not follow the pattern prescribed for unreality conditionals where the first clause takes irrealis marking as shown in (7.97) where the first clause is specified for the perfective aspect.

7.97 **Seve** *bas* *Ø-ti-ma* *je-v'an* *iekhe.*
COND bus 3SG:REAL-ASP-come 1SG:IRR-go DEM:LOC
'If the bus had come I would have gone by now.'
(Fieldnotes, elicitation)

7.5.5 Negative conditionals

In Nese, negative conditionals are signalled by the conditional marker seve and the negative verb *sikha* which means 'if not'. The subordinate clause introduced by *seve sikha* expresses the event or action which would have happened if the event in the main clause did not take place. Examples from the current available data on Nese indicate that the 'then' clause in Nese can only be either in irrealis mood (7.98 and 7.99) or marked with the dehortative marker *khota* (7.100 and 7.101).

7.98　*khina　　　ne-ve　　　　　kani　kirr-v'an　　lanus*
　　　1SG　　　　1SG:REAL-say　2PL　2PL:REAL-go　bush:LOC
　　　'I said, "you guys go to the bush",

　　　*ne-ve　　　　　**seve**　　**sikha**　khar　re-se-v'an　　re-se-jnejne*
　　　1SG:REAL-say　COND　　NEG　　　3PL　　3PL-IRR-go　　3PL-REAL-fish
　　　I said, "if not they will go fishing

　　　dokh　　　　latas.
　　　first　　　　sea:LOC
　　　first in the sea".'
　　　(204_01_19 naanhy01001 00:17:41.000-00:17:48.000 natural text)

In (7.98) the main clause is in fact the first clause with realis marked *v'an* as the head verb and the 'if not' clause being headed by two verbs in serial formation, both of which are marked for irrealis mood. The event described by the main clause occurred in real life, although the actions described by the 'then' clause are hypothetical situations which are presented as an option had the event in the main clause not occurred.

Example (7.99) presents a similar condition. The main clause has the transitive verb *viteikhor* 'block' with realis mood marking while the 'if not' clause is composed of the intransitive stative verb *nenelkhare* 'cold' marked marked for the irrealis mood. The main clause expresses an action that happened in the real world, and the speaker is stating, in the 'if not' clause, a possible consequence if the action in the main clause had not happened.

7.99 *Ne-viteikhor-o   kele   neten **seve sikha** Ø-se-nenelkhare.*
     1SG:REAL-block-3SGOBJ again PURP2 COND   NEG   3SG-IRR-be.cold
     'I closed it again because if not it's going to get cold.

   Rru-rongo   tenge te   khai Ø-ti-khavkhav.
   1PLINC:REAL-want   thing SUB   3SG   3SG:REAL-ASP-be.hot
   We want that which is hot.'
   (2012_06_12 obaksi01001 00:06:53.000-00:06:58.000 natural text)

Examples (7.100) and (7.101) differ from examples (7.98) and (7.99) in that the subordinate clause is not marked for irrealis mood but takes the prohibitive mood marker which occupies the slot prior to the head verb in the clause.

7.100 *Kanan   bir-se-woj   norrulnasasakh khe   buro,   kanan*
      1PLEXCL 1PLEXCL-IRR-eat   rice   DEM   GENMOD   1PLEXCL
      'We will eat this rice only, us

      min   vinelekh,   neten   te   khina   no-rong-o
      PREP2   daughter-in-law   PURP2   SUB   1SG   1SG:REAL-WANT-
                                                      3SGOBJ
      and my daughter in law, because I don't want

      *sikha   de-woj   nebetnekhev   khe,   **seve   sikha** khota*
      NEG   1SG:IRR-eat   bread   DEM   COND   NEG   PROHIB
      to eat this bread, if not

      s-bo-won-te   khe.
      1IRR-NEGI-full-NEGI   EMP
      we won't be full.'
      (2014_01_19 naanhy01001 00:02:34.000-00:02:43.000 natural text)

In (7.100) the intransitive head verb *won* in the subordinate clause is negated and the main clause is the initial clause with the transitive verb *woj* 'eat' as its head verb. The immediately following clause with the negated complement taking verb *rong* 'want' as the head verb forms a reason clause in a subordinate relationship with the main clause. Thus the negated conditional clause introduced by *seve sikha* presents a hypothetical situation which would arise if the action in the main clause has not occurred. While example (7.100) presents a case where a conditional clause is subordinate to a main clause containing another subordinate clause, example (7.101) presents a case where two independent clauses with the transitive head verb *takh* 'take' and the intransitive head verb *v'an* 'go' respectively precede the negative conditional clause introduced by *seve sikha*. The action encoded by the verb in the subordinate clause is a hypothetical situation whose occurrence is likely if the propositions contained in both preceding clauses did not occur.

7.101 *Ne-ve   wolei   vinelekh   kho-takh   khar*
       1SG:REAL-say   Oh   daughter in law   2SG:REAL-take   3PL
       'I said, "Oh my daughter-in-law take them

   kirr-v'an   maro   jin   nem-en   olfala   jokh-ok
   2PL:REAL-go   up   CLGEN   house-3SG:POSS   old   uncle-1SG:POSS
   you guys go up to the old man's house, my uncle

   *maro.   **Seve   sikha**   khota   nemere*
   up   COND   NEG   PROHIB   people
   up there. If not people will not

   bet   tengeterr   khe.
   make   thing   DEM
   be able to do these things.'
   (2014_01_2019 naanhy01001 00:36:58.000-00:37:11.000 natural text)

7.5.6 Concessive clauses

Nese uses the adverbial general modifier *buro* 'just' and the adversative *be* 'but' to form concessive clauses which mean 'X is still/just …but still X did…' The adverbial general modifier *buro* and adversative *be* occur at the end of the main clause and signal that although the event in the main clause happened, the event in the subordinate clause still occurred. Main clauses always have realis mood marking and subordinate clauses also take realis marking. This is illustrated in (7.102) and (7.103).

7.102 *Khai Ø-ti-roj* **buro** **be** *khai Ø-v'an*
3SG 3SG:REAL-ASP-sick GENMOD ADVS 3SG 3SG:REAL-go
'Although she was sick she went to the

lanus
bush:LOC
garden.'
(Fieldnotes, elicitation)

7.103 *Khai Ø-ti-sikha nav'at* **buro** **be** *rong-o yas.*
3SG 3SG:REAL-ASP-NEG money GENMOD ADVS want-3SGOBJ go
'Although she did not have any money, she still went.'
(Fieldnotes, elicitation)

References

Aikhenvald, A. Y. (1999). Serial constructions and verb compounding evidence from Tariana (North Arawak). *Studies in Language, 23* (3), 469–497. doi.org/10.1075/sl.23.3.02aik

Ariel, M. (2009). Discourse, grammar, discourse. *Discourse Studies, 11* (1), 5–36. doi.org/10.1177/1461445608098496

Barbour, J. (2012). *A grammar of Neverver*. Berlin: Walter de Gruyter. doi.org/10.1515/9783110289619

Bogiri, H. (2013). A descriptive grammar of Raga (unpublished PhD thesis), University of the South Pacific, Vanuatu.

Bresnan, J., & Mchombo, S. (1987). Topic, pronoun, and agreement in Chicheŵa. *Language, 63* (4), 741–782.

Bril, I. (2011). Noun-phrase conjunction in Austronesian languages: additive, inclusory and comitative strategies. In C. Moyse-Faurie & J. Sabel (Eds), *Topics in Oceanic morphosyntax* (pp. 235–286). Berlin: De Gruyter Mouton. doi.org/10.1515/9783110259919.235

Brotchie, A. (2009). *Tirax grammar and narrative: An Oceanic language spoken on Malakula, North Central Vanuatu* (PhD thesis), University of Melbourne, Australia. Retrieved from minerva-access.unimelb.edu.au/handle/11343/36956

Budd, P. (2010). Negation in Bierebo and the other languages of Epi, Central Vanuatu. *Oceanic Linguistics, 49* (2), 511–542.

Capell, A. (1962). *A linguistic survey of the South Western Pacific: Technical Paper No. 136*. Noumea: South Pacific Commission.

Charpentier, J.-M. (1979). *La langue de Port Sandwich (Nouvelles Hébrides): Introduction phonologique et grammaire*. Paris: SELAF.

Charpentier, J.-M. (1982). *Atlas linguistique du Sud-Malekula (Linguistic Atlas of South Malekula)*. Paris: SELAF.

Clark, R. (1985). Languages of north and central Vanuatu: Groups, chains, clusters and waves. In A. Pawley (Ed.), *Austronesian linguistics at the 15th Pacific Science Congress* (pp. 199–236). Canberra: Pacific Linguistics.

Clark, R. (2009). **Le Tuai: A comparative lexical study of North and Central Vanuatu Languages*. Canberra: Pacific Linguistics.

Codrington, R. H. (1885). *The Melanesian languages*. Oxford: Clarendon Press.

Comrie, B. (1976). *Aspect: An introduction to the study of verbal aspect and related problems*. Cambridge: Cambridge University Press.

Crowley, T. (1982). *The Paamese language of Vanuatu*. Canberra: Pacific Linguistics.

Crowley, T. (1990). *Beach-la-mar to Bislama: The emergence of a national language in Vanuatu*. Oxford: Oxford University Press.

Crowley, T. (1992). *A dictionary of Paamese*. Canberra: Pacific Linguistics.

Crowley, T. (1995). *A new Bislama dictionary*. Suva, Fiji; Port Vila, Vanuatu: University of the South Pacific.

Crowley, T. (1998). *An Erromangan (Sye) grammar*. Honolulu: University of Hawai'i Press.

Crowley, T. (1999). *Ura: A disappearing language of southern Vanuatu*. Canberra: Pacific Linguistics.

Crowley, T. (2002). *Serial verbs in Oceanic: A descriptive typology*. Oxford: Oxford University Press.

Crowley, T. (2003). *A new Bislama dictionary*. Suva, Fiji: Institute of Pacific Studies.

Crowley, T. (2004). *Bislama reference grammar*. Honolulu: University of Hawai'i Press. doi.org/10.1515/9780824850074

Crowley, T. (2006a). *The Avava language of central Malekula*. Canberra: Pacific Linguistics.

Crowley, T. (2006b). *Naman: A vanishing language of Malekula*. Canberra: Pacific Linguistics.

Crowley, T. (2006c). *Nese: A diminishing speech variety of North West Malakula*. Canberra: Pacific Linguistics.

Crowley, T. (2006d). *Tape: A declining language of Malakula (Vanuatu)*. Canberra: Pacific Linguistics.

Daily Post. (2021, 1 July). *Vanuatu population statistics announced: 301,695*. Retrieved from www.dailypost.vu/news/vanuatu-population-statistics-announced-301-69/article_8f4d8b6e-da02-11eb-b0d3-13b4f45e24a4.html

Dimock, L. G. (2009). A grammar of Nahavaq (Malakula, Vanuatu) (unpublished PhD thesis), Universty of Wellington, Victoria, New Zealand. researcharchive.vuw.ac.nz/xmlui/handle/10063/1183

Dixon, R. M. W. (2003). Demonstratives: A crosslinguistic typology. *Studies in Language, 27* (1), 61–112. doi.org/10.1075/sl.27.1.04dix

Dixon, R. M. W. (2006). Complement clauses and complementation strategies in typological perspective. In R. M. W: Dixon & A. Y. Aikhenvald (Eds), *Complementation* (pp. 1–46). Oxford; New York: Oxford University Press.

Dixon, R. M. W. (2010). *Basic linguistic theory: Methodology, 2*. Oxford: Oxford University Press.

Dodd, R. (2014). V'enen Taut: Grammatical topics in the Big Nambas language of Malekula (unpublished MA thesis), University of Waikato, New Zealand. digitalnz.org/records/35768682

Duhamel, M. (2010). The noun phrase of Atchin, a language of Malakula, Vanuatu (unpublished MA thesis), University of Auckland, New Zealand.

Early, R. (1994). Lewo Grammar (unpublished PhD thesis), The Australian National University, Australia. openresearch-repository.anu.edu.au/handle/1885/132959

Elliot, J. (2000). Realis and irrealis: Forms and concepts of the grammaticalisation of reality. *Linguistic Typology 4* (1), 55–90. doi.org/10.1515/lity.2000.4.1.55

Evans, B. (2003). *A study of valency-changing devices in Proto Oceanic*. Canberra: Pacific Linguistics. doi.org/10.15144/PL-539

Foley, W. A., & Van Valin Jr., R. D. (1984). *Functional syntax and universal grammar*. Cambridge: Cambridge University Press.

Foley, W. A., & Olson, M. (1985). Clausehood and verb serialization. In J. Nichols & A. C. Woodbury (Eds), *Grammar inside and outside the clause* (pp. 17–60). Cambridge: Cambridge University Press.

Fox, G. J. (1979). *Big Nambas grammar*. Canberra: Pacific Linguistics.

François, A. (2001). *Une description du mwotlap, langue océanienne du Vanuatu* (PhD thesis), Université Paris-IV Sorbonne, France.

François, A. (2002). *Araki: A disappearing language of Vanuatu.* Canberra: Pacific Linguistics.

François, A. (2007). Four grammars of Malakula languages. [Review of the books *The Avava language of Central Malakula (Vanuatu); Tape: A declining language of Malakula (Vanuatu); Naman: A vanishing language of Malakula (Vanuatu); Nese: A diminishing speech variety of Northwest Malakula (Vanuatu)*, by T. Crowley]. *Journal of the Humanities & Social Sciences of Southeast Asia, 163* (2/3), 430–439.

François, A., Lacrampe, S., Franjieh, M., & Schnell, S. (2015). The exceptional linguistic diversity of Vanuatu. In A. François, S. Lacrampe, M. Franjieh & S. Schnell (Eds), *The Languages of Vanuatu: Unity and diversity.* Studies in the Languages of Island Melanesia, 5 (pp. 1–21). Canberra: Asia Pacific Linguistics.

Guerin, V. (2010). Nese, a diminishing speech variety of Northwest Malakula, Vanuatu. [Review of *Nese: A diminishing speech variety of Northwest Malakula*, by T. Crowley]. *Oceanic Linguistics, 49* (2), 595–600.

Guy, J. B. M. (1982). Bases for new methods in glottochronology. In A. Halim, L. Carrington & S. A. Wurm (Eds), *Papers from the Third International Conference on Austronesian Linguistics* (pp. 283–314). Canberra: Pacific Linguistics.

Haspelmath, M. (2013). Argument indexing: A conceptual framework for the syntactic status of bound person forms. In D. Bakker & M. Haspelmath (Eds), *Languages across boundaries: Studies in memory of Anna Siewierska* (pp. 197–266). Berlin: De Gruyter Mouton. doi.org/10.1515/9783110331127

Hayes, B. (1995). *Metrical stress theory: Principles and case studies.* Chicago: University of Chicago Press.

Healey, D. S. (2013). *A grammar of Maskelynes: The language of Uluveu island, Vanuatu* (PhD thesis), University of the South Pacific, Fiji.

Hill, D. (2013). Longgu. In T. Crowley, J. Lynch & M. Ross (Eds). (2013). *The Oceanic languages* 2nd edn. (pp. 297–391). New York: Routledge Taylor and Francis Group. doi.org/10.4324/9780203820384

Holmes, R. (2014). *Espigles Bay: Grammatical topics* (MA thesis), University of Waikato, New Zealand.

Hyslop, C. (2001). *The Lolovoli dialect of the North-East Ambae language: Vanuatu*. Canberra: Pacific Linguistics.

Ivens, W. G. (1937–1939). A grammar of the language of Lamalanga, North Raga, New Hebrides. *Bulletin of the School of Oriental and African Studies, 10*, 733–763. doi.org/10.1017/S0041977X00078514

Ivens, W. G. (1940–1942). A grammar of the language of Lobaha, Lepers' Island, New Hebrides, Melanesia. *Bulletin of the School of Oriental and African Studies, 10*, 679–698. doi.org/10.1017/S0041977X00087553

Jauncey, D. (1997). A grammar of Tamambo (unpublished PhD thesis), The Australian National University, Australia. openresearch-repository.anu.edu.au/handle/1885/145981

Jelinek, E. (1984). Empty categories, case and configurationality. *Natural Language and Linguistic Theory, 2* (1), 39–76.

Keenan, E. L. (1985). Relative clauses. In T. Shopen (Ed.), *Language typology and syntactic description* (pp. 141–170). Cambridge: Cambridge University Press. doi.org/10.1017/CBO9780511619434

Krämer, M. (2003). *Vowel harmony and correspondence theory*. Berlin: Mouton de Gruyter. doi.org/10.1515/9783110197310

Lichtenberk, F. (1985). Possessive constructions in Oceanic languages and in Proto-Oceanic. In A. Pawley & L. Carrington (Eds), *Austronesian Linguistics at the 15th Pacific Science Congress* (pp. 93–140). Canberra: Pacific Linguistics.

Lindstrom, L. (1986). *Kwamera dictionary*. Canberra: Pacific Linguistics.

Lynch, J. (1977). *Lenakel dictionary*. Canberra: Pacific Linguistics. doi.org/10.15144/PL-C55

Lynch, J. (1978). *A grammar of Lenakel*. Canberra: Pacific Linguistics.

Lynch, J. (1998). *Pacific languages: An introduction*. Honolulu: University of Hawai'i Press. doi.org/10.2307/j.ctv893h2b

Lynch, J. (2005). The apicolabial shift in Nese. *Oceanic Linguistics, 44* (2), 389–403. doi.org/10.1353/ol.2005.0040

Lynch, J. (2006). Some notes on the linguistic history of Malekula. Paper given at the Terry Crowley Memorial Workshop on Vanuatu Languages. Victoria Uuniversity of Wellington, 13–14 November. Retrieved June 2011: www.victoria.ac.nz/lals/about/news/Attachments/Vanuatu-Languages-November-2006.pdf (site discontinued).

Lynch, J. (2009). At sixes and sevens: The development of numeral systems in Vanuatu and New Caledonia. In B. Evans (Ed.), *Discovering history through language: Papers in honour of Malcolm Ross* (pp. 391–412). Canberra: Pacific Linguistics. doi.org/10.1075/dia.29.3.07mcg

Lynch, J. (2016). Malakula internal subgrouping: Phonological evidence. *Oceanic Linguistics, 55* (2), 399–431. doi.org/10.1353/ol.2016.0019

Lynch, J., & Crowley, T. (2001). *Languages of Vanuatu: A new survey and bibliography.* Canberra: Pacific Linguistics.

Lynch, J., & Tryon, D. T. (1985). Central-Eastern Oceanic: A subgrouping hypothesis. In A. Pawley & L. Carrington (Eds), *Austronesian linguistics at the 15th Pacific Science Congress,* 31–52. Canberra: Pacific Linguistics.

Lynch, J., Ross, M., & Crowley, T. (Eds). (2002). *The Oceanic languages.* Richmond: Curzon.

Lynch, J., Ross, M., & Crowley, T. (Eds). (2011). *The Oceanic languages.* 2nd edn. New York: Routledge Taylor and Francis Group.

Macdonald, D. R. (1891). *South Sea languages: A series of studies on the languages of the New Hebrides and other South Sea islands.* Melbourne: Trustees of the Public Library.

Maddieson, I. (1989). Linguo-labials. In R. Harlow & R. Hooper (Eds), VICAL 1 *(Oceanic Languages): Papers from the Fifth International Conference on Austronesian Linguistics* (pp. 349–375). Auckland: Linguistic Society of New Zealand.

McGinn, R. (2001). Review of *Pacific languages: An introduction. Pacific Studies, 24* (3/4), 93–100.

McGuckin, C. (2011). Gapapaiwa. In J. Lynch, M. Ross & T. Crowley (Eds). *The Oceanic languages,* 2nd edn (pp. 297–321). New York: Routledge Taylor and Francis Group.

Ministry of Education and Training. (2012). *Vanuatu National Language Policy 2012.* Retrieved from moet.gov.vu/docs/policies/Vanuatu%20National%20 Language%20Policy%20(English)_2012.pdf

Mithun, M. (1995). On the relativity of irreality. In J. Bybee & S. Fleischmann (Eds), *Modality in grammar and discourse* (pp. 367–388). Amsterdam: John Benjamins. doi.org/10.1075/tsl.32.16mit

Mithun, M. (1995). The relativity of irreality. In J. Bybee, & Fleischman. S (Eds), *Typological Studies in Language 32* (pp. 367–388). Amsterdam: John Benjamins.

Moyse-Faurie, C. & Lynch, J. (2004). Coordination in Oceanic languages and Proto Oceanic. In M. Haspelmath (Ed.), *Coordinating constructions* (pp. 445–497). Amsterdam; Philadelphia: John Benjamins. doi.org/10.1075/tsl.58.23moy

Musgrave, J. (2007). *A grammar of Neve'ei*. Canberra: Pacific Linguistics.

Naito, M. (2006). Tutuba apicolabials: Factors influencing the phonetic transition from apicolabials to labials. *Oceanic Linguistics*, 45 (1), 217–228. doi.org/10.1353/ol.2006.0017

Noonan, M. (1985). Complementation. In T. Shopen (Ed.), *Language typology and syntactic description* (pp. 43–139). Cambridge: Press Syndicate of the University of Cambridge. doi.org/10.1017/CBO9780511619434.002

Pearce, E. (2015). *A Grammar of Unua*. Canberra: Pacific Linguistics. doi.org/10.1515/9781614516590

Ray, S. H. (1893). Sketch of Aulua grammar, with vocabularies of Aulua and Lamangkau, Malekula, New Hebrides. *Journal of the Anthropological Institute of Great Britain and Ireland*. 22, 386–397. doi.org/10.2307/2842138

Ray, S. H. (1926). *A comparative study of the Melanesian island languages*. Cambridge: Cambridge University Press.

Ross, J. R. (1973). Nouniness. In P. Kiparsky, J. R. Ross & J. D. McCawley (Eds), *Three dimensions of linguistic theory* (pp. 137–257). Tokyo: TEC Company Ltd.

Ross, M. (1988). *Proto Oceanic and the Austronesian languages of western Melanesia*. Canberra: Pacific Linguistics.

Ross, M. (1998). Proto-Oceanic adjectival categories and their morphosyntax. *Oceanic Linguistics*, 37 (1), 85–119. doi.org/10.2307/3623281

Ross, M., Pawley, A., & Osmond, M. (2011). *The lexicon of Proto Oceanic: The culture and environment of ancestral Oceanic society: 2 The physical environment*. Canberra: ANU E Press. doi.org/10.22459/LPO.03.2007

Schachter, P. (1985). Parts-of-speech systems. In T. Shopen (Ed.), *Language typology and syntactic description, vol. 1: Clause structure* (pp. 3–61). Cambridge: Cambridge University Press. doi.org/10.1017/CBO9780511619427

Sperlich, W. B. (1994). Namakir: A description of a Central Vanuatu language (unpublished PhD thesis), University of Auckland, New Zealand. research space.auckland.ac.nz/handle/2292/2314

Spriggs, M. (2006). The Lapita culture and Austronesian prehistory in Oceania. In P. Bellwood, J. J. Fox & D. Tryon (Eds), *The Austronesians: Historical and comparative perspectives* (pp. 119–142). ANU E Press. doi.org/10.22459/A.09.2006

Takau, L. (2016). A grammar of Nese (unpublished PhD thesis), University of Newcastle, Australia.

Thieberger, N. (2006). *A grammar of South Efate: An Oceanic language of Vanuatu*. Honolulu: University of Hawai'i Press. doi.org/10.1515/9780824861254

Thompson, S. A., Longacre, R. E., & Hwang, S. J. (2007). Adverbial clauses. In T. Shopen (Ed.), *Language typology and syntactic description* (pp. 237–300). Cambridge: Cambridge University Press. doi.org/10.1017/CBO9780511619434.005

Tryon, D. T. (1976). *New Hebrides languages: An internal classification*. Canberra: Pacific Linguistics.

Tryon, D. T. (1996). Dialect chaining and the use of geographical space. In J. Bonnemaison, C. Kaufmann, K. Huffman & D. T. Tryon, *Arts of Vanuatu* (pp. 170–181). Bathurst: Crawford House Publishing.

Vanuatu National Statistics Office. (2012). *2009 National Population and Housing Census*. Retrieved from vnso.gov.vu/index.php/en/census-and-surveys/census/national-population-housing-census/2009-census#executive-summary

Walworth, M., Dewar, A., Ennever, T., Takau, L. & Rodriguez, I. 2021. Multilingualism in Vanuatu: Four case studies. *International Journal of Bilingualism, 25* (4), 1120–1141. doi.org/10.1177/13670069211023132

Wessels, K. (2013). Malua Bay: A grammar of the Malua Bay language (Malekula, Vanuatu) (unpublished MA thesis), University of Waikato, New Zealand.

www.ingramcontent.com/pod-product-compliance
Lightning Source LLC
Chambersburg PA
CBHW061249230426

43663CB00022B/2953